GAME I

OPEN SOU

Game Developer's Open Source Handbook

Steven Goodwin

CHARLES RIVER MEDIA
Boston, Massachusetts

Cover Design: Tyler Creative
The publisher and author have attempted to provide accurate information and supply the Open Source license for each tool covered in the book on and the companion CD-ROM. Any oversight was without intention of infringement or harm.

CHARLES RIVER MEDIA
25 Thomson Place
Boston, Massachusetts 02210
617-757-7900
617-757-7969 (FAX)
crm.info@thomson.com
www.charlesriver.com

This book is printed on acid-free paper.

Steven Goodwin. *Game Developer's Open Source Handbook.*
ISBN: 1-58450-497-8
ISBN-13: 978-1-58450-497-9

All brand names and product names mentioned in this book are trademarks or service marks of their respective companies. Any omission or misuse (of any kind) of service marks or trademarks should not be regarded as intent to infringe on the property of others. The publisher recognizes and respects all marks used by companies, manufacturers, and developers as a means to distinguish their products.

Library of Congress Cataloging-in-Publication Data
Goodwin, Steven, 1973-
  Game developer's open source handbook / Steven Goodwin.
      p. cm.
   Includes index.
   ISBN 1-58450-497-8 (alk. paper)
   1. Computer games--Programming. 2. Cross-platform software development. I. Title.

QA76.76.C672G665 2006
794.8'1526--dc22

Printed in the United States of America
06 7 6 5 4 3 2 First Edition

CHARLES RIVER MEDIA titles are available for site license or bulk purchase by institutions, user groups, corporations, etc. For additional information, please contact the Special Sales Department at 800-347-7707.

Requests for replacement of a defective CD-ROM must be accompanied by the original disc, your mailing address, telephone number, date of purchase and purchase price. Please state the nature of the problem, and send the information to CHARLES RIVER MEDIA, 25 Thomson Place, Boston, Massachusetts 02210. CRM's sole obligation to the purchaser is to replace the disc, based on defective materials or faulty workmanship, but not on the operation or functionality of the product.

To Grandma and Granddad . . .
. . . who have always been proud of my work,
and made unlikely claims about understanding it!

Contents

Preface

With the cost of game development increasing with every passing month, studios are looking for innovative ways of reducing their budgets without compromising on quality. At the same time, developers are looking toward more complex and customizable software, tools, and libraries to build truly next-generation games. These goals have traditionally been mutually exclusive.

Open Source software can solve both problems by providing game developers with free, high-quality tools and libraries for every aspect of the development process. Graphics, audio, physics, networking, and movie playback code are all available for the taking; developed, written, tested, and packaged ready for anyone without fear or favor. This software is complemented by a wide range of end-user tools for both the programmer and artist including graphic editors, IDEs, MIDI sequencers, and 3D editors.

Free and Open Source software can increase the scope of the technology available and reduce the financial burden of the development studio.

This book uncovers the world of Open Source software for both the management and the game developers. It details what code is available, from where you can download it, how to incorporate it into your existing processes, and (importantly) how you can adhere to the license agreements. It introduces you to a new world of software, and a new way of developing games for the 21st century.

The book itself is split into the three key areas. I begin in Part I by looking at Free Software and the Open Source movement itself. I explain what it is, how it works, and how to make use of the software released. This is a largely theoretical discussion on the various licenses available, how to interpret them, and your responsibilities as a user. It also explains the differences between "free" (as in gratis) and "free" (as in freedom), and where (and why) the alternative term of "Open Source" is used. This section is essential reading for managers, the legal team, and the lead developers in all disciplines, along with programmers who are unfamiliar with the concept of Free or Open Source software.

Part II continues by looking at the wealth of software available and discusses specific Open Source projects of interest to the game developer. This covers all aspects of engine development such as graphics, audio, and physics, along with the game-related areas of AI and scripting languages. Programmers of all levels will learn the scope of software available and the various methods to incorporate it within their games.

Finally, Part III covers the various tools that may be used in the game development process. It details software that is generally not shipped with the game but is utilized in its production. This part is therefore of most use to producers, project managers, and studio directors. All the software detailed in this section is also available under an Open Source license and covers software for artists, level designers, and musicians.

As a whole, these three areas encompass everything you need to know to streamline your development processes using Open Source software.

Steven Goodwin
London 2006

Acknowledgments

Over the seven years in which I've been involved in Open Source I have learned a lot, from a lot of different people. There is such a density of information, knowledge, and ideas that this book can only represent a single view on that community. For it is just that—a community. And it is one of which I am proud to consider myself a part.

There are many developers, writers, evangelists, and hangers-on worthy of mention here. This includes all the active members of GLLUG, Lonix, and TULS, but especially those that have introduced me to so much in the community: Lisa and Paul Nasrat, John Southern, Colin Murphy, Shane O'Neill, John Hearns, and Dean Wilson.

To my friends with whom I've worked within the games industry, I thank you for putting up with me over the last 12 years. Most notably, Michael Braithwaite, Matt Cook, Ben Crossman, Dan Evans, Vlad Kaipetsky, Mal Lansell, David Manley, Jerome Muffat-Meridol, Alan Troth, and Dave Wall. Not forgetting the ever-growing list of development teams of which I've been a part, and continually impressed and inspired by: Edcom, Bits Studios, Computer Artworks (still R.I.P.), Criterion, Electronic Arts, and Glu Mobile.

Once again, I would like to thank Jenifer Niles and all her team at Thomson for this book and for continuing to make me appear competent!

To my network of friends, Janey Bartlett and Henry, Dean Butcher, Martyn Dicken, David Eade, Ed and Margaret Grabowski (without whom . . .), Justine Griffith, Phillip Hart, Phil Lunt, Colin Z. Robertson, and Fiona Stewart.

I want to thank Grandma, Granddad, Shirley and Ken, Juliette and Dean, Melanie, Mum and Dad, and Angela and Colin. And finally, to the newest addition of our family, Holly Goodwin. I look forward to the time she'll be able to read this book—and hopefully understand it!

Part

I

The world of Open Source is not new—the phrase was first termed in 1998—while Free software was quantified with the introduction of the GNU (GNU's Not Unix) system over a decade before, in 1984. But even that is not the beginning of the story because software was shared among users since even before the birth of C. And ideas, algorithms, and methodologies have been shared since time immemorial. With such a long history of sharing it seems remarkable that any industry, especially a high-tech one, can operate in secrecy and without the open exchange of ideas. Yet for the most part, that is how software is developed.

Open Source changes that approach by adopting that of the scientist. By exchanging ideas, and standing on the shoulders of proverbial giants, we all gain from these advancements. And with so much effort being spent on the development of software, it is usually released at no cost to enable the largest possible user base. This in turn results in more testers, developers, and a better final product.

Because of the long association of Open Source with Unix, some of the terms will be initially alien. But don't worry, as they're all explained within the text. Those with an appreciation of the field will quietly skip over the historical review in Chapter 1, "An Introduction to Free and Open Source Software," although everyone should carefully digest the contents of the specific licenses discussed at length within Chapter 2, "License Commentaries," and reprinted in full in the appendixes. This part ends with a practical discussion of games in the Open Source world and how it relates to the development process and the business of the games industry.

1

1

An Introduction to Free and Open Source Software

In This Chapter

- The Philosophy of Free Software
- Open Source Myths
- Licensing Open Source
- Open Source Development Practices
- Incorporating Open Source
- License Exceptions
- Free Content

THE PHILOSOPHY OF FREE SOFTWARE

There is a jungle of terms surrounding software rights: Free, libre, public domain, Copyleft, Freeware, Open Source, commercial, and proprietary. Each of these has a precise meaning relating to its licensing, copyright, and distribution rights. Although many of the ideas existed for years, Richard M. Stallman codified them for the software industry and projected them into the collective geek consciousness. These origins go back to the 1970s.

Richard M. Stallman

In 1971, Richard M. Stallman (or RMS as he is generally known) started working at the MIT Artificial Intelligence Lab in Boston. He was a systems programmer and was part of the hacker[1] community that existed at the time. Although they had a culture of sharing software, this was not common to everyone in the field. As time went on, more and more software became encumbered by proprietary licensing and nondisclosure agreements (NDAs). This led to various problems, most famously when RMS would not get the source code for his problematic printer driver at the MIT AI Lab. Although he *could* have acquired it, that would have involved signing an NDA. This in turn would mean he'd be unable to help fellow developers with similar problems. Knowing how frustrating it was to be on the other end of this predicament, he declined to accept the NDA and looked for an alternative solution.

His solution, announced on September 27, 1983, was the GNU project. GNU, which stands for GNU's Not Unix (one of the many geek-clever acronyms present in this story), became an umbrella for the many software projects he had envisioned. Every project would be available to all, unfettered by NDAs or fraught licenses. These projects were to cover the entire oeuvre of software found within a modern operating system such as compilers, text editors, debuggers, and, of course, the OS kernel itself. On January 5, 1984, GNU was formally founded to begin work on creating a completely free OS.

Even games were included in the original GNU task list because games were available in the original versions of UNIX.

NOTE

Around the same time, RMS quit his job at MIT, but by the grace of Professor Winston, was able to keep his office and use the university's facilities. By divorcing himself from the AI labs, he severed any legal responsibilities or claims MIT might have had to his work. This meant he could release the software according to his desires and visions—not those of anyone else. He began his first piece of GNU software, GNU Emacs, in September 1984, and by early 1985 it was ready for basic use.

At this point, to gain finances, RMS created the Free Software Foundation (FSF). This was (and still is) a tax-exempt charity for the development of Free software. GNU Emacs was its first product. It sold tapes of the GNU Emacs program to anyone who wanted one for a one-time fee of $150—and no NDAs. Today, funds for the FSF come primarily from donations. However, it also sells CD-ROMs of software, printed manuals, and other related services.

The Meaning of Free

Before continuing, it is important to clarify the meaning of Free. RMS has an often-quoted mantra of "free as in speech, not free as in beer." That means free is not the financial cost of the software, but the "free"doms you acquire by using it. Those freedoms are:

- The right to run the program
- The right to modify it
- The right to redistribute it
- The right to redistribute modified versions

The first three give everyone the rights to use some of the best software in the world without being encumbered. The philosophy was that if developers are going to devote a lot of time writing this software, they want the largest possible audience for it. These rights prevent the software being withheld from others.

The latter of the four freedoms ensure that the improvements you make are given back to the community, and applying these same rights to the new version allows the chain of freedoms to continue. This is how scientists have researched, published, and relearned for centuries.

However, the word Free itself is not without its opponents. In English at least, the word has multiple meanings, as you've seen. This produces an ambiguity that has caused some chagrin and a lot of confusion. For this reason, translators are encouraged to adapt a better word should one exist in their native tongue. In French, for example, the word *libre* is used.

The closest suitable English word is "unfettered." Other oft-suggested alternatives include "liberated", "freedom", and "open," but as the GNU website[2] says, they "either have the wrong meaning, or some other disadvantage." To help clarify the meaning, the word free is usually written with a capital F.

GPL: The Original Free License

The most famous quantification of Free software comes in the form of the GNU General Public License (or GPL for short). This describes the precise terms by which you can use and distribute the software. It is covered fully in Chapter 2, "License Commentaries," and quoted verbatim in Appendix B. Although it is the most widely known of all licenses, it is not the most widely used, especially in the games field. Knowing that game developers have traditionally been secretive with their source and about their methods, most of the Free software in this field has been released under different, slightly less restrictive, licenses.

The term GNU software should never be applied to code that uses the GPL license, as it is reserved for software developed under the patronage of the GNU project.

Free or Open?

Unconvinced by the "free" designation afforded by RMS in 1984, a strategy session was held to discuss and propose an alternate name for software that fulfilled the same basic ideas but wasn't as rigid in its proposals, as many found the ideals of Free software too confrontational.

This session was held on February 3, 1998, in Palo Alto, California, as an immediate consequence of Netscape opening the source code to its Mozilla browser.

While less code was available then than is available now (many parts of the browser required code that was used under license), it was a big news story, and the community knew it could capitalize on this by announcing a policy of openness while the proverbial iron was still hot. The meeting resulted with the naissance of the term *Open Source*. It also sparked the creation of a rule set that would determine if a particular license fell under the jurisdiction of Open Source. This mirrored the codification that RMS gave to Free software four years earlier. Such was the importance of this event that by the following day Linus Torvalds, creator of the Linux® operating system kernel, had lent his support to the movement.

The session itself consisted of many well-known developers of the time,

- Todd Anderson.
- Larry Augustin, from Linux International.
- John "maddog" Hall, also from Linux International.
- Sam Ockman, from the Silicon Valley Linux User's Group. This demonstrates that, even at this early time, policy decisions involved the community.
- Chris Peterson of the Foresight Institute. He ultimately coined the term Open Source.
- Eric S. Raymond, author of *The Cathedral and the Bazaar*, which discussed the development mentality of the community.

RMS was not invited to this meeting since it was believed that his insistence on Free software above all else would derail the process.

Bruce Perens was the project leader of the Debian® project, a purely Free (not Open) Linux *distribution*. This term is used to indicate that the included software features both a collection of GNU tools and a Linux kernel. Debian GNU/Linux, as it is known, was one of the first distributions to have a set of formal guidelines, to which all contributors should adhere. This was documented in the *Debian Free Software Guidelines*, which was created by Perens and honed (via the traditional email channels) during June 1997. Shortly after the meeting in Palo Alto, Perens gave his support to the term by removing the Debian-specific references from the guidelines, whereby it became the basic tenets for the *Open Source Initiative*, which are:

- Free redistribution, without restrictions.
- The source code must be available in an unobfuscated form, enabling it to be modified easily.
- It must permit derived works and modifications to be released under the same license. However, it does not *require* this is done. This allows new source code modifications to be kept secret, but still remain under an Open license.

- The authors' integrity must be preserved by allowing distribution of software with changes, but it *may* require those changes to carry a different name. Reputations are very important in the community-led world of Open Source.
- There must be no discrimination against people or groups. If it is illegal to use certain software in particular countries, the license can warn against it but not prohibit it.
- There must be no discrimination against fields of endeavor, thus giving the same rights to scientists as to hobbyists and governments.
- No additional licenses (such as an NDA) should be required to receive Open Source software.
- The license must not be specific to a product, since the software may be distributed in many different compilations.
- It cannot restrict other software with which it may be distributed, so one CD-ROM may contain many different programs without the problems of cross-checking for mixed licenses.
- It must be technology-neutral and therefore cannot require the inclusion of EULA or click-through licenses. This allows it to be downloaded from a website, or copied to a CD-ROM without restriction.

You can read the full explanatory text from *http://www.opensource.org/docs/ definition.php*.

The Open Source Initiative details the required terms in a license for it to be considered Open Source-compatible. If a license fulfills all of these, then it is compatible. It does not limit additional clauses that may be added, provided they don't contradict any of the terms in the previous list. This means it is permissible to release your source code under an Open Source license (because that fulfills your obligations), but consequently permit licensees to release their software under a non-Open Source license. This is different from the purest Free software licenses, such as the GPL, which requires you to perpetuate the terms of the original license. Open Source, in general, does not.

There is a list of the currently compatible OSI licenses at http://www.opensource .org/licenses/index.php.

Notice that on the surface, Open Source appears identical to Free software, but there are many differences. All Free software is, by definition, Open Source. However, not all Open Source is Free software—as dictated by the inventor of the term, RMS. For ease of reference, the term FLOSS is often used to encompass the general topic of Free, Libre, and Open Source software.

Ultimately, both Free software and Open Source are umbrella terms to encompass a basic viewpoint. At no point do the terms on their own dictate terms for the use of software. So, instead of assessing software based on its philosophy, consider only the license under which it is released and how it can provide you with solutions to solve your problems.

Licensing and Copyright

One of the biggest hurdles in understanding FLOSS is the distinction between the couplet of copyright and distribution.

Simplistically speaking, *copyright* is the right of the owners of a work to do as they wish with it. Copyright can be sold, assigned, or reassigned to anyone, but in most cases it rests with the author and is vested from the moment it's created. Even if software is given away, the software copyright generally remains with the creators, and it is their rules that govern how you may use it.

The license for *distribution* covers the rules by which you can pass on the software. This generally breaks down according to whether (or not) you can redistribute the software as given, or incorporate alterations, changes, or fixes you have made. It often includes whether you can pass the software on to any further users, and it may additionally include clauses indicating whether a fee may be charged for the software.

Source code is usually mentioned explicitly in the distribution license, although this is unnecessary, as having the freedom to make changes implies the source code must be present because changing any nontrivial software without it is incredibly difficult.

Let us now cover the basic terms prominent in FLOSS licensing. In each case, the traditional connotations are given. Some licenses may not fit exactly into any particular category, but all the common ones (such as the GPL) do and have been derived from these basic definitions.

The following demarcations were made in the first instance by GNU and have generally been accepted by the industry. However, there is no governing body that regulates the software industry, so some users may have alternative descriptions for some terms.

Free Software

The copyright remains with the authors, but everyone is permitted to copy, distribute, change, and use the software. Source code must always be available. This is Free as in freedom. All GNU software is Free with a capital F.

Open Source

As with Free software, this indicates that the copyright remains with the authors and all the usual rights are associated. The technical differences lie within the specific licenses, as many Open Source licenses include permissions that limit the freedoms that Free software seeks to offer. In most cases, however, the distinction is minimal. However, a lot of Open Source software does not require your source code to be given away.

TIP

Never refer to GNU Software as being Open Source. Always call it Free software, especially in the company of RMS.

Public Domain

This covers software that has no copyright, and is distributable freely. However, because no copyright is claimed[3] you are under no obligations to perpetuate your changes to another, nor may you be able to do so, because the person who gave you the code may have withheld the source—as they are at liberty to do with public domain code. Most software that comes under the heading of public domain usually exists on *shovelware* CD-ROMs and often only exists in binary form, making the idea of changing it a moot point.

Shareware

This covers any package that may be distributed freely but may not be altered or adapted. A license fee is traditionally payable once you use it for a fixed period of time, say one month. This was the origin of try-before-you-buy software, but may have been crippled through omitted features (usually Save and Print). This idea spawned a million imitators where, instead of asking for money, the developers asked for postcards (as in cardware) or beer (as in beerware), for example.

Generally, source code is not included and modifications are not permitted.

Freeware

This has no connection with Free software or Open Source. It is generally used to describe software that is available free of charge, but comes with no source code or the rights to modify it in any way.

Proprietary

This is effectively *permission software*, where you are required to acquire explicit written permission before redistributing, altering, or otherwise mess around with it. Source is only given in the rarest circumstances, and even then only under additional restrictions. These often prevent you from redistributing the source, changing it, or making use of it. This category covers most shrink-wrapped software.

Commercial

This covers any software created with the intention of making money from it. However, it is permissible for the software to be Free (as in Freedom), with money being made instead through support contracts or other value-added means.

Copyleft

This peculiar term is used to refer to specific license conditions whereby no one redistributing the software may add further restrictions when they do so. The GNU General Public License is the best-known example of a copyleft license. Other copyleft licenses exist but are discouraged because it can be legally impossible to combine source code from two or more different copyleft licenses.

One of the best examples of geek literary humor came from Don Hopkins when he wrote to RMS on this issue. On the envelope was the phrase "Copyleft—all rights reversed."

OPEN SOURCE MYTHS

The best word to describe the group of developers that produce Open Source software is *community*. And like any community, it has some zealots, advocates, and bad apples! Myths also abound, creating a stigma around particular products, or even Open Source in general, which prevent them from getting an honest assessment outside the community. Critical decisions are consequently based on these erroneous opinions that lead to inevitable problems in the future.

This section is dedicated to explaining the most common myths to show where the truth lies, enabling a qualified decision to be made.

Most of the myths presented here come from company-sponsored FUD, which stands for Fear-Uncertainty-Doubt. It is used as a negative form of advertising against someone else. While this is illegal in some countries, it can still slip under the radar when presented as legitimate research, such as statistics. On November 1, 1998, the "Halloween documents" were released, which documented Microsoft®'s dirty tricks campaign against Linux and Open Source projects in general. They are archived on Eric Raymond's site at http://www.catb.org/~esr/halloween/.

You Have to Give Your Source Code Away

This is not always true. Your source code belongs to you. If you decide to combine it with someone else's source code, then that license indicates the terms by which you can do so. Some licenses require you to make your source available. Some licenses will not. It is therefore necessary to check the terms of the specific Open Source license before finally deciding on a package. Chapter 2 details several popular licenses and what rights you have under each of them. Here is a rough guide:

GPL: You must release source code.

LGPL: You must release changes to the existing code base, but can retain all source you've written yourself that is separate to the original library. However, you must release the code as a precompiled object file so it can be relinked to the original LGPL library.

BSD or X11: You can maintain the secrecy of all your source code.

Naturally, there are other issues when combining code that use different licenses, and that topic is also covered in Chapter 2.

It Is Poor Quality

This is partially true. There is a lot of bad-quality, broken, and half-complete software in the world, and some of it is even Open Source. Using FLOSS doesn't instantly make the software poor, in the same way that spending a lot of money on something does not make it good. Where the Open Source community falters is that there is *a lot* of software out there. In the words of Theodore Sturgeon, "90 percent of everything is crud." In FLOSS, this is probably closer to 99 percent just by virtue of the sheer volume. Everyone in the community has written an online photo library, but only Flickr is prominent in most people's minds. Like all other software, each package should be used *in situ* to test its fitness for purpose.

Finding good software in such a large ocean can be difficult. In the case of 3D graphics engines, for example, there are nearly 650 packages listed on the *http://cg.cs .tu-berlin.de/~ki/engines.html* site alone. These include simple wrappers to OpenGL written by students for a first-year graphics course to professional-level game engines that have been used in commercial products. After all, the source code to *Quake® III (ftp://ftp.idsoftware.com/idstuff/quake3/source/Q3A_TA_GameSource_ 127.exe)* is now available as Open Source, and no one believes that this game is of poor quality or unprofessional.

There is no one best way to separate the wheat from the proverbial chaff. In the first instance, you should thoroughly read the product's website to look for sample code, tutorials, and documentation. A mature product generally has an abundance of documentation that has been created over time and by different people on other sites. Since there are more programmers than writers, only the best software has a manual beyond that written by the original developers. If the package has a book written on it, then that too is a good recommendation. The libraries featured in this tome, in Chapters 5 through 11, are by their nature among the better Open Source projects in their respective fields.

You can also determine the quality of the project by its volunteers because, after all, Open Source is very focused on its community. If the project has an active mailing list (which can determined by subscribing for a week or by reviewing the archive), then not only is development ongoing, but there is someone there to help understand the code that's gone before. You can also use the mailing list to determine the quality of information present, as the signal-to-noise ratio on some projects can be very low.

The Internet brings out certain character flaws more than other mediums. One unfortunate trait present (or at least, vocally present) in Open Source development is that of the zealot. They will be anti-establishment for no solid reason, because they like rebelling and behaving like the underdog. They can be vocal on any mailing list, even those of good projects, so do not reject work on this basis alone.

Projects on SourceForge[4] have an additional metric to consider: frequency of updates. With SourceForge being known as a general dumping ground for FLOSS, there are invariably a lot of bad projects and many projects that were started but never really got going. The software used on the site allows you to see how often edits are made and to what extent. This is not foolproof, of course, because some projects use SourceForge to save their own hosting fees and consequently will have their main pages hosted elsewhere.

You can sometimes determine the frequency of updates by using the Wayback Engine at http://www.archive.org, *which archives the home page repeatedly over time.*

Also, consider the quality of the releases made. One exception to the rule is in the case of the scripting language, Lua. This has had 12 releases in total over the last 13 years, with only three since the turn of the millennium. However, each one has been very stable.

The best and final way to evaluate a FLOSS project is to actually download it and test it out. This is not always the easiest of tasks because not all of them include binary packages—it is open *source* after all. And not all of them include Microsoft Windows® packages. However, these are more common in the games-development sphere. Evaluating a product should only be done by a senior software engineer.

With a spare day. This is because it is not unreasonable to require this amount of time to build the package from source. While this might seem like an instant deal breaker, you must remember that the software was developed in an entirely different environment. Nothing is guaranteed, so consider how long it takes a new hire to build your own in-house software without guidance, and then judge accordingly.

Finally, here are some comments about the multimedia exceptions. That is, when experimenting with multimedia software, do not judge the software upon the quality of its real-time output, unless the purpose of that software *is* real time. This is because the problems with skipped video frames and stuttering audio may be a problem with the underlying drivers and not just the package. This is more true under Linux, where free software drivers are not as good as their proprietary counterparts because they're written by the community without the insider knowledge from the hardware vendor. Therefore, it's likely that a movie-editor tool can export the film perfectly, but has great problems with the (simpler) task of playback.

There is No Support

This is very largely wrong. Any reasonably sized project will have a number of developers who maintain the code, answer questions, and run the mailing list. As you will have realized from the evaluation phase mentioned earlier, if there is none of these standard resources, then very often the project is dead and is no longer worth dealing with. That said, if no one is actively developing it (and you find it indispensably useful), then either you can take over or fork[5] the project for yourselves and the good of the software. The methods by which this should be carried out are outlined in the section on development practices later in this chapter.

No One Uses It

Sometimes true. Despite being held up as an issue with the uptake of FLOSS, it is not a good argument. In some fields, having a product that everyone else overlooks can be seen as a competitive advantage. This is not strictly true in the FLOSS world, where many eyes act as a natural crud filter, but the problem usually lies elsewhere. More often than not, it is usually fear of the unknown or a problem with one of the other myths detailed here—usually the belief that there's no support or that it doesn't work.

In 1999, Tim O'Reilly gave a talk in which he mentioned that the entire Internet relies on domain name system (DNS) that, at its heart, runs the Free software product BIND. And that 75 percent of all email is handled by Free software. And that 60 percent of websites use Free software. In 2006, he is still right, although the numbers have improved, since Apache alone commands about 70 percent of the world's web traffic, according to *http://news.netcraft.com/archives/web_server_survey.html*.

You Can't Make Money

Sometimes true, but it very much depends on what you're selling. If you try to sell software that everyone can already download for free, you might find it easier to sell fire to Satan! On the other hand, if you provide value-added code (which runs faster, smaller, or across a network), then this is something for which people would pay money. When written under a suitable license, these code changes do not have to be released back to the community, so it's a very definite addition.

Some projects, such as the Portable Document Format (PDF®) and PostScript® (PS) viewer GhostScript, work on this idea. The product is Free, but a commercial version can be bought with new features and an improved code base, along with better support and documentation. This commercial release becomes the Free version the following year, giving a 12-month industrial advantage for those who wish to pay.

As game developers, there are many revenue avenues to explore other than pure code. First, because the license terms only apply to the source, you can release any amount of graphics and new-level data and charge whatever the market will pay, since the license does not apply to any assets loaded from disk. Consider the modding community; the graphics and animations of *Quake* and *Half-Life* mods may be highly variable, but a professional add-on pack always triumphs over the student projects and hobbyists and thereby provides a very direct route to market. *Counterstrike* did good business for its developers and could have been developed as a standalone game using nothing but Open Source software.

Chapter 3, "Open Source in the Game World," explores this, and other, business ideas.

It's Insecure

Sometimes true, but no more so than proprietary software. This argument is usually leveled at networking applications and not games, where insecure software could result in a cracker[6] taking over your web server, email system, or worse. The closest analogy is in online games, where an insecurity could lead to crackers breaking the balance of gameplay making the game less fun for the paying public.

The belief that Open Source is insecure stems from the various benchmarks that monitor reported insecurities. And like all benchmarks, it's important to understand what the figures mean. In the first instance, there are many more flaws highlighted in Open systems because many more people are able to report them. This is in stark contrast to closed operating systems where each security problem is never announced to the public but kept hidden on private email lists. These numbers are also tarnished by the reporting methods often used. A security bug in the Linux kernel should count as one bug. However, many people are unaware that SuSE® Linux, Red Hat® Linux, Debian GNU/Linux, and Novell® Linux use the same kernel underneath, despite being listed as four different systems. Consequently, that one bug shows up as four, skewing the figures.

In reality, there is little difference in the *number* of bugs that either system has. But the severity of the problems, and the speed at which they're fixed will differ. This is where Open Source generally wins out.

It's Unenforceable

Untrue. There are lots of different Open Source licenses available, and many have been tested in court. This includes the GPL, where the Free Software Foundation takes action against violations around 20 to 30 times a year[7]. In most cases, however, it is unnecessary to take the case into court because it is obvious to the lawyers involved that the case against could never be won. This is covered in more detail in Chapter 2.

It's Only for Linux

Sometimes true, but it's always dependent on the specific software. For most people, their first brush with Open Source is through Linux, X Window System™, or some other Unix-oriented software. All of these projects were initiated as a means to support the creation of an entirely free Unix-based operating system, which meant programmers trying to port this software to Microsoft Windows often had problems because the software was never intended to run cross-platform. This implied a greater symbiosis between free software and Linux than really existed.

However, it is true to say that a lot of free software began on Linux, and that there is a lot of (game irrelevant) software available under an open license. This situation has now changed, and much free productivity software is now available for Microsoft Windows, as covered in Appendix G, and made available through *http://www.theopencd.org*.

Furthermore, games software is different. Those working on game libraries know the market has been very Microsoft Windows-focused and will usually accommodate. This is particularly true of graphics code, where the drivers have historically been superior to those available under Linux. Consequently, to show off their code in the best possible light, they ensure a Microsoft Windows version exists to benchmark their frames-per-second statistics.

TIP

If you do not have the resources to keep a purely Linux machine available, it is now very easy to create a virtual Linux machine on any Microsoft Windows desktop to experiment with Linux code when no native version exists or is several revisions behind. Chapter 4, "Development Environments," covers this.

And don't forget, in those cases where Linux is the only officially supported platform, you as a company will earn great kudos from the community by creating and maintaining the Microsoft Windows port. This is still cheaper than rewriting the whole code from scratch. Furthermore, electing to have your name attached to it ensures a more prominent Google™ ranking, which in turn can make recruitment easier as many geeks prefer to work for Open Source-friendly employers. It's the software equivalent of doing charity work!

One additional myth that is usually given in rebuttal is that the maintenance of your work in the community is time consuming. However, the bugs need to be found anyway (and you now have additional, unpaid, testers), and new features can be added as and when you, as a company, decide it appropriate. This is no different to how Open Source development works when there is an individual maintaining the project and not a company.

You Cannot Change It

Completely untrue. The focus behind FLOSS is that you *can* change it. What is sometimes meant by this argument is that you can't force the changes into the maintainer's main branch. *This* is true. This occurs because, essentially, it is their project, and they have the right to include—or exclude—any change they don't believe is of benefit to the community. If you do have trouble having changes accepted, it might be for any number of reasons:

- Your change is too specific.
- The change would detrimentally affect too many people.
- It breaks compatibility.
- It's not in keeping with the aims of the package, that is, you favor speed, whereas the code is designed to be small.
- The source is not submitted in a sensible, or the required, format.
- You've submitted source under a different, or incompatible, license.
- The project is no longer being maintained.
- A new drop of the source code hasn't been made yet.
- The maintainer is stupid and doesn't realize the benefits of your code.

All are possible, including the last one, as there can be some very zealous developers out there. Think of the difficult one in your development team . . . now imagine how difficult he would be to persuade if you *weren't* paying him.

This area is covered in more detail later, when discussing the development practices within FLOSS.

Programmers Won't Accept It

Largely untrue. While bad programmers might be concerned about job security, this is usually true of any code that's "Not Invented Here." However, the good programmers generally embrace it as they would any other middleware. While it is often true that engine and library programmers, whose roles are subject to more changes, are the most nervous, they are ultimately rewarded by the amount of opportunities their new roles allow because they can now concentrate solely on cutting-edge features instead of reimplementing the wheel—again.

LICENSING OPEN SOURCE

Unlike proprietary software, where shrink-wrapped agreements and EULAs are present before you even install the program, there is no formal signup process involved in Open Source. As with most other software, there are rights and obligations, but none of those attached to Open Source comes into effect until you intend to redistribute or release your (potentially) modified program. At this point, you have agreed by your actions to adhere to the inalienable rights and principles of Open Source. If you elect not to rerelease this code, then you are under no obligations whatsoever to do so.

The following section looks at these principles.

Principles

Despite the plethora of licenses in use within the Open Source community, they all follow very similar principles. These govern:

- The rights you have to the copyright of the code
- The rights you have to distribute the code
- How you should indicate the license to your end user
- What warranty and fitness for purpose is provided

The specifics are detailed in Chapter 2, but it is fair to say that the only commonality among them is that you are given no control of copyright (except in public domain software), and there is no warranty implied or otherwise in the software.

Warranties

Here are a few words about the warranties supplied with Open Source. There are none. Period.

Due to complexities in modern software development, no generally available software (including proprietary) comes with any of the three main forms of warranty. They are as follows.

Express Warranty

This is usually given as part of a sale. It is used when the product being sold has an explicit claim that it will perform a particular function. The express warranty generally entitles the purchaser to a refund or replacement if it fails to perform this function. These are usually only found on sales in the physical world where a television, for example, has a one-year express warranty.

Implied Warranty

This is sometimes termed a *Warrant of Merchantability*. It states that the product, as sold, will perform in a manner that is generally accepted to fit its description. This is to say, if you buy a piano it will work as a piano. This only exists with purchases from a vendor who is recognized as someone capable of selling pianos. A private individual who happens to be selling a piano wouldn't be able to give an implied warranty because their knowledge of pianos is limited to nonexistent. The determination of whether an individual can provide an implied warranty is governed by the operation of law.

Software comes with an explicit exclusion of implied warranty because, in part, the developers are not necessarily recognized as being professionals. (Although many are, legal matters always err on the side of caution, as it's easier to say "No" and ignore the problem than it is to say "Yes" and have to support it.)

Warranty of Fitness for Purpose

This is an implied warranty, also governed by the operation of law, but with the ideas of an express warranty. So when purchasing your piano you say you want to stand on it to announce each song, and the salesman says, "Of course it'll take your weight," he has made a warranty that it is fit for the purpose. This applies whether the seller is qualified in the area or not. Since Open Source software can be broken up into so many different routines and applied to so many different scenarios, it is impossible to claim whether the code is suitable in any given situation. Therefore, no warranty of this kind is given.

A Warranty Against Infringement

This is a comparatively new warranty and only truly exists in the field of intellectual property. It guarantees that the seller owns the necessary rights to sell it on—the right to copy (copyright), the appropriate patent clearances, and so on. Naturally, with the state of software patents and disparate retention of copyright, this cannot be offered on Open Source software. However, some companies insure against this and/or provide this warranty to provide a blanket of security for cautious developers.

Distribution

The distribution of Open Source software, as it is passed onto you, will vary. This is because the requirements of the various licenses are usually not specific about how you should release the source; only about what should be released. Consequently, source code is released in a manner the developer believes is easiest for him. This is usually a source archive in either .zip or .tar.gz (a.k.a. a GNU zipped tarball) format, but it may be available only through CVS access. Although CVS may not be installed on many machines by default, CVS *is* Free software, so this does not count as an additional restriction. In all cases, the license must be included.

There are even situations where the software does not come with source! In these instances, the license dictates whether the source should be available (the BSD license doesn't require it, for example), and from where it can be obtained. In some cases, a binary distribution references the source archive on a different server, or it may provide only a written license to provide it, in which case you must officially request it.

At no point do you ever need to notify the author that you are downloading, using, or even selling Open Source software. This is fortunate since this could potentially create some very long notification emails.

Giving Back

Different licenses have different requirements as to what you should give back. This is the area in which Open Source licenses differ the most, as you will see from the examples in Chapter 2. In all cases, it is traditional to pass patches, fixes, and new features to the maintainer for future inclusion. Even if you are not required to do this and intend to close your version of the source, you will be helping yourself in the long run because the reintegration of this source will be much easier. The maintainer will generally recommend the format in which these patches should be sent. Usually it is a *diff* file that shows only the lines that have changed between one specific previous version and yours. Chapter 11, "The Tools Pipeline," details some of the tools necessary to accomplish this.

If you are not intending to change the Open Source code you have been given, then you must still supply the source yourself and should not direct the user to the existing source code.

Regardless of license, you must always declare the terms under which your software is distributed. This is often governed by the license of the Open Source software from which you derived your own. But in any case, the end user cannot know the terms of the license unless you make clear what that license is and where to get it. For this reason, most software dictates a reference to the license in all source files, and the README.TXT file in the root directory, which directs the licensee to the LICENSE.TXT file in the same directory. Capitals are generally used for these filenames due to the fact they stand out more, especially in Unix-derived operating systems that are almost exclusively lowercase.

OPEN SOURCE DEVELOPMENT PRACTICES

For most developers, writing computer games is an understood process. More important, it is a *process*. They know the people with whom they are working, and are generally sitting next to (or very near) them. If they have issues with them or their code, they can raise it with the lead programmer, producer, or CTO. Everyone on the team is there to create a specific game, so ultimately must pull in the same direction. Open Source developers are working on their own projects, with their own focus. Your need for a small memory footprint might be the antithesis of their requirement for faster code. Their want for a larger feature set might contravene your minimalist architecture, and your deadlines will rarely coincide. It is the gentle equivalent of writing third-party middleware, but without knowing your customer requirements.

One of the oft-repeated mantras against Open Source software is about getting changes and bug fixes rolled back in to the main source. But this doesn't need to be a problem. Understanding how these developers work will help you approach them and how to best use their software.

Who Are They?

The first Free software released under the official banner of GNU Software was created specifically to create a purely free operating system. Which developers wrote which tools was governed by what Eric Raymond[8] calls "scratching a developer's personal itch." This is similarly true of most of the projects on SourceForge or FreshMeat[9]; the originator of a project generally has a specific interest in the project and a specific reason for writing it. This even includes Linux, an Open Source operating system kernel created (initially) by Linus Torvalds, which was begun "just for fun[10]."

From this time on, the originator assumes the role of *maintainer*. They are called the maintainers of the project even if there is only one programmer working on it. Throughout the lifetime of the project, it is the maintainer's responsibility to fix bugs, accept patches, and release new versions as and when they become available. The maintainer, therefore, is a combined lead programmer and producer. They rarely have anyone to answer to. Sometimes they bow to community pressure, but not always. Sometimes they are paid to make changes, but not always. Sometimes they delegate to other developers they personally trust, but not always.

When the project grows, other people become interested and submit their own features and bug fixes. To use the Open Source vernacular, they are called *contributors*. At the discretion of the maintainer, these changes may become part of the main source code, be ignored, or be placed alongside in a separate `contrib` folder. When the source is incorporated into the main code the copyright is consequently shared. The proportion of work is immaterial, but because the code is freely distributable, this is not an issue. Where the notion of copyright holders becomes important is when, or if, the source wants to be released under an alternate license, either to support a dual license or to replace the existing one entirely. Because only the copyright holder has the right to change the license, this must be agreed on unanimously by all contributors. For large projects extending over many years, this becomes an increasingly difficult and time-consuming administration task. If anyone objects, then the project can either not change license or developers must rewrite the contrary author's portion of code. But to do that they must know what code they submitted, and not all maintainers keep such detailed records. The increased use of source control within the Open Source community has helped this, however.

Bug fixes are not covered by copyright and therefore do not carry any claim to partial copyright of the product. Therefore, you can't submit a bug fix with the intention of forcing a change in license or for the purpose of vetoing license changes in the future. If you submit a feature with similar intentions, your code will be rewritten very quickly and you will most likely be blackballed from future development on that project. With Open Source being such a close-knit community, you may even find yourself at odds with other projects, too.

The alternate option, using a `contrib` folder, keeps these copyright issues at bay by isolating new code from the main branch. Additionally, some developers only accept code to their projects with the proviso that all copyrights are assigned to them to prevent this scenario. This also avoids the problem, albeit in a less community-friendly manner.

In larger projects, the maintainer may entrust some level of control to comaintainers. Linus Torvalds, for example, calls this group his lieutenants. They also have commit rights, which gives them the ability to make changes to the main source code held in a CVS repository. This is not an exclusive group, however, and by regularly contributing good code to a project you can often be rewarded with similar access. Despite being termed Open, most FLOSS source control repositories are targets for crackers and virus writers. Consequently, read access is generally available to everyone, but only the trusted few get commit access.

The structure of Open Source development teams is generally more fluid than in bricks-and-mortar businesses, but ultimately follows the same guidelines of trust. The maintainer retains full control of the project at all times, and it is not possible to forcibly remove his control. However, there are some extenuating circumstances.

Orphaned Projects

When a project has not been updated for a long time, it usually means one of two things. First, it can mean that the project has been made redundant by one or more other projects currently available. By reading old mailing lists or newsgroups and the release notes from the last couple of versions you may be able to ascertain which software has superceded it by comments such as "Add feature ABC to compete with XYZ." The same is true in reverse, as the announcements for XYZ will usually say "much better than ABC by supporting . . ."

Second, a project may become orphaned because the author no longer has the time or impetus to continue working on it. Free software created for university courses or as CV fodder often languishes untouched on websites for many years.

If you find an orphaned project that you wish to make use of, then it is possible to take over as maintainer by adopting it. The first step is to contact the last-known maintainer. This is usually by the email address on the web page, or it may be included in the README, but remember to check for addresses stored as image files, or written as name <at> address-<NO_SPAM>.com, both intended to fool spambots. If no reply comes from this, then post to any connected mailing list and the relevant newsgroup(s), and announce that the maintainer can't be contacted and you intend to become the new maintainer. If no one steps up after two or three enquiries, and no one else has been previously working on the project (in which case their claim trumps yours), then it is safe to assume the role. Even if the original maintainer does return to the scene, it is very likely he'll assign the maintenance to you anyway.

Copyright is assigned to the individual who authors it, not their role. So, if the original maintainer is also the author, assuming the role of maintainer does not give you the copyright. Also, asking to acquire the copyrights when you take over a project often offends and is treated with suspicion.

If the maintainer does turn up and refuses to help, you still have options. One of which is forking.

Forking the Project

Forking means to split. So, what was once one project, with one maintainer, now becomes two projects with two separate maintainers. At the point of forking, they both retain exactly the same source code, but the forked project (i.e., the new one) has to create a new name and identity for itself. Because you are not taking control of the copyright, you cannot repackage the forked code under a different license or turn it into proprietary code. But you can build on it under the same terms, without having to request permission from the original maintainer.

In large projects, and even small active ones, it is very rare to fork a project. There are many reasons for this. First, it creates a rift in the community. This not only generates ill will, but splits the development effort in half—or worse. Forking is such a religious issue with developers that they often adopt a particular fork based on personal alliances and not technology. Second, with both forks of the project attempting to solve the same problem, it becomes increasingly difficult to reconcile the two code bases. Any time and effort you save by forking the project is often insignificant when compared to the perpetual integrations between two forked versions, and it would be easier to maintain your own local version.

Paying for Changes

It is possible to persuade some developers to accept code changes with financial inducements. This may be in the form of cash, but generally is done with more subtly, and exists in the form of web hosting or a new computer to help compatibility testing. In this way, the maintainer gets something they need, and you get the goodwill by being associated with the project in a nonobtrusive manner. And it's more difficult for someone to turn down code changes in this situation.

The best way to approach FLOSS developers, if this is a long-term goal, is to tell them you're using their code and want to help with the project. Ask them what they need to make a better product. Their answers will vary, but most hardware and financial requests of a hobbyist individual are not unrealistic for many professional (and even independent) developers.

Paying for Developers

As an extension to the previous idea, it is possible to pay the developers a wage to develop their software. On the face of it, this can appear counterproductive as you are essentially paying to give your competitors a better product. However, what actually happens is that you are paying to give yourself a better product—which your competitors can gain from, but only if they work in the same way you do. Bear in mind that your reason for adopting a pay-to-play idea is because your prospective changes weren't accepted into the main code branch. Because you are now in charge and focusing the project more directly at your needs, it is more likely that any competitor will be hampered by your changes, not helped by them.

Since the employment of Open Source developers is a gentle way to massage the direction of the code, many companies, including Red Hat, Novell, and Fotango, have been doing it for years.

TIP

Many FLOSS developers are free-spirited types and would be repelled at the thought of being offered cash to change their opinions. So don't try.

Paying for Rights

Money can buy you love. It can also buy copyrights. Recall the discussion on copyrights and licenses earlier in this chapter. Once software has been released under a particular license, you, as the licensee, cannot change it. However, copyright holders can. They can release the same piece of software under any—and as many—licenses as they choose. Consequently, if you're a big enough company to buy the developer(s), you can actually own the software. Many companies do this (including Microsoft), and some of them even continue to keep the software available under a FLOSS license. Some buy other software (and software developers) to clear the market of competition for their own product or to close them down. While there is nothing illegal about closing once-Free software, it does not earn brownie points in the community.

The license ramifications of this move are considered later.

INCORPORATING OPEN SOURCE

With very few exceptions, most of the Open Source libraries you find are monolithic in structure. That is, they are all-encompassing and they cover much more functionality than their remit would originally suggest.

Take the example of a physics engine. While the solver is unique and the crux of any physics engine, the rest of the code usually comprises of mathematics functions, file I/O, and scaffold rendering code. In most cases, this just reinvents the wheel, but there are several reasons why.

First, programmers generally write applications, not libraries. Therefore, to produce a working prototype they must include general code, such as a graphics renderer and math library.

The second reason is that no code is an island. It *needs* that math library. Without it, the physics engine is but a theoretical concept. And when beginning to develop such a code base, it is typical to begin with a library that you have:

- Already written yourself and will mold to fit the new project.
- Downloaded and changed yourself. These changes are usually local to your own machine, requiring them to be merged back whenever a new version of the library is released.
- Begun writing anew when starting the larger project.

All these reasons are signs of typical programmer behavior. This should be quelled.

Originally, the C standard library was intended to provide a low-level abstraction to much of this functionality. There's `stdio.h` for the I/O system, `math.h` for mathematics, and so on. But C, and by virtue its standard libraries, are intended for general-purpose programming. Games are anything but general purpose. Consequently, the standard libraries are woefully underspec'd in many areas and the games' programmers must create their own. This is also true of the cross-platform supplementary libraries, such as Boost.

If you want to effectively use loosely coupled components, then you must only develop with unmodified code; otherwise, your components depend on those changes and become tightly coupled, relying on the quirks (and even bugs!) of the other code.

However, library code should be just that—a library. It should be taken off the shelf and used verbatim. Any corrections or fixes should be made and resubmitted back to the author. They should then incorporate your changes into the next version to the benefit of everyone else and to save you remerging the changes when you get the new version.

Notice that it says *should*.

The maintainers are not obliged to incorporate your changes. Even if they fix bugs that are detrimental to the project as a whole, maintainers may not accept them for the reasons detailed in the Open Source Myths section covered previously. One solution to this is to create your own private fork. This exists solely within the company, but is released (as per the license terms) with the game executable.

Creating Your Own Repository

While the technical problem of creating a repository is down to your source control package, there is sometimes confusion as to which version should be used as the fork. Despite the software industry's zeal to push the latest and greatest release, it is not always true that the most recent version is the best. Many people will hold back from the bleeding edge and only incorporate software (of any persuasion) once it has been tested in the wild. When code is initially released, there is no hard evidence as to whether this is a good release or not. Time will tell. However, there are clues you can pick up along the way.

Point Zero Releases

These are generally bad—1.0, 2.0, 3.0. All are developed from brand-new code, redesigned and rearchitectured from the version before. The term *lunatic fringe* has been used to describe users who trust a point zero release without qualification. Instead, wait for version 3.0.1 that usually occurs within the week. If it doesn't then either no one is using it (look at the mailing lists to see if this is true), or it's actually a stable release.

Developer Releases

Anything labeled as a developer release should also be avoided. These might work effectively, but may require very specific development environments to get them to work that it's not worth the trouble.

Repeated Releases

If there are many releases in a very short time frame, usually by one person, then it can be a sign of software being tested by the end users—and not the developers. Linus has said publicly that beta testing is what users are for, but he has clearly indicated which versions these were.

The Odd-Even Rule

This applies to Star Trek® films and Linux kernels. Essentially, any point release with an even number (1.2, 2.4, 3.8, and so on) is considered good, while those ending in an odd number are bad. The developers themselves, however, generally use terms such as *production* and *experimental* instead of good and bad. Note that this convention has not been adopted by all projects, so apply this logic only where it is known to work.

LICENSE EXCEPTIONS

As with all rules, there are exceptions, and Open Source is no different. Due to the split between copyright and distribution, it is easier to create exceptions than under other licenses.

Changing the License

Initially, consider the case where you wish to use Open Source software that is under a license to which you are unable (or unwilling!) to adhere. Having the rights to redistribute software does not give you the right to change its license. However, having the *copy*rights, does.

The copyrights in a piece of software are held among all the contributors, and it requires the authorization from *all* these developers before a license can be changed or released under an alternate one. If the software has been developed by a company, then it is likely the copyright remains with it.

The Free Software Foundation holds the copyrights for most of the code developed as GNU Software, which enables it to relicense its code at will. This includes the GNU Compiler Collection (GCC), which is a staple of many console-development environments. Under the normal rules of the license it would not be possible to produce a console's cross-compiler based on GCC without redistributing those changes to the masses. Naturally, with the secrecy surrounding console development, this is not an option. Consequently, a compromise is made with the FSF (that often involves money changing hands) to release a specific version under an alternate license so it can be used. This proves it is possible to negotiate with FLOSS developers for alternative licenses, no matter what their size.

The FSF also permits developers to assign their copyrights to the foundation so that similar decisions can be made on your behalf. However, most have not done so because to successfully sue for GPL violations, you have to be the original author, which is easier as an individual.

These rules apply to all software whether it is to be released under multiple licenses or if there is to be a retroactive change of license.

Mixing Licenses

This is an area fraught with danger because each specific license in use must be checked for compatibility with every other. While such an exhaustive list is beyond the scope of this book, solid guides for a small subset are certainly possible.

To understand the issues involved, the fundamental requirements of the licenses that can become deal breakers when licenses collide are considered. However, for a full discussion involving specific licenses, refer to the full commentaries in Chapter 2.

Redistribution of Code

The fundamental issue here is whether the program you write using licensed code must be released back to the public in its entirety. It covers any code that is compiled into the same executable with licensed code, or linked with it. Therefore, look at all the licenses involved for those that require you to release the source. All GPL software has this requirement, as does the interface package called QT (whose free version is under the QPL[11]). Therefore, the inclusion of a single piece of code from either of these licenses requires that the entire product be released under a similar license. It is an all-or-nothing situation.

So, if you mix GPL code with a proprietary library, then the GPL requirement wins out. Even if the other software has an NDA, a high price tag, or promises to curse your hard drive, you must still release the source code. Naturally, the onus is on you, as the developer, to acquire this permission from the vendor. So if any part of your released software requires GPL code, you must make sure that everything else is Open Source, in some manner, and you're prepared to release your own changes.

Even if you have your own 1-million-line program, and use a single 100 function from some GPL code, then you are required to open up the other 999,900 lines of your source. There are no worst-case "gotchas" here—the license is written in plain English, with no intention to trap you—but one of the libraries that may become a sticking point in the games field is *gettext*, the localization suite featured in Chapter 10, "Utility Libraries."

Redistribution of Changes

This differs from the former insomuch as only code based on the original must be given back, but any code that links to it can remain proprietary and closed. Using the example of a graphics library: you can keep the game code secret, but any improvements to the graphics engine must be kept open. Additionally, you might have to include the game code in object format so that future developers can relink your game to *their* improvements in the graphics library. The Lesser GNU General Public License (LGPL) is the best example of this kind of license. This has lesser restrictions than previously seen.

Additionally, because you are only linking to this code, you can place any other libraries you don't want to share in object files and link them in directly. This doesn't work with object files created from GPL code because that code must *always* be open. So GPL effectively trumps LGPL.

Additional Restrictions

The spirit and letter of Open Source law is to introduce and maintain freedoms, so if one license can only be used when those freedoms are maintained, and another disregards one of them (or requires inclusions or restrictions), then those particular pieces of software cannot be used together. Again, this is an all-or-nothing situation.

There are comparatively few cases where this occurs, but the most prominent involves our old friend (or is it fiend?) the GPL. Specifically, the GPL includes the requirement that redistribution cannot include further restrictions than are present in the original license. What constitutes a restriction, however, is interesting (and covered in Chapter 2), but one example is the inclusion of advertising clauses. So, even another license requiring you to advertise the fact that it "Includes the XYZ library by Joe Bloggs" would prevent you from mixing the XYZ library into GPL code.

While these are very difficult cases to spot, it is fortunate that most licenses do not include such advertising clauses, and most library code intended to be grouped with other code is not under a GPL-like license.

GPL: Friend or Foe?

It may currently seem that the GPL is very problematic, although a survey of Source-forge (*http://sourceforge.net/softwaremap/trove_list.php?form_cat=13*) shows that 47,811 of the 69,499 projects (at the time of writing) are available under the GPL. Its nearest rival is currently the LGPL with 7,911. Just as quality is more important than quantity, so is games software more important than photo albums written in PHP! Consequently you will discover that a lot of games-related Open Source is not released under the GPL, and so becomes less of an issue.

The issues subside further when you're not looking to mix GPL code with that from another license, as would be the case when using a large monolithic GPL code base. One example here is the *Quake III* engine. Because it incorporates everything you are likely to need, any minor gaps that need plugging can either be found within GPL-compatible repositories or rewritten yourself. After all, if you save $500,000 on a middleware license, it's probably worth that little extra effort.

A list of all the licenses that are currently compatible—and incompatible—with the GPL can be found at *http://www.gnu.org/licenses/license-list.html*.

As always, if one specific piece of software proves difficult to fit into the mix, then you can always ask for (or buy) the software under an alternate license.

Different Projects—Different Licenses

Curiously, the rules for mixing software apply only to its source code. Furthermore, this is only source code that is combined with other source code to create a derivative product. Using an Open Source compiler doesn't require that any code compiled with it becomes Open Source. Nor does using an Open Source paint package require you to assign any of your rights to the image you create or edit within it.

Furthermore, there are no license restrictions that apply to aggregation. That is, you can place your Open Source game onto a CD-ROM, supplement it with non-Open Source-level editors and game content (such as the art assets), and retain all your rights to the editor and assets.

Using Open Source on Consoles

In many cases, it is perfectly feasible to use Open Source in console development. Granted, in most circumstances, there is no prepackaged binary or known-good source archive, but it is not impossible to create one. The precise workloads vary according to the license.

BSD- and X11-style licenses

In the simplest of cases, any software that has been released under either a revised BSD or X11 license will suffer no ill effects. Briefly, these licenses put you under no obligation to release any part of the resultant source. Therefore, you can adapt the code with impunity. The worst you may be required to do is include a copyright notice in the manual.

One typical example of this license is the FreeType package, which uses a BSD license with a credit clause.

The Lesser GPL

This is stronger than BSD, insomuch as it requires you to provide access to the LGPL code you have modified but not any of the code that links to it. So, should you be using an LGPL graphics engine, you don't have to reveal any of the source code to your game—just the engine patches necessary to make it work. This is a fairly good trade-off because if your changes are specific, no one else will have a use for them, and you are not helping any competitor by doing so.

The only potential issue stems from the second part of the requirements. That is, you must make the object files for your game available so that they can be re-linked to the LGPL engine code. While this is a benign requirement, it does mean that others can rebuild your game, possibly with hacks and security flaws in the engine component. However, in order to compile both object and LGPL code back into a usable executable, you must have a suitable compiler. The LGPL states that you must provide such tools if they are not readily available. However, they're generally only available to licensed developers, which makes this clause impossible to fulfill without opening a dialogue with the licensors of the software and the console manufacturers.

CAUTION

You may think you can placate the manufacturers by including the object files on the game disk, which is usually under its own protection. However, this means the object files are not freely available, and so this trick will not adhere to the license.

Chapter 2 looks at the specifics of the LGPL.

The GPL

This is the strictest of the licenses presented in this book. It requires that any and all changes made to the source code under it are subject to the same conditions. That is, its source is freely available. While this is not a problem with PC games because the underlying API of DirectX or OpenGL is known and published, it is an issue with consoles because their programming guides and APIs are covered by NDA. Consequently, GPL code cannot be used directly in console games.

A Cure to All

Some FLOSS *is* available in console-friendly archives. One such package is *OpenAL*. This is able to exist in two formats because the authors have released the package under a free license, in addition to a proprietary one for the two Xbox consoles.

This is only possible when the software is released explicitly under an alternate license. Therefore, it never hurts to ask the authors of contentious packages whether they would consider releasing their software to you under an alternate license. This follows the same rules as detailed previously under License Exceptions, so it is impossible for them to relicense it unless all contributors agree. To this end, ensure you perform due diligence by reading the documentation to see who these contributors might be, and ensure that any requests for an alternative license covers these people. In most cases, this work can be done simply by asking the maintainer directly, and a CC: to the developers' mailing list.

Potential Problems

While there is nothing inherently dangerous about using FLOSS, it can become problematic when multiple licenses are used. Furthermore, because the source code is available to all, it is much easier to see if copyrights have been violated. Other problems are not so obvious.

Patents

In the last years of the 20th century, patent affairs were being applied to software. The reasoning for this was intriguing, as software is already covered by copyright and needs no more protection. However, patents were granted to various ideas, although the legitimacy of software patents has yet to be tried. Every company with an idea was patenting anything and everything it could think of. The overworked patents clerks allowed many of these through without the usual rigorous checks for prior art or unique inventiveness.

As a consequence, there are now so many patents for trivial things in computer science that developing software without violating at least one of them is impossible. Every month there is usually one new story of a previously-granted patent that would cause a very large percentage of existing software to be in violation of it, such as one-click ordering or command line macros. Until these patents are tested in court or are officially granted, there will be problems with patents. Indeed, the Patent Commons Project (*http://www.patent-commons.org/*) has been recently established to acquire patents under a pledge scheme. Many big names are involved, such as IBM®, Sun®, Novell, Red Hat, and OSDL, who have pledged the rights to their patents for the good of the community, allowing any user who wishes to make use of the ideas present within them.

While FLOSS suffers no more here than any other software (including that which you write yourself), its openness does allow it to be scrutinized more closely by others, so any potential patent infringement can be spotted earlier. Novell covers this very well at *http://www.novell.com/company/policies/patent/*. This is a good thing because it allows a Free version to be developed before it becomes a major problem. Conversely, any skullduggery on the part of the programmer will also be spotted.

With very few exceptions, no software will indemnify you against patent infringement. Recently, however, there have been companies that sell patent insurance, and larger companies (such as IBM) will protect you against infringement if you align yourself with them. The reason behind this last point is interesting: if you infringe on another company's patent, IBM will open its patent portfolio and attack the other company on your behalf. Since IBM has more patents than anyone else, there's a very good chance the other company will infringe one of its so it agrees to swap patent rights—eliminating any costs. IBM also gains immunity from another patent. This also unwittingly proves that patents do not help the small inventor.

When an infringing patent is found in your code, your options include:

- Change the code by finding a new solution to the problem.
- Prove that the patent is invalid by demonstrating prior art or that it contains no inventive step.
- Ignore it, hoping it will go away. This can court legal wranglings, however, and is not recommended.
- Pay the appropriate fees.
- Go without the feature.

None of these is a good option because development time is too precise to worry about such things. Unfortunately, there is precedence.

LZW Compression

One of the most famous cases of patents being used to the detriment of the software industry was the use of the LZW compression algorithm in compressed GIFs. This patent was filed in 1983 and published in *IEEE Computer* magazine the following year. The infamy of this case occurred because the article made no mention of a pending patent. Nor was any comment made when the compression method was used in the Unix compress tool (version 1.2 because you asked!) Nor was any comment made when the GIF format was formally released in 1987.

The patent holders (the UNISYS® corporation) accepted license fees from various high-profile developers (like Adobe®) but said nothing more concerning the patent until Christmas Eve 1994. While no licenser needs to publicize this fact, nor is it required to act against infringers, it did cause developers to panic. As a consequence, all GNU Software was changed to remove the offending code as quickly as possible.

As a direct response to this, a new format was devised called PNG (unofficially standing for PNGs Not GIF) and has since been termed Portable Network Graphics and become the de facto standard on the Internet.

FreeType

One of the patent cases you're likely to come across in games is with the Apple patent in FreeType, the Open Source font library for TrueType® fonts. This patent affects version 1, but not version 2, of the software. Although Apple has shown no signs of wanting to enforce its patent (unlike Unisys with LZW) a replacement algorithm was created anyway, which found its way into version 2. This is detailed fully in Chapter 5, "Graphics."

As with LZW, this replacement algorithm is nontrivial and can introduce unexpected issues in the development software, whether Open or not.

OpenSSL

One of the patent-heavy areas of software development is in encryption, such as the Open Secure Sockets Layer (OpenSSL) used to ensure safe traffic across the Internet. The developers of this particular software have included code that implements specific patent-encumbered technologies—specifically IDEA, MDC2 and RC5. While this is not illegal or against the terms of the license, it does require you, as the end user, to ensure you have the rights to use the patent-related code. For those who don't, you can configure the compiler to avoid that code:

```
./config no-idea no-mdc2 no-rc5.
```

Not Distributing Source

Despite Open Source software licenses being straightforward to understand and adhere to, there are still occasions where software is released, using GPL code, but the source code is not forthcoming. This happens for several reasons, but it usually boils down to ignorance, apathy, or intentional deceit.

Ignorance

Ensure that at each stage of the project you ask all the programmers from where particular algorithms came and what implementations they used. Because, although rewriting a piece of Open Source code (using the algorithm and ideas) is not covered by the software license or by copyright, there is the potential of it breaching a patent, such as the marching cubes algorithms (United States Patent numbers 4,710,876 and 4,885,688). Make sure all the programmers know they will not be penalized for using someone's code where they are permitted to do so.

Apathy

Creating a suitable source package of your latest game is probably the last thing you want to do—literally. It's an unforgiving task, and at the end-of-project crunch time, none of the development team ever wants to see that source again. Therefore, it's likely to be left—and forgotten.

In most licenses, you only have to ensure that source code is available—it doesn't have to be shipped at the same time as the game. Therefore, you have some breathing space between projects to create the archive and fulfill each specific license. GamePark Holdings (creator of the Linux handheld console, GP2x) got into trouble in January 2006 for not releasing the *exact* version of the code used to run its console. Such is community zealousness that the Slashdot forums had nearly 300 comments proclaiming the death of the GP2x because of this.

Intentional Deceit

This induces the most negative karma of all, and there is no excuse for it. The belief is usually that company X is so big that sole programmer Y will not try and file a suit against it because it doesn't have enough money. Or it thinks that no one will ever find the Open Source code inside the closed-source product. Both are wrong.

In the first instance, organizations like the Free Software Foundation (FSF) and *http://gpl-violations.org* can offer financial assistance in cases like this. Also, not all countries are created equally, and therefore legal aid may be available to private individuals, eliminating the usual problem in the U.S. where the biggest checkbook wins.

The second case also stems from two primary fallacies. That is, geeks (particularly Open Source geeks) have a lot of time on their hands to check code for violations. And although the EULA says "you will not reverse engineer this product," it is not binding because developers are allowed to do so under certain circumstances. It is reasonably simple to read the binary executable and match portions of code compiled under various options. If the case goes further, then the offending party is required to reveal the source code. From here, the similarities will be obvious.

Many developers are aware of these situations and intentionally put features into their code that would not normally be there so as to trivially prove it was stolen. For example, they may add code that is never called, add a cheat that's only executed when a special key press is entered, or they might misspell the original variable names so that, if it does come down to a line-by-line source code comparison, the same erroneous misspelling would rat out the culprit immediately.

But, Is It a Problem?

In a word—yes. Apart from the obvious facts that it is illegal[12] and unethical, it hinders the progress of Open Source, and can prevent developers from releasing more code. And from the point of view of someone wanting to use the modified and bug-fixed code, you can't!

To see the extent of the problem, the aforementioned *http://gpl-violations.org* site details many of the small—and not so small—companies that have been caught ignoring the rules of the best-known license, the GNU General Public License, a fuller description of which is given in Chapter 2.

FREE CONTENT

One of the most recent developments in freedom has been the creation of licenses like the Creative Commons[13], which cover all forms of media, including literature, photographs, music, and movies. An artist can generate content and give away *some* rights to others, enabling them to build on it, or take their art in a different direction. Since artists are purported to have a greater artistic temperament than programmers there are more restrictions in these licenses than there are for source code. However, with careful searching, you can find useful content to use within a computer game that costs nothing.

Creative Commons

This license is also know as CC, and unlike the licenses in the software world, where one license covers a specific set of terms, the Creative Commons license can be combined to allow you to tailor the precise license for your work without having to create a brand-new license each time. This makes it easier to determine, at a glance, which rights you are granted.

One noticeable difference, however, is that the parameters of the license are left to the individual creators. For example, the "by" license requires the work must be attributed, but it makes no requirement on how that must occur. It could be by a simple copyright line in the credits or to place the authors' names on the box packaging; it's up to the creator to specify anything more abnormal than "Written by Joe Bloggs."

As with Open Source software, the copyright to this media is not granted by the license, rather the scope with which you can use it and redistribute it. As with source code, you can always persuade artists to provide their work under other licenses through inducements.

The BBC has its own BBC Creative License, which is only available for residents of the United Kingdom and closely matches the ideals of the CC. However, it has very little useful content with respect to games development.

When CC-licensed work is included on a website, the icon shown in Figure 1.1 is usually accompanied with a link back to the CC website with a description of the full license. This description is abbreviated with one or more mnemonics: by, nc, nd, sa.

FIGURE 1.1   The Creative Commons logo.

These terms have the following meanings:

Attribution (BY): If you use this work, you must give credit to the author. The credit usually recommended is a single line in the manual, but the precise method can be described by the author. While not difficult to do, it does mean you have to be a meticulous librarian. Much of the material available at *http://commons .wikimedia.org/wiki/Main_Page* falls into a category similar to this.

Non-Commercial (NC): Quite simply, you cannot use the work for anything to make money, either directly or indirectly. This would therefore prohibit it from any commercial game.

No-derivative Works (ND): This means that although you may use the work, you cannot add to it. Nor can you transform, build upon, or take away from it. If it's music, you cannot remix it, add lyrics, or use it as a backing track to a video. Since everything in a computer game would be considered a derivative work, you cannot use any ND content. This is the only deal-breaker for the games developer.

Share-Alike (SA): Anything labeled with an SA brand means that you must reoffer your adapted works under the same license as you were given. That is, it must also be SA, along with whatever additional qualifications were given. This mirrors the function of the GPL with source code.

A share-alike license can only be used in combination with the attribution agreement, producing six different valid licenses.

In addition to the license, you may find additional limitations being placed on the work, such as "not to be used to promote seal clubbing." Naturally, these must also be followed.

The best place to start looking for free content is from the Creative Commons website itself. This site has specialized search facilities, which return only those works that are suitable for games development; that is, those without an ND component to the license.

There is also a trick whereby you can look for any website that links to the appropriate CC license page. *http://wholinkstome.com/* among others, supports this kind of search. So to search for all the electronic music released under an attribution-only license, you need to type the search URL *www.creativecommons.org/licenses/by/1.0.*

While it is technically possible to license content under licenses such as the LGPL, it is only truly understood in the context of distributing source code, so it suggested you use a Creative Commons license instead.

Open Source Open Content

In all currently-known cases, there are no restrictions in the way Open Source code and Open Content assets can be combined. Additionally, there are no restrictions in the way FLOSS code can use proprietary assets. This allows the games developer to use Open Source code throughout the game, but combine it with custom-made art assets and sell the two as a packaged game. Furthermore, because the code and content are separate entities, they can be combined into one package, without the licenses conflicting. This means your content does not have to become Open; you still maintain full copyrights and can easily sue for copyright violations if the assets to your game are reproduced without permission.

Very few games developers have taken the next step and opened their content for others. One of those that has is *http://www.nexuiz.com*, which has based its game on the original *Quake*.

ENDNOTES

1. As I'm sure readers of this book appreciate, "hacker" is the correct term for someone that enjoys technical challenges. Conversely, "cracker" is used for those that break (and attempt to break) into computer systems.
2. *http://www.gnu.org*
3. Under the Berne Convention you have to explicitly disclaim your copyright to place a work in the public domain.
4. *http://www.sourceforge.net*
5. In the open source world, a "fork" is the process where one project is split into two parts. Each continues as an individual project, under separate leadership.
6. The term "cracker" is used for those that break systems. The more common "hacker" keeps its more correct meaning of "programmer and tinkerer" within the open source community.
7. *http://www.vnunet.com/vnunet/news/2126778/open-source-licensing-minefield-looms*
8. For a greater understanding of the Open Source community read Eric's book, *The Cathedral and the Bazaar.*
9. *http://www.freshmeat.net*
10. This, not coincidentally, was also the name of Linus Torvalds' autobiography.
11. QT is also available in a commercial version where this rule does not apply.
12. The Sarbanes-Oxley Act can also be used in cases of GPL violation, *http://www.wasabisystems.com/gpl/sox.html.*
13. *http://www.creativecommons.org*

2 License Commentaries

In This Chapter

- The GNU General Public License
- The GNU Lesser General Public License
- The BSD and X11 Licenses
- Other Licenses

It is not an exaggeration to say there are hundreds of Open Source licenses in existence. When Open Source was new and the Open Source Initiative was still very young, most developers released each project under a specific license—their own. Each was concocted without lawyers and with specific purposes in mind, according to the developers' own whims. This proliferation makes it difficult for a newcomer to understand the exact ramifications of any particular license, especially when compared to the GPL, for example, which is well understood. Even when the license fully conforms to the OSI, and even when a big company is involved (such as Sun), people still create their own licenses to protect their own interests[1]. Consequently, the number of licenses has grown disproportionately to the size of the apparent Open Source market.

Over time, the more prevalent licenses took hold, and these are the licenses that most new projects will use. There are 58 licenses listed on the OSI-approved list (*http://www.opensource.org/licenses/*), although most of the source code pertinent to game development is generally released under one of the big four:

- GNU General Public License
- Lesser GNU General Public License
- Revised BSD License
- X11 License

Each Open Source license is like any other license—it is a contract. As with all contracts, the license agreement lays out what is, and what is not, possible under its terms. Also, like all contracts, it covers two sides because without being given something in return for something else, no mutual exchange has happened, and it is not a contract. The exchange in all Open Source licensing is the same: you are offered code (as a licensee) with which you can do various things. In return, you agree to redistribute it in a specific manner, as specified by the contract. In all the licenses given here, the only obligations you are required to make occur when the software is modified and/or passed on to someone else. There are no requirements about having to pay license fees to use or modify it.

The main licenses mentioned previously are covered here. You will see the history involved, why the license was created (and where it differs from the others), a breakdown of the license text, and what is necessary in order to conform with the license should you wish to use software published under it. This also includes information about mixing it with other licenses, and is probably one of the most important areas to study.

The discussion that follows has been culled from use cases and historical documents relating to the use of Free and Open Source Software over the last 15 years. Laws and jurisdictions change. This does not constitute legal advice. Always check with your lawyer concerning your specific circumstances.

THE GNU GENERAL PUBLIC LICENSE

Of all the licenses available, this is probably the most famous. It was created in 1989 by Richard Stallman using the Emacs General Public License as a base. In the early days, GNU created separate licenses for each product, too. These were often peppered with specific references to the program to which they were attached, making it difficult to transfer licenses. It was named the GNU General Public License; the first-ever version is available from *http://www.gnu.org/copyleft/copying-1.0.html*, although you are unlikely to find much games-related software released under it, as the industry hadn't understood or embraced the concept in 1989.

This general license was then upgraded to version 2 in 1991 and is the license under which most GPL software is released. It is also the license covered here.

Version 3 of the GPL began a 12-month public consultation in 2006, although the first games-related software released under it is not expected until 2008.

When the first GNU public licenses were released, it was a marked departure for most software of the day. In the academic field from which it was born, software was either given away free with the hardware needed to run it, or sold as a commercial package. When software, on its own, was given away, it usually fell into the public domain or was done so under very casual agreements. The GNU GPL solidified the intent of free distribution and provided the obligations to return any changes back to the community.

License Breakdown

As with most contracts, the GNU GPL is broken down into clauses, stating your rights and obligations at each stage. The complete legal text can be found in Appendix B.

The Preamble

This introduces the license and contains the brief philosophy of GNU, although the first important point to note comes just before the main preamble and is one that prevents you from changing the terms of the GNU GPL itself. For a license dictating freedoms, this might appear ironic, but it is within keeping of the license. This ensures that substandard licenses bearing the GNU title cannot taint its good name. This in turn assures readers that anything bearing the name GNU GPL is, in fact, an untainted version of the GNU GPL and that they can use the software knowing the terms implicitly. This also prevents you from creating a derivative license from the GPL.

The bulk of the preamble specifies the three main purposes of the license:

1. Keep the software free.
2. Highlight the lack of provided warranties.
3. Disclosure of patents law.

Freedom

This has been covered before—the use of Free to mean freedom, and not cost. Furthermore, once the software has been made free under this license, it must be kept free. This is so it can be distributed and modified without the original owner's permission. This is perpetuating, so others who receive the program must allow *their* licensees unfettered access of the code without having to acquire permission from the original author.

Only access to the code is granted, however. This opens two questions: copyright and patents. The copyright within the program is still owned by the original author, or authors, of the code. These rights are not transferred with the license. In fact, whenever GPL code is distributed you should see a copyright declaration before the preamble indicating who owns the copyright. Although this notice is not necessary (anything written down is automatically copyrighted under the Berne Convention), it is more usual to see it present, as it prevents misunderstandings later.

Warranty

Most FLOSS comes with an explicit statement disclaiming all warranties. This includes fitness for purpose. It is possible for any company to sell a warranty to the software, but none comes with the license itself. Clause 1 of the license explicitly mentions this as a business opportunity for middleware vendors. It does not affect the use of modified software for the games developer, as the agreement for any supplementary warranty must be distributed in a separate license.

Patents

The question of patents falls into two halves. Any patent created *as a consequence* of the implementation of program code is covered by the license. This ensures that should the creator, intentionally or otherwise, develop a new technique that someone else later patents, then the software in which it first appears does not become patent-encumbered. Prior art will rest with this software.

However, any existing patent whose algorithm is adopted within the software is not covered by the license, and you (as the licensee) must acquire the appropriate rights to use that patent. Generally, this will not be a problem in the games field since, with very few exceptions, each game is based on the same ideas and principles and the ones before it. Only a couple of well-known patents, such as the marching cubes algorithm[2], are likely to affect us. But if existing patented algorithms are used, then a license must be acquired for each licensee of the software. The problems come not from the licensing, *per se*, but knowing *what* features of the software are patented and need to be licensed.

Furthermore, any patent that has been implemented in GPL code is only provided for the GPL licensed version. If you reimplement that code, you need to acquire patent licenses as you would normally. Alternatively, if you obtain the code under a different license, this will need an explicit or additional, agreement to use that patent. Since only the patent holders can grant such licenses, and only the copyright holders can release GPL code under a different license, the original authors *must* also have been the patent holders, and so both rights would be provided together. There is no other combination possible in this situation.

Scope of the License

As mentioned in Section 0, the GPL only covers the acts of copying, distributing, and modifying the program. The act of using the program is not covered. Nor is the output[3]: so a GPL paint package does not lay claim to any pictures you draw with it, and the use of a GPL compiler does not require that any code you compile with it is forced under that license.

The initial section also mentions the phrase *derivative work*. This has specific meanings in copyright law and is an important part of the license. Essentially, any program that borrows from another is a derivative work. So if you take a GPL graphics engine and add a special effect to it, that resultant engine is a derivative work. Similarly, if you take the aforementioned engine and rewrite it in Java (with or without modifications), then your new engine would still be considered a derivative work. The reverse situation is also true. So, if you take the smoke effect from a GPL'd graphic engine and incorporate it into your own proprietary engine, then the smoke code is considered a "portion" of the work, and your engine would be a derivative of that code.

While this might appear overly protective, there are only two cases here that can cause some chagrin.

A Portion

Taking a piece of code, such as the smoke routine cited earlier, might appear under other laws as fair use. Quantitatively speaking, the smoke code might equate to a line of text in a novel. And you can legitimately quote a single line under the terms of fair use. Software, particularly FLOSS, does not work in that way because the qualitative aspects of the code are undeterminable outside a court of law.

Technically therefore, using any line of code is considered a portion. In reality, however, software is an amalgamation of everything that has gone before. So a single line that iterates around a set of objects is not really copyrightable. Instead, you should think of a portion of code in terms of function. The code that draws the smoke particles would be a portion, but the line that calls the graphics engine with a set of coordinates and a texture would not be.

If the only code of interest in a particular graphics engine is the smoke effect, then the license does not prevent you from learning the method by which it is handled and reimplementing it under a different license. It is best to do this using a *clean room implementation*. This can be achieved by Programmer A writing a specification for the smoke effect, based on his understanding of the GPL code, and then implemented and debugged by Programmer B using nothing but this specification, and certainly without consultation to the original code, the original program's output, or any input from Programmer A. Then, even if Programmer B creates a line-for-line copy of the original, there is a defensible argument against infringement.

Translation

This shows that the effort applied to the GPL has no bearing on the terms of the license; a complete translation may take many months, but the result would still come under the GPL. There isn't any real "work around" for this, although you can adopt the same clean room implementation as seen previously.

In reality, however, most people never want to translate a piece of code. They usually want a similar implementation in a different language—at which point they will usually internalize their own clean room structure, changing the original design so that the ideas are employed, but not the code. This avoids conflict with the GPL.

Alternatively, programmers might want to utilize a specific engine, but have it accessible from a different language; that is, the one they're more used to, at which point a wrapper is made, so the two pieces of code can communicate. This wrapper then becomes a derivative work and must be distributed under the GPL, as you see later. The code that then uses this wrapper must, in turn, be released under the terms of the GPL along with any code that uses it.

The Rights Given and Taken Away

Clauses 4 and 5 provide a simple pairing. Section 4 says that this is the only license you may use for the software. No sublicensing is allowed. This mirrors the text before the preamble that states no modifications can be made to the GPL license itself. Any attempt to do so will terminate the license, at which point you are in possession of code to which you have no rights because the law of copyright is still in effect. Therefore, you must explicitly license this code from the licensor under whatever terms he deems acceptable, or you must stop using the software.

This section also provides a safety mat, so should the licensor from whom you got your source code is found to contravene the license, it does not affect you, provided *you* conform to the terms of the license.

Enforceability

The enforceability of the GNU GPL is handled in Sections 5 through 7. This covers several distinct areas. The first begins by making the very open statement about the GPL, "you have not signed it." This does not make it unenforceable. Indeed, most proprietary software uses shrink-wrap or click-through licenses that forces you to agree with the demands before you even know if the program is suitable for your purpose. In contrast, the GPL allows you to install, use, and experiment with the program verbatim without ever being concerned about the license, as the license only comes into effect when you want to redistribute it in some way. By the time you are in a position to do so, you have experienced the license conditions and are able to make a valid judgment call as to whether you are able to comply. Shrink-wrap licenses have been passed as acceptable licensing mechanisms in some jurisdictions, and Clause 5 is equivalent to that.

One myth that often arises at this juncture is that the GPL has never been tested in court; if it were, it would break. A broken GPL could mean that everything written under the GPL enters the public domain, or it could mean you're liable to pay for every piece of GPL software you've used. Both scenarios are falsehoods, spread by the fear, uncertainty, and doubt (FUD) of other companies. First, the GPL doesn't *need* to be legally enforced to be enforceable. Taking a case to court would create such bad publicity for the company found stealing something marked as free that it would probably destroy them, as SCO are finding to their cost in related fields. The first time it's proven in court the law will make an example of them and introduce very stiff penalties. As Eben Moglen says, "Would you like to volunteer?"

Second, the GPL has been tried in court—and it won. A company called Fortinet™ took some GPL code owned by Harald Welte and used it without adhering to its obligations under the license. Although many GPL works were involved in the Fortinet product, it is necessary for the copyright holder to pursue an injunction and/or legal action against the offending company, and Harald was the one individual with copyrights who decided to press ahead and won the case. The jurisdiction in question was Munich, Germany. However, it is likely that this will set precedence in other western countries with similar copyright law. Failing to adhere to the GPL, in this case, led to an injunction halting all sales of Fortinet products until they were fully GPL compliant. This is an exception, and most developers and lawyers would rather see the case settled out of court without publicity rather than in court with the media watching.

You can learn about the ongoing GPL violations movement from the *http://www.gpl-violations.org* website that covers the Fortinet case and many others that have taken place since the start of the project in January 2004.

GPL and the Courts

One area in which control can be taken away from the GPL is with court judgments. These can stem from patent infringements, but need not. If the terms of the GPL conflict with any judgment handed down to you, then you must rectify the situation before continuing to distribute the software. In the example of a patent infringement, you must therefore acquire the appropriate patent rights before propagating derivative works.

NOTE

The courts can only annul portions of the license. Since the license covers only redistribution, they cannot stop the software from being used.

Section 8 continues this argument by clarifying this case on a geographical level. Should a country legally prevent the distribution of particular software within its border, then the copyright holder (i.e., the authors) can prevent it from being distributed to that country because doing so is a waste of time due to the all-or-nothing situation found within the GPL. This is the only circumstance where the author can limit the spread of his software without contravening the license, or the Open Source Initiative[4].

Distributing Open Source Code

The GPL allows distribution of the program in either its original or modified form. These are dealt with in Sections 1 and 2 of the license, respectively.

Original Form

Clause 1 is straightforward and indicates that the licensee can sell or give away original copies of the source code, provided all the original notices are included, also. These notices are generally:

- The copyright notice
- Disclaimer of warranty
- Reference to the license
- The license itself

But it can also include any specific notices provided by the programmer. For example, "This program requires you to acquire the rights to patent number 123456."

The concept of *original program* is also described here as being a verbatim copy. Even the slightest change marks it up as a derivation work and therefore comes under Section 2.

Modified Form

This section is the crux of the GPL. This gives you the right to make modified copies of the program and the right to pass these copies on to others. It also clarifies that you only have the rights to do this, if you adhere to the restrictions laid out.

Of course, if you modify the program but do not give it out to anyone, keeping it private to yourself, then you are not distributing the derivative work, and the GPL does not apply. However, if anyone (including coworkers) receives a copy of the modified program, then you must adhere to the GPL.

The restrictions for distributing derived works are as follows.

Make Your Changes Obvious

This is so future licensees know they're working with a modification of the original source so they won't expect it to be the same. The license also requires you to place your name on the files that you change as to not adversely affect the reputation of the original developers. This can be done on whatever granularity you choose; either one big file describing the changes and their dates, or separate messages in each file itself. The Unix program diff, which is also available for Microsoft

Windows, does this automatically and will create a list of every difference between two sets of files.

The Derivative Code Must Be Available Under the GPL

This is to ensure the future freedom of the software and to bring all good changes to the notice of the community. This is the clause that people most think about when they talk about Free software and that "you always have to release your source," as this section introduces the viral nature of the GPL. While this license requires you to make the source code available for anything you write that uses GPL code, it is one of the few that does. The methods by which you must redistribute your source code are covered later.

The Program Must Announce Its License

Because most games aren't run from the command line or take interactive input from it, this does not always apply. Some games begin with a welcoming splash screen showing the title, author, copyright, and license information. If you base your game on a GPL product where no license announcement is normally made when the program starts, then none needs to be made. That is, the splash screen doesn't need to be created, unless such a screen already existed. This lets end users know that these rights are available to them, so that they can apply them if they wish. It is normal, however, to include such details in the Help-About menu and in the documentation.

One other restriction made by the GPL states simply that any code that can work on a standalone basis, outside of the GPL'd program, is not itself affected by the GPL. But if it is integrated directly into GPL software, then it too reverts to being GPL. For example, the code to design an RPG character could exist outside the main RPG itself and could be under a non-GPL license. However, if that code is added to the game itself, it also must be released under the GPL.

Finally, Section 2 states that GPL code can be shipped with code under any other license. This allows your installer (probably not GPL'd) to reside on the same physical medium as the game itself.

Making Source Code Available

The GNU GPL, Section 3, reveals how the derivative source code must be made available. You know that the source code must be made available, as otherwise the derivative works (as required by the license) are not possible. This stems from the Unix world where most software was distributed as source code; consequently it believes that the default distribution should be with a source archive (a.k.a. tarball) of the modified work. Game developers always distribute executables. This is permissible, provided the source is made available in one of the following ways.

With the Program

This is the easiest to do. However, this doesn't necessary mean it has to be on the same disc. The phrase "a medium customarily used" means users must be able to access the source as easily as they can the executable. This allows you to package the disc, produce a gold master, and ship it off to the distributors one day and, at some point before release (and after your programmers have had a postcrunch holiday,) you can upload the source code to the company website.

In this and all subsequent cases, the source provided must be identical to the source used to compile the final version of the game. No bug fixes or supplementary features should appear, otherwise it is impossible to re-create the original executable, thereby breaking the license agreement.

With an Offer to Provide

If you are following a just-in-time development model, then you do not need to provide an archive of the source until someone actually asks for it. Clause 2b allows you instead to provide a written offer that you will provide the source at any point over the next three years at cost. Here, at cost means the physical cost of the disc, cost of burning the CD-ROM, and postage. Although no guidance is given as to cost (because CD-ROM duplication is getting cheaper by the day) it should generally be no more than five dollars. The cost mentioned applies to the physical cost; you cannot charge for the developer's time to prepare the disc.

The license dictates that any third party may request the source. So, even if you are distributing an internal tool, based on the GPL, without source then it is permissible for any competitor to request the source[5]. However, if you distribute the source with your program in the first instance, this section does not apply, and no one outside the existing distribution channels can access your code.

Also note the "three-year" phrase here. This means that your secrets will be lost if no one requests a copy of the source within the first three years. This is also known as auto-closure. However, if someone sends a request 2 years, 364 days after its release you are still bound by the GPL and must provide the source. This can cause problems because the lead programmer may no longer be at the company, and the source may have even become lost within the company itself. If you adopt this approach, it is recommended you create a complete source package after release and keep it safe at the company, creating specific discs when requested, as to not fall foul of the GPL. The penalties of noncompliance are detailed later.

With an Indirect Offer

If you had previously received a GPL'd graphics engine, for example, without source code, then it is impractical for you modify or create derivative works from the object code. Therefore, you cannot deliver the source onto your licensees. Instead, you can pass the buck to the licensors that gave you the object files in the first place, so that they can provide the source.

As the license says, this only applies to noncommercial distributions.

In all cases, the license clearly states that the source code must include all the build scripts (such as a `Makefile`, .NET solution files, and so on) necessary to recompile the original executable. This must also include any custom scripts your developers have written to ease the build process, even if the scripts themselves are not covered by the GPL. This is not an attempt to secure as much software as possible under the GNU GPL banner, but to ensure all users have the ability to work on the code, making it better, or change it to their needs. While many have argued that games do not fall into this category because of the perceived barrier to entry, the success of the modding community and the ease by which most games can be made more (or less) challenging by third-party developers negates this argument. Having a player adjust the game to his playing style is certainly within the realm of possibility.

How the Source Should Not Be Provided

The license makes it quite clear that you should provide the source to your application. Even if you have not changed the code, *you* must be prepared to supply the *source*. You cannot suggest that end users download it from another website, even if it's the same code, because your application might outlive their websites.

It is also true to say that the source must be provided in a state that can be compiled. That means that all special build scripts and `Makefiles` are included, but also that the format in which the source is supplied is readable; that is, no console-specific custom disc formats are allowed.

Applying the Terms

The typical GPL license document comes in two halves. The first half describes the rights and obligations of both parties, related to the software. The second provides a template that you should copy to your code to make the public aware that this software is Free. In most cases, this will have been provided by the originator of the GPL software you're using.

If you're starting a new project, you can copy and paste the information from Appendix B into a separate file and include it with your project, remembering to change all names and dates present.

Beware of the Future

To specify that your project is being released under the GPL, one of the lines you may want to change begins, "This program is free software; you can redistribute it and/or modify it under the terms of the GNU General Public License as published by the Free software Foundation; either version 2 of the License, or (at your option) any later version."

The last phrase can unnerve some developers due to the fact that the licensing control has been taken out of their hands and given to the Free software Foundation. Although the FSF will not change the spirit of the GNU GPL, it is possible that some clauses in version 3 or above could cause an issue with the existing software. Conversely, it is possible that a future version will close any discovered loopholes in version 2, making your investment in Open Source even safer.

This phrase is not part of the license, and therefore can be changed to suit your needs. You have three alternatives.

Name a Specific Version

By removing the last part of the sentence you can dictate an exact version that must be used. This is recommended for those who do not like surprises (for good, or ill) and want everything told upfront. Although the last change to the GPL was in 1991, another is planned for 2007; and so stating a specific version might be wise precaution until the dust of version 3 has settled and its ramifications become understood.

Specify a Version (or Later)

This is the default option as the FSF is largely benevolent and will only use later versions to close off problems. It also ensures longevity because it will still be possible to use your software in 10 years time under whatever license is then applicable. Although it is unlikely that any game engine developed now will still be cutting edge in 10 years time, it does ensure that whatever is usable is still licensable.

Remove the Version Number

In this instance, the licensee is free to use any version of the GPL, right back to 1.0. Since virtually no games software uses version 1.0 there is no need to be compatible with it, and so is not recommended.

Note that in all cases, while you can change the determination of the license, you cannot add further restrictions (Section 6 prohibits it.) While this generally is taken with the section stating you cannot change the license, it has wider implications when combining GPL code with other licenses, as you see next.

Compatible Licenses

Despite initial appearances, the GPL is not so restrictive that code released under it cannot be combined with code from other licenses. However, it is easier to discuss which licenses definitely will, and will not, be compatible with the GPL than to make sweeping statements about generalized licenses. Any edge cases, particularly those that do not use a standard OSI-approved license[6], must be checked on a case-by-case basis.

Clause 10 of the GPL indicates that you can combine software from compatible licenses without the authorization of the author.

The Simple Cases

The GPL is naturally compatible with all other code released under the GPL, including those of different version numbers. It is also compatible with the LGPL and public domain works. You may also incorporate work published under the X11 license because that has no restrictions.

Proprietary code cannot, in general, be used in combination with GPL code because by doing so the resultant code must be GPL. The exception to the rule is when proprietary vendors are willing to cross-license their software.

The Edge Cases

There are two sides to this edge, and both must be satisfied. The GPL must be compatible with the other license, and the other license must be compatible with the GPL. Surprisingly, these two ideas can be mutually exclusive. The most notable case was with the original BSD license.

The BSD Issue

The original BSD license allowed licensees to include the code in any project they liked, and even distribute it under a different license if they so wished. This would make it seem GPL-compatible. However, one clause in the original BSD license conflicts with one clause in the GPL making that impossible. Clause 6 of the GPL states, "You may not impose any further restrictions on the recipients' exercise of the rights granted herein." However, the original BSD license mentions that "All advertising materials mentioning features or use of this software must display the following acknowledgment:" Under the terms of the GPL, this is considered a further restriction, making the original BSD license incompatible, which in turn prevents you from combining software under these two licenses.

The revised BSD license *is* compatible because, in 1999, this "obnoxious BSD advertising clause" was removed. The full history of this change is documented at *http://www.gnu.org/philosophy/bsd.html.*

TIP

The quickest way to determine whether the license is revised or not is to count the clauses. The old BSD license had four, while the new revised version has just three.

Licenses in the Style

There are many variations of license that are considered BSD or X11 style. It is not safe to assume that any BSD-style license is compatible with the GPL (or any other license, for that matter) on the sole premise that the revised BSD license is compatible with the GPL. Due diligence should be employed to check the specific terms. However, this designation makes it much easier to determine if the licenses are not compatible, as opposed to if they are. To comply fully with the GPL, there can be no further restrictions, and are determined by the obligations of the license that you, the licensee, must carry out. If any of the obligations in the non-GPL license do not have a direct parallel in the GPL license, they are incompatible and you may not mix them.

The list of existing licenses is, unfortunately, growing all the time and so any attempt to list all those that are known to be compatible and incompatible is a mammoth task and one that dates very badly. Fortunately, work is ongoing to detail as many license incompatibilities as possible, with the current list maintained at *http://www.gnu.org/philosophy/license-list.html.*

Current Compatibility

What follows are the licenses you're more likely to uncover when downloading Open Source game code.

Compatible

- GPL and LGPL
- License for Guile (see Chapter 9, "Scripting Languages," to learn about Guile)
- X11 (for X Window software)
- Expat license (the XML file parser)
- Lua (for scripting)
- Revised BSD
- Zlib (for compression code)

Incompatible

- Original BSD
- OpenSSL (secure sockets layer for networking)

■ Academic Free License (versions 1.1 and 2.1), used in some graphics demonstration code

Applying the Terms

Determining that two licenses are compatible is the first half of the battle. The second half comes when you need to fulfill the requirements of both licenses. The GPL half of the equation means that any derivative work that utilizes GPL code must be released under the GPL. This includes any portions that come from other sources, such as BSD-licensed code, for example. This is permissible because the BSD license allows the code to be released under any other subsequent license, provided they carry the obligatory acknowledgments.

Because the more flexible licenses, like those from BSD and X11, allow their license to be changed, they instead require you to carry the acknowledgment of copyright. Note that this list can get quite long if you're drawing from separate sources.

Typical GPL Software

Because the GPL requires the distribution of source code, many game developers have shied away from releasing under the GPL. Consequently, the available code falls into one of two categories: complete engines that require no additional code to build a game (like the *Quake* series), or supplementary libraries. Because the inclusion of even the smallest library results in the entire game becoming GPL'd, you may wish to avoid this by restricting the libraries to your internal tools or learning the methods and performing a clean room implementation.

Recent software released under the GPL license includes:

■ *Quake* and its derivatives, such as *Nexuiz*
■ *Quake II*
■ *Quake III*
■ *Stratagus*
■ MAD: MPEG Audio Decoder.
■ Libraries to supplement SDL, such as 3DS parser, Collision Detection, GIME 2D Game Toolkit, and GUIlib

THE GNU LESSER GENERAL PUBLIC LICENSE

The first GNU LGPL license was created in 1991 to supplement version 2 of the GNU GPL. At the time is was known as the *Library* General Public License because its intention was to provide a mechanism whereby non-GPL programs could link directly to GPL libraries without breaking the terms and spirit of the GPL. Without the LGPL, any program that linked to a GPL library would be considered as a derivative work of that library and be required to appear under the GPL. Instead of relaxing the rules of the GPL, it was decided to create a completely separate license that allowed users to make use of the functions within the library without having to expose their code. However, when shortened to LGPL, it is not possible to infer whether it's *Library* or *Lesser* that is intended. However, the version numbers provide a clue. That is, any correctly labeled reference to the GNU LGPL 2 will involve the *Library* GPL, while the GNU LGPL 2.1 refers to the *Lesser* GPL.

Comparisons to the GPL

Both licenses are intentionally similar, with the original term "Program" being generally replaced with "Library" throughout.

NOTE

Due to vast similarities, the sections that are common to both GPL and LGPL will not be repeated here. Consequently, you would do well to study the section on the GPL first. This is recommended in any case, as it covers many of the traditional FLOSS concepts in addition to giving an insight into the mindset of the developers who originally composed the license.

A side-by-side comparison is inevitable between the GPL and LGPL, so that is where we start, because despite being termed a "lesser" license there are still some things that make us all the same. Where clauses are given, the LGPL section is given first, followed by its equivalent in the GPL.

Both licenses require you to:

- Highlight modifications to the source.
- License the work as whole—no sublicensing is allowed.
- License any separate work under the LGPL if it is derived from the Library itself. As with the GPL, if the same code is available as a distinctly separate work, then any license can apply to that code when used in isolation.
- Release the source to any derivative works. The LGPL applies only to extensions to the library, not the code using it, and refers to this as a "work based on the library." Even if you haven't changed the original LGPL source you must still, technically speaking, offer to provide that source, and linking to the original archive is not enough (since the site might have since disappeared).
- Include copyright notices that LGPL software is used in production.
- Provide the source code to derivative works, either with the executable or on demand over the next three years.
- Provide all data, utilities and build scripts necessary to compile.
- Forgo sublicensing, which is not permitted (8, 4).

- Use the license to redistribute the code because nothing else lets you (9, 5).
- Pass the license on (10, 6).

Naturally, the importance of the LGPL lies in its differences to the GPL, so those are covered next.

Differences to the GPL

The most obvious difference from the GPL is the fact that only source code related to the *library* needs to be released. This introduces two new phrases to the lexicon: work based on the library and work that is used with the library. Both are present in the legal definition, which is presented in Appendix C.

The first term refers to any derivative works of the library itself, so any changes made to the library itself are considered derivative works and have to be released with their source.

The second term covers any program that uses the library to provide some of its functionality, but whose primary focus is completely different. For example, a game that uses an LGPL graphics library would come under this term, whereas a library of vector drawing code that used the same library to provide its bitmap capabilities would not.

This duality is permitted to allow proprietary applications into the space occupied by the GNU system by giving all software access to standard libraries. Without it, it could discourage the uptake of GNU entirely and lead to many duplicated libraries that would evolve into more maintenance problems. The creation of the LGPL can be therefore seen as a strategic ploy because there is no ethical reason why a system focused solely on Freedoms should not allow the freedom of proprietary applications.

Defining Derived

By allowing code to use LGPL source it is important to stipulate what constitutes linkage and a derived work as to follow the correct side of the license. The most obvious case is static linking, where the LGPL library is combined into the same executable as your original code. This is considered a derived work, because portions of it are contained within the program. This poses deal-breaking issues for console development with LGPL software, but there are more issues for console developers, as you see later.

Conversely, should the original code use dynamic linking or an existing shared library mechanism (such as DLLs or .so files) to access the LGPL code, then the work is not derived and may be distributed under a license separate to the library. Section 6b clarifies the meaning of a suitable shared library by saying it must already exist on the computer, and a compatible library can be used in its place without destroying the function of the original application.

The first instance might appear problematic, especially if your game requires a slightly modified LGPL library. However, this license (through Section 6b1) applies to the game itself. It is perfectly reasonable to include the derived library on the user's computer as part of the installation process to conform to the license. This is also true if your game is an upgrade to a previous version.

The second case exists so that the user needs only one version (the latest) of any particular library in the system. The stipulation in 6b2 includes the phrase "interface-compatible." This means that if someone else adds new functions to the library, its interface as a whole is now different and you (as the original author) are not obliged to support it in any way.

A more interesting distinction occurs when using data structures within the libraries because these structures must (for compatibility reason) match the original binary. This would mean that any software that used numerical constants (even those as simple as TRUE and FALSE), data structures, macros, and inline functions from header files would mean the game gets classified as a derived work. Fortunately, the LGPL gives an exception for these cases at the end of Section 5. It also limits the size of an inline function to be "ten lines or less in length." Authors of LGPL software will not generally count the number of lines in every inline function, however, so you can generally assume any inline function written by the original author is safe to be used. However, when releasing a modified LGPL library, rewriting every function as inline would exceed this 10-line limit, break the intention of the LGPL, and be considered illegal. Because every version of the library must indicate what changes were made, this is easy to spot.

The Word "Library"

There's an important difference between *Library* and *library*. For most cases the word Library (capital L) is used to describe the software covered by the license itself. This can also mean a standalone application. However, Section 2a uses the term library (lowercase L) indicating that any modified work must be a library (again, lowercase L).

This means you cannot base your game on an LGPL library and release the whole game (with library incorporated) under the LGPL. Instead, you must release a modified version of the library and include the game as a supplementary program under the GPL that uses that library. For example, if you took an LGPL chess engine and programmed it with your rule variations, you would have to release `chess_ai_version2.lib`, alongside `chess_interface.exe`, that uses it.

The original purpose of the LGPL was for the redistribution of libraries. This in itself dictates that all code must be generic and not tied to any specific application. This is underlined by Clause 2d.

Other Differences

Clause 3 gives the ability to release any LGPL code under the GPL. This is in contrast to the GPL that prohibits changing the license under any circumstance. Moving the code to the GPL then counts as a derivative work. Consequently, anything produced from this derived work is then under the GPL and always under it. You can change the license on any LGPL software without notifying or seeking permission from the original author. Because the LGPL is compatible with the GPL, there are few reasons why this conversion should occur. One of them is that it helps with the problem of releasing nonlibraries using the LGPL.

CAUTION

If your code is statically linked with LGPL code, then the original LGPL can only be updated with access to your full source code. To ensure this can continue to happen, any statically linked code becomes a derivative work and its source must therefore be released. Since the resultant work is no longer a library, but a game, it effectively puts the new product under the GPL license automatically.

If you are not the copyright owner, you can only revert GPL code back to the LGPL by using the code from the last LGPL version of that library.

Combining with Other Licenses

Like the GPL, the LGPL is compatible with the major licenses in use today—that is, the GPL, the revised BSD license, and the X11 license. In short, anything that is compatible with the GPL is also compatible with the LGPL.

You may also combine LGPL code with other Library licenses (Section 7) providing you supply the source to the LGPL Library and a reference to the other libraries involved.

The Console Issue

One important difference between GPL and LGPL software is that LGPL software is required to release all "data and utility programs" necessary to rebuild the executable, if they're not readily available. The GPL only requires the built scripts to be made available, not the utility programs. The added stipulation of "utility programs" isn't necessary with GPL software because all source code is provided and can therefore be rebuilt under any suitable compiler. Even if the code is targeted for a PlayStation 2, for example, then that platform-specific source code is available so it can be ported to the PC.

In the console world these utility programs are generally protected by NDA and only available at great expense. This therefore prohibits the use of LGPL software in the console arena if your manufacturer does not allow you to redistribute the compiler tools for their platform. Instead, you should substitute the LGPL license for the GPL, which only requires the build scripts be made available. This change of license is actually permitted under Clause 3 of the LGPL, as shown previously.

In many instances, the compilers and linkers used in the console world have derived from GPL-based software, with the blessing of the FSF. It might therefore be possible to persuade it to extend that same courtesy to you.

The Simple DirectMedia Layer (SDL) library has been released under the LGPL, but the author has made an explicit exclusion for embedded device. That is, because such environments don't have an open development system, there is limited ability to recompile the software using the static libraries the LGPL requires. However, the author, Sam Lantinga, indicates that technically violates the LGPL and to "be cautioned."

Interesting, if the build tools are not available for zero cost but the licensee is able to purchase the software, then you still can't release it! This is because the licensee no longer has the freedom to use the source code because he would be impinged by the finances. Again, this rule is different to the GPL. If all the source code is available, it would be possible to port the code using GNU tools without any financial investment. It costs time, which the GPL allows, but not money.

This also means you cannot release an executable using LGPL code that has been compiled by a commercial compiler because you must supply object files that can relink into the published executable. This does not prohibit you from working within .NET, but the final builds must come from gcc *or a similarly free compiler. This can produce a significant extra workload, so it is suggested you adopt cross-platform techniques from the outset and periodically compile under* gcc.

What may become an additional issue is that the console manufacturer will not allow you to release object files. They may not even give a reason, although some will try to argue that it infringes their NDA with you or that it allows crackers to exploit the code. Because they hold the technical veto on releasing products, you should get this agreed to up front. BSD- and X11-licensed code does not have this problem.

Releasing New Code as LGPL

If you're planning on releasing new library code under a GNU-based license, then you should consider using the LGPL—but only if competing libraries already exist, as this doesn't limit anyone else from linking to it and therefore achieves the highest possible penetration for your code, allowing it to become a standard. On the other hand, should no alternative exist, then the GPL may be preferable as all software subsequently with it will also be free.

However, if you're after the largest market possible for your code (regardless of attribution, freedoms, and so on), then you may prefer to consider the use of the X11 or revised BSD licenses. These allow the end user to do almost anything with the code, as you see next.

Typical LGPL Software

The LGPL is a breeding ground for game engines with most of the code currently available falling under its auspices:

- CrystalSpace
- SDL
- PLib
- ClanLib

THE BSD AND X11 LICENSES

These two licenses are very similar and offer a very lax charge when licensing the code as both allow previously Open code to be closed. This means that you can compile BSD or X11 source code into your game without having to release the original code or your changes back to the world.

The BSD (Berkeley Software Distribution) license originated from the University of California, although the exact birth date of the license is unknown. It's either as early as 1977 (when Bill Joy released the code from Berkeley) or as late at 1989 (when the networking utilities were released). Whenever it was, Berkeley's code, and its license, have been widely used and even featured in versions of Microsoft Windows, controlling the network TCP/IP.

The X11 license began at the Massachusetts Institute of Technology and was used in the popular X Window System, a GUI for Unix machines, and is consequently known as the X license, despite the divergence of that particular project.

The X11 license is often called the MIT license because of its origins in Massachusetts. However, MIT has used several different licenses during the last few years, so the X11 tag is less ambiguous. As always, be warned of what pertains to be an MIT or X11 license since they are known to differ.

The BSD License

The BSD license comes in two main forms: the original pre-1999 version and the revised version. Both provide you with the same rights as each other, and the two can be interchangeable *if used on their own.*

The structure and text of the license is very simple and gives the user the right to use and distribute BSD code in either source or binary form with or without modifications. This, in its first sentence, covers all the combinations of distribution you will need, allowing you to do anything with the code providing the conditions are met. Those conditions are simply:

1. Inclusion of the copyright notice, license, and warranty disclaimer. This information must be present in the manual (or other supplied materials) if binary versions are used. This avoids the problems of introducing the text into the Help>About options in-game.
2. Nonendorsement of the derived product from the originators. This is similar to most other licenses where authors deserve to keep their integrity should a slipshod version of their code get released.

This second point is the nonattribution clause that the X11 license doesn't have, and is the only real difference between the two. This requires explicit permission for the originator's name to be used when endorsing or promoting the product, which prevents the marketing department from announcing "Made with the XYZ engine," which is still common when purchasing commercial middleware or existing game engines.

The complexity in using this license comes from its brevity. With so many rights given away in less than 100 words, it can be difficult to know whether something has been subtly retained. In short, however, if the license doesn't restrict something, you may enlarge on it. This includes, but is not limited to, the right to:

■ Change the license
■ Create a derivative work
■ Keep any derivative source code secret

Combining with Other Licenses

Being as open as the BSD license is, it would appear that it is compatible with any of the other Open Source licenses. Indeed, the GPL, LGPL, and X11 can be combined with the BSD license without issue. But this only applies to the revised BSD license. The original version (pre-1999) is not compatible with the GPL or LGPL because of the "obnoxious BSD advertising clause."

Pre-1999 BSD

The original BSD license had one additional clause over recent versions that prevent it from being used with GPL or LGPL software. That is:

All advertising materials mentioning features or use of this software must display the following acknowledgment: This product includes software developed by the University of California, Lawrence Berkeley Laboratory.

Clause 6 of the GPL considers this an additional restriction and consequently incompatible. This was covered when discussing interlicense options in the GPL section earlier in this chapter. The full history is documented at *http://www.gnu .org/philosophy/bsd.html*.

However, it is hoped you will discover this problem rarely, if at all. In 1999, the BSD license was changed to remove the advertising clause, and all subsequent versions have been compatible with the GPL. However, there are still developers using the old license.

CAUTION

Be aware of similar custom licenses with similar "advertisement" clauses. While this causes no direct issues for the game developer because the advertising usual credits your workforce and the developers whose work appears under such a license, it will still be considered an "additional restriction," prohibiting you from combining it with any GPL code.

The X11 License

This is similar to the BSD license, but it is even shorter and disclaims the same quantity of rights. That is, you have complete control over the source you have received under the X11 license and can redistribute it with or without changes as you see fit. The only conditions are that if you redistribute the code (in either its original form or substantial portions thereof) you must include the copyright notice as given. You must also give notice to future owners detailing their rights to the work. This latter point is common in all licenses (how can the licensees know what they can do with the code if they're never told?), but the X11 license spells this out explicitly.

You can mix this with code using the revised BSD license.

Typical BSD and X11 Software

With the extreme freedom afforded by the BSD and X11 licenses, it permits the source to be closed after release, making it difficult to determine which software has benefited from Open Source. The libraries that use them, however, are better known:

- FreeType font handling
- The OpenGL® GUI library for games[7]
- G3D[8]

OTHER LICENSES

A lot of companies and developers have jumped on the proverbial bandwagon and used the term Open Source in their material as a clever marketing buzzword, even when their company or product has nothing to do with the movement. What follows are some of the other licenses you may encounter, which can only be used with care. None of those presented here is compatible with the GPL, and most do not fall under the auspices of Open Source.

The IBM License: This requires that any code submitted to a project using this license includes all necessary patent clearances.

SCSL: This license from Sun requires strict adherence to certain compatibility suites.

Microsoft Shared Source Initiative: This falls short of its intended goal as it restricts the usage of the code, in many cases, to Microsoft Windows.

Mozilla® Public License (MPL): This also requires patent clearance for any code submitted.

QPL:[9] This applies to the TrollTech® Qt® user interface library, but is likely to only affect game tools. It requires that developers use a specific license for any software that is released commercial.

ENDNOTES

1. Although Sun voluntarily derecommended its SISSL license in September 2005. Information such as this comes from the OSI's License Proliferation Committee mailing list, which you can read at *http://crynwr.com/cgi-bin/ezmlm-cgi?9.*
2. Covered by United States Patent, numbers 4,710,876 and 4,885,688.
3. In some circumstances the program output is covered, such as those cases where the program outputs its own source code as part of the program. This is covered since the output is not independent of the program.
4. Section 5 of the OSI covers discrimination against persons or groups.
5. How any competitor would know about your use of the GPL is beyond the scope of the argument.
6. *http://www.opensource.org/licenses/*
7. *http://www.bramstein.nl/gui/*
8. *http://g3d-cpp.sourceforge.net/*
9. *http://www.trolltech.com/download/opensource.html*

3 Open Source in the Game World

In This Chapter

- Game Considerations
- Business Models
- id and the GPL
- Enforcing Licenses

GAME CONSIDERATIONS

Of the many ways in which you may integrate FLOSS into your game, two methods usually prevail: either you begin with an Open Source engine—consisting of either a graphics engine or complete game framework—and add your gameplay code to it, or you begin with an existing code base (perhaps your own proprietary source code) and add Open Source components as you need them.

Both approaches are correct.

For brand-new projects or studios the first case is preferable. This ensures you begin with the ideals of Open Source in your mind, so as each new FLOSS component is added its license can be checked for compatibility with the existing code base. It also means that you have to think explicitly about every piece of code you write for the engine and whether such proprietary code can be added legally, and—if you're required to release this code under an Open Source license—whether you're happy about presenting such work to the Open Source community as the best you can do.

With the second method, you can integrate new Open Source libraries as if they were any other piece of code, remembering, of course, to check the license. If you're adding code from only BSD- and X11-style licenses, then you are obliged to do nothing except make notes of which code has been included so the appropriate attribution notices can be added as per the license. If GPL components are used, you must release the rest of the game under the GPL, also. At this point, you will have to retroactively audit your game for any proprietary code that has been included over the years, or company secrets that you don't want released. This might include server passwords, intranet URLs, network encryption methods, and (potentially) libelous comments from disgruntled programmers. (Chapter 11, "The Tools Pipeline," details some helpful auditing tools in this respect.)

In either case, you need a set of common conventions from which to work. This also means the provision for a set of common types and protocols, such as function naming conventions and whether you return success as true or 0, for example. This does not mean, however, you should reformat the entire source code because this is a waste of time, it adds nothing, makes future integrations more problematic, and limits the library's use as a black box. Instead, new functions and wrapper libraries should be made to conform to the existing style of that module, with their interface using common arguments and return types used by the main code base, but passing on these arguments in a suitably massaged form. This keeps any casting localized to the wrapper libraries and makes it easier to change the underlying types.

Reintroducing SGX

In many places, we reference the SGX engine, or the SGX Core. This engine framework was first highlighted in the book, *Cross-Platform Game Programming*, and features more fully here. Its purpose is to provide a common grounding for all code so that disparate modules can be coupled more easily. It does this by providing a set of basic, abstracted, types and a number of game-related interfaces for the usual tasks in games development, such as file handling, mathematics, and so on. Knowing that the graphics library will utilize the same matrix functionality as the physics code, it makes sense to unify them. However, since physics is usually more dependent on fast math code, these developers may take the lead in optimizing it.

TIP

There is rarely agreement on whether the physics-based math code should be used in over the graphics-based one or vice versa. Therefore, it is best to isolate the math code into its own module and assign its own lead programmer who has no allegiances to either side, thereby acting as an arbitrator.

The SGX Core provides a reference implementation for all common components that help abstract this type of problem in the general case. As a third-party library, it provides some independence to the individual modules but more importantly, it specifies a set of types and interfaces that all modules can use, so that if the implementation is changed, no other code needs to change. Most development studios work like this automatically, as they build the companywide engine from the bottom up, starting with these core components before moving on to physics and graphics. Where Open Source differs is that these components have been developed by different people with different base components.

Since there is no governing body controlling Open Source game code, the libraries featured here do not utilize the base types and functionality laid down by the SGX Core. This is unfortunate because, as you will see, there is a lot of common functionality between the libraries. Therefore, many of the library components featured in this book have been wrapped by the SGX types and presented in addition to the original package.

If you start by using a large engine or game framework, such as CrystalSpace, then all the basic components already exist in an abstracted and common form, so it is not necessary to adopt the SGX conventions. This adheres to the traditional notion: if a standard already exists, follow it. The SGX Core approach is primarily of use for those building their own frameworks, incorporating separate libraries from disparate sources, or looking to adopt a more loosely coupled approach.

Problems in Use

What follows are the typical issues discovered when moving a module of Open Source code from its isolatary dispersal to its residence within larger projects.

Windows and Linux

While most games-oriented source code has archives suitable for your development platform of choice, it is not guaranteed. It is certainly not required under any of the Open Source licenses currently in existence. The most obvious of these differences is between the Windows and Linux environments, which have a number of subtle, and not-so-subtle, differences in their handling. Code compiled for one will not necessarily recompile flawlessly on the other—even if it's written in compliant ANSI-C. *Cross-Platform Game Programming* details this topic in detail. What follows are the more usual problems discovered.

Filenames

In Windows, filenames control most operations. In Linux, they control everything. This is because Linux follows the Unix metaphor where "everything is a file." This means more relevance is placed on the Linux filesystem than its Windows counterpart.

Therefore, any filename that is referenced—by either the source code or the in-game filesystem—must be converted to the appropriate format because they are not equivalent. The usual problems are as follows:

Slash direction: All Windows paths are separated by the backslash (\) while Linux uses the forward slash (/). At the very basic level, this requires that any hierarchical directory structure must be accessed through slightly different file paths, such as game\data\level2\file instead of game/data/level2/file. Sometimes the filesystem will have been abstracted and the paths are converted automatically, but the standard library does not guarantee this. Additionally, it means that all source code (generally the #include directives of the preprocessor) must use the correct slash, in case the preprocessor does not understand it. Fortunately, the latter is a minor case because most Windows compilers are able to understand both forms of directory path.

Case sensitivity: The Linux filesystem is case sensitive, making filenames SDL.H and sdl.h different files. This can be a big problem for Linux programmers making use of Windows Open Source (admittedly, a smaller minority), where the previous programmers have been sloppy with their naming convention and particular files are claimed to not exist. The same is also true when accessing named asset files from disc.

Filesystem operations: In the lower-level file-handling code, there are marked differences in what functionality the filesystem supports. Linux, most obviously, supports a set of nine separate attributes for each file (read, write, and execute flags for the current user, their group, and everyone else) whereas Windows is limited to read-only, hidden, and archive flags on a more global basis. This invariably leads to different code paths. What complicates matters is that the functions required to set and query this functionality will differ between platforms, both in terms of the function prototype and its name. The best examples of this exist with the open function that is used in most Linux software. Instead of using the ANSI-C standard fopen, most developers need to capture the extra power of the Linux filesystem and so use _creat. However, the difference also exists with the Linux function fsync (which uses the Windows extension _commit), mkdir (which has two parameters in Linux to handle the file attributes, instead of one), and fchmod (that has no direct equivalent). These must all be abstracted.

Compiler-Based Differences

Although in theory these are numerous, most game developers need only suffer very few of them. This is because gcc is available across most platforms, giving a strong common base from which all source code can be derived.

One typical difference between compilers is highlighted with the code example:

```
if (a = b) {
   // ...
}
```

This is perfectly legal and in some cases will not even produce a warning. However, code such as this can defeat the Visual Studio programmer that expects his code to work flawlessly under gcc. Creating local variables in statement blocks can confuse, too.

```
if (a = b) {
   int newVar; // this sometimes remains in scope at the close of the
   brace
}
```

What can also change are platform-specific headers, despite holding common functionality. Although both Windows and Linux have networking capabilities, the method by which each is implemented differs vastly. Taking sockets as an example, both platforms support them. And both use identical function signatures. However, they have differently named header files. Attempting to unify them is a pointless task as there are better solutions to the same problem. The most prominent solution involves the creation of common_networking.hpp, a generic file that includes all the necessary platform-specific header files and abstractions. As an example, MingW32 would require its Windows version to include just #include <winsock2.h> while any Linux-oriented version would require the triplet of:

```
#include <sys/param.h>
#include <netinet/in.h>
#include <arpa/inet.h>
```

Using third-party abstractions such as the SGX Core as a base, you can switch between these two variations by wrapping code with #ifdef SGX_PLATFORM_WINTEL32.

These switches may also need to consider the compiler, too, because MinGW32 and Cygwin use more Linux-based conventions, and those generally differ from those used in Microsoft Windows.

Library Conventions

Some study domains have different approaches to the same problem. Two of the most obvious examples are matrix orientation and endian order.

In the first example, matrices can be stored as either row-major or column-major. Both are correct, although it is more common for mathematicians and computer scientists to use the row-major method, with engineers sticking with column-major. Consequently, any processing carried out with such a library must place its matrices in the same order so that the code looks correct when performing matrix operations.

Problems of this type occur when two formats are present in the code. The obvious solution is to convert them on the fly. However, this is a very bad idea because, in games especially, performance is very important. Sometimes you can use the overloaded operators in C++ to access individual elements transparently, making a switch much simpler in the short term. However, this causes further problems in the long term, as you have to remember which matrix format is being used on each specific line of code. This removes the transparency traditionally valued by the object-oriented programmer. There is little option, therefore, and you should determine which part of the code is easier to rewrite—the matrices or the code that uses them—and do so.

The matrix ordering problem might enforce a specific solution if you are programming close to the hardware or a specific API, as the driver might require its matrices in a specific format. OpenGL, for example, uses a 1D array of floats.

Handling endian differences is a much smaller problem because it only affects the byte order when data is loaded into, or saved from, memory. This gives you a very specific region inside the file I/O code at which to place your conversion routines. Because any libraries compiled on the same platform will be of the same endian, there should be no problems in sharing raw data between the library and the main source code.

Problems can occur when the source code originated on an architecture that is differently endianed to your own because the original programmer may not have made his code endian-safe. Converting data is straightforward and handled by inline functions in the SGX Core:

```
SGX_INLINE tUINT16 sgxEndianSwap16(tUINT16 var)
{
    return (tUINT16)((((var)&0xff)<<8) | ( ((var)>>8)&0xff));
}
SGX_INLINE tUINT32 sgxEndianSwap32(tUINT32 var)
{
    return ((((var)&0xff)<<24) | ((((var)>>8)&0xff)<<16) |
            ((((var)>>16)&0xff)<<8) | ((((var)>>24)&0xff)) );
}
```

Many operating systems, such as Linux and MacOS X, exist in both big- and little-endian versions, so check the architecture (if given) used by the original developer before volunteering an endian-based bug.

A Typical Linux-Oriented Archive Structure

For the Windows user, the extraction of a tarball (usually ending in `tar.gz`, but more recently using `bz2`) is a surprising revelation. Instead of a simple EXE file featuring either an installer or a self-extracting ZIP archive, it is comprised of 100 or more files that constitute the source of the project. What follows is a guide to help you appreciate its contents.

`Makefile:` This is perhaps the best known. It is the equivalent of a .NET solution file. It is processed by a binary called `make` or `gmake` and describes the compilation methods and dependencies involved in creating a new executable. Alternatively, you may also see `makefile.mgw` indicating that the `makefile` has been specifically coded for a particular compiler—in this case MinG W32. Sometimes, neither file is present and will be generated automatically, as highlighted in the autotools section later in the chapter.

`COPYING:` This describes the full terms of the license agreement that applies if you decide to redistribute, and its presence is more blatant than with Windows software. This text file lives in the root directory, whereas Windows software would usually place the license in the EULA of the installer. This file might also be called `LICENSE`.

`INSTALL:` A text file describing the process for compiling the package. Often, this will come from a standard template that indicates you should perform the trio of `./configure`, `make`, `make install`. In this case, it's a sign that the package uses autotools, as you learn shortly. Otherwise, it should give details of the package's dependencies and compilation method.

`README:` A standard text file with the basic instructions for using the package. Convention dictates that no compilation instructions are included, but that is not always true. This should also detail the maintainer and a reference to the license. The copyright owners are often mentioned here.

`AUTHORS:` Sometimes called `CREDITS`, this lists everyone who has ever worked on the project. It is generally bad form to send an email to any of them for help, because they may no longer be working on the project. Instead, direct all questions to the associated mailing list, or in the worse case, the software's maintainer, who should be listed at the top of the file. Should you wish to acquire a version of the software under a different license you need to get consent from *everybody* involved, and while this is the best place to start searching, you should always start with the maintainer.

`HISTORY:` Sometimes called `NEWS`, this covers the basic revisions of the package and is useful when deciding whether to upgrade.

`NEWS:` This may be zero bytes long since autotools requires it to exist in order for the packaging to work correctly.

Autotools

Much of the current brethren of Linux software have been built using autotools. This package attempts to ease the compilation process on Unix-like machines by automatically generating a standalone configuration script for the software that details the setup of the machine on which the software was originally built. This configuration script is then run on the local machine to generate the files necessary for it to be recompiled in an identical fashion. These scripts have to be highly portable and are consequently quite complex. All of the files listed here play some part in the autotools process and may additionally appear in the directory.

> `configure:` This is a BASH (Bourne Again SHell) script that automatically generates an appropriate `Makefile` for the application, along with a `config.h` header file describing the basic configuration for the current machine. For Windows users, the most prominent BASH interpreter comes in the form of Cygwin[1]. `configure` checks the current configuration to determine whether the software can be built safely without introducing subtle errors (such as the `sizeof(int)` being too small) and unsubtle ones (the required library is not present). The script itself is self-contained, but uses the supplied `Makefile.in` file to generate an appropriate `Makefile`.

> `configure.in:` This is often included with the source, but not necessary for compilation as it is this which generates the `configure` script. However, the `configure` script itself is very complex and would not generally be edited by hand. Therefore, it is considered one of the files necessary for compilation and so must be included under the terms of the GPL.

> `aclocal.m4:` This is a file of user-defined macros for the M4 preprocessor language. It is an addition to the autotools package. Its use is being deprecated, however, in favor of new functionality in `autoconf`.

Networking Problems

Games that send encrypted data across a network may be at risk if the source code becomes available because the security of network traffic was previously realized through obscurity. That is because no one knew the protection was only handled with rot13, for example, it didn't have to be any better. When the exact method of transmission is known, you have to adopt stronger methods, which usually involve industry-standard algorithms such as RSA or PGP. These methods are well documented on both the web and in the security literature currently available. Furthermore, most are supplied with completely free source code under BSD licenses. This benevolence stems from the fact that those who develop cryptography want a reference model that can be tested on as many platforms as possible, and to be visible to as many people as possible. Just as "many eyes make bugs shallow" so do many eyes help raise the awareness of any flawed encryption logic that may exist. This approach has only one problem—the government. Or, more precisely, *some* governments who consider the use of encryption mechanisms as munitions. This means the same laws that govern the selling of weapons to foreign countries also govern the act of copying encryption-based source code from one computer to another.

The best documented case is of PGP where its author, Phil Zimmermann, was investigated by the U.S. government for exporting munitions as a "defense article under category XIII(b)(1) of the United States Munitions List." However, a *printed* copy of the source code does not contravene it under the International Traffic in Arms Regulations (ITAR)! Although the case against Zimmermann was dropped, possibly because the NSA has found a way to crack PGP, the legal ground is very unclear and can change as regularly as the evening news. The EFF page on encryption[2] has more background information on this area.

According to the terms of all Open Source-compliant licenses, you are only providing a right to access the code—not necessarily use it—as there may be patents or legal issues that prevent you from doing so. Documentation as to what these might be is usually included in the README file.

It *is* possible to get around these laws if you're so inclined. Because the law indicates that you may not transfer the code across the country's borders, there is nothing to prevent you from creating one specific encryption for your own territories and have another developed physically outside it for the others.

One school of thought says that because encryption is impossible to police, the laws are already outmoded and will be revised and removed in due course. Another says encryption is only necessary if you have something to hide, so encryption (in all forms) will become illegal and everyone must accept a lack of privacy in return for the illusion of safety. Only time will tell.

Performance

One of the things you will notice most about strong encryption is that execution speed is comparatively slow. Remember that all encrypted traffic occupies CPU time for both the encode and decode portions, and a server having to handle data from multiple machines gets very slow, very quickly. If the encrypted message contains an AI's position that is being sent several times every second, there is almost no processing power left the game logic. Furthermore, this processing time doesn't decrease substantially if fewer bytes are encrypted. And finally, the encrypted data packet is usually larger than the original data, which can negate the optimizations often performed to fit all frame-oriented data inside a single UDP packet.

The solution to all these problems comes in several parts—literally. While the strong encryption methods *do* take a comparatively long time to process, they are not needed for all traffic. Also, consider that the sensitivity of the basic information (such as the AI's position) is only useful for a few seconds, after which time the character moves elsewhere and a new position is sent. This produces a solution of parts, where the strong encryption is used to exchange the basic game lobby information and login details about the player's machine, while a weaker method (possibly even rot13 or simple XOR mask) is used for the everyday data. In these cases, the weak methods can be made stronger by sending the key as a data block inside the strongly encrypted data periodically. For example, one moderately secure packet could be sent every minute to change the XOR mask that is to be applied to all insecure data. Or, 1000 XOR masks could be sent during the (highly secure) login procedure, and the moderately secure packet could specify which of these 1000 should be employed next. Consequently, if a cracker is trying to brute force the method used to learn this information, there is a limited time in which to do so before the data he has thus far amassed becomes obsolete.

What You Lose

The section is reticently titled *lose* because it highlights what you don't get with Open Source, as opposed to the problems associated with it. However, it is untrue to say that you lose anything by using Open Source. Even if the license requires you to release your source code changes, you haven't really lost anything. But there are intangibles you should consider.

Credibility

It used to be true that no real men ate quiche, and no real developer used the software of others! This has not been so prevalent in recent years with the uptake of middleware hitting the mainstream developers as project scope has increased at a seemingly exponential rate. However, there are still some cases where the use of Open Source makes it look like you, as a developer, are not good enough to write your own engine. This is clearly preposterous, and the days of homebrew development where you had to write everything yourself (including the compiler) are largely gone.

Anonymity and Mystique

Very few Open Source projects harbor any mystique around them or their code. Indeed, the fact it can be downloaded from a million and one websites removes any naughtiness that might have been associated with the opportunity to read the code. In contrast, a leak from Microsoft featuring *any* of its source code gets lengthy articles and public dissection on Slashdot—despite only a fractional percentage of the development world being able to comprehend it.

Should your image be of a super developer who has mustered a reputation for solid, ingenious, code then you should:

1. Avoid using the GPL license that requires you to reveal your entire source code.
2. Rewrite any changes of LGPL-licensed code as a game-specific feature so it can be part of the non-LGPL game code, and not part of the library (because that code must be rereleased to the community).
3. Appreciate that your secrets will be available to the public. Secrets means "the dirty little hacks required to get the game gold."

If the source is available, developers will be able to tell how good you really are at writing structured code. But who's to know? Truth be told, most don't care. If you're developing casual games then no one is going to be interested, as the mechanics are invariably honed to a specific problem, such as a SuDoku solver, and are described on many web pages around the world. Furthermore, the engine code in these games is usually trivial, and probably Open Source anyway.

Developers of large FPS games may still make their source available with carefree abandon because anyone capable of understanding that size of code base probably has the knowledge to create the code themselves and would be generally uninterested in following it. This is typical of those working in games development professionally. They will also be the ones who know which hacks were employed to complete the game on time, and will generally be more forgiving. The (illegal) release of the *Half-Life 2* source code highlights this point well, since the theft made it a newsworthy item, although very few people were able to learn from it (particularly those who distributed it around the Internet) because the code base was too large for junior and curious programmers to understand.

Before releasing any source code, be sure to audit all comments for potentially libelous text. Many game developers don't feel constrained by the rules of professionalism (usually citing reasons of pay and conditions) and so may include derogatory remarks about the boss, publisher, industry, or government. In this prosecution-happy world, vulgarity is the least of your problems. Chapter 11 details some useful auditing procedures.

CAUTION

Making your code available to the world is scary. In fact, it's akin to losing your source control virginity! Now your employer can see exactly how many times you *fixed* a particular function, or what nastiness lies inside the loop. This is a fear that is overcome with time, and releasing small portions of the game ahead of time, even if not officially announced, should help calm these fears.

Even when the source must be made available, it doesn't have to be included on the CD with the game. It can be included on a website, where you can track downloads.

NOTE

Verbal Feedback

Very few, if any, developers give out their mobile number. Nor are they generally in the same office as you, or their fellow developers. This means it's more difficult to get an immediate, real-time response to questions, and nearly impossible to *shout* at them in a way that would make them care. In reality, the situation is not much different from asking an ex-employee for advice on a system they wrote under the company's auspices before they left. While email and public forums may help, it is preferable to have someone inside your own company who is the liaison for each particular piece of Open Source. Issues can be directed toward them, and they maintain it for the rest of the team.

What You Gain

There are several direct, and indirect, benefits from using Open Source. Although cost is the most obvious, benefits can manifest themselves in other ways, too.

Cost

One of the biggest benefits of Open Source in the short term is undoubtedly the financial savings. Not only are you saving on the cost of the initial purchase price, you will save more if the game gets a sequel or moves onto another platform because there is no additional cost involved in relicensing the engine for each SKU, as often occurs with middleware products.

Middleware vendors may also charge additional fees to provide the source code. This is something Open Source provides naturally and for free. While publishers feel safe just by using middleware, most programmers only feel safe when they have its source, regardless of the support contracts in place.

You can also save money on the evaluation period. This is often free for commercial middleware, but only for a limited time. Without good project management, this evaluation period may not coincide with the lead programmer's R&D month, meaning you might only get three weeks of effective evaluation. Requesting an extension might cost more money for that extra week, or means the evaluation is rushed and possibly in error. FLOSS has an indefinite evaluation period.

A Head Start

When starting with any new code base, there is a lot to learn. Not even Open Source can eliminate the learning curve. But what it can do is make it smoother. For example, new hires and other developers can begin learning about the specific engine before they start work on the project. This can extend to home study for existing developers, too, since publishers cannot object to nonproprietary code leaving the physical building[3].

Open Source also has the benefit of books and websites. While all proprietary middleware has its own documentation, and typically an online forum, access is usually restricted to licensed users from specific IP addresses. This limits access. It also draws from a much smaller pool of talent.

Recruitment Savings

A direct consequence of being able to study the engine code at home is that you're open (no pun intended) to more potential employees than usual. In the first instance, using an engine with which hundreds (if not thousands) of developers have familiarity helps to shorten lead times and provides a wider net of experienced people. Those using the larger graphics engines, such as CrystalSpace, may have already completed games as part of university projects that help both parties. And because your potential developers already have experience of the technology you are using, it enables you to interview them more effectively.

Second, it is possible that some of these developers will seek you out directly because they know you use the same engine they do. Despite many tarnished company reputations, the games industry has kept its fun and cool image of which many people would like to be a part. Having employees seek you out has the obvious effect of lowering your recruitment agency fees and demonstrates the candidate's keenness.

A third situation can occur when soliciting advice on mailing lists. There are a lot of talented people out there, and those that are working on these projects in their spare time might be glad for part-time or full-time work coding the engine they love. Some may even be doing it for the sole purpose of entering the industry on a paid basis. Again, you save money on agency fees.

No Lock-In

What ultimately becomes the biggest selling point of Open Source is the inability of anyone to lock you in to a particular engine or library. This is something very few commercial enterprises can guarantee. This was brought home to many users in the summer of 2004[4] when Criterion was bought by Electronic Arts. Overnight, the users of RenderWare saw their biggest competitor charging them to compete. Those developers who were not in the EA stable had concerns and, while existing contracts where honored, the investment of those companies in RenderWare was now wasted as future projects were required to use other engines.

It also prevents the very real problem of price changes. While the big-selling games may be given a license for free (or at cost) to maintain the prestige of the middleware product it uses, the rest of the industry will be paying in full. This will naturally rise every year, often over and above the rate of inflation because extra work has gone into the product with the middleware company having to pay another year's wages to its development staff. Having invested several developer years into a technology, people are loathe to change it and often pay the increase. But with Open Source you don't have to pay the increase, so there isn't a problem. Also, if you haven't paid $500,000 in the first instance for the code, the money you save (which may equate to five or more developer years) can be used to seek out new alternatives.

Finally, remember that once the code has been released under an Open Source license it is impossible to rescind it. This can be a good thing and a bad thing. From the view of a customer, it is a good thing because there is no controlling company behind it, so there's no danger of liquidation, bankruptcy, or takeover that might remove those facilities (such as source code or discussion forums) as was seen with the RenderWare case.

Conversely, it can be a bad thing since the companies and individuals providing Open Source may decide to close it[5], make it proprietary, and start charging money for it. This may be necessary to protect their revenue streams or through management persistence. The reason such a procedure turns bad is because any change in the path of free software can mean the project is forked by other developers who believe more strongly in the freedoms that FLOSS provides. In the best case, the original project and its new fork may continue happily as separate projects, each with half of the original developers and users. What is more likely, however, is that everyone will migrate to the free version leaving the original company with no customers. This pattern of development can dissuade some companies from entering the FLOSS field.

BUSINESS MODELS

One of the popular myths exploded in Chapter 1, "An Introduction to Free and Open Source Software," is that you always have to release your source code. Because this is not true, the existing development business models are still applicable when using Open Source, and nothing different needs to happen. If you therefore intend to avoid those licenses that require exposure, such as the Copyleft licenses like the GPL, then you can ignore this entire section and continue with your business as normal!

On the other hand, if you are releasing your source code or are concerned that the existing business models will not work, here are some ways to make money from Open Source game development. These are but starting points from which most explorations start. And again, they apply predominantly when you are required to distribute the source to your game code.

Sell the Design

So much of the development schedule is devoted to programmers and their problems that it is often very easy to forget that what you are actually selling is a game.

The code is a means to achieve that end. However, it is the uniqueness and ingenuity of the gameplay that causes people to put their hand in their pockets and buy the game. Drops in frame rate can be forgiven and less-than-stellar visuals are pardoned (the original *Half-Life* being the most obvious example), but only if the gameplay is engrossing. And gameplay code is a very small proportion of the whole.

So, what constitutes gameplay in this scheme? From a low level, all the AI code written into the game engine itself to handle pathfinding, state machines, or min-max tree searches would have to be considered. This needs to be as fast as possible, and so will have to be compiled into your executable and will therefore be considered as a derivative work. Much of this code, however, merely *facilitates* the true AI code that determines *when* those routines should be called and with which parameters. This is usually implemented using scripts that support character movements, player interactions and conversations, level-specific puzzles, and set pieces—all of which are usually considered gameplay. If you use a scripting engine (as detailed in Chapter 9, "Scripting Engines"), then much of this code will be placed in external scripts that are dynamically loaded which, because they sit outside of the main code, are treated like any other data asset and can be copyrighted as you see fit.

Media files, like graphics, sounds, and movies are always loaded by the executable from external files, and therefore never come under the jurisdiction of the source code license. Therefore, any artwork loaded by your GPL-compatible game can remain under your copyright.

While it is certainly possible to encrypt scripts to prevent the casual prying eyes, you will never stop ardent hackers from understanding them, so it is rarely worth the hassle of trying.

Effectively, by selling an implemented design of the game, you are becoming a games company first and technology developer second. The most famous *company* of this ilk is the CS Team that created the *CounterStrike* mod for *Half-Life*. To prove the point even further, this itself was later modified!

Online Subscriptions

With the uptake of broadband, especially among gamers, it is no longer an unreasonable expectation of games to require it. Indeed, Valve's Steam initiated the realization of this idea by providing game content through the Internet as early as 2002 for the beta of *CounterStrike*, version 1.6.

By requiring an online server, and consequently a subscription, you achieve the typical scenario of a Massively Multiplayer Online Game (MMOG) whereby the money made from the initial sale pales into insignificance next to the power of the (forced) subscription. A lot of games are moving this way anyway, as it provides a solid revenue stream and a simple means to eliminate piracy in one motion. In fact, it is very possible to give the game away for free, charging only for those that play online. This online content would consist of art assets and script code—essentially nothing that could be considered as a derivative work of Open Source, and remains copyrightable by the company, preventing others from stealing your revenue.

For the Open Source developer, online play has the additional benefit of being able to exploit the socket hole without any effort. This hole is not strictly a back door around Open licenses, but it can appear so. What happens is that instead of linking two parts of the source code together with the compiler, they are connected through a network socket connection. One side acts as a server, while the other is the client. Two separate processes can then communicate information about the game state. This connection can join two processes on the same computer or across a network. What is important is that both processes can be written under different licenses without affecting either of them because they are not linked together. It is a tightly coupled form of the communication that happens between web browser and web server. Furthermore, the work involved in converting such a game to a network-based client-server architecture is very much simpler, because the bulk of the work has already been done. This allows the gameplay logic and AI to reside and run on the back-end server in your data center using closed-source software, while the game engine just receives messages saying "draw this object here" or "play this sound now" and utilizes Open Source throughout. At no point are your secrets or game logic compromised.

Back-End Servers

While many games do not require a server, there are important points to consider should you take this route. First, although it is completely within the letter of the license, it can sometimes be considered to be lacking in spirit. The extent to which your community kudos will be bruised has yet to be tested.

Second, there is a strong backlash against many server-only games. Even when the remote server is used solely for authentication, the reliance on the server causes some chagrin because it is not available when:

- The user has no access to a net connection, such as when on the train.
- The server has broken, for whatever reason.
- The company has liquidated, and the server doesn't exist.

In all cases, users feel aggrieved that they are unable to play the game they paid for. This is mitigated in games such as *World of WarCraft* or *Second Life* that *require* the server for gameplay, but is a nuisance in others as legitimate users are inconvenienced for the sake of profits and the pirating populous.

One potential solution is to provide an executable-only server so the game can run locally on a user's machine using it if the official server cannot be found.

The Open Source community may be able to write an Open Source, clean room implementation of your game server, but the ruling of Blizzard/Vivendi vs. Bnetd in 2002 allowed Blizzard to shut down the battle.net servers that provided a similar service. So, as developers, precedence is on your side.

The Real-World Goals

This focuses primarily on casual online games, most notably poker. By making the heart of the game something desirable in the real world, such as fun, friends, and money, the emphasis moves away from the code and onto online services.

The biggest websites in the world—Amazon, eBay, and Google, for example—run almost exclusively on Open Source software. All of these companies make money, and both the user's client software (i.e., the web browser, like Firefox) and the company's server-side technology (such as Apache) are completely free! By looking at gaming portals and friend-matching services as fundamental to your game you can bring visitors to your site, which in turn can produce the profit necessary to develop more games.

Sell Support or Consultancy

This is an oft-quoted money-making idea put forward by the Open Source community. For most developers, however, it rarely works. Large companies are able to sell support contracts because they're large enough to support a large user base. For a small company this rarely applies since the people using the Open Source software are usually the same ones writing it, or are good enough to have written it and can consequently invest their time to solve the support problems.

In the games field, there is less of an opportunity due to the comparatively small size of the industry and the general reluctance to invest in software that "wasn't invented here." It may be possible, however, to make money through support by selling the source alongside it, as you see next.

Sell the Source

Because it is possible to dual license software, any code you write under the GPL can also be sold for money under more restrictive nonopen licenses if you wish. This plays into fears and myths you learned to oppose in Chapter 1 as other companies might not be so open with their source code. All forms of engine component fit in here because to work within an existing code framework the new code is likely to be more modular, and therefore easier to transplant into another game. It also allows the potential end consumers (developers in this case) to experiment with the software before paying for it. They can develop using your existing Open Source tools and code, and purchase the commercial license later once they successfully integrate it into their proprietary engine. The market for good middleware components is growing proportional to the complexity of the current platforms and tool chains. Good software, such as the *Quake III* engine, can still command hefty license fees despite being available as Open Source.

Many vendors supplement their GPL version with a commercial distribution. This is usually badly—namely, because you may use the GPL version in commercial software provided you follow the GPL. You do not need to buy the commercial license to use Open Source in a commercial product. The only correct legal interpretation of this clause is that the company own all copyrights to the code and will provide you with a version that it is not under the GPL, in return for a license fee that permits you to keep your source secret. The Augmented Reality toolkit[6], among others, adopts this approach.

ID AND THE GPL

The takeup of the GPL by id Software is a modern success story of Open Source in the games arena. It is proof that giving away your source code, the once regarded crown jewels of development, does not noticeably affect your bottom line. True, id only released its source once the paying licensees had completed their games, but as John Carmack has noted,[7] there "won't be nearly as sharp a cutoff as before."

The Engines

All three of the Quake engines are currently available under the GPL, which means you can do with them as you wish, but you must release all source changes back into the wild. The *Quake I* engine may be old now (it was first released in 1996), but it can still be used for many games, even if the graphics do look dated. The same is true of the *Quake II* engine. However, with age comes wisdom and bug fixes. As a consequence, *Quake* has been ported to nearly every device on the planet (including the Open Source handheld console GP2x), so you can be assured of a solid code base. These engines utilized a software rasterizer and therefore do not require a 3D graphics accelerator card; however, today's machines are powerful enough to handle this engine without resorting to difficult assembler optimizations present within its belly.

Should you be looking to create more complex levels, however, then a step up to the *Quake II* engine is recommended. This was the first prominent commercial game to require 3D graphics acceleration and is a more suitable base from which to start. There is even a Java™ port of the *Quake* engine available at *http://www .vertigosoftware.com/Quake2.htm*.

These engines have the additional benefit over most Open Source engines because the copyright for the whole engine is owned by id. This means, because of the distinction between copyright and distribution, that id may distribute the engine to you under a different license, allowing you to keep your source code secret. The cost of each engine under a proprietary license clocks in at $10,000 per title, but without per-copy royalty payments.

Quake III Arena is a little different. As well as being the most modern, it is also the most powerful. However, only the engine code is available under the GPL. The tools exist, but they're not all available under the GPL. The code is very usable though, and it is id's best-designed engine yet. The problem comes if you ever want to release your game under anything other than the GPL. Like the engines for *Quake I* and *II*, you can purchase a commercial license from id, but in this case the cost is $250,000 for a single title, guaranteed against a 5% royalty of wholesale. Furthermore, id has said[8] that the number of licenses will be regulated to limit competition in the marketplace.

Despite this, the spirit of Open Source is still prevalent because *Icculus* has taken and extended *Quake III Arena* so that it works natively on x86_64 and PowerPC. It has also been ported to BSD. You can read more at *http://icculus.org/quake3*.

Going Further

Although id stopped developing *Quake I* nearly 10 years ago, many people have built great things upon it all under the GPL. One of the most famous enhancements in this field has been the *Dark Places* engine. The developer behind this goes by the name Lord Havoc and has been working on it for six years, so the changes are numerous (see *http://icculus.org/twilight/darkplaces* for details). Among the most important is the switch to an OpenGL rendering engine (removing the need for (slow) software rasterizing), and the inclusion of real-time lighting and shadows. The visual difference between the original *Quake* game and the new engine is quite remarkable and demonstrates the benefits of having a good Open Source base from which to start.

The reason this particular engine has gained a following is due, in part, to *http://www.nexuiz.com*. This is taking the idea of Open Source development further by incorporating open content, so even the meshes, map data, and levels can be taken (by you) and changed, appended, and even sold. The team has chosen to release content under the GPL, so any changes you make must also be under the same license.

There is a similar project at *http://tenebrae.sourceforge.net*, which among other things adds per-pixel lighting and stencil shadows to *Quake*.

Finally, there is open content available because the company originally producing it went into liquidation. One such unfortunate was *http://catmother.sourceforge.net* who released both its code and assets under the GNU GPL.

ENFORCING LICENSES

There are always questions surrounding legal issues, especially among software engineers who would rather write code than legal documents. For them, this section splits into two halves, depending on who is doing the enforcing.

Enforcing Your Own Work

The first thing to understand is the extent of rights to which you can enforce. Because Open Source licenses do not prohibit the *use* of the software, the enforceability can only occur if the person redistributes the source in either a pure or modified version.

If you have not released your game under an Open Source license but have still used Open Source in your work (as could occur when using BSD- or X11-licensed code), then the whole product is under a proprietary license and you can enforce any copyright violation as you would with any traditional product without Open Source.

If you have chosen to use GPL or LGPL code, then you must supply (at the very least) source code (for GPL) or object files (LGPL) for the game. These can be redistributed at will by anyone, and therefore are not subject to legal ramifications. If you distribute source code with your game, then this too can be redistributed without issue. However, should any of this code appear within a closed project, you can seek legal redress.

In both cases, the resource assets (sounds, animations, meshes, and so on) are under a separate license. With most commercial games development, this prevents others from using identical assets in any other game and can be legally pursued as normal.

Enforcement Process

In many cases, an email to the CEO explaining the violation is enough to force the change, as he may be unaware that the problem exists. In the initial correspondence, it would be wise to state that failure to comply with the license is a *copyright violation*, as this is a term most CEO's understand. Many, especially those that haven't read the myths explained in Chapter 1, believe that Free software means cost-free and may disregard the email as a crank or someone trying to extort money.

From here, a written notice must be made.

NOTE

You can only bring a case against someone for GPL violations if you are the copyright owner of the original work. If others have contributed their copyrighted material to the project, then you each need to make individual contact or have an agreement that you will all be represented as one.

Highlighting Violations of Others

In the real world, most people would call the police if they saw someone breaking in to another's house. The same zeal should be applied to the virtual world, too. In this instance, the first step is to notify the original copyright owners, as they are the only ones who can bring charges against the perpetrators. Furthermore, they may already know about the violation and sold additional licenses to cover proprietary use.

Private notification is the only thing you should do—or need to do. You should *never* announce the discovery on a website, newspaper, or Internet forum. Never. This is because in some territories there is a time limit during which all claims must be made. This is often as short as 30 days from the time the information is made public. If you don't publicly announce the problem, the original author(s) can attempt to solve the problem discretely over whatever time frame they deem necessary. If the information is made public, then the proverbial clock starts ticking, and you will do the Open Source movement more harm than good.

Avoiding Open Source Violations

No professional company would intentionally ignore the license agreement of proprietary software, such as Windows or .NET, but there seems to be a more placid approach with the violation of Open Source licenses. The reasons for this are immaterial; it is illegal. It is not possible to ignore the license of any software. Anyone who elects to ignore the license must then follow the law as if no license had been explicitly given. That is, you are using copyright software, but without a license to copy it. This translates as an illegal practice in any language.

Even if you use FLOSS secretly, it is no guarantee that you will be safe. There are two obvious scenarios here. The first is that the code will be discovered accidentally by hackers studying the binary of your game. This will happen whether or not you place a license clause indicating "no reverse engineering."

The second method of discovery can appear as the result of litigation. If someone brings a case against you believing you have stolen their code, then the courts can require that the source to both products is opened up. At this point, both pieces of source are visible, highlighting the incorporation of FLOSS you have not correctly licensed. This invalidates all claims you have to the copyright on, and money made from, that game. This is a heavy price.

Naturally, these rules of law work in reverse, too. So, if you believe a competitor has stolen your code, in order to press charges, you must expose your code. Doing so may reveal yourself to have misappropriated code from an Open Source project. Again, you can lose all your rights to the source code that incorporated the original project.

Whether this is likely to happen is a matter for the specific companies. Whenever a star employee, or group thereof, leaves one company and starts an independent studio there is always the veiled belief they are taking their existing engine with them. As in poker, it can cost a lot of money to see if they're bluffing.

Remember that in spite of whatever secrecy you harbor, it is possible that your infringement will be noted by an independent developer outside the loop, just having a poke around. Consequently, the only safe option is compliance[9].

The penalties and legal outcomes will vary depending on which license has been violated, as the terms of that license must now be adhered to. Free software licenses have been carefully constructed as to apply in most countries around the world, so this should have no effect. The only difference is likely to be the specific penalties for copyright infringement proffered by a particular country.

TIP

The Free software Foundation has a compliance lab at compliance-lab@fsf.org, *which offers consultancy services for those companies that are unsure of the ramifications of the GPL and other Free software licenses.*

BSD and X11 Licenses

If you had violated the rights of software written under the BSD or X11 licenses, you would have no copyright over the resultant game, which in turn means you do not have the exclusive right to sell it in the future. Furthermore, it is possible for the original authors to bring a suit for damages through a mechanism known as *unjust enrichment*. If such a motion were made, all profits earned from the game up until that point could be reassigned to the original authors. It is likely your source would remain private, however.

GPL and LGPL Licenses

All existing code must now be released under the GPL as per the terms of the original license. Failure to do this (as detailed in Section 2b) contravenes the license according to the terms in Section 4. This states that the infringer no longer has any rights to the code. As previously mentioned, having "no rights" actually means "default rights," which is the assumption of copyright. At this point it is no longer a violation of a license, but a blatant copyright infringement. As with BSD and X11 infringements, it is likely you would lose any profits made from the game.

Unlike many laws involving intellectual property, copyright infringement is covered by both criminal and civil penalties. Not only is a conviction easy to obtain (in the Western world), it also carries subsidiary violations because every day that these rights are neglected adds to the time during which the company, its directors, and its lawyers are considered to be "aiding and abetting" criminal action.

Community Enforcement

The developers that create FLOSS are often obsessive individuals. They are writing the best code they can for the biggest audience they can get. While they personally might not be particularly zealous over the tenets of the license agreement and ideology of Free software, there will certainly be others to take their place on the Internet soapbox and blogosphere. Peer pressure has always been a very powerful persuasion tool. The FLOSS community has this skill in spades.

Once a developers name is known as a GPL violator, the community will react. Typically, you will be named and shamed on various websites around the world, especially community sites that cannot be influenced through advertising budgets. This includes the GPL-violations site, Slashdot, and The Register. This in turn alienates the early-adopter, high-quotient geek demographic, which is the very audience you need to create a positive buzz for your game.

The community's typical response will rarely involve expensive legal action. Instead, you may soon find that your questions on forums and notice boards go unanswered, or worse, include misinformation. You may additionally be flamed or insulted on public mailing lists, using language or content that goes beyond the usual bounds of being "on topic" or clean. While this is considered unethical, and potentially illegal, it has strong parallels to the mob mentality found in the real world. Some may go as far as cracking your email and web servers[10] or committing an illegal distributed denial of service (DDOS) attack. The people involved in these operations are themselves criminals, and will probably have nothing to do with the original software. But their zealousness makes them Internet heroes and modern-day Robin Hoods.

You may also find that future projects refuse your input and will not let you join. This will require you to create your own fork or use your own repository (as you saw in Chapter 1), which can hinder development.

And finally, on a more subtle note, developers may refuse to work for you or buy your product[11] and will encourage others to follow suit.

There are only a vocal few that will engage in such antisocial behavior. They are also the ones who will shape the next generation of game players, influencing them for or against a particular product. When two similar games are available from different developers, one who is known to violate Open Source licenses, and one who isn't, which game will get recommended by those with the loudest voices?

The extent to which this affects the bottom line is questionable because no good data exists. The industry is small enough for the bad words to travel, and large enough for Google to remember everything that was said.

For real-world examples of the bad press geeks can generate, consider the ill will created when Sony installed PC root kits on its music CDs[12]. Regardless of the processes involved, this was a violation against the common good and many FLOSS developers launched a backlash. Regardless of the violation, there is a very audible community wanting users and purveyors of technology to do the right thing. Note also that the Sony root kit fiasco was not highlighted by disgruntled employees or litigation in obscure court cases, but by a solitary geek by the name of Mark Russinovich who was curious about a CD he'd just bought.

ENDNOTES

1. *http://www.cygwin.com*
2. *http://www.eff.org/Privacy/Crypto_export*
3. It is in fact a contractual term in many cases that any code written for them does not leave the building without a special license.
4. Known to some as The Dark Summer.
5. This requires the consent of all copyright holders, which means everyone who has contributed code to the project.
6. *http://www.hitl.washington.edu/artoolkit*
7. *http://www.armadilloaerospace.com/n.x/johnc/Recent%20Updates/ Archive?news_id=290*
8. *http://www.idsoftware.com/business/technology/techlicense.php*
9. Otherwise, as in the case of Leaf (*http://www.animenewsnetwork.com/ article.php?id=8465*), you may be forced to release your source code.
10. As happened when Unix vendor SCO launched a case against Linux.
11. The fortunes of Metallica after the Napster debacle highlights this.
12. *http://www.boycottsony.us*

Part

II

One of the biggest problems in choosing an Open Source solution is choice. Lots of choice. Too much, in fact. Almost every game component has a number of very viable solutions to the same problem. And many extend their original design brief. What started life as a small graphics 2D library may now exist only as a complete 3D engine with all the trimmings. There is no absolute answer to whether this is a good or bad thing; it can only be judged in context, knowing what you intend to do with the code. What *we* can do, however, is highlight the possibilities of each package.

Sometimes, the package will constitute an entire game engine. Consequently, it is not feasible to discuss the whole engine, its features, or how to use it (that's what *its* documentation is for!), but we can cover principles behind its design, how existing code can be integrated into this design, and of what components the developer should be wary. When the code encompasses a lot of functionality that we might want to access in an alternate way, that is, not through the library or its interfaces, then that approach is detailed, too.

In some instances, we might be discussing a small self-contained library. In this case, the focus will be on its subcomponents and how to use them within the context of a complete game, or integrating into a large environment or engine.

4 Development Environments

In This Chapter

- Compilation Tools
- Debugging
- Complete IDEs
- Machine Virtualization

COMPILATION TOOLS

In the same way that there are several parts to the compilation process, there are also many tools that facilitate software development in the Open Source world. Under GNU/Linux, these tools integrate seamlessly into the environment because the operating system as a whole is reliant upon it to compile itself and its modules. Consequently, a lot of work has been put into this predominantly GNU/Linux-oriented area.

Historically, Microsoft Windows users have not been so lucky. This has been changing—and improving—steadily for the last few years, with many components now available in a number of simple packages with their own installers. Therefore, although this section will detail the use of Open Source tools in games development, the installation commentary will focus on the tools and the manner in which they are provided on the Windows platform.

GCC—MinGW

The primary Open Source compilation tool is gcc, and has been in existence since 1984 where it was one of the first tools to come from GNU. The gcc package has been ported to Microsoft Windows several times since its inception, with Minimalist GNU for Windows (MinGW) being the current ruler of the roost and available on the companion CD-ROM. Previously, this post had been held by DJGPP, but it wasn't as strongly maintained and fell out of favor. It is still available on some sites, but since it doesn't support DirectX; only the MS-DOS holdouts make use of it.

MinGW comprises of natively compiled tools from the GNU compiler collection (gcc) providing the same quality as, and compatible with, those under GNU/ Linux. These tools include make, the C and C++ compilers, assemblers, and their associated linker. This is supplemented with a Windows resource compiler, command shell, and debugger.

MinGW has its own website at *http://www.mingw.org* with all the component software being available on *http://sourceforge.net/projects/mingw*.

NOTE

With most of the GNU development taking place outside of the Windows environment, the versions of the tools present with MinGW may lag behind those of their GNU/Linux counterparts. This is not a problem for game developers because less importance is generally placed on the implementation of new language features.

Installation

As the MinGW documentation mentions, you can either install it as a self-sufficient toolset, or from individual packages, with the former being recommended. This will place all the necessary files into a self-contained directory (such as c:\mingw) ready for use. This subtree can be relocated anywhere on the hard drive, and is therefore trivial to hold multiple versions on the MinGW tools on the same machine.

NOTE

Upgrading individual components is also easy because you only need to overwrite the specific files with their upgrades. The Unix philosophy of many small components doing only one job works well in this situation, particularly because each tool is interface-compatible with the previous version.

Once installed, it is only necessary to connect the tools to your IDE of choice and you can begin development immediately. For those whose preferred IDE is the command line, you can simply add c:\mingw\bin to your path. You can change this at the Windows command prompt with,

```
PATH=%PATH%;c:\mingw\bin
```

A more permanent change can be applied by using the Environment Variables option on the Advanced tab of the Control Panel's System Properties feature. To confirm it's working, open a new command line window (it *must* be a new one, since these changes are not applied retroactively to any already open windows), and type,

```
gcc −v
```

This should detail the current configuration, options, and paths used by the compiler. For example,

```
Reading specs from c:/mingw/bin/../lib/gcc-lib/MinGW/3.2.3/specs
Configured with: ../gcc/configure −with-gcc −with-gnu-ld −with-gnu-as
−host=MinGW −target=MinGW −prefix=/mingw −enable-threads
−disable-nls −enable-languages=c++,f77,objc −disable-win32-registry
−disable-shared −enable-sjlj-exceptions
Thread model: win32
gcc version 3.2.3 (mingw special 20030504-1)
```

This version of the compiler will generate native Windows applications as singular executables that do not require any of the MinGW libraries.

You should be careful to only build native applications with these tools. Some versions of MinGW, such as MSYS is a Cygwin derivative and allows you to build under a GNU/Linux-like environment that produces smaller executables by making use of the functionality in its core DLLs. This adds an unnecessary dependency and can introduce unsuspecting QA problems. In the obvious case, this occurs with mismatched DLL versions, but can also occur when the DLL is not shipped because no one realizes that there is a dependency on the DLL (because everyone in the company now has it installed), and users are unable to run their game without it.

Workflow Integration

Compilation with additional libraries is no different under gcc than it is with any other compiler. Essentially, you need to specify an additional include directory in which new header files reside, such as,

```
gcc -I c:\devlib\include mycode.c
```

In most cases, this must be supplemented with a corresponding library directory, using the −L flag,

```
gcc -I c:\devlib\include -L c:\devlib\lib mycode.c
```

Furthermore, because the specific name of the required library cannot be determined from the code alone, each library must be explicitly named on the command line. In each case, however, the .a extension (used in gcc, instead of .lib) must be ignored.

```
gcc -I c:\devlib\include -L c:\devlib\lib -lSDL mycode.c
```

Some compilers use #pragma lib to indicate the required library for the current file. This pragma is not supported across all compilers, such as gcc, and should be avoided.

Code such as SDL usually comes with precompiled, MinGW-friendly libraries that can be linked without any further effort. For those who are supplied with only source, you can manually compile these into the main executable or as libraries. Alternatively, you can rely on someone else performing this library build step for you, perhaps using the prepackaged binaries found at *http://www.devpaks.org*. The problem of libraries that come only in proprietary formats, such as DirectX, including neither source nor suitable .a library files is covered later.

Debug and Release

Unlike the popular proprietary compilers, gcc makes no distinction between debug and release builds of the software. Instead, it uses the same compilation engine for all builds, but is able to use different postcompile optimization routines on the resultant code.

There are numerous options, all prefixed with –f, that control specific optimizations. A full list can be found at *http://gcc.gnu.org/onlinedocs/gcc/Optimize-Options.html*. For example,

```
gcc -finline-functions myfile.c
```

Some of these optimizations have parameters that control the extent of the optimization. Continuing the above example, you can supplement it with,

```
gcc -finline-functions —param max-inline-insns-auto=90 myfile.c
```

Because these option strings are invariably long, common groupings have been made that invoke a predetermined selection of optimizations. The default is –O0, which performs no optimizations, with –O1, -O2, and –O3 adding progressively tighter optimization sets to the code. These are all speed-oriented optimizations and are the most useful for games development. However, for those working on handheld consoles the size optimization flag, -Os, may also be useful. This derives its working flags from the –O2 optimization set, excluding those that typically enlarge the code, and including some additional processes.

All the options mentioned thus far could be termed *release mode* compile options. But, as already mentioned, there is no strict demarcation between this and debug mode. Instead, gcc is able to include symbol information into the executable irrespective of the compiler optimizations so that the debugger can work in all modes. This is an improvement over the traditional scenario because it is simpler to debug optimized code if the symbols are present. Anyone that's resorted to .map files to debug a problem that only happens in release mode can attest to that!

There are several options to introduce symbolic information into a build, all detailed at *http://gcc.gnu.org/onlinedocs/gcc/Debugging-Options.html*, but the most common is,

```
gcc −g myfile.c
```

This introduces debugging information in a format suitable for the underlying operating system. It should be compatible with most debuggers, such as gdb that you come to later. If your tools expect a different format or can support additional debugging information, you can utilize one of the other options such as −ggdb or −gstab.

If you invoke the compiler and linker separately, as you would when compiling several different files through a Makefile, *the −g option must be passed to both compiler and linker.*

As an added bonus, this debug-laden executable can be pruned into a more streamlined version by removing the symbol information without recompiling the whole game, using the strip tool like this,

```
strip game.exe
```

Note that in addition to symbol information, the Windows version of this command also removes information from the PE header that is not needed for execution.

Resource Compilation

Although not usually part of a game developer's arsenal, the tools programmers will be pleased to know that .rc files (containing icon, dialog, and menu descriptions) can be compiled using the free tool windres.

```
windres  myresources.rc compiled.res
```

Creating .rc files is not particularly difficult because they are text descriptions, but finding a good WYSIWYG editor is. This is because the format is very Microsoft-centric, and few developers have seen the need of supporting a proprietary interface format when so many free versions (like GTK and QT) already exist. One exception to this rule is the wedit program that comes as part of lcc package. This can be downloaded from *http://www.cs.virginia.edu/~lcc-win32*. It is a functional editor, capable of generating most of the traditional GDI widgets such as lists and check boxes, although the newer Windows 2000 functionality is missing.

Make

Naturally, building an entire project using gcc on the command line is prohibitively obstructive. Even batch files do not handle the basic nuances of dependencies that are handled automatically within IDEs such as Microsoft Developer Studio or .NET. Instead, you can adopt Makefiles that describe a number of different source files and how they relate to one another for this particular game.

The principles of makefiles are well understood and documented in numerous places, including the GNU book on the subject, which is available for free at *http://www.gnu.org/software/make/manual*. In essence, a Makefile is comprised of two parts: declarations and dependencies.

Declarations allow you to specify global options for the entire build process, such as compiler switches and optimization levels. Most makefiles begin with a structure similar to,

```
CC=gcc
CFLAGS=-O2 -Wall -Werror
LDFLAGS=
```

These names are not only historically meaningful, but are de facto standards, and you would do well to adopt them, particularly as some commands use them implicitly.

Note that these settings can be changed externally, too, by specifying name= value pairs on the command line. It is more usually, however, to trigger changes internally by using a special variable that can amend multiple options.

```
ifeq ($(BUILD),debug)
CFLAGS+=-g
LDFLAGS+=-g
endif
```

You can then switch between the different builds with,

```
mingw32-make.exe BUILD=debug
```

Note that under MinGW, however, the GNU make's executable is called mingw32-make.exe so as not to conflict with other executables in the current path called make.

You can also use command line arguments to switch between different compilers to handle cross-platform builds. However, because there is likely to be different file groups and dependencies between those platforms, it is better to handle each platform as a different target and switch between compilers according to the target using

```
ifeq ($(MAKECMDGOALS),ps2)
CC=gcc-ps2
endif
```

The second part of the Makefile consists of dependencies between files, so that when one is updated, make knows which of the others needs to be recompiled as a consequence. This step is often taken for granted as most IDEs handle this automatically. When presented literally in a Makefile, they look like this,

```
pacman.o: pacman.h render.h gameloop.h
player.o: pacman.h player.h ghosts.h pills.h board.h
ghosts.o: pacman.h ghosts.h board.h
```

In fact, the creation (and maintenance) of these dependencies scales so badly that there are a number of tools to assist you, including the compiler itself. It can be invoked with the –M flag and a compliant list of dependencies will be generated. However, the GNU gcc compiler supports the better –MM option, which ignores the system dependencies, like stdio.h, since they are unlikely to change.

```
gcc -MM -I c:\devlib\include ghosts.c
```

You must specify the same list of include directories on here that you would when compiling.

A simple MS-DOS script can then combine a common stub, containing the standard compilation flags, and join it to the list of dependencies to produce a full Makefile.

```
copy /y stub.mak Makefile
gcc -MM -I c:\devlib\include *.c >>Makefile
```

The same effect can be achieved through the Unix tool makedepend, which also has Windows ports available[1]. This works like the previous script, but is the more traditional approach to the dependency problem because it replaces the dependencies in the Makefile directly, eliminating the additional steps of the previous script. It does this by placing a marker in the Makefile (# DO NOT DELETE) that is then used to delimit the user- and machine-generated portions of the Makefile. This tool can also be invoked as part of a depend target,

```
depend:
    makedepend – $(CFLAGS) – $(SRCS)
```

This allows the dependencies to be updated using nothing more than the call of, make depend.

It also makes a backup of the Makefile *called* Makefile.bak.

When migrating from other environments, there are other tools to assist you. For example, dsw2mak generates Makefiles directly from the Developer Studio workspace files. Those are covered in more detail later.

MinSYS

This is short for Minimal SYStem and consists mostly of additional tools and configuration files to provide a POSIX system inside the Windows environment. It is derived from Cygwin and is available in several different parts, each providing a defined set of tools. The main page at *http://www.mingw.org/download.shtml* contains three distinct packages:

MSYS-1.0.10.exe: The main package that features the standard commands, such as touch and cp. It also contains the vitally important msys-1.0.dll. Any MSYS-oriented download requires this file as it provides the base services to all tools. This is available on the CD-ROM.

msysDTK-1.0.1.exe: This contains a lot of advanced functionality, such as the automake system, as well as a Perl interpreter and libtool. This is also available on the CD-ROM.

bison-2.0-MSYS.tar.gz: This is the only other MSYS tool available from the MinGW website that is not featured in either of the previous two packages. It provides both bison and yacc, which are useful tools in generating language parsers and lexical analyzers.

The installation of MSYS will add the binaries (placed by default in c:\msys\1.0 \bin) to your path.

If you choose to use the Bash shell through Cygwin, remember to adjust your paths so that the newly installed MinGW tools are found first, and not the original versions supplied with Cygwin.

MSYS exists to make the compilation and development process easier by providing an environment that is closer to the one expected by the underlying tools, like gcc. This means that the typical pre- and post-compilation commands have the expected functionality—using the same command line switches—as they do everywhere else. This means, for example, that the copy operation must be invoked with the cp command.

The majority of MSYS tools have not been compiled into native code. This means that they can only be executed through a suitable command shell, such as Cygwin, or the equivalent shell provided from msys.bat *installed to* c:\msys\1.0.

The Transition to Open Source Development Tools

For those used to proprietary development environments, the Open Source way can appear a little haphazard and fragmented. This is actually by design, as it fosters competition by allowing any individual link in the chain to be replaced with a better one as and when it becomes available[2]. As a consequence, every part of the proprietary environment needs to be mimicked by separate Open Source components. So, instead of one new learning experience, there are several. There is an oft-quoted argument that C++ is easier to learn if you *haven't* already learned C, as there is less to unlearn. The same can be said of Open Source development. So, if you begin game development in an Open Source environment, everything will appear logical and natural, whereas those coming from a proprietary background will be required to make wholesale changes to their thinking and their tools.

There is also a common myth surrounding Open Source development that it is complex. This is a fallacy. The difficulty in any form of development comes from the problems that need to be solved, and this rarely involves the tools. True, the tool set is *different* but not necessarily any more complex with Open Source, but it can require a learning curve to learn the new features, options, and error messages of a new compiler, for example.

Furthermore, with a lot of software being developed with Open Source tools, the language incompatibilities of C come to the fore, as covered fully in Chapter 2 of *Cross-Platform Game Programming*. Notably, many proprietary compilers adopt the standard in a lax manner or provide language extensions that many believe are generic. This can require changes to the code before it will compile, and is often seen as a source of frustration, and complexity. The myths exploded in Chapter 1, "An Introduction to Free and Open Source Software," which covers this in more detail.

Link Libraries

One of the perceived problems with Open Source is its interoperability with proprietary solutions. This is somewhat ironic given its open metaphor, but it does contain a kernel of truth. But it is a problem where both sides are guilty.

In the first instance, the more zealous members of the Open Source community will refuse to work, or interact, with proprietary software. These members are often the loudest, and so is the only message many other developers will hear. However, they are in the minority, and where one fool refuses to tread, 100 (quieter) angels will, and take on the task of proprietary interoperability.

Second, the vendors of proprietary technology often refuse to release full details or specifications of their work. This lack of disclosure is most common with hardware vendors refusing to release Linux drivers (or even enough information for the community to write its own), but is also prevalent with the linkable object files of many common libraries.

Each compiler has a different format with which it creates its link libraries. This makes it impossible for one compiler to link to the libraries of another, for which it doesn't understand the format. This was a big problem in the two-horse race between Microsoft and Borland in the 1990s when the latest version of any particular library became available to Microsoft users first and Borland second. This staggered release meant that Borland users were always behind the curve.

The solution then, as now, is to convert Microsoft object files (`.lib`) into something gcc-compatible (`.a`). There are two approaches to this problem.

The first method is to convert the `.lib` into `.a` files and link to them. This can be done using a tool called `reimp` that can be found as part of the standard MinGW archive. This is run simply as,

```
reimp -c vendor.lib
```

which creates a compatible `vendor.a`. This can be copied into the standard MinGW library folder (`c:\mingw\lib` by default) or included in a separate directory for third-party conversions.

An alternative conversion tool involves the pairing of `impdef` and `dlltool`. This two-step process extracts the definitions from the DLL, rather than the import library. Because the format of the DLL must have backward compatibility beyond the next compiler release, this can be a more reliable conversion. So, first build the definitions file,

```
impdef vendor.dll > vendor.def
```

and then rebuild a linkable library from that definition and its associated DLL:

```
dlltool -k -def vendor.def -dllname vendor.dll -output-lib vendor.a
```

The second possibility is to link the library files into your code directly, as if they were normal object files[3]. This is possible because an understanding of vanilla `.lib` files (that is, those without C++ name mangling) has been built into the MinGW version of gcc. Using a command line such as

```
gcc -I c:\vendor\include myfile.c c:\vendor\lib\somelib.lib
```

allows the compiler to add the binary for this library directly into the executable. As you can see, it must be specified using its full path and extension. Also, when including it on a single compile line such as this, it *must* be placed after the source code, otherwise the symbols will not be found.

It has been discovered that some native `.lib` files do not work with this approach. In these cases you can simply convert them and include them directly as was done previously. This is notably true of the DirectX libraries.

Despite all the free software license agreements requiring the code be provided as source, many developers will additionally supply precompiled link libraries to expedite the development process. It is an intriguing fact to note that many of these libraries appear in the proprietary .lib format, and not .a! These can be converted in the usual way or, more preferably, recompiled natively through MinGW and released for the good of the community.

DirectX

Of all the PC third-party libraries necessary to games development, the most important is undoubtedly DirectX. Although it can be downloaded for free[4] and is purported to work with any Windows compiler, the only libraries included are for Microsoft Developer Studio and .NET.

For most DirectX applications, older versions of the libraries exist in the current version of MinGW inside the w32api package (most recently, version 31 of DirectX 9) and are available on the CD-ROM. For more up-to-date DirectX versions, you can download archives from *http://alleg.sourceforge.net/wip.html* or *http://www.libsdl.org/extras/win32/common*.

ON THE CD

Naturally, for the most up-to-date versions, it is necessary to convert these yourself using the methods detailed earlier.

As an alternative to static linking, it is always possible to call functions inside DLLs without using a .lib at all. This removes all the previous problems, at the expense of an extra indirection at runtime and additional development work at the start of the project. The method is to use the pairing of LoadLibrary and GetProcAddress, the latter being used to retrieve the function pointers themselves. For example,

```
// One of many necessary type definitions
typedef void (APIENTRY *glBeginProcPtr)(Glenum mode);

// Non-standard initialization
HINSTANCE hInstLib = LoadLibrary("opengl32.dll");

// There will be many calls like this
glBeginProcPtr glBeginProcAddress =
    (glBeginProcPtr) GetProcAddress(hInstLib, "glBegin");

// The glBegin call is made like this, instead
(glBeginProcAddress)(GL_TRIANGLES);

// Free when necessary
FreeLibrary(hInstLib);
```

Note that it is still possible to use the OpenGL header files here, and that APIENTRY is necessary to ensure an external linkage. DirectX functions can be invoked using the same method.

OpenGL

This is much simpler than DirectX, as these libraries have been made freely available by many developers. Also, since the API has remained stable in recent versions, with new functionality being confirmed largely to extensions (that are accessed in a different manner), you generally only need the version supplied with MinGW.

Header Files

The counterparts of link libraries are their header files, which provide the function prototypes, data structures, and macros that interface with the library. Being plain text, they can be moved between compilers more easily. The problems here come from intercompatibility and not interoperability.

It is a sad fact that so much software is poorly written and incompatible with the standards to which they aspire. For compilers, this generally means the ANSI C standard. To combat this problem, GNU has provided an implementation of the standard libraries (known as glibc) that intends to be as compliant as possible. But this can still leave problems when trying to compile header files from other vendors, as they may have had their contents massaged to overcome problems with their vendor's original compiler. The largest collection of include files likely to exhibit this problem is undoubtedly the STL, but because the compiler vendor supplies their own files, this is unlikely to be apparent. But you're more likely to use STLport instead (for cross-platform compatibility), so problems can lurk there. STL covers such a wide range of functionality that it is fundamental to most software and cannot be simply ignored or manually amended to circumvent compiler warnings.

STL is part of the C++ standard, so any ANSI-compliant compiler must provide it.

NOTE   Fortunately, many developers are already using STLport with gcc so these vagrancies are unlikely to exist in the current versions. As always, however, if you intend to use cutting-edge versions of either gcc or STLport, it is possible that some combinations will produce errors; so be warned.

Combining Multiple Development Libraries

When incorporating libraries into a large product you will, in almost all cases, be supplied with (or will compile yourselves) a static link library and a header file. The installation instructions in all cases involve copying them to locations that your development environment can see. The precise location, alas, is never specified. Therefore, establish consistent naming ahead of time.

This problem is not unique to Open Source development, but with the all-in-one approach of proprietary development systems it is less prevalent.

So, create a directory called `c:\devlib` and add `include` and `lib` directories inside it to take all new library code. This keeps it away from the system libraries, with which some filenames may conflict, and in a common location so that the directory can be copied, en masse, for new hires.

There are three potential structures to this direction hierarchy.

A Flat Directory

This ignores the problem entirely by placing every file in the root of `c:\devlib` and adding a single line to the compile flags.

```
gcc -I c:\devlib source.c
```

This ensures every header will be accessed correctly, without source changes, by the library code and any other libraries that depend on it. It will stop collisions of header filenames because Windows will complain when you attempt to overwrite an existing `name.h`, for example. In this case, you can rename the file and amend the source files that reference it. Consequently, only one header with any specific name will be visible to the compiler because there is only one include path pointing to these files.

However, this makes the root directory quite messy and awkward to audit. Also, it can cause problems for developers and third-party code that expects to find a particular header named as `xyz.h`, only to find that (due to naming collisions) it is now `lib_xyz.h`.

When a particular library has many header files, they will usually already be in their own subdirectories. These do not need to moved out of this folder since they where already in their subdirectories and will be referenced by the code as

```
#include "sub/header.h"
```

Multiple Subdirectories

An alternative approach is to place every header file in a subdirectory that reflects the library name. This keeps the root uncluttered, at the expense of having several directories with maybe only one or two files in it. This approach may also require you to add each directory to the "additional include path" option because the C standard doesn't dictate whether the relative paths should begin with directory of the current file or where the `#include`-chain began. Therefore,

```
#include "sub/name.h"
```

might not be found until it is changed to,

```
#include "library/sub/name.h"
```

depending on the compiler.

Here, the developer has two equally valid choices. The first is to amend the `#include` line to incorporate the library subdirectory, and then carefully integrate these changes from the project's main repository. This is the better approach when the project doesn't change much or bug fixes will be made in a fragmentary, as opposed to wholesale, manner. The downside is that dependent libraries will expect `name.h` to be in the root `c:\devlib` directory, not from a subdirectory, and so they too will need to be changed in the same manner at some point in the future.

The second method involves adding the `library/sub` directory to the list of additional include directories. If the project changes regularly, then this is the preferred option. One issue that can arise with this configuration concerns duplicate filenames as two libraries might have a `name.h` in their project, and some files will be confused with the correct one. Sometimes you can avoid this problem by carefully ordering the `include` directories, as is often necessary for the compiler to use the most recently installed version of DirectX, and not the one bundled by default with the compiler. If the ordering cannot be suitably massaged, the only solution is to rename the header files with explicit paths from the `devlib` root, ensuring the root is the first directory in the list of additional locations. So, `#include "name.h"` becomes

```
#include "library/name.h"
```

Of Projects, Workspaces, and Solutions

Within the various Microsoft development environments there are different ways to group files into their respective projects. Under Microsoft Developer Studio 6.0 there are projects (`.dsp` files containing one linkable unit) and workspaces (`.dsw` files encompassing several projects). With .NET, these were combined into one XML-structured `.sln` file, called a solution. All three formats are incompatible with your Open Source tools and so need conversion.

There is an Export to `Makefile` *option within DevStudio, although the resultant file is only compatible with* `nmake`, *the Microsoft tool.*

Converting `.dsw` files can be handled with the `dsw2mak` tool, presented as part of the standard MinGW installation. It uses `gawk`, which is also supplied in MSYS, and can be run as

```
c:\msys\1.0\bin\gawk -f c:\MinGW\bin\dsw2mak myproject.dsw
```

This generates a new standards-compliant `Makefile` in the current directory, replacing any that previously existed. If the workspace contains `.dsp` project files (which it invariably will), these are converted as well.

The Language and the API

Despite the difference in tools, there is no real complexity in developing using Open Source as opposed to proprietary. There are certainly new things to learn, and some of the tools (such as gdb) can appear archaic, but they present their own power and stay true to the oft-repeated Unix mantra of doing one thing well.

Furthermore, to develop Windows applications requires a Windows-compatible compiler. And to interface with the Windows GDI library, for example, requires you to use the GDI interfaces through its own DLL. This is no different whether you use Open Source or not.

The main difference, and the reason many perceive Open Source as being more difficult, is that most people's introduction to Open Source comes through Linux. With Linux libraries. And Linux interfaces. And Linux graphics toolkits. So not only is there a difference in tools, but the different operating environment introduces extra complexities into the transition. This section, therefore, details the primary differences between the Windows and Linux operating environments to assist in the reading of Linux code, and provide a lexicon so that a Windows user can understand a Linux-based source commentary.

Graphics

Under GNU/Linux there are several ways to improve on the basic text mode that is synonymous with Unix-like operating systems. The most prolific is the X Window System, which is sometimes called X11, Xfree86, or just X. This provides a client-server architecture for a window manager to draw and handle application windows as a graphical environment. The window manager itself controls only the appearance of the windows, and is separate to the underlying X Window System. This allows for replacement interfaces without needing to rewrite the whole system, and differs from the Microsoft Windows approach. Typical window managers include Sawfish, Blackbox, and Enlightenment. There are many detailed at *http://xwinman.org*.

The window managers of the X Window System have been supplemented in recent years to include *desktops*. The most famous of these have been KDE and Gnome. These provide a library of typical interface widgets necessary in desktop applications to limit the proverbial reinvention of the wheel, and a Windows-like system bar and icons designating a My Computer equivalent. They both use the underlying X Window API, and so applications written for Gnome can be used on a KDE system, and vice versa, because it's nothing more involved than a graphics library. The Gnome library is called GTK (Gnome ToolKit), while KDE uses the QT GUI toolkit. However, because the *desktop environment* controls the screen real estate, it is only possible to run one desktop component at a time.

Older systems provide graphics through a frame buffer device (fbdev), where the physical graphics hardware is mapped into memory so each pixel can be individually controlled. This is rarely used in modern development environments, however, but it still applies to some embedded devices.

For most Linux developers, graphics means OpenGL. Or at least Mesa, which is the Open Source implementation of that particular standard. It uses the same API and handling as OpenGL, but cannot be named as OpenGL because that term is trademarked by SGI[5] who requires all OpenGL implementations to conform to its compatibility test suites before being bestowed with the moniker of OpenGL. Most implementations of Mesa work on top of X Window and are therefore compliant with any other components that sit on top of X Window—that is, all of the window managers and desktops.

Not all graphics cards are supplied with 3D accelerated drivers for Linux, so rendering can be an order of magnitude slower. For those that do, X Window needs to be suitably configured to make use of it. This requires changes to the server portion inside /etc/X11/XF86Config-4 *and should be explained fully in the appropriate documentation.*

Audio

For the longest time, audio development has been difficult under Linux due to the different driver-level options available. There are currently three in common use.

The Open Sound System (OSS) provides freely available and commercial drivers for many sound cards under Linux, Solaris, and BSD. It also provides support, for a fee, and provides improved drivers over those available with the standard Linux kernel. More can be found at *http://www.opensound.com.*

ALSA, the Advanced Linux Sound Architecture, provides MIDI and audio support through a combination of low-level drivers and high-level API functionality. It also provides OSS support through a compatibility layer. Details can be found at *http://www.alsa-project.org.*

JACK is a recursive acronym standing for Jack Audio Connection Kit and provides a way for different audio applications to talk to one another. It is a server-based technology, but requires special code on the part of each application for them to interact. It is usually used in audio applications (like SoftSynths and sequencers) as opposed to standard game audio. Its website is at *http://jackaudio.org.*

System

Most of the system functionality is taken for granted, until you change environments. After all, many programmers believe that anything that is not obviously graphical or auditory must be part of the standard C library, such as the ability to yield a process or start a new thread. Alas, both exist as platform-specific extensions.

Fortunately, there is only a small amount of system functionality utilized by game code and so is abstracted easily. The main case, threading, is generally handled under

Linux with the pthreads system. This doesn't need to be abstracted since an implementation (*http://sourceware.redhat.com/pthreads-win32*) is available for Windows. The other primary Windows functions of `Sleep` and `Yield` are presented within Unix as

```
#include <unistd.h>
void sleep(unsigned int seconds);  // not milliseconds, as it is in
Windows
int usleep(useconds_t useconds);   // this uses microseconds
```

and

```
#include <unistd.h>
void yield(void);
```

respectively.

DEBUGGING

No matter how good a compiler is, it will be shunned if it cannot add useful debugging information into the final executable. You have already seen that gcc is very capable of writing this data into the program, so now you have to look at the applications that read it.

GDB

There are a number of graphical debuggers that all take their core code from `gdb`. They include `xxgdb`, `ddd`, and `kdb`, and are generally available only under Linux. For Windows users, a natively compiled `gdb` is perfectly capable of handling the traditional debugging tasks and is controlled by a command line interface that is briefly covered in the following section. For those requiring a GUI, the *Eclipse* IDE integrates `gdb` into its framework, enabling multiple debugging windows to be open at once.

Gdb is available in the standard MinGW package outlined previously and can only be called on executables supporting `gdb`-compatible symbol information. This is invoked in gcc with

```
gcc –g file.c
```

or

```
gcc –ggdb file.c
```

which is invariably set inside the `Makefile` with

```
CFLAGS=-g
```

The format of the debugging information differs between MinGW native executables, and those built under Cygwin, or similar (such as MSYS). Be very careful not to mix them, otherwise the program is likely to crash unexpectedly or not start at all.

Using the gdb debugger is easy once you learn the basic set of commands. They are given in Table 4.1.

TABLE 4.1 Basic Debugging Commands in gdb

Command	Short form	Description
run	r	Begin a program
continue	c	Continue running
next	n	Next instruction, stepping over function calls
step	s	Step into next line, of function
break	b	Add a breakpoint
print	p	Print the value of the given variable
ptype	pt	Print the type of the given variable, or structure
backtrace	bt	Detail the current stack
list	l	List a portion of the programs source code
help	h	Retrieve help information
quit	q	Stop executing the program

Each gdb session begins with

```
gdb game.exe
```

followed by run. From here, it's debugging as usual. There are several productivity gains with the gdb command line interface, such as the use of a carriage return on its own being used to repeat the last given command, and the ability to execute functions within your game code while still in the debugger, using call function(). This can be used to enumerate lists or serialize complex structures to the screen, for example.

The breakpoint command (also known as *tracepoint*) has several other variations, given in Table 4.2, although in each case, the filename can be omitted if there's no ambiguity in doing so.

As always, the best way to experiment with gdb is to use it, and there are several tutorials on the Internet, such as the original GNU one at *http://www.gnu.org/software/gdb/gdb.html*, giving guidelines and tips on this very useful tool.

TABLE 4.2   Breakpoints in gdb

Command example	Description
b main.c:302	Set a breakpoint on the specified file and line
b player.c:setVelocity	Set a breakpoint on the specified function
b ai.c:54 if characterID==12	Set a conditional breakpoint
watch memoryBlock[22210]	Set a watchpoint that fires when the expression changes
info break	List all breakpoints and watchpoints
delete 2	Delete breakpoint number 2 (or all, if the number is omitted)
disable 1	Disable breakpoint number 1 (or all, if the number is omitted)
enable 1	Enable breakpoint number 1 (or all, if the number is omitted)

Valgrind

This is a very powerful tool that tests the validity of all memory accesses made by a program. It doesn't need the program to be compiled in any particular way, but instead traps all accesses to the standard memory manager (through either new, delete, malloc, or free) to look for double-free'd blocks, memory bounds errors, and the use of uninitialized memory.

To support this array of low-level functionality is a complex task, and impossible with any platform-agnostic approach. Consequently, Valgrind can only be used on the x86 and AMD64 Linux platforms. Although other Linux-oriented platforms, including MacOS X, are planned in the future, it is unlikely that a Windows port will become available soon. If you are anchored to the Windows platform for all your development, you might therefore wish to consider proprietary solutions such as Purify from IBM or the more traditional BoundsChecker.

Valgrind can be downloaded from its home page at *http://valgrind.org* with a front end available from *http://alleyoop.sourceforge.net*.

Profilers

Very little exists in the way of free profiling tools, although in recent years Valgrind has exceeded its original goal of being just a memory tool to become a general-purpose debugging framework. However, it is still lacking the profiling department. Indeed, as with Valgrind, the complexities present in developing a good Windows profiler has been left to proprietary software development teams, such as IBM, because no Windows port exists.

For game developers, however, this is not a vital omission because they usually have their own profiling tools built in to their games. This enables a more customized profiling library to be written that, by being part of the native code, doesn't impinge as heavily on the system resources as more traditional third-party debuggers. Second, it allows the profiling tools to work cross-platform enabling the developers to see how their code is handled across the different consoles. Furthermore, it is also true that some developers cannot (or will not) spend money on these traditionally expensive tools, particularly when the same tool is needed for each platform.

The brightest star in this traditionally barren sky is gprof, the GNU profiler. Like gdb, it requires the source code to be built specially. This uses the compile flags

```
CFLAGS=-pg and LDFLAGS=-pg
```

When linking these object files into the main executable, you should replace the traditional crt0.o common runtime stub with the gcrt0.o file. Furthermore, it is recommended you use the gprof-specific object file c_p with

```
LDFLAGS+=c_p
```

That will enable the profiler to count the number of times the system functions are called.

The executable is run as usual (but with the expected slowdown that profiling code incurs) and generates gmon.out on completion.

The program must complete cleanly for the profiling file to be written. This means either main *finishes normally, or* exit *is called. If necessary, wrap your game code with a simple exception handler to ensure this.*

The gmon.out file is then processed with the gprof command thus,

```
gprof mygame gmon.out >results.txt
```

This typically begins as

```
Flat profile:

Each sample counts as 0.01 seconds.
  %   cumulative   self              self     total
 time   seconds   seconds    calls  s/call   s/call  name
 80.03     3.60      3.60      674    0.01     0.01  Pac_DrawPills
  8.67     3.99      0.39   526057    0.00     0.00  drawTiledIcon
  6.00     4.26      0.27   460475    0.00     0.00  Pac_GetMap
  2.45     4.37      0.11   452928    0.00     0.00  drawSquare
  0.89     4.41      0.04      734    0.00     0.00  Pac_EventLoop
```

This is the then followed by a call graph and functions by index. The explanations for each section are also thoughtfully provided in the resultant output text.

A graphical interface for `gprof` also exists in the form of the Linux program, `kprof`. More documentation on `gprof` is available at *http://www.cs.utah.edu/dept/ old/texinfo/as/gprof.html#SEC2.*

Garbage Collection

Many developers, especially those destined for cross-platform compatibility, will have no need for automatic garbage collection or memory profilers because they will have their own versions, intercepting every `new`, `delete`, `malloc`, and `free` in the game.

For those that don't, you might like to consider `mmgr`, from *http://www. FluidStudios.com.* This library uses macros to redirect any call from the standard memory allocators to its own functions. Here it keeps track of all memory allocated and free'd. It works automatically, once the line

```
#include "mmgr.h"
```

has been added at the top of your first header file and the supplementary `mmgr.cpp` has been added to the project.

`mmgr` has been successfully integrated into the FreeType GL font library (`ftgl`) covered in Chapter 5, "Graphics."

COMPLETE IDES

The Integrated Development Environment is a large and complex beast. Even in the proprietary world, very few exist, with Microsoft Developer Studio and .NET being the most well known[6].

Eclipse

To many, Eclipse is an IDE written by IBM to overshadow Sun in the arena of Java development. That, unfortunately, is jingoistic and only half the story. While it is certainly true that Eclipse began life inside the walls of IBM as its follow-up to the VisualAge IDEs, it was always intended to be a complete development *framework* rather than a single IDE. There was a common workbench that could be amended by various plug-ins and components in order that the same environment could be used to build any large-scale application, on any platform, and using any language. In addition to its formidable Java tradition, there is also support for the development of testing and performance tools, GUIs, UML, and C. Eclipse can also handle integrated source control and automatic documentation creation.

Eclipse is sometimes also used to refer to the organization behind the software, known as the Eclipse Board of Stewards. It is a not-for-profit consortium and was formed in 2004 when IBM first released the Eclipse Platform as Open Source.

Homepage: *http://www.eclipse.org*

License: Eclipse Public License (not GPL compatible)

Distribution: Source and binaries

Current version: 3.1.2 (stable since January 19, 2006)

Platform(s): Extensive, including Windows, Linux, MacOS X and Solaris

Dependencies: Several, but included in Windows binary

Other resources: Several mailing lists, forums, online tutorials, books, and IRC channels

The license, although not compatible with the GPL, does not prevent anyone from using Eclipse in any way they find useful, and so should not hamper development.

Installation for C Development

Four components need to be in place before Eclipse will compile C and C++ source code.

MinGW

This is the same compiler suite covered at the start of this chapter and should be set up identically as before, with the `c:\mingw\bin` directory added to the environment path so that the various commands can be found automatically from inside Eclipse.

It is recommended that you also install MSYS and add its `bin` *directory to the search path. This is because when Eclipse automatically generates* `Makefiles`, *it does so in style of a traditional Unix system using compliant commands such as* `rm`, *that are traditionally unavailable in a Windows system. This means that even simple operations, such as* `make clean`, *will not work. Naturally, Linux users will not need either step.*

Java

The Eclipse framework is written in and built upon Java. Therefore, an installation of version 1.4.2 or above is required that can be downloaded from *http://java.sun .com/j2se/1.4.2/download.html*. This is a vanilla install and not special in any way. The extra GUI functionality present within Eclipse is included within the Eclipse package itself and automatically added to the Java *classpath*[7].

The Eclipse Framework

For a package that is intended to be only a lightweight framework, the 120 MB archive for Eclipse might appear a little disconcerting. However, once extracted into a sensible working directory, Eclipse is ready to run without any further installation or configuration! Therefore it is wise to choose an appropriate directory before experimenting and not leave it in your downloads folder or on the desktop.

CDT

This stands for C/C++ Development Tools and exists as a number of plug-ins that enable Eclipse to perform syntax highlighting and code completion for the C language, along with GDB integration, application launching, and `Makefile` generation. Its home page is at *http://www.eclipse.org/cdt* that also indicates the appropriate version of CDT for the corresponding version of Eclipse.

Installation of CDT is very easy because the archive needs only to be extracted into the existing Eclipse directory for it to be complete. When Eclipse next starts, it scans the `features` and `plugins` directories and loads the CDT functionality. You can verify its installation by reviewing the contents of the Help>About dialog box.

Using Eclipse

At first glance, Eclipse is awash with windows and nonconventional interface controls, as shown in Figure 4.1. However, they are all grouped into *perspectives*. The currently available perspectives are shown at the top right of the window. Each of these configures all the windows in the workspace to match a chosen configuration, such as C/C++ development or debugging. You can add and customize these as much as you wish.

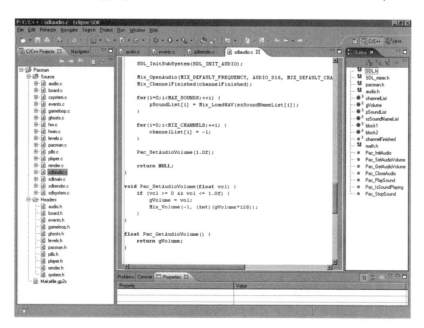

FIGURE 4.1   The typical view of Eclipse.

Where many people get confused is with the individual windows themselves, as these can react within the entire workspace. So, by double-clicking the caption bar, the window will maximize to fill the workspace. Also, the minimize and maximize icons do not apply to the currently open window, but to the tabbed group of windows, which differs from some windowing systems.

The final common annoyance with Eclipse is the amount of information present, but this is soon realized as one of its great strengths, as there is complete transparency between the workspace and the tool. For example, once it has compiled an executable, Eclipse allows you to view all the symbols present within each object file or review a list of every include file or method used within the project.

Preparing Eclipse for C Development

With the CDT installed, the first thing to do is to deselect the Build Automatically option from the Project menu. This is because it has no value in C development because the current tools do not support the necessary functionality. However, they are still able to support other useful operations such as syntax highlighting and CVS integration.

From here, you can use Eclipse to begin building projects. Eclipse makes a distinction between C and C++ source files and requires you to indicate your preference when the project is created. In reality, there is no difference in the code output, because the gcc compiler that drives the process determines the appropriate compilation method based on the file's extension, so you should select C++ to ensure maximum functionality. However, because Eclipse treats them differently, you need to duplicate the build instructions in the Project>Properties dialog box, as shown in Figure 4.2, for both the C and C++ compiler options if your source files contain both extensions.

The following sections briefly consider the two methods by which most projects are built: manual and assisted.

Manual Make

This adopts the traditional approach whereby you are expected to create and maintain the Makefile. While this is not difficult, it can become a maintenance problem, and so is the kind of task that should be generally allocated to a machine.

For those still eager on working harder than necessary, you should create the Makefile in the project directory and write the targets as normal. Note that because you're using MinGW, you must explicitly modify the command line options, as shown in Figure 4.3.

From here, the build process occurs as usual using your Makefile.

FIGURE 4.2   Project-specific properties.

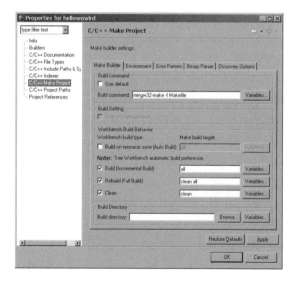

FIGURE 4.3   Using the MinGW make program
from within Eclipse.

Assisted *Make*

This is the more usual option for larger projects. As each project is created, new files
are placed into the workspace folder given upon installation, and any source files

added to the project are copied underneath this directory structure. This new directory is also used to store folders called Debug and Release that hold the automatically generated Makefiles, dependency lists, and executables built by Eclipse.

Again, you need to modify the make command to use mingw32-make. Due to the differences between manual and assisted builds, this is located in a different dialog box and is shown in Figure 4.4.

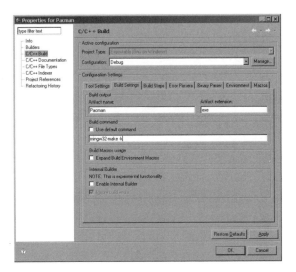

FIGURE 4.4 The MinGW settings for an assisted build.

By default, Eclipse places all project files into the unconventional directory of C:\ Documents and Settings\your_username\workspace, *which is difficult to get to from Explorer. You can select an alternative directory when running Eclipse for the first time or changing the configuration in* eclipse/configuration/.settings/org .eclipse.ui.ide.prefs.

Executing and Debugging from within Eclipse

Finally, you must configure an instance of the appropriate template within Eclipse. To debug a C program, for example, select Run>Debug and right-click C/C++ Local Application to create a new configuration.

The defaults will generally suffice here, but remember to switch into the Cygwin GDB debugger if you are not running a native Windows executable. In contrast, if you are running native Windows code, then you will need to ensure that the PE Windows executable format is understood by Eclipse. This is done with a single check box inside the Binary Parser option of Project>Properties>C/C++ Build, but is one of the most overlooked features.

KDevelop

This, like Eclipse, is a behemoth package. The approach in this case, however, was to build a development environment focused around C, C++, and QT applications for Linux that would match the style and functionality of those available for Microsoft Windows. Consequently, any similarity between Microsoft Developer Studio version 6 and *KDevelop*, is completely intentional!

Since its first incarnation, *KDevelop* has branched out to include software typical of more modern IDEs by including integrated source control, Doxygen, and internal documentation. It has also taken advantage of its Linux foundation to include the free debugging tools available on the platform, including Valgrind and Kcachegrind.

Despite its Linux bias, KDevelop can be installed under Windows through Cygwin. Although it contains the same functionality as its Linux brethren, some of the advanced tools (such as Valgrind) have no analog in the Windows world, and so are not available.

> **Homepage:** *http://kdevelop.org*
>
> **License:** GNU GPL Version 2 (Appendix B)
>
> **Distribution:** Source from the developers, with many Linux distributions, including their own binaries
>
> **First release:** Summer 1998
>
> **Current version:** 3.3.3
>
> **Platform(s):** Linux, Cygwin under Windows
>
> **Dependencies:** Several, but usually handled by the Linux package manager
>
> **Other resources:** Several mailing lists, forums, on-line tutorials, books, and IRC channels

The main window, as shown in Figure 4.5, contains a main editor window supplemented with a number of tabbed panels around three sides. Each panel opens a separate window that either allows the user to make selections (left-hand side), report on current and recent operations (lower panel), or interactively read documentation or code (right-hand side.)

The workflow method follows that of Eclipse, allowing you to either create and manage your own `Makefile` or have one built for you. In the case of the latter, KDevelop begins by asking for a suitable template from which to create the project. This prepares the additional header and library directories, and there are built-in

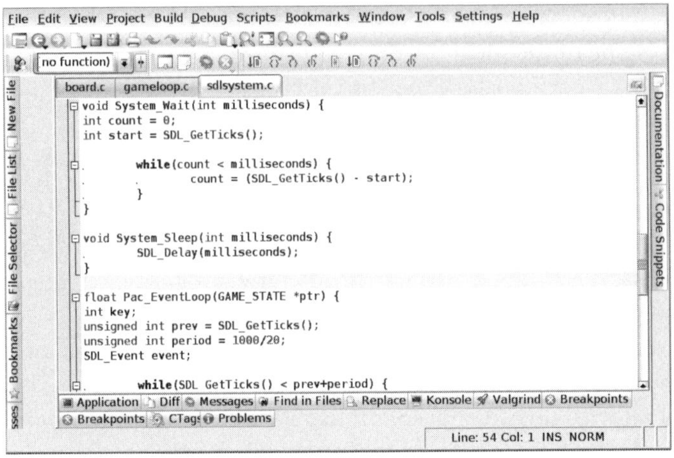

FIGURE 4.5 KDevelop in operation.

templates for SDL and ClanLib development. This results in a `.kdevelop` file. The vanilla template also provides a basic C project directory containing all the standard files found in a typical project such as the license (`COPYING`), installation instructions (`INSTALL`), and the change log (`ChangeLog`). However, while you are working within KDevelop, these files are unused, as it uses the `.kdevelop` file and dependency information generated from automake. These tools are reused when the project is exported as a source archive (through Project>Packaging & Publishing) when suitable `configure`, `configure.am`, and `Makefile.am` files are generated.

As with most Linux development software, the tools are integrated automatically and simply use the package manager of whichever Linux distribution you are using. This means that no extra tricks are necessary to configure the debugger (which uses `gdb`) or source control package, such as CVS, Subversion, or even proprietary offerings such as Perforce and ClearCase.

More information can be found on its FAQ page at *http://kdevelop.org/mediawiki/index.php/FAQ*.

MACHINE VIRTUALIZATION

With many Open Source projects originating on Linux, it is usually quicker to try the software on its native platform. This is particularly true when building from source, as Linux has significantly better package management systems, such as Apt and Yum, enabling their own unified repositories to store mutually compatible software and the necessary libraries so that the software can be downloaded and run automatically. For those who do not wish to have a dual-boot machine or waste space with a separate physical machine, it is possible to run Linux using your existing Windows machine. Furthermore, this is possible without repartitioning your hard drive or damaging your Windows install.

This is the only section in the book that highlights non-Free software.

Some of the methods described here are not usually termed virtualization, but the English language lacks a better word.

Knoppix

This is a Live CD distribution of Linux that allows you to boot from a single CD or DVD directly into Linux. It doesn't install anything to the hard drive, but automatically configures the graphics display, sound card, and network on the fly. This gives you immediate access to a complete development environment and all the standard libraries. It works by booting the entire Linux filesystem into memory, but using soft links to the data still held on the CD. In fact, the CD stores a compressed filesystem, enabling a standard CD to hold over 4 GB of data. This ensures enough space for all the drivers, libraries, and tools necessary to give the user a full picture of the GNU/Linux operating system.

Since it is running from a read-only medium, you cannot install new libraries or create new files within the system. However, you can mount your existing Windows partition under Linux and use the files on it as if they were native.

If you plan on sharing a drive between Windows and Linux often, you should ensure one partition is formatted to FAT32 because there is no free software that can safely write to an NTFS partition safely.

Alternatively, instead of using the Windows partition, you can make use of the USB socket for either pen drives or external hard drives. These are both mounted as SCSI devices, so you should create a directory for them. For example,

```
mkdir /pendrive
```

and mount the appropriate device so that its contents appear in the `pendrive` directory. For example,

```
mount /dev/sda1 /pendrive
```

The first SCSI device is sda0, followed by sda1, and so on. If you already have SCSI devices on your machine, then look at the end of the Linux kernel log file to determine which device was last inserted. This can be done with

```
dmesg | tail
```

Downloads are available from *http://www.knoppix.net*. Note that Knoppix has a powerful customization facility, allowing similar incarnations of Live CD to be built with a minimum of effort. This is primarily responsible for the large number of Live CDs currently available, and the many versions of Knoppix itself, tailored for different types of users.

Other Live CDs

Knoppix was not the first live CD distribution, but it is probably the best known. It has also spawned a sibling, Gnoppix, which adopts the Gnome desktop instead of the Knoppix favorite, KDE. There are other live CD distributions available; most are detailed at *http://www.frozentech.com/content/livecd.php* and *http://distrowatch.com/dwres.php?resource=cd*. The more prominent ones are given in the following list.

Ubuntu

Coming from the African word meaning "humanity to others," Ubuntu is the latest Linux distribution to have enchanted the Linux fraternity. Using the package management system called Apt (that originated from the heavyweight distribution Debian) this provides its own packages and versions of software that are tailored "for the human being." The focus is always on usability and functionality, rather than features. Consequently, the source code (which must be supplied to comply with the GPL) is not included with the standard discs, because that would confuse the novice and occupy much-needed space on the CD. If you have been sent a CD by Ubuntu, however, it will send you the source code as required by the license. If you have received Ubuntu, you should ask the person who gave you the disc, and they must fulfill *their* obligation to the GPL! You can also download the live CD (and installable versions) from the Ubuntu website at *http://www.ubuntu.com*.

SuSE

SuSE began as a German-language version of Slackware Linux in 1992. From there it grew to become one of the leading Linux distributions in the world, before being sold to Novell in 2003. Historically, it was the best distribution for computers using exotic hardware, as its hardware-detection system was the best around (despite being mostly closed source). This lead may have lessened in recent years, but it is still a powerful distribution backed by one of the biggest networking companies in the world found at *http://www.novell.com/products/suselinux/downloads/suse_linux/index.html*.

It supplies a live DVD version of SuSE Linux, along with an installable version.

VMWare

This product lets you install an instance of Linux in a complete virtual machine that runs inside a window on your desktop. The VMWare kernel acts like a hardware device for the virtual machine, controlling all of its input and output through the host operating system. There are separate versions depending on whether the host machine is running Microsoft Windows or GNU/Linux, but once the virtual machine is running, any operating system can be installed and run on it. VMWare is available in several versions; some are specifically tuned for Linux virtualization, for example.

Where the VMWare approach scores highly is that by being a true virtual machine you can save the entire memory and processor state to disk, and recover and rewind through previous experiments quickly. Also, because the time taken to virtually boot up is much quicker than a dual-boot system, enabling a faster turnaround for smaller virtual experiments.

Homepage: *http://www.vmware.com*

License: Proprietary

First release: VMWare Workstation in 1999; VMWare player in 2005

Current version: 5.5 (VMWare Workstation); 1.0.1 (VMWare Player)

This is not a free tool, as the Workstation version currently costs $199[8]. However, there is also a VMWare Player[9] that allows you to run *existing* VMWare images for no cost. You still need a license for the operating system itself, but when that is Linux, no such requirement exists.

The important point to note here is the word "existing." You cannot create new virtual machines with the VMWare Player. However, you can download existing machines from *http://www.vmware.com/vmtn/appliances*. This list includes versions of the most popular Linux distributions (such as Debian, Fedora Core, and Ubuntu), in addition to numerous other specialty applications.

This power comes at a price—a good host machine specification—because there is a noticeable drain on the host machine while running a virtual operating system. Although this isn't as bad as you might think, considering the processing necessary to run two operating systems side by side. The recommended minimum specification is 500 MHz CPU and 256 MB of RAM, but all new machines exceed this specification significantly, so only the most cash-strapped developers need worry. The biggest necessary resource is hard drive space, however, as the full install of most Linux distributions is now several gigabytes. So this is one area where it is recommended that you don't scrimp. Although you can store the virtual disc image on any drive, you can get some good performance gains by placing it alone on its own physical drive.

TIP

The quickest way to install a complete Linux distribution inside VMWare is to download the smallest Debian virtual machine image (for example) and a Debian ISO disc image. Then install the small virtual machine, but use all the software from the CD image.

There are many benefits to using VMWare for virtualization, not least of which is its ability to run on non-Windows architectures, such as Linux, and handle complex virtual networking configurations hosted on a single machine. This can be vital for debugging complex MMOGs that require various network problems to be simulated in a repeatable environment.

If you are unable to use the full screen area within a virtual Linux machine, you may need to change the configuration settings inside /etc/X11/XF86Config-4 *to provide a more generous HorizSync and VertRefresh rate.*

VirtualPC

This Microsoft[10] product performs tasks similar to VMWare insomuch as it creates complete virtual machines with their own memory space, hard drive, and networking. It is primarily available for Windows hosts, although a Mac version is also available.

> **Homepage:** *http://www.microsoft.com/windowsxp/virtualpc*
>
> **License:** Proprietary
>
> **First release:** 1997 (for Mac)
>
> **Current version:** 5.3

This software is also not free and costs $129[11]. There is, however, a trial version downloadable from *http://go.microsoft.com/?LinkId=319394*. Its focus is to enable developers to have multiple versions of Windows running on a machine for compatibility testing, although it is able to run Linux targets, too. This option, however, is not available on the wizard, so you have to create an MS-DOS virtual PC and use it to boot from an installable Linux CD-ROM. A compatibility list of which operating systems are supported is independently maintained at *http://vpc.visualwin.com*.

By adopting the same virtualization techniques, both VMWare and VirtualPC have the same problems and need large amounts of memory and disk space to run. In the performance stakes, however, VMWare is still ahead. Part of this problem is attributed to the manner in which VirtualPC handles its virtual disk. That is, it dynamically increases the size of the file on the hard drive until it reaches the formally agreed maximum size. This in itself introduces performance problems as the (real) disk becomes fragmented. Although VirtualPC has an option to create a large hard drive up front, the performance of VMWare is still ahead despite this.

It is not necessary to run purely VMWare or VirtualPC sessions within the same company because there is a tool that converts a VirtualPC-generated virtual machine into one that is compatible with VMWare.

Xen

This is a truly remarkable piece of machine virtualization. It works by booting the host PC into a wafer-thin Xen kernel, which in turns boots the other target kernels. Because each target kernel communicates with the hardware through Xen, it requires small modifications to the kernel source. With this approach, it is possible for multiple operating systems to cooperate without special hardware. Although some high-specification functions are not currently possible, this truly free solution works very well.

> **Homepage:** *http://www.cl.cam.ac.uk/Research/SRG/netos/xen*
>
> **License:** GNU GPL (Appendix B)
>
> **Distribution:** Source, binary and demo CD image
>
> **First release:** October 2003
>
> **Current version:** 3.0.2

The biggest problem with Xen is that it requires changes to *every* kernel that wants to run on it. This means the developers must have access to the Linux source code to support virtualized Linux under Xen—they have done this. Similarly, they must also use the Windows source to support virtualized Windows. This is a problem area because, although a version exists in its laboratories, Microsoft has not made a license available to Xen for this to be released commercially. An announcement was recently made, however[12], that the Windows operating system code-named "Longhorn" will support Xen virtualization sometime in 2008.

Consequently, this is a good solution for those wanting to virtualize only Open Source operating systems. For your purposes, the best approach to take involves a stand-alone machine running Xen, then install different distributions of GNU/Linux on top to provide the configurations that the majority of Linux-based developers will be using. These would include SuSE, Debian, and Red Hat (or Fedora Core).

ENDNOTES

1. Including the native build at *http://unxutils.sourceforge.net/*
2. By contrast, consider how you'd change the debugger in .NET or even if it's possible to do so.
3. Gcc uses the `.o` suffix here, instead of `.obj` with which most Windows developers are familiar.
4. From *http://www.microsoft.com/downloads/details.aspx?familyid=EDB98FFA-A59C-4C23-9B92-BA304F188314&displaylang=en*

5. During development of this book, SGI unfortunately went bust. At the time of writing there is no word on whether these test suites will be resurrected by another company.

6. There also a cost-free version called *Visual C++ 2005 Express Edition* available from *http://msdn.microsoft.com/vstudio/express/default.aspx.*

7. The *classpath* is the mechanism that dictates which directories and JAR files (Java ARchives) Java will use to discover code for the Java Virtual Machine (JVM).

8. *http://www.vmware.com/products/ws*

9. *http://www.vmware.com/products/player*

10. Using the technology purchased from Connectix.

11. *http://www.microsoft.com/PRODUCTS/info/product.aspx?view=22&pcid =ba9e68ed-9571-4d10-82d2-b51828c33297&type=ovr#HowToBuy*

12. *http://www.microsoft.com/presspass/press/2006/jul06/07-17MSXen SourcePR.mspx*

5 Graphics

In This Chapter

- 2D Graphics
- 3D Graphics
- Fonts
- Movie Playback

2D GRAPHICS

Despite the merry abundance of 3D games, many genres work better in 2D, with strategy, management, and puzzle games being the obvious choices. But shooting and platform games are also well suited to 2D environments. Furthermore, with the increase of casual games on both mobile phones and handheld devices, and the Microsoft Live and Live Anywhere platforms, there is still a market for a well-positioned 2D game.

Additionally, 3D games will usually have a strong 2D component in the form of front-end screens, in-game menus, and heads-up displays. The 3D drivers generally support the 2D component with simple sprite and overlay handling, but have very little support for complex 2D manipulations such as fades and wipes. These have to be developed manually. This provides a renaissance opportunity for the 2D engines that can handle these operations, providing a single surface that can then be written to the screen using the 3D driver.

On the PC, most games will make use of 3D in some fashion. This is not always "just because they can" but for a very real practical purpose. That is, the 2D component of most graphics drivers has not been updated for many years. The benchmarks that once tested the speed of *Quake* (which used a software rasterizer and 2D blitting) now test *Quake IV* and its ability to send 3D vertices and textures through the graphics pipeline as fast as possible. Consequently, it can often be faster to render a complex 2D scene using a 3D graphics engine applying parallel projection and/or overlays than it is to switch render states back to 2D.

SDL

SDL stands for Simple DirectMedia Layer and is the most popular cross-platform 2D solution currently available. It was started by Sam Lantinga in 1997 as a means to ease the porting of *Maelstrom* from the Macintosh to Linux. Since then, a small army of developers and writers has helped in the development of the project, producing a very large array of tutorials, demos, and extra ports. It is included on the CD-ROM.

ON THE CD

SDL itself is not just a rendering package, however. It provides a full game-development solution providing all the basis components necessary to create games, such as:

- Audio
- CD-ROM handling
- Joysticks
- Threads
- Timers
- Video (i.e., graphics)

These are known as *subsystems* and can be initialized at will during runtime.

In all cases, these provide low-level support to the hardware device in question. This can make it rather cumbersome, as every menu screen must be written by hand in its entirety: from the handling of the input, the drawing of the buttons (in up and/or down positions), and the moving of the window itself. Although SDL itself doesn't provide any support to make this easier, there are a number of libraries that do. These are covered by other licenses, which can make sublicensing your own code more difficult, but this is covered later.

Homepage: *http://www.libsdl.org/download-1.2.php*

License: GNU LGPL version 2.1 (Appendix B).

Distribution: Source and binary.

First release: 0.8.0 (1998).

Current version: 1.2.10.

Platform(s): Extensive, including Windows, Linux, Macintosh, GP2x, Playstation Linux, and Dreamcast.

Dependencies: None.

Other resources: SDL has one of the best online resources in the community. This includes the usual collection of mailing lists and websites, but also a very good set of API documentation in several languages. Magazine articles and books have also extolled its virtues. There is also a large selection of third-party libraries to simplify the development process. While not all of these are as well documented, they are generally written solely using code from the basic SDL distribution, which limits the problem of broken dependencies, ensures cross-platform compatibility, and makes them easier to understand.

Installation

As with most packages, the biggest problem is the first one: installation. Due to its age and user base this has been simplified over the years making this a nonissue. In the first instance, the basic package contains all the necessary files to build natively under most (if not all) of its supported platforms. For GCC-based development, the standard `Makefiles` are enough to build SDL as a set of dynamic libraries for the platform itself. Those using Visual C++ or .NET will need the `VisualC.zip` file present in SDL's root directory. This contains the workspace and solution files necessary for Visual C, so you must extract these to the SDL root directory and load them into your IDE.

Although SDL is fairly up to date, it is not always as up to date as the file formats of .NET. Consequently, you may be asked to upgrade your workspace when loading older dsw or sln files. Just say "Yes" to this.

From here, you can build both the DLL and LIB files necessary, copying them to a suitable directory. You must also copy the `include` files, too. Due to the frequent updates of SDL, it is recommended you use a version-based directory structure, such as

```
c:\devlib\sdl\1.2.9\include\SDL
```

In this way, you can easily experiment with different versions and upgrades by a single change to the "Additional Include Directories" parameter.

Handling the Monolithic Structure

Due to its monolithic nature, all of the subsystems (audio, threads, etc.) are built into the standard SDL library. This increases code size in return for an easy integration. The runtime hit, however, is much smaller as only the necessary subsystems are initialized. The developer determines what subsystems are considered necessary. Most SDL programs begin with

```
SDL_Init(SDL_INIT_VIDEO);
```

that prepares the graphics subsystem. If you are only interested in the cross-platform timer, you would instead use

```
SDL_Init(SDL_INIT_TIMER);
```

and so on. Individual subsystems can later be initialized, or released, with the pairing of

```
SDL_InitSubSystem(SDL_INIT_JOYSTICK);
```

and

```
SDL_QuitSubSystem(SDL_INIT_JOYSTICK);
```

While not a problem on the PC, this redundant code size can be perceived as an issue on smaller and embedded, platforms. Each SDL subsystem is designed to work together, and so the threads library makes use of the standard types in SDL_types.h, and in turn the video library makes use of the threads library to provide mutual exclusions around critical sections, and so on. If threads are not supported on a particular platform, then that code will exist as a null driver, but it will not contribute significantly to the overall size. However, removing unused subsystems entirely (such as CD audio) is not a task to be taken lightly and is best left to a static compile and an intelligent linker.

As an example, the size of the main DLL (on Windows) is around 232 KB, with a 39 KB link library and 7 KB stub loader. If it is necessary to reduce the size of the SDL libraries, however, it can be done by removing the redundant functions from the exports file (src/main/<platform>/export) that details which functions should appear in the DLL. The resultant library should be renamed to something specific to your game, so as not to conflict with the standard version of SDL that may appear on another user's system.

 Some embedded systems, like the GP2x, have the standard SDL libraries present because of other game installs. Consequently, creating a minimal version actually increases the space used.

SDL Development

While there are good guides available elsewhere, some caveats in SDL should be mentioned.

First, all include files in SDL begin with SDL in uppercase. This goes against most standards and conventional thinking that state they should be lowercase. Generally, it is too much effort to rename all the header files locally, and a maintenance problem to keep your own repository of alternatives. Instead, you should make all developers aware that (in some development environments) SDL.h is a different file to sdl.h, and they should always use the former, lest their code not compile elsewhere, such as case-sensitive filesystems like Linux.

Second, note that the cross-platform file-handling code (SDL_rwops.c) isn't a complete solution. Although it does support device transparent file loading from disc and memory files, and abstracts the basic file operations (such as read, write, and seek) away from the end user, it still requires the use of the standard library for functions such as fopen in its typical entry point of SDL_RWFromFile. Most cross-platform filesystems have this abstraction elsewhere. It also has some hard-coded changes to handle the differences between directories delimited with / and \. If you're building a game on an operating system that supports the standard library, then it is likely that the fopen function will handle both slashes identically. However, this is not guaranteed; so to implement a truly cross-platform system you need to provide your own abstractions here. The process of loading an abstracted file typical function begins:

```
SDL_RWops *rwopsMyFile(const sgxString &filename) {
    SDL_RWops *pMyRWOps = SDL_AllocRW();
```

with the custom, I/O-specific data being held in an unused field inside the SDL_RWops structure,

```
pMyRWOps->hidden.unknown.data1 = (void*)new sgxFile(filename);
```

You can always add fields to this structure (held in SDL_rwops.h) if you wish, or introduce more meaningful names, but be mindful of any future updates of SDL. From here, you can simply fill in the callbacks,

```
pMyRWOps->seek = sgxFileSeek;
pMyRWOps->read = sgxFileRead;
pMyRWOps->write = sgxFileWrite;
pMyRWOps->close = sgxFileClose;
```

and return the pointer,

```
return pMyWROPs;
}
```

These functions will generally be of static scope and begin with the SDL_RWops structure, followed by the traditional parameters for each operation. That is,

```
int (*seek)(struct SDL_RWops *context, int offset, int whence);
int (*read)(struct SDL_RWops *context, void *ptr, int size, int maxnum);
int (*write)(struct SDL_RWops *context, const void *ptr, int size, int
    num);
int (*close)(struct SDL_RWops *context);
```

You cannot remove the SDL_Rwops structure from the SDL build entirely, however, because the audio and bitmap loaders make use of it when loading resources. Unless you already have your own import library, you should make use of the existing code and wrap the filesystem calls with RWops if necessary.

As is hinted by the `SDL_AllocRW` function, SDL makes use of the standard `malloc` function for its memory management. This must be substituted through a standard search-and-replace if you require more control in this area.

Finally, the use of types is mentioned. SDL provides a set of basic types (such as `Sint8`) with guaranteed sizes. Most developers will have already created their own. If you are focusing on using the entirety of SDL as a basis for your game, it makes sense to use their names and provide a `typedef` wrapper for other libraries.

```
#include "other_library_types.h"
#include "other_library.h"
```

Where `other_library_types.h` contains code such as,

```
typedef Sint8 tOtherLibsInt8;
```

When working on a more disparate code base, or it's likely that SDL will not remain the focus of your development, create a library-independent set of type definitions (such as found in the SGX core) and use them instead, as this ensures you never feel obliged to stick to external conventions that are no longer applicable.

Surface Interoperability

The surfaces created by SDL are abstractions. This ensures that every platform is source-compatible with the others. This in turn, however, means that the surface cannot be used with other graphics libraries without an element of conversion.

At the lowest level, each surface can be *locked* to provide a pointer to a bitmap. This lock can be read-only (for querying pixel-perfect collision data, for example) or read-write, enabling per-pixel modification and algorithmic textures.

```
if (SDL_LockSurface(pSurface) < 0) {
   // Error locking surface !
}
// pSurface->pixels now points to valid data
SDL_UnlockSurface(pSurface);
```

As with most other graphic APIs of this type, the surface may be in the memory of the graphics hardware. This requires separate DMA transfers, which may take a long time and can severely damage performance. Furthermore, if you are locking with a view to changing the data, there must be another memory copy back to the surface. Consequently, only lock if you really need to, and don't lock for read-write operations if you will never write any data back. If your game needs to query the surface data regularly, to perform collision checks say, then it is usually worth the extra memory to create a collision-specific surface. This will be a two-color version of the original image, created as a software surface (to save memory copies), and kept permanently locked. This surface is often termed a bitmap mask.

When a surface is locked it cannot be used as either the source or destination of a blit operation.

With the surface now locked, the pixels can be enumerated to extract RGB color information. However, because each surface can be of any bit depth and size, the code needs to be data-driven. The main problem occurs when the surface itself is not in the format that you requested when creating it. This can occur only when creating hardware surfaces that are not supported by the user's graphics card. Therefore, you must either query the format after creation to check for compatibility with your graphic resources, or handle multiple formats. When blitting graphics from one surface to another, SDL will perform this conversion automatically and choose an optimal code path for the copy. When performing per-pixel operations yourself, such as collisions, or when rendering primitive shapes such as lines and circles, you need to consider these format differences manually. The typical handling code would appear as,

```
pSurfacePtr = (Uint8 *)pSurface->pixels;
iBytesPerPixel = pSurface->format->BytesPerPixel;

if (iBytesPerPixel == 1) { // palettized
   pixel = *pSurfacePtr;
} else if (iBytesPerPixel == 2) { //16-bit, in either 555 or 565
   pixel = *(Uint16 *)pSurface->pixels;
} else if (iBytesPerPixel == 3) { //24-bit color
   pixel = *(Uint32 *)pSurface->pixels;
   pixel &= 0x00ffffff;
} else { // 4 bytes per pixel, aka 32-bit
   pixel = *(Uint32 *)pSurface->pixels;
}
```

You can then increment your surface pointer correctly with

```
pSurfacePtr += iBytesPerPixel;
```

Despite these variations in format, you still don't know the color of any particular pixel. There are two supplied functions for this, SDL_GetRGB and SDL_MapRGB, along with their alpha-compliant equivalents of SDL_GetRGBA and SDL_MapRGBA. Retrieving the component RGB values from a pixel is handled with

```
Uint8 r, g, b;
SDL_GetRGB(pixel, pSurface->format, &r, &g, &b);
```

while the reverse operation uses `SDL_MapRGB` to convert the individual components into a pixel in a compatible format,

```
pixel = SDL_MapRGB(pSurface->format, 155, 0, 32);
```

This can then be written back into the surface using the same care about format shown previously, and only write the correct number of bytes per pixel for each on-screen pixel. In both cases, you may need to consider the endianness of your machine with a check, such as

```
if (SDL_BYTEORDER == SDL_BIG_ENDIAN)
```

However, there is one further problem to overcome with hardware surfaces: their size. Most graphics cards only permit the creation of power-of-2 surfaces. That is, those that are 32, 64, 128, or 256 pixels wide and high. If you require one that is 24-pixels wide, for example, SDL has a choice of either failing, switching to software surfaces, or being clever with hardware. What *actually* happens is implementation specific, but the necessary solution is general purpose. Each surface, along with a width parameter, stores a value called `pitch`. This is sometimes called `stride` or `span`. It describes the number of bytes between the first pixel on one line and the first pixel on the next line. This might *not* be the same as the width multiplied by the number of bytes per pixel. Therefore, to enumerate every pixel on the surface requires this to be considered thus,

```
for(y=0;y<pSurface->h;++y) {
    for(x=0;x<pSurface->w;++x) {
        // Read the pixel, as previously shown
        pSurfacePtr += iBytesPerPixel;
    }
    pSurfacePtr -= pSurface->w * iBytesPerPixel;
    pSurfacePtr += pSurface->pitch;
}
```

In a real game, this operation would be very slow because of the continual structure references and the if-else chain according to pixel formats. Because this format won't change once the game has started it is better to perform this check outside the inner loop.

TIP

Note that in all cases the surfaces can be created without being shown to the user, allowing for offscreen rendering to use SDL in the same manner.

SDL Libraries

As previously stated, much of the legwork in SDL involves creating the basic scaffold for your game: sprites, audio mixing, and interfaces are all suspiciously absent from the basic SDL package. However, a good set of libraries will fill this gap. The following sections cover the most useful.

SDL_Mixer

Home page: *http://www.libsdl.org/projects/SDL_mixer*

License: GNU LGPL version 2.1 (Appendix C)

The core SDL audio subsystem provides a single audio buffer (of variable format) and the ability to dynamically mix new waves into it. There is no built-in support for multiple buffers, 3D-sound positioning, and other essentials, although it's possible to build such code using the given base. Consequently, the SDL_Mixer library was born of this frustration. It is covered in full detail in Chapter 6, "Audio."

SDL_image

Home page: *http://www.libsdl.org/projects/SDL_image*

License: GNU LGPL version 2.1 (Appendix C)

The SDL core provides the basic facilities for loading bitmap images using a simple BMP loader. However, the scope of images you can handle using only BMPs is limiting, so Sam Lantinga created SDL_image, which loads other formats (including JPEG, PNG, and TIFF) into the same SDL_Surface used by the rest of the SDL system. This library is a standard feature of many SDL games because the PNG format is more compact and full of features than that of BMP for lossless images.

ON THE CD This is also on the CD-ROM.

3DS Parser

Home page: *http://scene3ds.sourceforge.net*

License: GNU GPL 2 (Appendix B)

This library will load the binary-chunked format of 3D Studio into memory. Although the software that created these files has since evolved in 3ds Max and its own improved format, many people are still using it due to its compact name, well-understood format, and wide deployment. Although many parsers exist, this one is cross-platform and supports lights, material, scenes, and objects.

The documentation for this is sadly lacking, comprising only of an example in the README file, and a sole tutorial at *http://www.gamedev.net/community/forums/ topic.asp?topic_id=313126*. However, its operation is fairly simple, so this should

suffice. This is also on the CD-ROM.

SDLTk

Home page: *http://developer.berlios.de/projects/sdltk*

License: GNU GPL 2 (Appendix B)

Alternative: GG (*http://gigi.sourceforge.net* under the GNU LGPL 2.1)

Alternative: GUIChan (*http://guichan.sourceforge.net* under the Revised BSD license)

Alternative: ParaGUI (*http://www.paragui.org* under the GNU LGPL 2.1)

SDLTk is in stable beta and provides a good number of GUI toolkit functions to render the standard array of widgets, such as scroll bars, menus, buttons, and trees. Although much of the functionality is targeted toward more serious applications, SDLTk does provides skin styling code to allow the visual appearance to customized, allowing it to gel better to your game's graphical style.

There are many libraries competing to become the de facto SDL GUI library because the base install comes with nothing in this area. Among the other worthwhile competitors are GG, which uses OpenGL for the render component, GUIChan under the more liberal BSD license, and ParaGUI that contains many customizable widgets

with gradient colors and background images. These are also on the CD-ROM.

SDL-collide

Home page: *http://sdl-collide.sourceforge.net*

License: GNU LGPL 2 (Appendix C)

This is a very simple library, consisting of just two source files, that performs pixel-perfect collision on two arbitrary surfaces. For most 2D games, this is likely to be handled by custom code for performance reasons. However, by using a two-color surface, this algorithm can be used directly to handle generic collisions.

If you are using surfaces to hold data, such as the collision mask, ensure it is flagged as a software surface and/or always kept locked. This ensures the memory containing the data is always available to CPU without having to transfer it there first.

It is available on the CD-ROM.

OGLCONSOLE

Home page: *http://oglconsole.sourceforge.net*

License: GNU GPL 2 (Appendix B)

Alternative: SDL Console (*http://wacha.ch/wiki/sdlconsole* under the GNU LGPL 2.1)

This library provides a text input console that can be overlaid onto an existing OpenGL screen to provide an easy method of invoking debug commands or setting parameters that change the game. The idea was first popularized in *Quake*, but has been used in many places before and since. Console developers may care to map their joypad's buttons to predetermined keywords to make use of this library because its reporting and trace facilities are very useful. This is available on the CD-ROM.

SDL_mmap

Home page: *http://burningsmell.org/SDL_mmap*

License: GNU LGPL 2.1 (Appendix C)

This library is available for Windows, Linux, and MacOS X, and performs cross-platform memory mapping. This enables a game to reference the entire contents of a file as if it were a block of memory, without first loading it into RAM. The operating system in most cases supports this functionality directly, but SDL_mmap is a useful abstraction and so has been included on the CD-ROM.

SDL_resize

Home page: *http://members.cox.net/dolsen6/resize.zip*

License: Freeware

Despite the functionality provided by SDL for its surfaces, the ability to scale sprites is largely lacking. This small library fills that gap by providing functions to stretch and scale a given surface, using various interpolators, such as hermite, B-spline, Mitchel, and Lanczos3. It is also available on the CD-ROM.

SDL_rwlib

Home page: *http://burningsmell.org/SDL_rwlib*

License: GNU GPL 2 (Appendix B)

As the name suggests, SDL_rwlib makes use of the file abstraction mechanism in SDL, RWops, to provide an alternative set of file types and streams. Important for game developers, it provides zlib compression and decompression, and thread-safe ring buffers that are useful in network programming. It is also available on the CD-ROM.

It also supports the ability to read directly from HTTP sources, given a URL, so that web pages can be loaded and parsed directly in-game. If your game is using the web to retrieve assets or data (such as high scores) and you don't need a fully interactive experience with the site, then this is a very easy addition to make. It requires the SDL_Net library.

The SDL License

While the license is a standard LGPL, the lead developer has indicated[1] that exclusions apply for embedded devices, where relinking to the original code is problematic because the software is often unavailable. However, as mentioned in Chapter 2, "License Commentaries," he advises caution if you do not intend to release the source or object files. Although not yet tested, at least one SDL-based game has quoted this exception (*http://h-world.simugraph.com/thanks.html*) and subsequently remained safe. However, should the rights to SDL be bought out, this exception may no longer apply. Although it's likely you would be able to continue to use existing SDL implementations in embedded systems under the current license (which include the caveat), any new version would essentially be released under a new license—most probably the GNU LGPL minus the exception—causing divergence, and two separately licensed versions.

A commercial license is planned for SDL version 1.3, but no details are currently available.

Allegro

Allegro is a game-programming library initiated by Shawn Hargreaves as a library for the Atari ST®. Since then, many platforms have come and gone, but Allegro remains; albeit as a slightly left-field library, with less visibility than SDL. This may be due, in part, to the old-school philosophy employed within the project and the promotion of obsolete technology, as far as games developers are generally concerned. Also, the documentation begins in a very light-hearted and jokey manner, which can belie some of the technology within. However, if you are interested in working with older or obscure operating systems (such as DOS or BeOS), or your project must avoid C++ code, then Allegro is probably your most viable option.

Homepage: *http://alleg.sourceforge.net*
License: Giftware (essentially freeware)

Distribution: Source; separate binary packages recommended for some compilers

First release: 1995

Current version: 4.2.0 (stable since November 7, 2005)

Platform(s): Fairly wide, including Windows, Linux, DOS, QNX, and Macintosh

Dependencies: None

Other resources: Mailing lists, forums, IRC channels, on-line tutorials, a wiki, and at least two books

Allegro has existed for a long time and, as a consequence, has a comprehensive graphics library, along with sound code (supporting both MIDI and WAV play-back), a math library (including fixed-point processing), joystick handling, and a useful GUI library. There is also 3D functionality, including a software rasterizer. However, the 3D support is slightly lacking compared to the other options available. So, while it is useable for those needing some occasional 3D images in their 2D application, those wanting primarily 3D graphics should perhaps look toward solutions covered later.

Installation

ON THE CD

The easiest way to start working with Allegro is to download both the source and binary packages, or copy them from the accompanying CD-ROM. The former gives you all the documentation, source code, and test programs, while the second includes the Microsoft Windows DLL files and a "more useful than you think it'll be" makemsvc.bat script. This batch script builds the necessary compiler-specific library (.lib) files, compiles the test suite, and converts the documentation into several formats, including HTML and RTF. After copying the DLLs into a suitable directory (which the script does automatically if you let it), all of the test programs can be run.

Integrating Allegro

Allegro is a monolithic code base, and as such should be used as the foundation of any software using it, although the basic header system is quite involved and includes lots of include'd includes. Searching for any particular prototype invariably begins with allegro.h. The important files to seek out from here are base.h (which handles all the standard version numbers) and alconfig.h (which acts primarily as a redirect to the compiler-specific header files in the allegro/platform directory).

Those using C++ may wish to modify base.h to remove the existing versions of the typical MIN and MAX macros and replace them with the safer template functions found in the SGX core,

```
template <typename T>
const T sgxMin(const T &v1, const T &v2)
{
   if (v1 < v2) {
      return v1;
   } else {
      return v2;
   }
}

template <typename T>
const T sgxMax(const T &v1, const T &v2)
{
   if (v1 > v2) {
      return v1;
   } else {
      return v2;
   }
}
```

One more important area of note, however, is the lack of type abstraction through the code. All parameters are explicitly given as char, int, or long, as the situation calls. While this removes the need to create platform-specific header files, it also opens the code up to a lot of warnings on machines where an integer is not 4 bytes wide, and you need to cast from your own tINT32 type back into an int.

Memory abstraction is a more complex issue. This is because Allegro has none of its own; every allocation goes through the standard C functions of malloc and free. While search and replace is a simple enough operation, you will need to make the changes (and *remember* to make the changes) whenever new versions or bug fixes appear. That said, Allegro has been stable for a while, and changes will be rare. Changes that affect you will be even more rare, so it is safe to adopt an internal repository with a modified version.

The file-handling capabilities of Allegro are mostly standard. That is, it abstracts the standard fopen function with its own code, but does no more. This means that all file paths are unchanged, requiring the correct format of directory slash and case for it to work cross-platform. However, where Allegro scores highly is in its use of pack files. These files allow you to package several individual files into one, but still access them individually. It is more often used in console development, where the platform limits the number of files that may be stored, but it can used elsewhere to improve load times or obfuscate the resource data.

Unicode

Allegro is one of the few libraries that utilizes Unicode as standard. This is done by storing each string, regardless of format, in a `char *`. It then supplements these with constants, such as `U_ASCII`, `U_UTF8`, `U_UNICODE`, and `U_ASCII_CP`, which describe the format of the string internally. Holding this information within each string is generally a waste of space; so in most cases, you will switch Allegro into a specific encoding, and leave it there. This is achieved with

```
set_uformat(U_UNICODE);
```

However, conversion between formats requires the description of each `char *` to be supplemented with its type, often through the `do_uconvert` function. There is also a version that will convert text into the current encoding:

```
uconvert_ascii("Welcome to Unicode", szEncodedString);
```

The current encoding is simple in its implementation as it defines which of the low-level functions are used to process the string. Naturally, the traditional string-processing functions, such as `strlen` and `strcat` are unsuitable for Unicode strings, and so Allegro provides a set of cross-platform variants prefixed with u. Each relies on the current encoding being set correctly.

Failure to use the Unicode-compliant functions will result in very hard-to-find bugs.

Allegro also supports string pools and localization, using the `get_config_text` function. This is a double win. In the first instance, it allows the text to be translated automatically if the string argument exists within the localization file. Second, it stores the text internally using the correct encoding in its own table. This means there is no duplicate text processing to be done, and memory is saved since only one copy of it needs to exist.

The localization functionality is usable outside of Allegro, but is not too easy to extract is because of its reliance on the Unicode implementation contained within.

3D GRAPHICS

The growth of 3D over the past 10 years has been staggering. As a vehicle for games development and high-end visualization, it is possible to achieve effects in the home that were previously thought impossible. Consequently, everyone and their dog has written a 3D engine of some description. The Open Source world follows this trend with the 3D engines list at *http://cg.cs.tu-berlin.de/~ki/engines.html* detailing over 640 different options. As with all software, some is useless. Some are merely wrappers to OpenGL, and some are true renderers with full scene management and special effects. However, some can be used to develop entire games without any third-party code. Indeed, the full source to the *Quake* series (up to and including version 3) is now available under the GPL, upping the ante even further.

The solutions covered here are the prominent engines that are generally self-contained and work as standalone middleware. This includes the renderer, file-system, GUI, and a good selection of importable file formats. While it is possible to build complete games with these engines out of the box, developers that are also considering console development will have to understand what changes are necessary in each case. Similarly, any individual components not featured in the particular engine will need to be integrated manually to the existing source base. Both areas for each engine are covered.

In some cases, these engines are available in console flavors. Due to the NDA nature of console development, any Xbox port (for example) is likely to only work on chipped machines using a homebrew SDK.

NOTE

Ogre

Ogre stands for Object-oriented Graphics Rendering Engine, but can do much more than just rendering. While it is true that it has extensive graphical capabilities (including particle systems and GPU programming), it also has abstractions for the filesystem, Zip file handling, and animation. Furthermore, the basic package (available on the CD-ROM and weighing in around 29 MB) also includes Crazy Eddies GUI library (CEGUI), and the physics solution Open Dynamic Engine (ODE), making this a very good one-stop shop for 3D game development. Additionally, code is also included to load BSP maps and levels from *Quake III* making it useful to those wanting to retain their *Quake III* assets, but move away from its GPL license.

ON THE CD

Homepage: *http://www.ogre3d.org*

License: GNU LGPL 2.1 (Appendix C).

Distribution: Source and binary.

First release: December 29, 2000.

Current version: 1.2.1 (stable since June 11, 2006).

Platform(s): Windows, Linux, and MacOS X. Later versions do not include Visual Studio 6 binaries.

Dependencies: zlib, openil, zziplib, CEGUI, FreeType2, and ODE. All included in the binaries. A separate archive called `OgreDependencies_VC6_1.0.3b.zip` is also available.

Other resources: Mailing lists, forums, IRC channels. and documentation wiki.

Integration

This engine covers a lot of ground technologically because it is able to employ many other Open Source projects. The font handling, for example, is carried out by the FreeType code, while the memory manager uses the code from MMGR. This not only provides a near complete engine, but also proves the Open Source philosophy can work when developing game software by combining multiple libraries (under different licenses) together. You can also use it as reference when looking to understanding some of the integration methods others have chosen.

Ogre uses two main methods to include code from other sources. The first is to incorporate the source directly into files, named and formatted in the Ogre style, wrapped with its naming convention. MMGR is one such example.

The second approach is to encapsulate the library with an entirely separate class, and instantiate the external library objects as is necessary, and using Ogre to abstract their interface and well as their types. The compression handler, for example, uses Zzip in this manner.

Despite the scope of the Ogre components, everything lives within a single C++ namespace (to prevent name clashes with other libraries) and in a moderately flat directory structure, with all the cross-platform components living in the OgreMain/src directory, while each platform-specific component has its own directory, such as PlatformManagers and RenderSystems. The only variation is in the definition of the base types, which are in the main include directory and wrapped by platform-specific defines.

> **OgrePrerequisites.h:** This is the first header that most source code will include and prepares the basic types, forward references classes, and prepares the compile environment, using the other header files listed here.

> **OgreConfig.h:** This is a generic control header that governs which features are built into Ogre, and the method by which that happens. Although it is not platform specific, per se, changes may need to be made in some instances; for example, when handling exceptions or defining the maximum number of lights permitted per render pass.

> **OgrePlatform.h:** This prepares the basic definitions of platform and compiler. It's approach is simple: map the define OGRE_PLATFORM to one of OGRE_PLATFORM_WIN32, OGRE_PLATFORM_APPLE, or OGRE_PLATFORM_LINUX to allow other code to easily determine its platform by reviewing the (already set) defines for the specific compilers. This also provides the generic OGRE_DEBUG_MODE and OGRE_ENDIAN defines.

> **OgreStdHeaders.h:** The compiler-specific variations are handled here. This includes the loading of the standard STL headers. If you were moving to STLport, changes here might be necessary

The naming convention for the Ogre header files include uppercase characters, so type carefully if you're developing on Windows but intending to port to a case-sensitive system like Linux.

Handling Memory

Due in part to the large number of third-party libraries, Ogre has decided it would be a waste of time to convert all the existing code to use a single form of memory manager. Instead, it uses MMGR to overload the global new and delete operators, and call the singleton MemoryManager class. This is generally considered a bad idea because it also removes the predictable of operation of any third-party libraries that are using new and delete properly. In this particular instance, the only external libraries are ours and so you can be moderately sure the allocations will be correctly handled.

There are two steps to the allocation overload procedure. The first is the macro inside OgreMemoryMacros.h, which replaces all instances of new with a special function call that records details of the current allocation attempt,

```
#define new    (::Ogre::MemoryManager::instance().setOwner(__FILE__,__
LINE__,__FUNCTION__),
    false) ? NULL : new
```

This then causes the global new operator to be invoked. For example, with

```
inline void *operator new(size_t reportedSize)
{
  if(!gProcessID)
    gProcessID = Ogre::MemoryManager::instance()._getProcessID();
  return Ogre::MemoryManager::instance().op_new_sc(reportedSize,
  gProcessID);
}
```

which completes the memory tracking handler. The same approach is taken for new[], delete, and delete[].

This approach is not foolproof. Any memory allocated by a third-party library (compiled without MMGR) but released inside your code (with MMGR) will cause a mismatch in the known number of allocations and deallocations.

Conversely, the standard C allocators are handled much more simply by re-defining the functions with macros that call the memory manager directly,

```
#define malloc(sz) ::Ogre::MemoryManager::instance().allocMem(
    __FILE__,__LINE__,__FUNCTION__, ::Ogre::m_alloc_malloc, sz,
    gProcessID)
```

The Math Library

As with most modern math libraries, this is split into separate files for each of the standard types (vectors, matrices, and quaternions) and supported by general-purpose OgreMath.cpp/.h files containing the standard trigonometry and algebraic functions. This also contains the random number generator.

There are two features to highlight here. The first is that the standard trigonometry functions can all take an extra parameter indicating whether they should use a lookup table or not. The second is that there are two separate classes covering Radians and Degrees that introduces an often-unnecessary layer of conversion.

Exceptions

Ogre throws exceptions by using the wrapped macro, OGRE_EXCEPT. This allows any one of the predetermined exceptions codes (such as ERR_ITEM_NOT_FOUND or ERR_INTERNAL_ERROR) listed in OgreException.h to be thrown and caught by the parent function through the try-catch mechanism. Unfortunately, this second stage has not been abstracted, meaning that exception handling in Ogre is mandatory. As the comments in OgreException.h say, "OGRE never uses return values to indicate errors", so we must therefore handle them.

However, few game developers use exceptions, particularly on consoles because they increase code size by about 10 percent. Furthermore, few junior and midlevel developers understand the principles and intricacies behind exceptions, so will have purposefully ignored them. Consequently, this becomes a feature you must either learn or remove.

In the general case, removing exceptions from the code is not trivial and requires a global replace throughout the source, followed by a manual check that no exceptions are intentionally thrown as a means to avoid returning error codes; for example, an exception when no file can be found, as opposed to returning a NULL pointer.

The first step in this process is to replace each instance of try and catch with macros that can get switched on and off between builds. These macros might appear as:

```
#define SGX_TRY         try
#define SGX_CATCH       catch
#define SGX_THROW(thro) throw thro
#define SGX_RETHROW     throw
```

Then check that there are no "illegitimate" exceptions hiding in the source. That is, modify the code to any explicit SGX_THROW that could be rewritten in a different way to return a sensible error code or value. In this way, the removal of all exceptions will not cause a problem with the legitimate working of the software.

Next, confirm that the exceptions can be removed by changing the macros:

```
#define SGX_TRY        if (1)
#define SGX_CATCH      if (0)
#define SGX_THROW(thro)
#define SGX_RETHROW
```

and that the compile is still clean and the code still works.

The final step takes the most time. It involves reviewing every instance of OGRE_EXCEPT and confirming that should the condition be reached, it is possible for a clean exit. This is a change in development philosophy because any invalid data must now be sanitized and/or a sensible NULL value returned from the function. Unfortunately, this now becomes an error code, and must therefore be passed back to the parent function all the way up the chain until it reaches the original main function. At least, it should in theory. In practice, an exception will not occur unless something is badly wrong with the code. These bugs will have been worked out during development and will no longer occur. Therefore, the removal of exceptions should have no effect.

Of all the exceptions in Ogre, most are in the serialize and script compiler, and when caught do nothing more exotic that log the error. The memory manager also uses them, but note that some of its functions use the standard C++ keyword throw instead of its abstracted macro, and that the prototype for these functions appears as

```
void *allocMem(const char *szFile, size_t uLine, size_t count) throw ( );
```

Controlling the GUI

As mentioned previously, the GUI components come from the separate CEGUI. Therefore, you need to tie in all input and output mechanism to this library. The GUI sample program in the Irrlicht program demonstrates how this can be accomplished. It simply involves the injection of each input event (mouse move, key pressed, etc.) to the CEGUI system, so that it can handle them. For example,

```
void keyPressed(KeyEvent* e)
{
  CEGUI::System::getSingleton().injectKeyDown(e->getKey());
  CEGUI::System::getSingleton().injectChar(e->getKeyChar());
  e->consume();
}
```

Each type of input mechanism must involve a listener of some kind. This is akin to the Java methodology. Typically, a new input receiving class is created that derives from each type of listener,

```
class GuiFrameListener : public ExampleFrameListener,
        public MouseMotionListener, public MouseListener
```

This input is then paired with the output rendering command,

```
CEGUI::System::getSingleton().renderGUI();
```

The later versions of CEGUI, from 0.5 upward, will be licensed under the MIT license, as opposed to the LGPL.

Like most modern GUI systems, this too can be reskinned by created XML files describing the layout and supplying alternate textures. Several skinning tutorials can be found at *http://www.cegui.org.uk/wiki/index.php/Tutorials*, with some sample screenshots located at *http://www.cegui.org.uk/gallery/thumbnails.php?album=2*.

The License

Because of the extensive use of third-party libraries in creating Ogre, there are a lot of acknowledgments to consider. Under the terms of many licenses, you have to acknowledge the use of Open Source code in the documentation, even if the code itself doesn't have to be rereleased. Consequently, your manual must contain the appropriate packages acknowledged in the ReadMe.html file of Ogre itself. At the time of writing these are:

- Wild Magic engine 0.2
- Aftershock and Bart Sekura's ROGL
- Singleton template class from Scott Bilas
- MMGR by Paul Nettle at Fluid Studios

Also, the unmodified contributions from:

- Zlib
- DevIL
- Zziplib
- Crazy Eddies GUI
- SDL
- FreeType2
- ODE

The tutorials and demo programs that come with Ogre are not released under the LGPL, but rather a completely free license. Consequently, you can do anything with them. This includes making use of them in closed software or (if you wrapper the Ogre-specific code) apply them to a completely different engine.

CrystalSpace

Of all the Open Source 3D engines, this is probably the best known. It has gone through many iterations and is now comprised of much useful code including KD-trees, shaders, and particle systems. Furthermore, like the other engines presented here, it is not limited to graphics rendering, but also contains abstractions for the filesystem, Zip file handling, and animation.

CrystalSpace has consciously split its technology into core libraries and modules, thereby making components very easy to add, which might explain why other Open Source projects have been incorporated into it. These include ODE physics (as covered in Chapter 7, "Physics"), Crazy Eddies GUI (detailed in Irrlicht later), and FreeType fonts.

As part of the community around CrystalSpace, the website also includes a large number of textures and models available for free use. Furthermore, the downloads section also provides an artist-friendly binary archive enabling them to test level walkthroughs. This encourages artists to experiment with known-good assets without the involvement of a programmer.

This community also provides links and screenshots to its current projects utilizing CrystalSpace. This includes games, tutorials, demos, and examples of shader code. All can be accessed through the site at *http://community.crystalspace3d.org/tiki-galleries.php*.

Homepage: *http://www.crystalspace3d.org*

License: GNU LGPL 2.1 (Appendix C).

Distribution: Source and binary.

First release: August 26, 1997.

Current version: 0.99 (stable since January 27, 2006).

Platform(s): Windows, Linux, and MacOS X.

Dependencies: zlib, libpng, and libjpeg. Windows users are provided with cs-win32libs that supplies them all. Other components are optional; FreeType 2, CG, ODE, Cal3D, lib3ds, Ogg/Vorbis, libmng, MikMod, CEGUI, and CAC. These are also included in the cs-win32libs install.

Other resources: Mailing lists, forums, IRC channels, and documentation wiki.

With such an impressive feature list, it is sometimes difficult to know where to start with CrystalSpace. However, the core of the engine is actually very small, as the majority of its components (including the renderer) are presented as separate modules, or *plug-ins* as CrystalSpace calls them. This gives us three areas of interest: the basic libraries (inside CS\libs), the plug-ins (CS\plugins), and the header files for both of them within CS\include.

Upon traversal of the source tree, you will notice several Jamfiles. *This is the preferred building mechanism of CrystalSpace. If you're only using the engine internally, then the* make *emulation layer will build suitable libraries you can distribute to the team without porting your game development build system to Jam[2]. However, if you want to help with the ongoing development of CrystalSpace, it would be in your interests to build the engine (at least) with Jam.*

The Header Structure

The include directory contains the header files for both libraries and the bundled plug-ins. Each library and plug-in has its own header file, such as csutil.h, that contains every header file within the associated directory, csutil in this case. Additionally, the CS/include root contains many other useful includes and the all-important system definition headers, which are spread across five main files.

crystalspace.h

This is the daddy[3] of all CrystalSpace headers as it includes everything else that is generally needed in a build; that is, all the basic libraries, the most often-used plug-ins (such as the graphics renderer), and the system definitions. If you do not have precompiled headers in your development environment, it would be a good idea to use them before blindly including this file.

cssysdef.h

This is the system definition file that you should use to declare type abstractions and so on because, although they do not live in this file, this is the one that allows the platform-specific headers to override the default settings and prepare compiler-specific fixes.

csplatform.h

The configuration data for *CrystalSpace*. This file is always included before any of the system headers, so macros and switches can be set up beforehand. There are two main platform configuration files, one for Microsoft Windows (csutil/win32/ csconfig.h) and one for everyone else (csconfig.h). The latter is usually generated by the platform-specific configuration script.

Additional platform-specific macros (such as CS_EXPORT_SYM_DLL) are defined in the csutil/<platform>.csosdefs.h file.

cstypes.h

The generic type abstraction definitions, so that variables can be declared with a specific number of bits. The naming convention uses uint16, int32, and so on, and supports long long, and wide characters.

csdef.h

This is a cross-platform definitions file that handles different compile configurations based on the capabilities previously defined in csplatform.h and cstypes.h, and their children. For example, if the platform is known to have a problem with new-style C++ casts, the platform-specific headers will have defined CS_USE_OLD_STYLE_CASTS. This header therefore switches between,

```
#define CS_CAST(C,T,V) ((T)(V))
```

and

```
#define CS_CAST(C,T,V) (C<T>(V)).
```

This then propagates to,

```
#define CS_STATIC_CAST(T,V)      CS_CAST(static_cast,T,V)
#define CS_DYNAMIC_CAST(T,V)     CS_CAST(dynamic_cast,T,V)
#define CS_REINTERPRET_CAST(T,V) CS_CAST(reinterpret_cast,T,V)
#define CS_CONST_CAST(T,V)       CS_CAST(const_cast,T,V)
```

so that all future cases can be handled correctly through a standard call to

```
float result = CS_STATIC_CAST(float, sin(value));.
```

This file also contains values for pi, epsilon, and old macros for MIN, MAX, ABS, and SIGN.

The Basic Libraries

These contain the main system abstraction core, along with general-purpose cross-platform code. The implementation of many features is spread between the source file and its header.

csutil

This comprises of three major areas: the Shared Class Facility (SCF), smart pointers, and utility system functions. SCF is CrystalSpace's way of differentiating between interfaces and implementations. As with systems like COM, Java, or CORBA, CrystalSpace uses only interfaces to describe particular objects, and passes them between functions. In this way, the implementation can change substantially, but provided the contract of interface is maintained between all components, the code will continue to work.

Using objects with SCF is a simple metaphor to use, and is engrained into the engine; so any new features you add would do well to adopt this approach.

SCF adopts a very similar interface to COM. Indeed, its origins are in an early implementation cross-platform COM, and as such contains methods such as `In-cRef`, `QueryInterface`, and `DecRef`. Previously, the reference counting was handled manually, with explicit calls to `IncRef` and `DecRef`. Now, however, CrystalSpace has smart pointers.

SCF is the only part of the engine to currently use Runtime Type Information (RTTI.) The general avoidance of RTTI is a heritage feature to prevent problems with non-compliant compilers.

The smart pointer implementation, held in `CS/include/csutil/ref.h`, provides the SCF components of CrystalSpace with an easy way to reference count and correctly free resources. Although this is a comparatively recent addition, it is already used throughout the engine and so removing or changing the implementation is likely to be fraught with danger.

Instantiating objects with reference counting is handled simply with

```
csRef<iEngine> engine;
```

These are usually coupled with SCF interfaces to save on the manual reference counting used by SCF.

The final major area of interest within *csutil* are the system functions, such as threading (`thread.h`), timers (`timer.h`), and memory mapped files (`mmap.h`). These comprise of both common and platform-specific header and source files. These often include a generic implementation, when no specific version is available. Be aware of this, however, since the generic implementation for memory mapped files will attempt to load the entire file into memory, through `fopen`, to support the feature.

Since the CrystalSpace engine is generally used in its entirety, these are points to be aware of when porting to consoles, but need less consideration in general usage since they exist and "just work." However, the features presented next permeate the engine, so any attempt to transport the feature set code elsewhere will have to consider them.

csgeom

This contains the basic mathematics for the engine, including matrices, vectors, and polygons. These all the use native `float` types without abstraction and contain separate classes for each dimension of vector (i.e. `vector2.h`, `vector3.h`, and `vector4.h`) instead of the templated version you may already be using. However, the implementation is straightforward and binary compatible with most other variations.

The equality of vectors does not use an epsilon value in CrystalSpace unless explicitly requested through the special `VectorN::IsZero` *method.*

NOTE

The rest of the math library utilizes the implementations of the standard library; no lookup tables for sine or cosine are to be found here. Console porters may wish to change that to ensure cross-platform compatibility.

Also, you do not have to worry about naming conflicts. Although a single namespace is used through the majority of the project, most types are also prefixed with a lowercase `cs`. This includes the perennial integration headaches of `min` and `max`. However, the standard macros `MIN` and `MAX` are already created by the system definitions.

csgfx

Despite the name, this is not the graphics component of CrystalSpace. Instead, this is a collection of cross-platform utility routines that manipulate graphic images and work with the shader language. The graphics driver is, instead, held within the `plugins\video\render3d` directory.

cstool

This is a collection of high-level utilities, such as collision wrappers and application frameworks. They are all cross-platform and rarely need tweaking.

The Main Plug-ins

All of the major CrystalSpace components, including the graphics driver, can be found within the plug-ins directory. The current version supplies 29 of them. This section briefly details the major plug-ins that importantly affects the porting and maintenance process.

Virtual File System (VFS)

This plug-in is probably the most irreplaceable because all internal CrystalSpace file operations, such as the graphics code and font server, utilize its code. As you'd expect, this abstracts the basic file-handling code with a solid cross-platform implementation. This code also transparently handles Zip files and can mount a virtual directory onto several real-world filesystems, allowing foreign language files to supercede their generic versions in a different directory.

The implementation for VFS is monolithic, living entirely in `plugins/filesys/vfs/vfs.cpp`, and requires an implementation of the standard I/O library. Consoles without this library, or those wanting to improve performance by using platform-specific functions, can use native methods by changing portions of the `DiskFile` constructor and `IsZipFile`. There are similar changes necessary to replace `fread` and `fwrite`.

To add support for alternate filesystems, such as the memory card of a console, you can derive classes from `VfsNode` to support them.

VFS uses blocking functions by default, unless you rewrite the methods inside the `DiskFile` *class. However, you may run it on a separate thread, since it is naturally thread safe, making use of* `csMutex` *for synchronization.*

NOTE

Video

Of interest to many is the rendering component. In CrystalSpace, this is split into four sections, all convened under the video plug-in moniker.

The *canvas* component creates a working surface using a specialized module. This can range from the platform-specific drivers of OpenGL, DirectDraw, or the X Window System through to the generic (but abstracted elsewhere) components like SDL.

Cursor is a cross-platform component for handling a mouse cursor. It uses the `csPixmap` class to hold the image and uses its draw function to render it. The position of the cursor is handled internally by listening to the appropriate event messages.

The *loader* component is also cross-platform and simply loads images from many different formats into a class dictated by the `iImage` interface. Some of these parsers have been implemented internal within CrystalSpace, such as BMP, while others use third-party libraries to process the data before copying it into the aforementioned generic structures. JPG is typical of this later approach.

CrystalSpace incorporates DDS image I/O, and is one of the few pieces of Open Source to both load and save the format.

TIP

Finally, the *render3d* component exists in three flavors: OpenGL, software, and null driver, and consists of the typically glamorous code of 3D rendering. Although the OpenGL is the primary driver of choice, its functionality is limited to the basics, relying on the other engine components to provide a suitable data set for rendering and manipulation. Consequently, the functionality here is limited to basic state handling, frame buffer creation, and texture assignment. This is supplemented with a very capable shader library.

Collide

This uses the OPCODE collision system—also used in the Open Dynamics Engine (ODE) physics engine covered in Chapter 7—for all the collision processing. The data types are abstracted on input and output; however, since all OPCODE functionality is wrapped by CrystalSpace. This modified version of the source places OPCODE in its own namespace (`cspluginOpcode::Opcode`) and uses newly created functions, such as `CollideRaySegment`, to collect the abstracted structures (in the form of `iCollider` and `csVector3`, for example) and build OPCODE-compliant data before calling this underlying code, and then copying the results back into CrystalSpace–friendly versions. This structure works very well for individual collisions, but the integration of a physics engine component (such as ODE) should access the OPCODE functions natively, and abstract the reports and results code at a higher level.

ODE is included inside the `plugins\physics\odedynam` directory, providing a thinner wrapper around ODE, while still using the singletons created through the Collide plug-in.

NOTE

Font Server

This applies a wrapper around the FreeType 2 libraries in much the same way that the Collide plug-in wrappers OPCODE. In this case, however, FreeType is not supplied with CrystalSpace and must therefore be compiled separately.

Please review the discussion on FreeType2 later in this chapter for important licensing information.

CAUTION

Once a font is loaded through VFS, you can render character glpyhs directly into buffers with the `GetGlyphBitmap` function; but it is more usual to make use of the video driver helper functions such as `csGLFontCache::WriteString`.

Cscript

This plug-in supports the scripting languages Python and PERL, both utilizing Swig in some way. Although Python is beginning to make its mark in the games community, PERL is more the reserve of data mongers. Therefore, it is likely you will take the premise of the Python implementation, and create your own handler for Lua or your own language of choice. See Chapter 9, "Scripting Engines," for more information on scripting languages and their integration.

Creating an Application

Although there is no strict requirement to base a game on the supplied framework, many developers do because it handles the event messages and ensures the quit message is broadcast appropriately. A typical application would therefore begin,

```
class MainApp : public csApplicationFramework, public
csBaseEventHandler {
{
```

with the derived OnInitialize method being used to request any necessary Crystal-Space plug-ins, and prepare any third-party data—which includes your own structures.

```
bool success = csInitializer::RequestPlugins(GetObjectRegistry(),
    CS_REQUEST_VFS,
    CS_REQUEST_OPENGL3D,
    CS_REQUEST_ENGINE,
    CS_REQUEST_IMAGELOADER,
    CS_REQUEST_REPORTER,
    CS_REQUEST_REPORTERLISTENER,
    CS_REQUEST_END);
```

From here, events can be received (through OnKeyboard(iEvent& ev), for example) and the world is then generated or loaded as appropriate. There are several examples, demos, and tutorials included with the basic install. The supplied documentation at CS\docs\html\manual\usingcs\ownprojects also provides screenshots covering all the project initialization steps for both the KDevelop and .NET development environments

Crystal Entity Layer

Most of the rendering and game engines available leave all game logic to the end user. This logic typically moves and rotates the render objects according to a set of rules or behaviors to make the world come alive. This code is generally very simple and begins with a simple base class, such as,

```
class GameObject {
   IEngineObject *pObject;

public:
   virtual void draw();
   virtual void update(float timeElapsed);
};
```

This is followed by any number of derived classes for each type of object; for example, the player, an AI, or an exploding crate. Adding this structure on top of an existing engine is not difficult, but necessary in all cases. To eliminate this extra work, the Open Source community has developed an analogous layer on top of CrystalSpace to achieve the same effect.

The Crystal Entity Layer (CEL) follows the same demarcation between the core library and plug-ins, and exists as its own plug-in to CrystalSpace. Consequently, there are no platform-specific components in CEL, and so they should work on the consoles should CrystalSpace have been previously ported to it.

CEL makes extensive use of the SCF and VFS of CrystalSpace, so although porting it to another engine is possible, it is probably not worth the effort.

Since CEL exists as a plug-in, it requires that it be initialized in the way shown previously, with RequestPlugins, resulting in,

```
bool success = csInitializer::RequestPlugins(GetObjectRegistry(),
   CS_REQUEST_VFS,
   CS_REQUEST_OPENGL3D,
   CS_REQUEST_ENGINE,
   CS_REQUEST_IMAGELOADER,
   CS_REQUEST_REPORTER,
   CS_REQUEST_REPORTERLISTENER,
   CS_REQUEST_PLUGIN("cel.physicallayer", iCelPlLayer),
   CS_REQUEST_END);
```

CEL comprises of two layers onto which game entities are placed. The first is the physical layer created with

```
csRef<iCelPlLayer> pl;
```

and is used to create and keep track of each entity within the world with

```
csRef<iCelEntity> player = pl->CreateEntity();
```

Persistence is also part of the physical layer and provides these entities with the ability to serialize their data to and from disk.

You can also add object-specific properties, such as mass, health, or weapons carried, to these entities so that they can be retrieved in a generic manner. These are governed by *property classes*, and several are supplied with CEL. Each must be registered before use. For example,

```
pl->LoadPropertyClassFactory("cel.pcfactory.mesh");
```

This permits the use of the pcmesh property class that assigns a mesh on disk to the current entity. The property class can then be assigned to an entity, such as

```
pl->CreatePropertyClass(player, "pcmesh");
```

and then queried and utilized to load the player mesh with, for example,

```
csRef<iPcMesh> pcmesh = CEL_QUERY_PROPCLASS_ENT(player, iPcMesh);
pcmesh->SetPath("/game/player");
pcmesh->SetMesh("test", "player_mesh.cal3d");
```

Other property classes include the ability to retrieve machine input, review timers, control movement, and maintain an inventory.

The second layer in CEL is the behavior layer. This allows you to send messages between entities when particular events have occurred. These events generally tie in with the property classes mentioned previously, so when a particular key is pressed or when the inventory changes, an event can be fired off. The control code for the behavior can be in C++, Python, or XML, although in all cases, control is passed back through the physical layer so that only valid movement that is physically possible occurs.

CEL is also released under the LGPL and is available from the same download page as CrystalSpace. A tutorial covering the basics is available from the same location.

Irrlicht

Irrlicht, which is German for a will-o'-the-wisp-like creature, is the personal project of Nikolaus Gebhardt. Despite these apparent humble beginnings, it is a competent all-encompassing engine with a lot of useful functionality (collision detection, *Quake III* map loaders, full GUI, and special effects) and graphics drivers for OpenGL, DirectX (versions 8 or 9), and even software rendering. Numerous examples are also available and are well documented, as is the API. An archive is available on the accompanying CD-ROM.

ON THE CD

Cross-platform compatibility comes as standard with precompiled libraries for Linux, MacOS X, Windows using gcc, and Windows using Visual Studio. In fact, Irrlicht is one of the occasions where the Windows user is equally favored as all 14 example programs are supplied with full source and binary executables for the platform.

One of the interesting facts about the management of this project is that all of the work has been carried out by the originator. He is keeping very tight reins on the project and not accepting features from other developers. While this means you will have to keep your own repository synchronized to the current release, it might be possible to buy alternate licenses if you wish because the copyrights are solely owned by Mr. Gebhardt.

Homepage: *http://irrlicht.sourceforge.net*

License: Custom (but similar to zlib and libpng).

Distribution: Source and binary.

First release: March 14, 2003 (0.1).

Current version: 1.0 (stable since April 19, 2006).

Platform(s): Windows, Linux, and MacOS X have binary libraries in the archive. Xbox and OS/2 must be built from source. It includes an OpenGL and software driver so other platforms should be possible.

Dependencies: None.

Other resources: Forums, tutorials and wiki.

Installation

As a package, Irrlicht is very Windows-friendly and includes ready-to-build libraries for both version 6 (Visual C++) and version 7 (.NET) of Microsoft Developer Studio. To make use of it, you simply need to add the include directory (such as `irrlicht-1.0\include`) and library directory (`irrlicht-1.0\lib\Win32-Visual Studio`) to your options and rebuild the examples as normal. Place `bin\Win32-VisualStudio\irrlicht.dll` in the current directory (or one that has been set up by Windows to be searched, such as `c:\winnt\system32`), and you'll be able to run the binaries as normal. Linux users also enjoy a simple experience. The standard package includes media, examples, tools, and documentation. Consequently, it is more usual to place only your version of the include and library files into source control and check them out to a minimal `devlib` folder, keeping the full archive contents for reference purposes only.

Integration

Irrlicht integrates well with other software due to its application of namespaces and its judicious use of interfaces. The namespaces prevent collisions with similarly named functions in other libraries and requires that functions are called either with

```
IrrlichtDevice *pDevice = irr:createDevice(irr:video::EDT_OPENGL,
    irr:core::dimension2d<s32>(640, 480), 16, false);
```

or the source must include

```
using namespace irr;
```

to resolve the function automatically for any function within the irr namespace. If you are solely using Irrlicht, you can create a separate myirrlicht.h file that begins with,

```
using namespace irr;
using namespace core;
using namespace scene;
using namespace video;
using namespace io;
using namespace gui;
```

However, including namespaces within header files is generally a bad idea and not recommended because it can transparently hide naming conflicts; but if you only include that header from source files (as opposed to other headers), the burden of guilt passes to the individual source programmer and not the original library writers!

Interfaces are used throughout Irrlicht allowing each component to be replaced with alternate implementations, without requiring changes to the rest of the code base—provided the interface is honored. This layer of abstraction makes it very easy to create a new type of file handle, for example, as the function

```
pFile = CFileSystem::createAndOpenFile("filename");
```

returns a pointer to an interface (IReadFile), not the class of any particular implementation (such as CReadFile). The virtual functions are then correctly identified at runtime by the appropriate vtable.

The Hierarchy

To provide the total level of abstraction that Irrlicht does, everything is accessible from a single object—the device. This holds references to the graphics driver, filesystem, scene manager, and all other major components of the engine. These are all created from a single call to

```
IrrlichtDevice *pDevice = createDevice(driverType);
```

as the driver type can insinuate the other components necessary. These are created through the base device class, `CIrrDeviceStub`. In most instances, the specific implementations are created through functions outside of this area, allowing for another layer of abstraction. So, when `CIrrDeviceStub` creates the filesystem, it actually calls

```
io::createFileSystem();
```

which is found in `CFileSystem.cpp` so that *it* can then govern the most suitable filesystem. Since graphics drivers are specific to a particular platform (for example, `EDT_DIRECT3D8` implies a Microsoft Windows-based operating system) the appropriate filesystem is created by the device class automatically. In those rare cases where one driver can work across two platforms, the distinction is made by the `CIrrDeviceLinux.cpp` or `CIrrDeviceWin32.cpp` file because only one can ever get compiled into the executable at any one time.

Having created this device object, all other components are then referenced from methods of `pDevice`, such as,

```
pDevice->getFileSystem()->createAndOpenFile("myfile.dat");
pDevice->getVideoDriver()->getTexture("brickwall.dat");
```

The File System

For the most part, the interface abstraction works well here, and the inclusion of Zip files makes it unnecessary to integrate external implementations of this traditional console feature. One slight issue is that the use of the standard library is not confined to the `CReadFile` class that uses it. So, in addition to changing this file (or, more preferably, creating a new implementation class based on the `IReadFile` interface) there is also one necessary change to `CFileSystem::existFile` (inside `CFileSystem.cpp`) to remove the `fopen` call.

Normal disc files are opened as shown previously, with Zip files requiring just one extra step that adds the contents into the filesystem structures, so it can be loaded with the usual functions.

```
pDevice->getFileSystem()->addZipFileArchive("myfile.zip");
```

The Memory

Irrlicht itself is written completely in C++ and makes extensive use of the `new` and `delete` operators. These will need to be overloaded if you intend to use a custom memory allocator. However, Irrlicht is comprised of other libraries—notably zlib, libpng, and jpeglib—that are C based and use `malloc`. Both need to be considered.

Basic Components

There are a number of essential features covered by the Irrlicht engine. The documentation covers the how-to of them fully, but those requiring porting or adapting within a typical game are briefly looked at.

Video Driver

There are six basic drivers included in the standard package: two for DirectX (versions 8 and 9), two software renderers, an OpenGL driver, and a Null driver. The latter is not only useful for debugging, but also comprises of much common functionality (such as image loaders) for the other drivers, so any new drivers would do well to use CNullDriver as a base.

CAUTION

Although Irrlicht is supplied with a software renderer, this is purely demonstrational, as it is has various issues (such as clipping, which introduces gaps in the geometry) and doesn't look particularly nice.

The driver itself, however, does very little rendering work. It supports standard device initialization and preparation (like viewports), texture and material handling, and basic rendering of triangle fans and meshes, and 2D components. This covers all bases in the issue of *how to draw*, but not *what* to draw. That is handled by the scene manager.

Scene Manager

This covers a multitude of functionality, including meshes, billboards, and particle systems. It also includes all the handling for the cameras and lights. Because there is only one cross-platform implementation of the scene manager, this approach ensures good code reuse between all drivers.

The manager itself is a hierarchical tree, and retrieved from the device with

```
irr::scene::IsceneManager *pSceneManager = pDevice->getSceneManager();
```

Each node contains either a feature to render (such as billboards or animated meshes) or a rendering approach such as the position and type of cameras or the parameters of a particular light. These nodes follow the rules of a typical parent-child hierarchy insomuch that if the parent moves, so do the children, and if the parent is not visible, neither are the children.

Because there is no integrated physics solution in Irrlicht, each node has to be manipulated manually with

```
pNode->setPosition(vNewPosition);
pNode->setRotation(vNewRotation);
```

Because both of these parameters are relative to the parent, additional work may be necessary.

Note also that the types used here are Irrlicht types, namely `irr::core::vector3df`. This is a standard templated class providing the x, y, and z coordinates in single precision IEE754 format. No other members are included, making it binary compatible with most other libraries. However, casting to `vector3df` is not recommended because of the extra functionality it provides. If the base vector class of your engine is not the one provided by Irrlicht, but lacks any methods and contains only x, y, and z members, then consider upgrading the basic class to `vector3df`. Otherwise, create a global set of `vectors3dfs` and whenever you need to move the objects use

```
pCache[nextFree].set(pOtherVertex->x, pOtherVertex->y, pOtherVertex->z);
```

to prevent unnecessary constructors.

The scene manager also includes asset loaders that allow you to assign a complete mesh or animation to a single node.

```
pMesh = pSceneManager->getMesh("filename");
pSceneManager->addAnimatedMeshSceneNode(pMesh);
```

Such files can be in many different formats, including 3ds Studio, Collada, and DirectX. There are also importers for the *Quake* data formats of .bsp and .md2. Additionally, if your tool chain is formatting the data in a special way, you can implement an instance of the `IMeshLoader` interface, and register it with the scene manager using,

```
pSceneManager->addExternalMeshLoad(pNewMeshLoader);
```

This enables you to incorporate other data in the format loaders that may be necessary for your engine, such as physics collision information or metadata.

The DirectX importer works cross-platform so it can even load .x files into Linux versions.

NOTE

The abstracted filesystem is used as normal.

GUI

The GUI presented in Irrlicht utilizes the basic primitives in the graphics driver to create a skinnable interface. It does this by generating a `CGUIEnvironment` into which the individual buttons, message boxes, and even entire windows can be added.

Because the process of adding individual buttons to pixel-perfect locations can be tiresome, there is a GUI editor available from *http://www.dracsoft.com/zips/ irr_gui_editor.zip*. This is not part of the Irrlicht engine or distribution, but it does have an official thread on the forum at *http://irrlicht.sourceforge.net/phpBB2/view-topic.php?t=4787*. It requires the .NET framework and does not come with source.

All the gadgets supported by GUI are drawn using simple 2D primitives such as draw2DRectangle. While the size can be changed through the creation code, the colors are assigned through another abstraction, representing the skin.

The IGUISkin interface is one of the more important ones for game developers because no game wants to spoil the illusion of the player being in a spaceship in the year 2525 by having the interface looking like a Windows 95 machine! Fortunately, the supplied skins provide good templates on which to base your own. There are two main components to customize within a skin: the colors and the button shapes.

The GUI colors are created by pairing each of the style enumerations (such as EGDC_3D_DARK_SHADOW, EGDC_3D_SHADOW, or EGDC_3D_FACE) to a specific color through the method getColor. This *is* as easy as it sounds. For example,

```
Colors[EGDC_3D_DARK_SHADOW] = video::SColor(101,50,50,50);
Colors[EGDC_3D_SHADOW] = video::SColor(101,130,130,130);
Colors[EGDC_3D_FACE] = video::SColor(101,210,210,210);
```

The button shapes and styles require slightly more work, as each method needs to be implemented from the IGUISkin interface. But even if you intend to create an entirely new skin, the default class CGUISkin provides a complete set of render methods on which you can base your own. Furthermore, by simply changing the color scheme you can get a good first draft of a custom skin.

The only font support provided is through bitmap fonts loaded as textures. This is generally good enough for most game GUIs.

System

There are two main areas containing standard system components, which are often replaced with each new engine port. One is irr::core. This contains the basic math libraries for vectors and matrices. All the standard trigonometry functions are handled using the standard library, although a specific set of constants is provided in irrMath.h, which also designates the rounding error epsilon and the standard min and max templates.

CAUTION

Several vector functions will return the f64 type. This is slow on most consoles and PCs, and consideration should be given to whether this is necessary or if the type (in irrTypes.h) can be downgraded to a standard f32.

irr::core also includes a string template type called string that may conflict with STL or other libraries. Therefore, you should either explicitly refer to them using their internal definition of core::string<irr:c8> or core::stringc, its type definition.

The second system area resides in the implementation collection called *other*. This includes the debug loggers and operating system timers. The platform definitions, such as _IRR_WINDOWS_ or _XBOX, are used to compile only compatible code. Much of this functionality can be found in the single file os.cpp. It is recommended that these macros are unified with other libraries, such as the SGX Core.

The License

The custom license chosen for Irrlicht is based on the zlib and libpng licenses. This means you do not need to release the source code to your game or any variations you make to the engine. However, any source versions that *are* released must be marked as being changed from the original. In either case, there is no acknowledgment clause; so you do not need to mention Irrlicht anywhere in the documentation or game.

FONTS

Font handling in computer games is generally provided by two alternate solutions. In the first instance, a game may render the score by displaying different regions of a simple 2D texture onto the screen using the overlay feature of the graphics engine. This will be fast, but look unappealing and have little flexibility. Many of the graphics libraries mentioned thus far include their own font handling, which, to a large extent, performs this exact procedure and draws nothing more than simple bitmaps. For more complex font images, including baseline control, proportional fonts, and kerning, a second—more complex—solution is needed.

 Although all the software covered here is under an Open Source license, the fonts themselves may have alternate copyrights.

FreeType

The only show in town right now, with respect to elegant font generation, is FreeType. Everything that has followed has been thanks to this project. Its purpose is to rasterize high-quality glyph images using TrueType fonts (TTF files) as its source input.

FreeType exists in two current forms, although both are very similar and show signs of the same solid vintage. While they both provide a good modular design and anti-aliasing render facilities, FreeType 2 has extended both the feature set and the quality of its output. In the case of the latter, this has included a TrueType bytecode interpreter[4] and automatic hinter module. It has also improved the method by which the file I/O and memory management are used, and abstracted it away from the code itself. This was developed as part of the FreeType 2 push to develop a powerful embedded solution for fonts (missing before this release) and benefits game developers because of this.

Homepage: *http://www.freetype.org*

License: Custom (similar to the original BSD license), or GNU GPL (at your discretion).

Distribution: Source. Some platform binaries available.

Current version: 2.2.1.

Platform(s): Windows, MacOS X, Linux, and most Unix variants.

Dependencies: None.

Other resources: Several mailing lists, on-line tutorials, and demos.

Despite the many accolades showered upon FreeType, it garners little attention here. This is because it provides only low-level control and rendering of the font information into an arbitrary block of memory. To make use of the glyphs within a game, some legwork is necessary to render this information into a suitable surface. Fortunately, this work has been done for us with solutions such as FTGL and SDL_ttf so it makes development sense to begin there. In all cases, anything derived from FreeType must consider its licensing rules, and so the following sections must still be considered required reading.

Licensing and Patents

Much is often discussed concerning the FreeType license. At first glance, it requires the developer to make nothing more than a simple choice between original BSD (that features the advertising clause) or the GNU GPL (that requires the opening of source). Indeed, that is the first step, but is solved simply by looking at which other licenses with which you have to maintain compatibility. However, despite the incompatibilities of the BSD-style license with other licenses, there is a larger problem looming: patents.

Portions of the TrueType bytecode interpreter infringe on U.S. patent numbers 5155805, 5159668, and 5325479, which are owned by Apple Computer, Inc. There are several ways around this. First, use version 2 of FreeType that omits these patented features by default. This is the recommended method. Alternatively, you can pay Apple for the rights to use this technology[5]. Finally, you can use an existing TrueType font-rendering package to produce a bitmap containing the nicely rendered font, and draw regions from within this bitmap using simple blit operations.

There are some binary versions of FreeType 2 (particularly in Linux distributions) that have compiled in the offended patented code. Consequently, it is recommended (to be perfectly safe) that you compile your own binaries of any FreeType 2 library you get, unless you can independently assess whether the offending code has been included. However, Apple has yet to enforce this patent; so the risk is minimal.

FreeType Integration

As mentioned previously, it is recommended that you compile your own FreeType library for your game to prevent licensing problems. Whether you decide to distribute that code to your developers as source or object files is a different question.

FreeType uses the standard I/O commands (include `fopen`) and standard memory management code (`malloc` and `free`) in its implementation. So if these need to be replaced with custom handlers, you will have to integrate this source with that of your engine. This will be true primarily for console developers. Those on PC-based systems will probably build standard linked libraries for the team. `Makefiles` and Visual Studio project and workspace files are available in the `builds/win32` and `builds/win32/visualc` directories, respectively, although you may find it easier to create a brand-new project and insert the source files manually, adding the `include` directory to the list of additional search paths.

FreeType is a very large project with its include files placed logically, but disparately, in a number of different directories. It is best to embrace this complexity and keep the existing directory structure, adding new search paths where necessary.

One file, `ftsystem.c`, contains the principle abstraction components necessary for porting FreeType. The first function under consideration is `FT_Stream_Open` that handles the filesystem abstraction for the whole FreeType library. The second are the memory handlers. Both can be abstracted or modified directly.

The File System

The main `FT_Stream_Open` function is passed two parameters: a filename that can be in any format you're prepared to parse and an `FT_Stream`. It is the responsibility of the opening function to fill this structure with the necessary file parameters, such as size and current seek position, and function callback pointers to the underlying file I/O system code, so that any subsequent call need no further data. For example,

```
FT_EXPORT_DEF(FT_Error)
FT_Stream_Open(FT_Stream Stream, const char *pFilename)
{
```

```
   if (!stream) {
      return FT_Err_Invalid_Stream_Handle;
   }

   CSGXFile *pFile = new CSGXFile(pFilename, "r");

   if (!pFile->IsValid()) {
      return FT_Err_Cannot_Open_Resource;
   }

   // Prepare data pointers
   Stream->descriptor.pointer = (void *)pFile;
   Stream->pathname.pointer = (char *)pFilename;

   Stream->size = pFile->GetFileSize();
   Stream->pos  = 0;

   // Prepare callbacks
   Stream->read  = sgxFile_IO;
   Stream->close = sgxFile_Close;

   return FT_Err_Ok;
}
```

You can then implement the callback functions using the typical signatures of,

```
FT_CALLBACK_DEF(tULONG32)
sgxFile_IO(FT_Stream Stream, tULONG32 iOffset,
   tBYTE *pBuffer, tULONG32 iCount);
```

and

```
FT_CALLBACK_DEF(void) sgxFile_Close(FT_Stream Stream);
```

Note that due to the specialization of the font code, no file writing capabilities need to be provided.

The Memory System

Memory management is handled in a similar way. At the start of the program, a call to

```
FT_Memory Memory = FT_New_Memory();
```

is made, which initializes the callbacks for the memory routines `alloc`, `realloc`, and `free`. These are used throughout the FreeType library using calls such as

```
ptr = Memory->alloc(Memory, 100);   // get 100 bytes
```

However, this is usually wrapped in the `FT_ALLOC` macro to hide the duplicate use of the `Memory` variable.

Incorporating a new memory manager is managed simply by replacing the `FT_New_Memory` function with your own. You may, optionally, decide to also replace those macros using it (such as `FT_Alloc_Debug`) to capture the extra debugging information FreeType has thoughtfully incorporate into the code.

FTGL

The FTGL package—short for FreeType OpenGL—provides a good wrapper around the FreeType system enabling fonts to be drawn using the standard OpenGL methods for maximum speed. Each font is loaded direct from disk as a standard TTF file, without the need for offline conversion, into an internal format suitable for rendering directly with OpenGL. The font can then be used to render text in many different forms, including bitmap, texture maps, outlines, extruding polygons, or polygon meshes.

This is generally accepted as being the most globally usable method of introducing fonts into the OpenGL arena. While the other implementations have disadvantages of one kind or another[6], this has become the de facto standard. However, the home page is rarely updated, and new versions are few and far between, making this appear as an unfortunate standard. Such neglect generally means the software is either irrelevant (having been replaced by something superior) or complete (since there is nothing new worth adding). Neither is particularly true in this case, but the reasons are more closely aligned with the latter.

This library is so tightly integrated into the OpenGL calls, users of DirectX are advised to either start work from SDL_ttf, or make use of the Microsoft Windows font handling code.

Homepage: *http://homepages.paradise.net.nz/henryj/code/index.html#FTGL*
License: GNU LGPL 2 (Appendix C)
Distribution: Source only
First release: July 22, 2001
Current version: 2.1 (stable since December 5, 2004)
Platform(s): Windows, Linux, and Macintosh

Dependencies: FreeType 2 (version 2.0.9 or above) and Glu

Other resources: Homepage, rarely updated

This project, also available on the CD-ROM, takes the same idea that spawned GLTT, which was also a TrueType rendering engine for OpenGL. This former project, hosted at *http://gltt.sourceforge.net*, is different insomuch as it requires an older version of FreeType (1.3.1) and does not currently work with FreeType 2. It is for this reason that FTGL is suggested.

FTGL compilation is only supported through Microsoft Developer Studio version 6, although there is no reason why other versions of tha, and other, compilers should not work.

FTGL Library Integration

Once FreeType has been prepared to your satisfaction, you can begin integrating FTGL. In the first instance, you should confirm that `ftgl/FTGL.h` contains the correct abstractions for the `float` and `double` types, along with the compiler-specific `FTGL_EXPORT` invocation. This is generally the case, but it never hurts to check. As with FreeType, there are a lot of header files present and they should be kept in the same directory hierarchy, using additional include paths if necessary to prevent their reorganization.

The file I/O is the simplest component to consider with this integration since all file handling functions within FTGL use the `FT_Attach_Stream` function. This is actually part of the basic FreeType system and uses the `FT_Stream` structure. This function was created and abstracted earlier when discussing FreeType. Therefore, no extra work is involved.

Custom memory handling is more cumbersome to maintain, but with the infrequency of releases, this shouldn't be a problem. The first thing to realize is that FTGL does not, unfortunately, use the existing `FT_ALLOC` from FreeType. Nor does it have its own allocators or overridden `new` operators. You must, therefore, resign yourself to a maintenance schedule to replace and maintain these changes. In many cases, this work can be safely ignored since the fonts will only allocate memory at the start of the game and never release it. Therefore, it cannot fragment memory any further, limiting the use of an alternate memory manager.

Using FTGL

Most people refer to "Arial" or "Times New Roman" as a font. In reality, these are typefaces, with each instance of this typeface—comprising of a specific size and style—being called a font. This idea extends to the method by which FTGL loads each font. That is, you must load a typeface by name, and then apply a set of parameters to create the specific font. Because FTGL processes the TTF format internally by caching the necessary OpenGL commands, you must specify the rendering style when you initialize the font using

```
pFT = new FTGLBitmapFont(filename);
```

or

```
pFT = new FTGLOutlineFont(filename);
```

Each requires inclusion of its own specific header, such as `lib/ftgl/FTGLBitmapFont.h` or `lib/ftgl/FTGLOutlineFont.h`. You can then specify the font parameters, such as

```
pFT->FaceSize(iTypeSize);
pFT->Depth(iTypeDepth);
pFT->CharMap(ft_encoding_unicode);
```

The font-caching process can be slow, so you should certainly prepare all necessary fonts at the beginning of your game.

The filename given to `FTGLBitmapFont` must either include a full absolute path or reference a relative filename. It does not search the operating system's standard font directory if the file cannot be found. Although this appears to cause a problem with cross-platform engines, the solution is simple because the calls to `new FTGLBitmap-Font` can be made very easily in platform-specific code.

As an alternative, you can always load the font into a block of memory, and the use the memory stream thusly:

```
pFT = new FTGLOutlineFont(pData, iSizeOfData);
```

Once the data is in memory, the drawing process is very simple. Because FTGL uses only OpenGL calls, you can set up the parameters for the rendering first, using standard calls such as `glColor3f` and `glRasterPos2f`, and any text written afterward will conform to the style you've already supplied. You may even care to wrapper this functionality from within the graphics engine. For example,

```
void DrawFont(const sgxString &name, const sgxVector2 &pos) const
{
    sgxColorRGBA col;

    CGfxEngine::Get()->GetColor(col);
```

```
glColor4f(col.r, col.g, col.b, col.a);
glRasterPos2f(pos.x, pos.y);

m_pFTFont->Render(name.c_str());
}
```

In this way, any platforms that are not using FTGL can call the same method and get identical cross-platform results. After all, the library is called *FTGL* for a reason.

Finally, you may have to incorporate any state information maintained by your OpenGL engine into the font rendering code. This is simple, since a typical Render method appears like this:

```
void FTGLBitmapFont::Render( const wchar_t* string)
{
   glPushClientAttrib( GL_CLIENT_PIXEL_STORE_BIT);
   glPushAttrib( GL_ENABLE_BIT);

   glPixelStorei( GL_UNPACK_LSB_FIRST, GL_FALSE);
   glPixelStorei( GL_UNPACK_ALIGNMENT, 1);

   glDisable( GL_BLEND);

   FTFont::Render( string);

   glPopAttrib();
   glPopClientAttrib();
}
```

As you can see, it begins with glPushClientAttrib and glPushAttrib and cleans up after itself with the expected pair of glPopAttrib and glPopClientAttrib. Anything beyond this, such as the grouping of blend modes, will require suitable modifications to the FTGL code itself in order to integrate it fully with your engine.

Alternatively, you may decide to remove all the code from Render and incorporate it directly into the suggested DrawFont call, shown previously.

 Remember that you need to make these changes to each type of font handled in FTGL.

In this way, the Render method can be hidden from the end user, and you are free to reorder the scene more efficiently, as the needs of your engine dictates.

SDL_ttf

This library follows the same principles as FTGL given previously and uses the FreeType library to render TrueType glyphs into a more suitable format—in this case an SDL surface. This text can be rendered normally in bold, italics, underlined, or any combination of the three. The surface is transparent, may be blitted to any other surface, and can be manipulated with any of the standard surface-oriented functions.

> **Homepage:** *http://www.libsdl.org/projects/SDL_ttf*
>
> **License:** GNU LGPL 2.1 (Appendix C)
>
> **Distribution:** Source and binaries
>
> **First release:** January 2000
>
> **Current version:** 2.0.8 (stable since October 2, 2005)
>
> **Platform(s):** Windows, Linux, and MacOS X
>
> **Dependencies:** SDL 1.2, FreeType 2.0 (except 2.1.3)
>
> **Other resources:** website and standard SDL mailing list

As a bonus, SDL_ttf also includes some special functions to render TrueType fonts using the standard OpenGL functions. This solution exists as a demo in the source archive and is neither as complete, or as useful, as FTGL.

Preparing FreeType

As always with these font libraries, the first step is to integrate the FreeType package. While it is possible to build from sources—and this approach is always recommended—Visual C++ users have a prebuilt library available inside the `VisualC.zip` file of the SDL_ttf archive. This file also contains the necessary header files to reference the library in the traditional FreeType hierarchy.

Library Integration

After copying the standard three files (header, library, and DLL) into the appropriate locations, you can use SDL_ttf right away because it follows the SDL guidelines and philosophies throughout. In this way, if you have already integrated SDL into your application, libraries such as this will fit in seamlessly, encouraging you to use them (rather than reinventing the wheel). The only addition is to initialize the SDL_ttf-specific structures in your code with `TTF_Init();`

The filesystem is, as you'd expect from SDL, handled through `RWops`, allowing you to reuse any underlying abstractions you might have already created in that area. Consequently, you can therefore either load fonts into memory with

```
pFont = TTF_OpenFont("c:\\winnt\\fonts\\arial.ttf", 32);
```

or

```
pFont = TTF_OpenFontRW(rwops, 1, 32);
```

with 1 indicating that you want SDL_ttf to close the RWops stream upon completely, and 32 representing the point size. As with FTGL, the full path to the font file must be specified.

Abstracting the memory handlers is done, as is common for SDL libraries, by renaming the calls to malloc and free into something more appropriate.

If you are not planning on using SDL_ttf with SDL itself (perhaps as a precursor to moving the text into other types of surface where FTGL is inapplicable for your needs) then it is possible to prune the SDL library to the necessary components. These are RWops, SDL_Surfaces, the endian macro code, and the standard error handling routines. However, a good compiler can remove this deadwood more easily than a human, and if you can't take the hit of the entire SDL library, then it's easier to add the necessary code into SDL_ttf, rather than removing those sections that are *un*necessary.

Handling Fonts

SDL_ttf works by rendering all text into a new surface as you request it. This means there is an overhead in the creation of a new surface and the blitting of the font surface to your screen, or back buffer. Typical render code appears thus:

```
SDL_Color color = {255,100,200,0};
SDL_rect rc = {320,100,0,0};

TTF_SetFontStyle(pFont, TTF_STYLE_NORMAL);
pFontSurface = TTF_RenderText_Solid(pFont, "Testing!", color);
SDL_BlitSurface(pFontSurface, NULL, pTitleScreen, &rc);
```

Individual characters can be rendered with the alternate glyph-oriented function:

```
pFontSurface = TTF_RenderGlyph_Solid(pFont, 'H', color);
```

Any surface returned from SDL_ttf is now your responsibility and must be released, manually, with the usual

```
SDL_FreeSurface(pFontSurface);
```

The solid rendering can be replaced with TTF_RenderText_Shaded or TTF_RenderText_Blended, although all variations build a cache of the used glyphs as they are rendered. Therefore, to maintain a constant memory footprint, and to eliminate the occasional slowdowns during the game as new glyphs are created, you can instigate the glyph caching at the start of the game by rendering the alphabet onto a new texture that is immediately discarded.

You can determine the size of the rendered text by using the dimensions of the new surface. Alternatively, if you need to know this information before the text is rendered, TTF_SizeText *has been thoughtfully supplied.*

TIP

MOVIE PLAYBACK

When employing movie playback code on a PC there is one major problem: codecs. Lots of them. For each approach to movie playback, there are a different number of potential codecs that suit the application. Naturally, these foci are mutually exclusive as the best encoding speed requires a different codec to the one used for the best decoding speed, and that is different to the ones that achieve the best compression, best visual quality, best dynamic color range, and so on.

The current solution to this problem is to adopt a two-pronged attack with container formats and codec-specific data. Here, one container format (say AVI) describes the structure of the file and references to the format used to encode both audio and video, while another format, such as DivX, handles the decoding of individual frames from arbitrary blocks of data. This enables the playback code to parse any suitable file, but assign control to a specific plug-in module (or modules) for the decoding of each frame. This is how software such as Windows Media Player and the Open Source mplayer work. The main problem with this type of structure is that it is possible to load the file but be unable to play all of its components. You may often notice the player software displaying a black screen while the audio whistles along perfectly, as can occur when the video codec cannot be found, but the audio can.

In games development, you have significantly more control over the data you use, and therefore can avoid the problems inherent in generic movie playback. The issue you suffer instead is a lack of choice since video compression is a difficult problem. And good video compression is a *very* difficult problem. Consequently, the number of Open Source codecs and playback engines are limited. Furthermore, the number of libraries that have suitably abstracted this functionality are fewer still.

Contrary to popular opinion, DivX is not Open Source, and therefore shall not be covered here. There is a free version of XviD available for download, but concerns over patents are still prevalent and shall consequently not be covered.

NOTE

mpeg_play

For many veteran developers, this is *the* implementation for mpeg video decompression. It began within the Berkeley Multimedia Research Center as part of its MPEG tools suite and has become the code base from which many other mpeg-based codecs have originated, because the implementation was based heavily in cross-platform C—without the forays into assembler that were common at that time, in an attempt to improve the performance.

Homepage: *http://bmrc.berkeley.edu/frame/research/mpeg/mpeg_play.html*

License: Custom (BSD style)

Distribution: Source and binary

First release: August 1995

Current version: 2.4

Platform(s): Most Unix machines

Dependencies: Various, including X11 and Motif

Other resources: Some historical websites

Unfortunately, the history of mpeg_play is fairly short because it depended on the (non-Free) Motif windows toolkit and did not provide sound. Other players became available (such as the one at *http://www.geom.uiuc.edu/software/mpeg_play*) but while this removed the dependency on Motif, it was—and is—still too Unix-centric to be of use to game developers. Fortunately, others have stepped up to the table to provide a suitable MPEG solution using mpeg_play as a base.

SDL MPEG Player Library

This library, called SMPEG for short, combined the original mpeg_play software from Berkeley with an audio decoder from Woo-jae Jung to produce a fully usable playback engine. It was originally developed by Loki Games as part of its cross-platform tool suite to help port various Microsoft Windows titles to Linux such as *Unreal Tournament* and *Soldier of Fortune.*

The intention of SMPEG is to decode mpeg 2 movies directly into an SDL surface, which can then be blitted directly onto the screen. This avoids the need for the base engine to decode the frame data into an arbitrary buffer and then a separate routine to copy it into the SDL surface, as both passes can be done at once. The audio data is decoded and passed directly to SDL's audio component.

Homepage: *http://www.lokigames.com/development/smpeg.php3*

License: GNU LGPL (Appendix C)

Distribution: Source and binary

First release: 1999

Current version: 0.4.3

Platform(s): Windows, MacOS X (but slow), and most Unix machines

Dependencies: SDL 1.2.0

Other resources: Some historical websites, a very low-traffic newsgroup

Because this is only a software decoder of the MPEG format, it is recommended you limit the use of playback to standalone cut scenes, lest the processor drain become too much for your game. For in-game film clips, such as playback on security monitors or advertising hoardings, you might care to use a simpler animation format (such as FLI), or even just change the region of the texture and synchronize it to the audio track manually. Alternatively, you might be able to build the scene within your game level, and use a render-to-texture solution.

System Integration

ON THE CD

With the ample download choices at *ftp://sunsite.dk/pub/os/linux/loki/open-source/ smpeg* (or from the CD-ROM), there is little chance you can't begin right away. The archives provide the necessary DLL, link library, and all header files that should be incorporated into the source tree in the usual manner.

The MPEG format provides movie data in an arbitrary number of streams. In most cases, there will be two: audio and video. The SMPEG implementation creates a new thread (through SDL_CreateThread) for each of these streams and assigns them to a suitable threading function for decoding.

There are a couple of implications with this approach. First, any code that uses the surface or movie playback data (such as the disc system) must be threadsafe. Since SMPEG is dependent on SDL, there is a built-in mutex facility (with SDL_ mutex) that can be used for this purpose. Indeed, several parts of SMPEG make use of the SDL thread handling code, and it is recommended you follow this library, even if the underlying implementation is an abstraction of your own code.

The second implication is the start-up time necessary to spawn these new threads, as this is a nontrivial delay. The traditional approach in software development is to create a number of threads at the beginning of your program and classify them as a thread *pool*. Then, whenever a *new* thread is requested, the next available thread from the pool is returned. There are two ways of employing this approach with SMPEG. You can either compile SDL into your game directly and change the implementation of SDL_CreateThread, or you can recompile SMPEG to use your thread pool-specific functions.

SMPEG also follows the SDL tradition when adopting memory management facilities. That is, it doesn't! It relies on the standard functions malloc and free to perform its management, so a global rename will be necessary. Furthermore, because SMPEG has been written in C++ you need to overload the `new` and `delete` operators, too.

File handling is simpler because it uses the RWops functionality provided by SDL. If you are not intending to use RWops as your lowest abstraction layer to the filesystem, you will save a lot of time by allowing RWops to use your underlying abstraction. This saving will scale well with each new SDL-oriented library you use.

Playback Integration

Much of the functionality is focused around the playback of an MPEG stream, as you'd expect. An SMPEG object is created from a data stream, such as

```
SMPEG_Info info;
SMPEG *m_pMpeg = SMPEG_new(filename, &info, FALSE);
```

and controlled with functions such as,

```
SMPEG_play(m_pMpeg);
SMPEG_pause(m_pMpeg);
SMPEG_stop(m_pMpeg);
```

The stream shown here originates from a file, which will be the standard mode of operation for most developers. However, the file abstraction mechanism in SDL, RWops, can be used to facilitate other types of input stream.

```
SMPEG *m_pMpeg = SMPEG_new_rwops(rwopsSrc, &info, FALSE);
```

These functions create a new object, but do not begin to play it or prepare the data in any other way. It is therefore necessary to assign an appropriate surface into which the decoder will write the data. This is performed with a combination of the three functions

```
SMPEG_setdisplay(m_pMpeg, pMovieSurface, NULL, null_update);
SMPEG_scaleXY(m_pMpeg, 640, 400);
SMPEG_move(m_pMpeg, 0, 20);
```

Only the first is necessary. The others provide a mechanism to scale the movie to a specific size and then offset it in the target surface. Because you have control over the files your engine will be playing back, you will rarely need SMPEG_scaleXY, although SMPEG_move is useful if you use identical movies for both NTSC and PAL versions and need to letter box one.

The `null_update` function given is a callback function. By default, the function will update the hardware screen surface with the latest frame residing in `pMovieSurface`. This surface will generally be in software since the MPEG decoder will be need to lock, and unlock, it at each frame to write the new pixels into it, and so it's quicker to keep the data in a software surface. Once a frame is complete, the surface is then blitted to the screen with `SDL_UpdateRect`, which is what happens if no callback is used. Using a null callback such as

```
void null_update(SDL_Surface *screen, Sint32 x, Sint32 y, Uint32 w,
Uint32 h)
{
}
```

allows you to handle this process manually at a later time or ignore it altogether.

Using a Single Surface

In any application, the fewer large memory copies you perform the faster it will be. Therefore, being able to write directly into the target surface is the ultimate goal. With all movie playback occurring in a separate thread, however, this needs to be carefully orchestrated to prevent the graphics engine using the surface while the MPEG decoder is attempting to write to it. This can be done by supplying a suitable mutex, such as

```
SMPEG_setdisplay(m_pMpeg, pMovieSurface, pMutex, null_update);
```

When `pMutex` is non-NULL, the mutex will be honored and the lock acquired before the frame is decoded into the surface.

In many cases, however, the movie decode cycle will occupy more time than a standard blit, so creating a mutex on the primary hardware surface will generally introduce stalls. The best approach here is to create a new surface, and blit from this surface to the screen.

Creating a New Surface

For most games, a new surface created solely for the movie image will be sufficient. This can then be blitted (or in some cases stretched) to fit the target hardware surface. In some instances, you will not want to create a new surface but rather use an existing piece of temporary scratch memory in lieu of this surface.

To tie this memory to a surface requires a special SDL function called `SDL_CreateRGBSurfaceFrom`. This takes your arbitrary memory pointer, and a description of the pixel format, and builds an appropriate surface structure for you. Obviously, these surfaces can only ever be software-based and so do not need any other format flags. This call appears as

```
pSurface = SDL_CreateRGBSurfaceFrom(pMemory, width, height, iBitsPerPixel,
    iMemorySpan, 0xf800, 0x07e0, 0x001f, 0xffff);
```

In some instances, it might seem that having a memory pointer provides a suitable hook for applying special effects to the video stream. Not so! SMPEG has already provided this functionality in the form of filters, which unify the approach and ensure thread safety.

Filters

Filters are assigned to SMPEG before playback by way of a callback function that is invoked automatically (and threadsafely) from within the movie playback engine. To ensure suitability across all types of filter, two buffers are used (current and next) to prevent premature obliteration of necessary pixel data. There is an example of a bilinear filter in the file MPEGfilter.c, along with a null filter to be used as a template.

The creation and use of filters are trivial. They are created with

```
SMPEG_Filter *filter;

filter = SMPEGfilter_bilinear();
```

assigned with

```
filter = SMPEG_filter(m_pMpeg, filter );
```

and destroyed with

```
filter->destroy(filter);
```

Audio Integration

Being based on the SDL, most developers will adopt SDL audio as the simplest method by which you can play the audio track from the movie. Even when SDL audio has not been used for the rest of the game, there is very little wasted space by including it solely to assist in the movie playback code. The performance increases you'd normally gain by offloading the audio processing onto the sound card (using OpenAL, for example) do not apply here because the original audio data has to be decompressed from the audio stream, making any copying time negligible by comparison.

Dirac

This began in the BBC R&D labs around January 2003 to provide a suitable codec for Internet streaming. Coming from the BBC, its remit is quite large, and the plan is to support both small size video clips and large HDTV broadcasts using the same software.

It was named in honor of British physicist Paul Dirac.

Homepage: *http://dirac.sourceforge.net*
License: Mozilla Public License 1.1
Distribution: Source only
First release: March 11, 2004
Current version: 0.6.0
Platform(s): Linux, MacOS X, and Windows
Other resources: website and forums

The project is still evolving, and the specification is still not finished despite several current working implementations being available from its website. To this end, the project is a useful one to mention as "one to watch" although its integration and use may not be practical at the current time.

Licensing

Although the Mozilla Public License is generally not compatible with the GPL or LGPL, the version chosen is 1.1, which *does* allow the code to be relicensed under alternative licenses such the GPL and LGPL.

With regard to patents, the BBC does own some patents with Dirac, but has provided them to the world by providing implementations of them within the software. They have also been careful to ensure that none of the existing work infringes on the patents of others.

ENDNOTES

1. The original comment is quoted in several places, including *http://osdl.sourceforge.net/OSDL/OSDL-0.3/src/doc/web/main/documentation/rendering/SDL-licence.html* with a recent thread on the developers list (*http://www.libsdl.org/pipermail/sdl/2006-January/072350.html*) further clarifying Sam's point.
2. *http://www.perforce.com/jam/jam.html*. This useful tool is also covered in *Cross-Platform Game Programming*.
3. Or if you prefer, the mother.
4. This code may involve patent problems.
5. Contact *iplaw@apple.com* for licensing information.
6. As highlighted at *http://www.opengl.org/resources/features/fontsurvey*.

6 Audio

OPEN SOURCE AUDIO

Game audio can be broken down into three generalized components: audio data, sound sources, and listeners. The audio data usually comprises of WAV files that are unchanging in nature and loaded at the beginning of the level, or game. Each piece of audio data has a set of properties that is unique to it and remains constant throughout the game world. This includes information such as its minimum and maximum audible range.

Sound sources refer to the characters and objects within the game that emit sound, in some manner. This can include footsteps, speech, bullet ricochets, and so on. Each source can emit many different sounds. The position and direction of each instance of the sound is determined by the object to which it is attached, and may move with the object.

Finally, the listener is a single object that reflects the game player's perspective on the world. This, like the source sources, will contain positional and directional information and is used to calculate the relative volume of each sound and its position within the stereo field. In general, the panning information is inferred from the final mix because complex audio engines may support surround sound where a simple left-versus-right calculation is inadequate.

OpenAL

As the name suggests, OpenAL takes its inspiration from OpenGL (the popular graphics API) with its first specification appearing in January 2000. It began as a project within Loki Entertainment to produce an open audio API that would help in the cross-platform development of games on which it was working, such as *Unreal Tournament 2004*, *Jedi Knight 2*, and *Lineage 2*. Creative Labs, of Soundblaster fame, was also onboard during its early development and produced hardware-accelerated drivers in 2001. This eliminated the software-only approach to audio that would otherwise surely have hampered its dissemination. It has also meant that new audio features, such as EAX, can be accessed from within Open Source code to allow hardware-processed echo and reverb, freeing up the processor for the main game code.

Among its many features, OpenAL provides direct control for multiple 3D sound sources, streaming, and multiple speaker configurations. It is available on many platforms including Xbox 360. The Microsoft Windows implementation, along with source code, is included on the CD-ROM.

ON THE CD

> **Homepage:** *http://www.openal.org*
>
> **License:** GNU LGPL version 2.1 (Appendix C)
>
> **Distribution:** Source and binary
>
> **First release:** January 2000
>
> **Current version:** 1.1 (stable since June 2005)
>
> **Platform(s):** Windows, Xbox, Xbox 360, Linux, Macintosh OS X and 8/9, BSD, Solaris, and IRIX (although not all are available with the 1.1 specification)
>
> **Dependencies:** None
>
> **Other resources:** Various tutorials, forums, and official mailing lists

OpenAL adopts a similar philosophy, coding style, and naming conventions to those found in OpenGL. Consequently, many people find it easy to adopt this API. Even those unfamiliar with the API will find it clean and approachable. Furthermore, the standard inclusion of the OpenAL Utility Toolkit (ALUT) to aid in basic file parsing, plus the inclusion of the library's source code and reference implementation, removes the guesswork of "how will this function react when . . . ?" Since the source base is relatively small, it is easy to navigate and is a good endorsement for Open Source.

The OpenGL Connection

On an organizational level, there is no connection between those who created the OpenGL specification and those involved in OpenAL. However, it is very clear from a cursory examination that both follow a lot of the same principles and ideas.

In the first instance, all buffers are given unique identifiers determined by the library using functions such as `alGenBuffers` and `alGenSources`. These IDs are then used as labels when assigning data into these aforementioned buffers with functions like `alBufferData`. This mirrors the texture handling of OpenGL, and, like its graphics predecessor, allows you to specify the format in which the data is held. For example, the positional vectors can be specified as either `floats` or `ints` through a solid naming convention.

```
alListener3f(AL_POSITION, x, y, z);
```

Furthermore, this information can also be supplied in an array, if that better suits the rest of your engine.

```
alListener3v(AL_POSITION, &position);
```

Second, the API specifies only the manner in which sounds are to be played and from where in the 3D environment they are heard, but not the minutiae of how it will be realized. This allows a high level of abstraction to exist, giving the driver more opportunities to optimize the audio rendering process.

Finally, OpenAL leaves all file handling and resource management to the user. This is a good move when it comes to cross-platform engine design, but a poor choice for those wanting to get their audio solution working quickly, as it raises the barrier to entry. This means you cannot load a WAV file to test OpenAL without first writing a WAV parser and resource manager. However, that is solved with ALUT.

ALUT

ON THE CD

Like OpenGL, OpenAL comes with a utilities library to supply the most often-used functionality in audio. This is provided in source and binary forms, and can be downloaded from *http://www.openal.org* or copied from the accompanying CD-ROM and is released under the LGPL. This code provides enough of a basis to load WAV files into a raw buffer and assign it to an OpenAL source. ALUT can either be used as part of the game or as part of the toolchain.

ALC

The Audio Library Context (ALC) is a set of operating system bindings that connect the OpenAL processing code with a method to emit sound from the attached hardware. This might involve the driver for a specific sound card, a software audio renderer generating a premixed waveform into a single stream, or any combination of the two. All commands must be made through an audio context; therefore a context must be created first.

ALC is included as part of the OpenAL library.

Integration

OpenAL is comprised of three basic header files and its associated library. These can be copied into the appropriate `c:\devlib\include` and `c:\devlib\lib` directories, and you're ready to go. It is recommended, however, that you place the header files into their own `AL` subdirectory because most of the sample and demo code expect it to be there. This includes the current implementation of FreeALUT, which you will generally incorporate into your game. Or, at the very least, will be included as part of the prototyping phase because it provides the standard WAV parsing code you will need early on.

The data types in OpenAL mirror those from OpenGL. That is, an `unsigned int` is represented with `ALuint`, and `signed shorts` are called `ALshort`. However, while these types are to be encouraged within the code audio engine itself[1] any external API calls should use the base types defined for your engine. Since OpenAL and OpenGL have differently named types, there is no existing convention to follow, so adopt whatever is used in your most major engine component. In the event of a tie break, use an independent set of types (such as those found in the SGX Core). The `al.h` header file ensures that every platform uses identically sized data types so you will not need to recast your parameters because a `tREAL32` is the same type as an `ALfloat`.

CAUTION

Identifiers in OpenAL usually use the ALuint type. The unsigned nature of this type can cause benign warnings if type safety is not observed. This will be particularly true when you're used to considering −1 as an error code or invalid handle.

Aspects of 3D

Because OpenAL is able to consider objects in 3D space, it stands to reason that there should be a 3D math component in the library. There is! It is integrated into the code itself and cannot be removed without recompiling the library. The calculations are scattered across the API but contained within specific files, and include matrix multiplications (`al_matrix.c`), vector normalization (`al_vector.c`), and fall-off distance calculations (`al_distance.c`), and rely on the standard math library for functions such as `sin`, `pow`, and `sqrt`. In all cases, the code is neither optimized nor externally modifiable. This raises two issues.

Initially, there is the case of audio-related math performance. This should not be a problem because the number of mathematical transformations undertaken by the audio code, compared to the rest of the engine, is usually insignificant, and consequently will be absent from the critical path.

The second issue follows the impact of being unable to replace the math functions without recompiling the OpenAL source code. Therefore, your game will duplicate code with these math functions, adding to the memory footprint. Because it is possible to get OpenAL implementations in nonOpen Source varieties, this may be unavoidable. But fortunately, this is not a large amount of space (because very few functions are used), and most linkers will remove any unused static functions anyway. In those cases where the math library is dynamically linked, you will incur a slight performance overhead as the external call is made, in addition to the extra footprint of the shared library being held in memory. Both cases should be minimal.

One undesirable side effect of using two math libraries is that the results may differ slightly between them. While this case is more problematic in theory, it has less of an effect in practice with the audio component because it is usually stand-alone. So, although a physical difference between an object's audible position in stereo field and its representation on-screen might exist, it is unlikely to be noticed. This is in sharp contrast to the graphic and physics components where visual tearing can occur in the scene if two collaborative functions calculated the same equations but produced different results.

CAUTION

Because the standard math library is used, ensure you link to a multithreaded version if your audio library is to be run on a separate thread.

One consolation is that the coordinate system used is right-hand Cartesian, just like OpenGL. If your engine uses the left-hand axis, then ensure all OpenAL calls are wrapped and that the Z-axis is negated.

Memory

Simply put, OpenAL is written in C without function hooks. This means all memory allocation is handling through the standard calls to `malloc` and friends. This occurs throughout the code and can only be overridden by rewriting these calls and recompiling.

File Handling

Because OpenAL relies on the user to perform all resource management, you would expect the `fopen` function to be absent from the code. Alas, no! There are, however, only three instances that need to be modified in the code: configuration file loading, loading raw data into a buffer, and saving an audio result to disk. All are superfluous to you.

Creation

Because OpenAL is capable of handling multiple contexts on a single system, the first task of any game is to determine which it will use, and then create it. This adopts the standard mechanism of enumeration and creation.

```
ALCchar *pDeviceList = (ALCchar *)alcGetString(NULL,
ALC_DEVICE_SPECIFIER);

while (*pDeviceList) {
   printf("%s\n", pDeviceList);
   pDeviceList += strlen(pDeviceList) + 1;
}
```

The text string in each case can be used as a parameter to `alcOpenDevice` to use that particular device. Naturally, the default device and context can be created simply with

```
ALCdevice *device   = alcOpenDevice(NULL);
ALCcontext *context = alcCreateContext(device, NULL);

   alcMakeContextCurrent(context);
```

This is the only setup required in OpenAL. Closing the device involves an unsurprisingly simple

```
alcMakeContextCurrent(NULL);
alcDestroyContext(context);
alcCloseDevice();
```

CAUTION

In these and all subsequent examples, the error handling code has been omitted for clarity. In most instances, errors are handled by setting an internal state flag that the user can query with `alGetError`. OpenGL users will be familiar with this convention, and details of the returnable errors can be found in the API reference.

Basic Structure

OpenAL takes a very literal interpretation of the three audio components given at the head of this chapter: audio data, sound sources, and listeners. All audio data, that is, the sound samples, is stored in buffers, each referenced with a unique ID provided by the system.

```
ALuint bufferID;
alGenBuffers(1, &bufferID);
```

The data for this buffer must be preformatted, loaded into a simple array, and assigned directly.

```
alBufferData(bufferID, AL_FORMAT_MONO8, block, sizeof(block), 11025);
```

Buffers such as this are assigned to sound sources, which would normally reference the various objects in the world. Again, you require a unique ID for each sound source, which can be provided by the system.

```
ALuint soundSource;
alGenSources(1, &soundSource);
```

The assignment of buffers to sound sources is simply,

```
alSourcei(soundSource, AL_BUFFER, bufferID);
alSourcei(soundSource, AL_LOOPING, AL_TRUE);
alSource3f(soundSource, AL_POSITION, pObj->x, pObj->y, pObj->z);
```

So, once you have set up a listener,

```
alListener3f(AL_POSITION, x, y, x);
```

you can start the sound playing with

```
alSourcePlay(soundSource);
```

Each sound source can only be assigned one audio buffer, so a player character that could emit footsteps, gunshots, and speech at the same time would require three individual sound sources.

One problem that can occur when sample playback is no longer under game control is beating. This is an unpleasant auditory side effect when two sounds are played within a very short time of each other and they interfere. To prevent this you can wrapper the alSourcePlay call and store the time (in milliseconds) of the last 32 sound sources, and the audio buffer it played. Then if an identical sound is played within, say, 5 ms the second sound is not played and the volume of the previous instance is amended to represent the loudest volume between itself and the one that would have been played.

Streaming

This is provided with the *queuing* mechanism inside OpenAL that assigns a number of buffers (prepared with the usual alBufferData call) to a sound source:

```
alSourceQueueBuffers(soundSource, 2, buffers);
```

Each buffer is then played in succession, one after the other, as the preceding one finishes. On its own, this doesn't stream data from the disk, but you can easily fill each buffer with audio data loaded from your filesystem as normal. As an added bonus, this allows compressed audio to be handled automatically because, as with Ogg Vorbis, most decompression libraries will return an uncompressed audio stream for you to plug directly into a standard buffer, as you see later.

This feature requires that the game programmer poll OpenAL every game tick to determine if any of the existing queued buffers have been processed (i.e., played) yet.

```
int numProcessedBuffers;

    alGetSourcei(soundSource, AL_BUFFERS_PROCESSED,
&numProcessedBuffers);
```

At this point, each buffer must be unqueued. New data is loaded into it and then requeued by OpenAL at the end of the queue.

```
ALuint buffer;

    alSourceUnqueueBuffers(soundSource, 1, &bufferID);
    streamNewDataIntoBuffer(bufferID);
    alSourceQueueBuffers(soundSource, 1, &bufferID);
```

Since you can remove these queued buffers—stored last in, first out—with alSourceUnqueueBuffers, the stream can be emptied with the simple loop

```
int numQueuedBuffers;
ALuint bufferID;

    alGetSourcei(source, AL_BUFFERS_QUEUED, &numQueuedBuffers);

    while(numQueuedBuffers-) {
        alSourceUnqueueBuffers(source, 1, &bufferID);
    }
```

The number of queued buffers is not limited to two, so you can vary the number used to compensate for imbalances between disk and processor speed.

ALUT

As previously mentioned, ALUT is an auxiliary library to OpenAL in the same way that GluT is a utility library for OpenGL. It, too, exists in source and binary versions, the latter comprised of a single header, link library, and DLL. Again, the header should be moved into the `c:\devlib\include\AL` directory as its de facto resting place.

However, unlike its OpenGL counterpart, this is considerably less useful in a real game as it contains only three main pieces of functionality, all of which need to be replaced by other engine code to ensure cross-platform compatibility.

The first is the file loader that parses a WAV into a raw data block. While this is undoubtedly useful, it employs the standard file I/O system that should have been superceded by a more powerful cross-platform filesystem early in the development cycle. However, ALUT may still earn its paycheck by finding a place within the tools pipeline to prepare the WAV data ready for the engine. The parser functionality can still be utilized without the initialization of an audio context, although ALUT itself still needs to be created using

```
alutInitWithoutContext(NULL, NULL);
```

This eliminates the possibility of errors if used on a server without a sound card. Data can then be loaded using a simple

```
ALsizei size;
Alsizei frequency;
ALenum  format;
ALvoid *pData;

pData = alutLoadMemoryFromFile(?filename?, &format, &size, &frequency);
```

From here, your toolchain can generate engine-ready data from the information provided. This data will generally contain a simple block holding all the previous information along with a unique ID for the waveform. This will be used by the engine as an *internal* handle so that it can be used by a reference-counting resource manager that prevents two copies of the sound being loaded into memory. This handle has no relevance to OpenAL because you cannot determine or generate OpenAL handles offline. Instead, a CRC32 of the filename is recommended as a handle for memory reasons, with the toolchain exporting an ordered list, so humans can map internal handles to filenames for debugging purposes.

CAUTION

No loop information is extracted from the WAV file. There is an additional function called `alutLoadWAVFile` *that will, but this has been deprecated, and the Macintosh flavors of ALUT do not support the final loop flag anyway. Looping information should therefore be provided as metadata.*

The second piece of useful ALUT functionality is the `alutSleep` function. This is no different to other sleep functions, insomuch as it suspends the current process for a short while, giving an opportunity for the processor to do other work. Most notably, it gives processor time to the audio thread and/or driver. But despite being useful, it is not worth importing the whole ALUT library for one function. You can create a simple abstraction yourself, with the function from the SGX Core:

```
void sgxSleep(const tREAL32 t)
{
    // WinTel32 version of 'Sleep' is in milliseonds
    Sleep(DWORD(t * 1000.0f));
}
```

Finally, ALUT provides functions that generate sound buffers containing the basic waveforms of sine, square, sawtooth, white noise and impulse. Even if you're writing a retro game, all sounds are likely to come from samples, not algorithms, so this code can be safely ignored.

Licensing

OpenAL is essentially a two-part solution to the cross-platform audio problem. The first is the specification itself. This dictates a solid API and governance that ensures a well-understood environment and wide community support. Second, it involves the implementation of the API itself. This implementation can exist as any combination of static library, dynamic library, and driver. The licensing around this split is interesting.

Any code written using the API is copyrighted by the author and available for release according to other licensing obligations. Unlike console audio solutions, the specification is available to all, so there are no NDA problems with which to contend.

However, the OpenAL implementation for most of the popular platforms, notably Microsoft Windows, uses a combination of library and driver codes that are released under an LGPL license, requiring the release of all linkable game object files, at a minimum. On platforms where the static library is used solely to call to a dynamic library, the intent of the LGPL can be preserved without releasing source or object files since the dynamic library can be changed (or updated) without needing to modify the original executable.

For the console market, LGPL code is usually a no-go area. Here, however, the distinction between copyright and licensing comes to the fore because the implementation of the OpenAL specification for the Xbox[2] (and Xbox 360) is owned by Creative Labs. This enables it to release its implementation under a separate license, which in turn is compatible with the closed architecture of the aforementioned consoles.

SDL AUDIO

As mentioned in Chapter 5, "Graphics," the base SDL package includes an audio solution out of the box. What is provided, however, is only a low-level API, giving control of a single audio channel and its basic abstraction to the audio device. This approach allows SDL to control even the most basic sound cards. However, games require multiple audio channels, and therefore a more complete solution.

Multiple channels can be handled in one of two ways. The first is that the hardware driver can be invoked natively to access specific channels. This may be handled through an abstraction layer, such as DirectSound, or programmed directly. Second, it is possible to mix several individual samples—in real time—into a single audio stream that can be played on simpler monaural hardware. This second approach works by creating a single looped sample, and then using the CPU to mix additional sample data into this buffer using a write pointer that is just in advance of the playback pointer. This allows multiple software buffers to be used and accessed individually, with the trade-off of a slight latency (typically 25-50 ms) between the sound being requested and it being heard. This is no different from the mechanism used in DirectX when software audio channels are used. Older readers may remember the same method was used in the forerunner to DirectSound and WaveMix.

The standard SDL audio package provides enough functionality for you to implement the software mixing approach yourself, but there is already an existing library to provide this functionality. It is called SDL_mixer. It provides sample playback, streaming audio, a simple effects chain, MIDI playback, and accessibility for Ogg Vorbis and Soundtracker MODs.

Homepage: *http://www.libsdl.org/projects/SDL_mixer*

License: GNU LGPL version 2.1 (Appendix C).

Distribution: Source and binary.

First release: January 14, 2000.

Current version: 1.2.6 (stable since September 15, 2004).

Platform(s): Extensive, including Windows, Linux, Macintosh, GP2x, PlayStation Linux, and Dreamcast.

Dependencies: SDL 1.2. libvorbis for Ogg Vorbis support.

Other resources: SDL has one of the best on-line resources, as mentioned in Chapter 5, and SDL_mixer is one of its most used extensions.

If you are using SDL for your graphics component, then this must be considered the essential audio solution. However, because the mixing is always done in software, you may discover performance issues on low-end PCs or consoles, where the audio is normally handled by hardware. Solutions to this problem are covered later.

Integration

ON THE CD
The binary package for Windows (also available on the CD-ROM) provides a single header, library, and DLL that should be copied to the usual places; for example, c:\devlib\include, c:\devlib\lib and c:\windows\system32. Because SDL_mixer derives its functionality from the standard SDL audio component, it is ready for use with the initialize and release pairings of

```
SDL_InitSubSystem(SDL_INIT_AUDIO);
Mix_OpenAudio(MIX_DEFAULT_FREQUENCY, AUDIO_S16, MIX_DEFAULT_CHANNELS,
1024);
```

and

```
Mix_CloseAudio();
SDL_QuitSubSystem(SDL_INIT_AUDIO);
```

This prepares a typical stereo audio device using a standard signed 16-bit audio format. The magic number 1024 is the chunk size. This indicates the number of individual samples that will be mixed from each sound into the playback buffer at each game tick. As all effects are applied in software, this same amount of data needs to be processed for each effect in the chain. This number, therefore, has a direct affect on the latency because smaller values process fewer samples before passing the data onto the sound card. However, there is a greater overhead due to the increased number of function calls (to handle the same quantity of data) and amount of thrashing that the caches have to endure.

CAUTION

If the hardware cannot support the format specified by Mix_OpenAudio, *an alternative format will be employed. This can change the way that effects code is written.*

In the current implementation, there is a default of eight available mixing channels, as determined by the value of MIX_CHANNELS. This can be changed by either recompiling your own custom library or, more conveniently, invoking

```
Mix_AllocateChannels(16);
```

A recompile of the library will be required to make one of the more important console abstractions: memory allocation. The standard SDL_mixer library uses the standard functions of `malloc` and `free`, and so may need to be changed for those using custom memory allocators. There are a number of these calls, but nothing a search-and-replace will not solve. How you then maintain these changes is up to you. You can either keep your own special repository of the modified code or store it as a set of differences (using `patch` and `diff`, as covered in Chapter 10, "Utility Libraries") and integrate on each new version.

The filesystem abstraction in SDL_mixer is handled in the same way as the base SDL package—that is, through `SDL_RWops`. This structure is created whenever a file is opened and holds callback function pointers for the standard file operations of read, write, seek, and close. If you have implemented your own platform-specific `RWops` to support SDL, then SDL_mixer should be already complete. Review Chapter 5 for more information on `RWops`.

The Provided Functionality

SDL_mixer provides a number of different mechanisms for handling audio data, although each is mixed into the same waveform.

Sound Samples

The most common use for an audio engine is to trigger individual sounds at specific points in-game. This is the typical use case for SDL_mixer and is handled very simply. Each sample is loaded into memory with

```
Mix_Chunk *pFootstepSound = Mix_LoadWAV("footstep.wav");
```

and then played on the next available channel with

```
Mix_PlayChannel(-1, pFootstepSound, 0);
```

If your engine wishes to assign channels manually, then the first parameter should be renamed to

```
Mix_PlayChannel(footstepChannel, pFootstepSound, 0);
```

This allows the game to allocate a certain number of channels to each type of sound, according to the needs of the game. However, a basic form of this functionality is already provided through the concept of *groups*.

Each group is assigned to a number of channels through a combination of the `Mix_GroupChannel` and `Mix_GroupChannels` functions

```
Mix_GroupChannels(0, 3, GROUP_TAG_PLAYER_SOUNDS);
```

The next available channel within that group is returned with a simple

```
footstepChannel = Mix_GroupAvailable(GROUP_TAG_PLAYER_SOUNDS);
```

Since SDL (and therefore SDL_mixer) follows the old school of C development, the return value for failure is -1. If this happens, you can find the oldest sound playing within the group (using `Mix_GroupOldest`) in order to free up an old channel. If any more control is needed, you need to create your own sound scheduling code.

Additionally, support is provided to fade the sounds in and out, affect their volume, change their position in the stereo field, trigger a callback upon completion, looping, and the usual methods of pause and resume.

Streaming Audio

Support is provided for a single music stream coming from either OGG, MP3, Soundtracker MODs, or WAV files held on disk. This data is mixed in real time into the existing channels and can be affected with its own set of functions. This feature is intended for long pieces of music where a memory load would be inefficient or impossible. Only a single piece of streaming music can be played at a time due to the structure of the interface, although it's technically possible to enhance the API if necessary while still making use of the underlying mixing code.

The functions to affect and query the streaming music properties (such as volume) are different from those used to affect single sounds.

Handling music simply involves retrieving a valid handle:

```
Mix_Music *pMusic = Mix_LoadMUS("background1.wav");
```

and playing with

```
Mix_PlayMusic(pMusic);
```

MIDI

In a word—don't! The MIDI sequencing facilities provided here employ an internal software sequencer, with each MIDI event triggering specific samples and mixing them dynamically into the output stream. This mixing needs to occur in real time, but the sheer quantity of sample data involved in realizing a MIDI file can overwhelm the processor and cause skips. This is due to the larger number of different notes generally played in a MIDI file (because each chord comprises of three or more individual sounds and not one prebaked sample) and the software mixing overhead of SDL. Unless you have very simple MIDI files or little other processing occurring in your game, it's better to sample the composer's realization of the MIDI file into an OGG or WAV file and use that instead. If you have many MIDI files, and converting them into OGG would occupy more disk space than you can afford, it's recommended you look for an alternate MIDI solution that can trigger the MIDI events using the sound card hardware.

The underlying software sequencer included with SDL_mixer is Timidity, released under the GPL, not the LGPL.

CAUTION

Adding a Listener

SDL_mixer takes an egocentric view of audio playback. That is, from wherever any sound is triggered, it always assumes the listener is at the center of the world or origin. If the player moves or rotates, then the parameters of every sound need to be updated. This includes both its relative direction and volume, which diminishes with distance. In simple games with short spot effects, this is not difficult to implement, since it only needs the relative position to be determined when the sound is triggered because the sound can be completed before the player can move or turn very far.

```
Uint8 left = getScaledAngle(vObject, vPlayer, 255);
Uint8 distance = getScaledDistance(vObject, vPlayer, 255);

channel = Mix_PlayChannel(-1, pFootstepSound, 0);

Mix_SetDistance(channel, distance);
Mix_SetPanning(channel, left, 255-left);
```

The scaling is necessary in both cases to ensure the distance fits in the range of 0 to 255.

NOTE

However, with looped and repeating sounds (such as water drips or the hum of electronics), the listener can move significantly between frames, making the original relative position incorrect. This requires the addition of a listener that can update the position of all currently playing sounds and make repeated calls to `Mix_SetDistance` and `Mix_SetPanning`.

In most games, any sound source (that is, an object that can omit audio data) will have an instance of its own class. Furthermore, with all objects often deriving from a common base it, is easy to add a method that retrieves the position from the audio engine. You can even create a simple class containing this method alone and employ multiple inheritance:

```
class AudioParameters {
public:
   virtual sgxVector3 getAudioPosition();
};
```

From here, you can store a pointer to each sound source that is paired to the channel:

```
class AudioEngine {
   int          m_NumChannels;
   AudioObjects *m_pObjectList;
   sgxVector3   m_vListener;

public:
   AudioEngine(int numChannels) {
      m_NumChannels = numChannels;
      m_pObjectList = new AudioObjects[numChannels];
   }

   void setListenerPosition(const sgxVector3 &v) {
      m_vListener = v;
   }

   void playSound(AudioObjects *pObj, const Mix_Chunk *pSound) {
      int channel = Mix_PlayChannel(-1, pSound, 0);
      if (channel != -1) {
         m_pObjectList[channel] = pObj;
      }
   }

   void update() {
      for(int i=0;i<m_NumChannels;++i) {
         if (Mix_Playing(i)) {
            Uint8 left = getScaledAngle(m_pObjectList[i], m_vListener,
            255);
            Uint8 distance = getScaledDistance(m_pObjectList[i],
                                    m_vListener, 255);

            Mix_SetDistance(i, distance);
            Mix_SetPanning(i, left, 255-left);
         }
      }
   }
};
```

You can then abstract the structures and types as much as you wish or expand it to handle calculations for effects such as the Doppler shift.

Audio Formats

For optimal performance, SDL always tries to work with data in the same format as the hardware expects. This is a standard tenet of game engine design: no work is performed on the target platform that doesn't need to be. It is therefore the responsibility of the toolchain to take the audio data and format it according to the specifics of the target platform.

The format of audio data can be surmised with the following parameters:

Number of channels: This is usually mono (1) or stereo (2) but more recently can be six or seven for the specialized surround modes (5.1 or 6.1) currently available.

Playback frequency or sample rate: The number of individual samples per second, usually 44,100 Hz for CD quality, although the Sony PlayStation 2 has adopted 48,000 Hz.

Bit depth: Usually 16-bit, giving CD-quality audio, but 8-bit can suffice for sounds like footsteps and rumbles.

Byte order: Little endian or big endian.

Signed or unsigned: For example, the range of a 16-bit sample would be from 0 to 65535 for unsigned data, or –32768 to 32767 with signed.

These parameters can be used to describe the format of both the hardware properties of the playback channel or the individual sounds played upon them. This also extends to the file formats (such as WAV) although these are generally standardized; so although not every logical format might exist in the real world, it must be considered in general-purpose middleware such as this.

SDL combines the last three format parameters above into a single format type.

NOTE

Format Conversions

The SDL_mixer API supports many different audio formats, but converts all of them on load into that of the hardware. This is supported through the base SDL audio function `SDL_BuildAudioCVT`. It accepts a source and destination format (such as `AUDIO_U16LSB` or `AUDIO_S8`) and generates a structure that can be used to convert data between the two formats with the function call `SDL_ConvertAudio`, also in the base SDL audio code. This ensures the heavy processing of determining the appropriate conversion, and then carrying it out, is only done once upon load.

The result of the SDL_BuildAudioCVT process includes a callback function that is ultimately used to convert the data from one format to another. Raw data should then be loaded with

```
cvt->buf = malloc(lengthOfSourceData * cvt->len_mult);
memcpy(cvt->buf, sourceBuffer, lengthOfSourceData);
```

and converted with

```
cvt->len = lengthOfData;
SDL_ConvertAudio(&cvt);
// the resultant data is now in cvt->buf
```

The reason for the specific malloc is that the conversion routine may result in a larger data set than was supplied for the source data. This is usually true when converting 8-bit data into 16-bit.

As supplied, SDL audio has several conversion routines included in SDL_audiocvt.c that understand the differences between the two formats and populate a chain of routines to perform the conversion. This can handle all the general cases that SDL supports, at the expense of speed, because some conversions may require five (or more) filters. Most games, however, will perform these conversions offline by using SDL audio in the tools pipeline to produce suitable engine-ready files.

Sound Effects

All effects in SDL must be registered on a channel-by-channel basis. This ensures that at the time an effect is applied, the code can determine all the necessary parameters to perform the effect as efficiently as possible. This usually involves looking at the properties of the hardware format, as determined by

```
int channels;
Uint16 format;

Mix_QuerySpec(NULL, &format, &channels);
```

The format of the sound playing on the specified channel will already be of a suitable format because it is converted on load with the SDL_ConvertAudio function you saw previously. Note, however, that this may not be the format specified by Mix_OpenAudio. To limit the amount of extra processing required, it is recommended you create specific functions for each likely format and process them natively. This would involve writing, for example, _Eff_myeffect_u16lsb_c2 when working on stereo 16-bit unsigned samples, using little endian data. Console developers, or those with fixed hardware, have an easier task here because only one function is necessary.

In SDL_mixer, even seemingly simple processes like panning are handled as effects.

By controlling the pan and spatial position of a sound through the SDL effects system means that neither operation is cheap in terms of processing power.

However, this panning code (which varies the volume of each sample added to left and right audio channels) gives you a canonical example of effects programming and some sample code you can reuse—either by a copy-and-paste into your own code or by including your processing into the SDL_mixer library directly and recompiling a custom version.

Including the code in the SDL_mixer library means that you must release those changes back to the community under the terms of the LGPL.

A study of `effect_position.c` will yield the `get_position_effect_func` function that determines a suitable callback function from the 20 available that place a positional sound into the final mix. These positional sounds reference the distance from the listener and the panning angle, and apply the process to a small chunk of sound data. Because most action games require these audio properties by default, any additional effects will introduce further latency and an increase in CPU usage. One method of limiting this is to include your effects as part of the standard positional effects package inside the SDL_mixer library itself. This involves amending the `position_args` structure to include your effects-specific parameters and then supplementing each of the processing functions (which all begin with `_Eff_ position_`) with the appropriate code.

Overcoming Software Mixing

Like most libraries, SDL_mixer promotes a wide range of functionality. Its most valuable feature is that of compatibility. By building on top of the simple base functionality of SDL audio, multichannel audio is supported by any platform available to SDL. However, this is also its undoing as this requires that every operation is performed in software. As you'd expect, this includes the effects chain, but also—and more controversially—the basic operations like volume and pan control. While the library has been optimized in many places to prevent data from being copied unnecessarily, this still adds a significant overhead in some games, especially those requiring full 3D audio, such as first- and third-person shooters. This overhead is also further damaging in console development, where specific audio chips traditionally handle these operations and remove the load from the main processor. Overcoming this problem can be done in a number of ways.

Use SDL as a Wrapper

This is the most effective solution from a cross-platform and performance point of view. By rewriting SDL_mixer using the native API of your console, you can call identically named functions from common game code while ensuring that all the audio functionality is handled optimally for the platform. This might include a special library that utilizes DirectSound on the PC, for example. It also means you have a reference implementation with the original SDL_mixer code to verify the locale of any bugs that might occur.

The first, and most obvious, problem with this approach is that of development time. Creating a good library is a time-consuming occupation, and it is not helped by forcing programmers into the straightjacket of being API-compatible with a library they might not like or agree with—particularly if the platform already has a perfectly good audio engine. In practice, the SDL_mixer API can be adapted quite easily because there are very few entry points to the library. The only troublesome areas are the handling of custom effects filters, such as echo. These can either be converted into platform-specific DSP functions (with suitable abstractions) or generated using the processor, as SDL_mixer would normally.

The second problem involves the quality of your cross-platform port. Every code difference that exists between the API layer and hardware introduces another possibility for problems and errors that can affect the game in subtle ways. These are covered fully in the book *Cross-Platform Game Programming*, but can be summarized by remembering to support:

- The Utopian Development Environment. This is where everything is deemed possible, even if the functionality is mimicked silently in the background.
- Abstractions between the format of the sound data and its use. So `PlayBackgroundMusic()` is a better abstraction than a more specific `PlayMusic("background1.mp3")`.
- Standardized scales (such as 0-1) for all audio parameters (like volume, or pan).
- Null driver handling for debugging.

Use an Independent Audio API

If you're working in-house or on the core team of engine developers, you may prefer to design your own independent API to suit the type of games you generally develop. This API will be an abstraction of the functionality you require and will be compatible across all necessary platforms. This will then call out to the SDL_mixer library for basic support, or use the native functions for console development or where a more involved usage is required. This adds benefits because of the willing buy-in from the NIH (Not Invented Here) bastions and your ability to adapt the API for those platforms you are specifically targeting. Furthermore, since the API belongs to you, it can be added and amended with fewer integration problems or concerns of breaking backward compatibility.

Avoid SDL

It is sad to say, but the simplest short-term solution is to avoid SDL_mixer entirely. If your reason for using it is to simplify the process of writing audio on a single plat-form, then you are probably better off being pragmatic and sourcing a hardware-accelerated library for that specific platform. This may even extend to buying the license to a non-free solution. Since the SDL graphics solution—and several others—is available under the LGPL, the licensing requires you to only release ob-ject files to your game. In this case, the third-party libraries can be statically linked to your game code, and that will often satisfy the license requirements[3].

PortAudio

This package provides a cross-platform audio solution for streaming sounds. It can handle both input (i.e., audio capture) and output (i.e., playback) streams and adopts one of the fundamental Unix philosophies—do one job, and do it well—by providing an abstraction for only streaming audio. At no point are spot sounds po-sitioned in the stereo field as they are with OpenAL, nor are they mixed down into a single stereo track like SDL_mixer. What happens instead is that the user creates a number of streams that are filled with pertinent data upon each invocation of a special callback function. This provides two options for the games programmer wanting to use positional audio.

The first way is to use only the streaming logic from PortAudio and integrate the driver code into your existing audio engine so it can coexist with your code for positional sounds and spot effects. This acts like the software mixer approach of SDL_mixer.

The alternative approach is to treat every sound in your game as a stream. In-dividual sounds can be played by copying the sound's sample data into the stream buffer at the first opportunity. This is not dissimilar to the method used by Direct-Sound under the hood. It is also equivalent to SDL_mixer. This has benefits in small memory environments since sample data can be held in either main memory or disk, and its location moved between them with little change in code. Therefore, sounds can be reassigned from memory streams to disk streams until the memory footprint has been suitably reduced because the streaming playback code does not need to change.

Politically speaking, one concern for the developer is the apparent lack of significant releases over the past few years. In most cases, this can signal a stalled or dead project. However, in this case the current implementation is very usable because it only does one job and consequently doesn't need a lot of maintenance. However, the mailing list is still active, with bug reports, changes, and announcements appearing regularly. Furthermore, V19 has undergone an active design and review process and has a stable API. The current progress toward this new version can be found at *http://www.portaudio.com/docs/proposals/status.html*. Version 18 has been included on the companion CD-ROM.

ON THE CD

Homepage: *http://www.portaudio.com*

License: Custom (BSD-like)

Distribution: Source

First release: 1999

Current version: V18 (stable since 2000)

Platform(s): Extensive, including Windows, Macintosh, and Unix machines using the Open Sound System (OSS) such as Linux, Solaris, and FreeBSD

Dependencies: None

Other resources: Mailing list

PortAudio comprises of both halves of the software/hardware divide. In the first instance, any data that has been loaded from disk or recalled from memory must be written into the streaming buffers using software. This utilizes processor power to some extent and cannot be avoided. On the other hand, each streamed buffer can be assigned to a different hardware channel by making the appropriate calls to the library. This generally provides you with the best of both worlds.

No console drivers currently have published implementations because that would breach NDA agreements. However, there is nothing in the license that would prohibit a developer from creating (and selling) them independently because it is only "requested" that you "send the modifications to the original developer."

Basic Usage

With only source archives available, the installation process can take only one route: compilation. This is simply a matter of combining the common PortAudio code (inside the `pa_common` directory) with the specific driver for your platform. Microsoft Windows developers have a choice of components: `pa_win_ds` (which wrappers *DirectSound*) and `pa_win_wmme` (which utilizes the standard Windows multimedia layer). The documentation suggests the `pa_win_wmme` version since DirectSound is not well supported on NT. However, the landscape has changed since those documents were written, and DirectSound is perfectly suitable to the task.

Installation requires only the three common headers (`portaudio.h`, `pa_trace.h`, and `pa_host.h`) to be copied into `c:\devlib\include` because the support code is compiled directly into the game. This also makes it much easier to change any code that uses the standard library, such as `malloc`.

Due to the age of the package, there can be conflicts between the PortAudio, DirectSound, and Microsoft Developer Studio header files. The most common problem is with version 8 and above of DirectSound on pre-.NET installations where an

```
error C2061: syntax error : identifier 'DWORD_PTR'
```

can occur. This exists because the `DWORD_PTR` type (as used in DirectSound version 8) is not defined in older DevStudio versions, and so must be defined explicitly with

```
typedef unsigned long * DWORD_PTR;
```

at the head of `dsound_wrapper.h`. You will need also to include `winmm.lib` under Windows to gain access to the high-resolution multimedia timers.

Memory Handling

All memory allocated by PortAudio falls in one of two categories; both are allocated differently. First, there is memory for the audio streaming buffers and structures. These are the common data structures that exist across all platforms and are allocated through the `PaHost_AllocateFastMemory` function. This is implemented in platform-specific code, such as `pa_dsound.c` and has the typical prototype

```
void *PaHost_AllocateFastMemory(long numBytes);
```

The second type of allocation covers internal driver data, and as such appears only in platform-specific code. The current drivers generally use `malloc` for this.

The distinction is made (and termed *fast*) because this data is used for filling the stream buffers with audio data and needs to be as close to real time as is possible. This performance can be achieved by allocating physical memory that is not, or could not, be paged into virtual memory. Most operating systems have special functions to support this, as do consoles, but that information is under NDA.

File I/O

There is no functionality in the standard PortAudio library to read data from the filesystem. Even the provided sample code does not demonstrate any mechanism to load a WAV file and then apply it to a stream. For games, however, it is usual for this information to have been processed by the toolchain into a game-specific format. This can be handled by your existing code, perhaps even ALUT and OpenAL.

Using the Library

The technical usage of the library is very simple with

```
if (paNoError != Pa_Initialize()) {
    return FALSE;
}

// Game code here...

if (paNoError != Pa_Terminate()) {
    return FALSE;
}
```

surrounding the game code. Streams are created at the start of the game and generally left running until the end, although they can be stopped and started at will if necessary. The initialization routine for individual streams is quite complex and covers much of the functionality attributed to each stream. This is exacerbated as just one function is used to create both input and output streams. Its prototype is

```
PaError Pa_OpenStream(
    PortAudioStream** streamPtrPtr,
    PaDeviceID inputDeviceID,
    int numInputChannels,
    PaSampleFormat inputSampleFormat,
    void *inputDriverInfo,
    PaDeviceID outputDeviceID,
    int numOutputChannels,
    PaSampleFormat outputSampleFormat,
    void *outputDriverInfo,
    double sampleRate,
    unsigned long framesPerBuffer,
    unsigned long numberOfBuffers,
    unsigned long streamFlags,
    PortAudioCallback *callback,
    void *userData);
```

The important points of note follow. The `PaSampleFormat` describes how each sample is to be represented. For games, you use the same stream format as your output buffer, as queried from platform-specific capabilities structures, but it will normally be 16-bit integer data paInt16.

PortAudio also guarantees a cross-platform implementation of samples that use 32-bit floating-point numbers. This incurs nothing but processor overhead for you, but is very useful for those writing software synthesizers.

We also note the userData argument at the end. This is always passed to the callback function, such as

```
int
paCallback(void *inputBuffer, void *outputBuffer,
        unsigned long framesPerBuffer, PaTimestamp outTime, void
        *userData);
```

This can include any data, but it is usually a structure indicating the sample(s) to play on this stream. For disk streaming this needs to include a file handle and offset within the file, and for memory streams this will be a pointer. The number of individual samples to copy into the buffer is supplied as the framesPerBuffer argument, since this value can be set externally.

The data enters the stream by the outputBuffer pointer, which contains interleaved sample data in the format specified by the Pa_OpenStream function. For convenience, it is recommended the structure pointed to by userData include this information also.

The source of the data will usually be the disc, however you are strongly advised to load this information in a separate thread and copy it to the buffer afterward. This is because disc access is very slow, and the callback needs to return as quickly as possible to prevent the audio from skipping. One method is to write all streamed data into a FIFO that is copied by the callback. A sample of this can be found in the PABLIO sample.

Engine Integration—Stream Everything

As mentioned in the introduction, the first way to integrate PortAudio into your audio solution is by streaming everything. This is the simplest to implement and takes the SDL_mixer approach of mixing the individual sounds together in software to form a new stream.

A Single Stereo Stream

This approach creates a single stereo stream and mixes each individual sound into one stereo buffer. To do this you must manually affect each sound playing at any particular interval to reflect its relative position, orientation, and velocity to the listener. If your game is under a GPL- or LGPL-compatible license, you can adapt the effect_position.c code from SDL_mixer (an LGPL-licensed product) and include it in your game. Otherwise, you will have to either borrow from BSD-licensed sources or write it yourself.

The basic processes necessary to reflect positional sound data are its distance and angle from the listener. The distance is modified by two properties—the inner and outer cones. The inner cone is the distance from the sound source within which the volume is at its maximum, whereas the sound is inaudible at the outer cone, as shown in Figure 6.1.

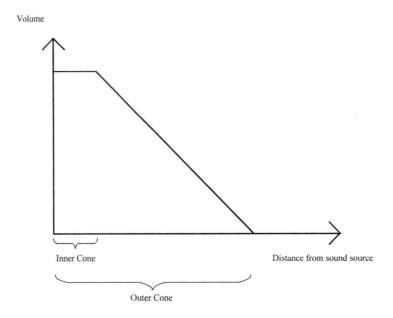

FIGURE 6.1 Sound fall-off.

Note that the orientation between listener and sound source changes only the relative volumes of the sound from the left and right speakers.

The final mix-down occurs at the end of the pipeline when each sample is combined into a single 16-bit stream. This involves affecting the volume of each sample individually according to the present mixer values. The most important consideration when mixing is to avoid distortion. The most common form of distortion is clipping distortion that occurs when the sum of each sample exceeds the range of the data. A signed 16-bit buffer, for example, will clip when the total exceeds 32767 or drops below –32768[4]. Avoiding clipping in a dynamic system is a difficult problem because you don't know in advance how loud the loudest sound is likely to be. In prerecorded sound, the buffer is usually *normalized* by finding the loudest part of the sound, boosting it to the maximum extent, and then scaling the rest of the sound to match. However, because the loudest peak in a dynamic system fluctuates all the time, you cannot normalize the data at all. Instead, you must opt for sensible mixing defaults that will not clip the sound. This can be achieved empirically.

One alternative is to mix the multiple 16-bit buffers into a single 32-bit buffer. Because it requires 65536 fully utilized 16-bit channels to overflow one 32-bit channel, you can be safe knowing you will suffer no distortion with this approach, even if the sound is not as loud as it could be. The data in the 32-bit channel must then be scaled back into a 16-bit buffer to be compliant with the hardware. This scaling can be accomplished with a simple division by an arbitrary factor. Again, this is determined empirically.

Because division is slow, you can optimize the code by shifting the bits along to the right. Furthermore, if you know that there will be no more than 16 sounds mixed into this buffer, it follows that the loudest peak cannot exceed 16*32767. Therefore, you can trim the sample data with

```
newMixedData16 = (oldMixedData32 >> 4) & 0xffff;
```

This also achieves the benefit that no clipping detection needs to be performed, such as

```
if (scaledValue > 65535) {
    scaledValue = 65535;
}
```

Multiple Streams

This adopts the same logic as a stereo streaming, but it uses multiple mono streams, each placed at specific points spread across the stereo field. This eliminates one set of software calculations because the sound can be mixed at its normal volume into a single stream, as opposed to incorporating it separately into both left and right streams. This saves processor time, in return for less granularity in sound placement, and the added cost of the extra streaming buffers. There should be no additional performance hit, however, because these buffers can be located in hardware and played at a fixed volume.

Reusable Streams

If you only have a small number of potential sounds playing at once, you can create enough streams for them all, and reposition them individually in the stereo field as each new sound is played on them. This requires even less software processing because the data is copied directly from the sound buffer into the channel, and the hardware mixer is used to set the volume and pan values. The trade-off comes from the channel limit, which is fixed in hardware. Those focused on cross-platform development will know of the problems and issues involved here.

Some PC drivers allow you to query the number of hardware channels available on the sound card. However, some of these drivers will lie and report more channels than are truly available. When this happens, the audio mixing will still occur, but it will do so in software, eradicating any benefits you once gained.

Engine Integration—Driver Integration

If you are using two libraries that both abstract the features of, say, DirectSound, then it is possible to integrate both libraries to form a single entity within the code. This involves the adoption of the *Miss or Ms* principle.

The Miss or Ms Principle

This is the formalization of a technique to combine two or more pieces of code, both with singleton-based functionality, into one. Audio fits this mold well because there is only one sound card, but two or more libraries might want to make use of it. The two alternatives are Miss (master-slave-slave) or Ms (master-slave). In the first instance, a completely new master library is written. This abstracts the basic functionality necessary to implement both slave libraries. The abstraction is wafer thin because both libraries have previously used it directly but it gives the master a mechanism whereby it can regulate channel allocations and the like. In addition, the new master handles all the standard start-up and shutdown code, which it consequently removes from each slave.

The master-slave (Ms) approach selects one of the existing libraries to become the new master. The slave then acquires resources from, and utilizes the functionality within, the new master instead of going to the DirectSound driver directly.

The master-slave-slave (Miss) approach is usually best because it scales better if new or alternate libraries are to be used. It is also the more useful approach if both libraries are small, or offer limited functionality because neither would want the burden of the extra wrapper code.

In contrast, the Ms technique is favorable when one library is already powerful enough to become a master in its own right, or there would be significant overhead in abstracting the resource allocation code away from one or the other of the existing libraries.

PortMusic

Building on the success of PortAudio, PortMusic provides cross-platform MIDI support and a basic playback sequencer. Because this utilizes only the MIDI hardware, you will need an additional way to upload samples to the soundcard if you are aiming for anything other than General MIDI (GM) sounds in your composition. It would be possible to combine these libraries so that a MIDI out message would generate a sound on a PortAudio stream, but unless you have specific audio requirements for automatic or real-time generative music, you are unlikely to use this library. It also suffers the same performance problems as Timidity, the MIDI solution with SDL_mixer.

Ogg Vorbis

Ogg Vorbis is a two-stage audio codec for high-quality audio playback. Ogg is a container format that holds generic information about an audio file, such as its name, length, and encoding mechanism. The second part is the audio data itself, and usually encoded in Vorbis, but this can be replaced at will. One example of this is the Speex decoder (pronounced speaks) that was built for VoIP systems, but can be used for encoding off-line speech, too.

Ogg Vorbis relies on an offline lossy compression algorithm to generate a file suitable for real-time playback. It uses less memory and disk space than an equivalent MP3 at the same quality, and uses approximately the same amount of processing power to decompress it. Furthermore, it is patent-free allowing it to be used without fear of legal litigation[5]. Because of this, Ogg Vorbis has been integrated into many Open Source projects and game engines.

Homepage: *http://www.xiph.org* and *http://www.vorbis.com*

License (API): Custom (revised-BSD-like)

License (Utilities): GNU GPL (Appendix B)

Distribution: Source

First release: 1993

Current version (libogg): 1.1.3 (stable since November 27, 2005)

Current version (libvorbis): 1.1.2 (stable since 2005)

Current version (libspeex): 1.0.5 (stable since 2005)

Platform(s): Extensive, including Windows, Macintosh, and Linux

Dependencies: None

Other resources: Wiki

Because Ogg is a compressed format, it requires a decompressor (usually in software[6]) occupying a slice of CPU time. Consequently, it is primarily used where a memory and disk space trade-off can be made—usually in background music.

Both Ogg and Vorbis libraries have been included on the CD-ROM along with the Vorbis tools.

Basic Usage

The Xiph website contains the source packages necessary to allow Ogg Vorbis to be built with the minimum of effort, including workspace and project files for Microsoft Developer Studio. Once built, using Ogg is simply a matter of opening a file, such as

```
FILE *fp;
OggVorbis_File vorbisFile;

    if (ov_open(fp, &vorbisFile, NULL, 0 ) < 0 ) {
        // Error
    }
```

and using the newly assigned vorbisFile reference in all subsequent operations.

Under normal circumstances, Ogg uses the standard file I/O functions to load data from disc. Because this is not applicable to most games, the developers have thoughtfully provided a set of callback functions to override this. They can be set up with ov_open_callbacks.

```
ov_callbacks callbacks;

callbacks.read_func  = my_read_func;
callbacks.seek_func  = my_seek_func;
callbacks.close_func = my_close_func;
callbacks.tell_func  = my_tell_func;

ov_open_callbacks(myFilePtr, &vorbisFile, NULL, 0, callbacks);
```

Speex

The API for Speex looks significantly different from that of the Vorbis codec. That is because it's heritage is in the VoIP field where the library must encode as well as decode. Consequently, the API was built to make both halves of *this* equation look similar, as opposed to looking like Ogg. Initialization occurs with

```
SpeexBits bits;
void *dec_state;
```

```
speex_bits_init(&bits);
dec_state = speex_decoder_init(&speex_nb_mode);

speex_decoder_ctl(dec_state, SPEEX_GET_FRAME_SIZE, &frame_size);
speex_decoder_ctl(dec_state, SPEEX_SET_ENH, &enh);
```

with the individual data being read by

```
speex_bits_read_from(&bits, input_bytes, nbBytes);
speex_decode(st, &bits, output_frame);
```

A comprehensive manual details these more fully, but this should give you a head start.

One consequence of using Speex is that the optimal code footprint can only be achieved with careful removal of the encoding portions of the library. If you compile the source directly into your game (as opposed to building a link library) then the compiler will—hopefully—remove this deadwood. This source is available on the CD-ROM.

ON THE CD

Preintegrated Solutions

With most engines using Ogg in some capacity, you can often find a preprepared solution that makes integrating the code a trivial or nonexistent operation.

SDL

The SDL_mixer library comes complete with an Ogg Vorbis module. You need to link the SDL_mixer source with the compiler-specific libraries (or compile the source in directly) and use the functions prefixed with OGG_, such as OGG_play and OGG_stop. The uncompressed audio from the Ogg Vorbis library is read from the stream with OGG_getsome and converted immediately into the currently format of SDL audio. This data is then mixed into the standard audio stream whenever the music is playing.

CAUTION

SDL supports a number of different music playback formats, although each is handled through API functions such as Mix_LoadMUS. *The way in which this works, however, requires that any new codecs, or variations in older ones, are added to the various switch statements within* music.c.

Again, SDL uses its filesystem abstraction, RW_ops to read data from the disc.

OpenAL

Using the queued buffers of OpenAL means that Ogg Vorbis support is very easy to add, as you only need to fill the next buffer with audio data when the AL_BUFFERS_PROCESSED state indicates the more recent buffer(s) have completed. Uncompressed Ogg data can be imported with function ov_read as normal.

There are several tutorials on the web covering this process[7], and a custom extension (*http://www.openal.org/docs/EXT_vorbis*

ENDNOTES

1. This is so your OpenAL code matches the style of the API, which allows others understand the code easier (to assist in bug tracking), and helps you provide a clean-looking minimal sample to demonstrate any bugs you might find.
2. The PlayStation 2 does not have an OpenAL implementation due to licensing issues. However, an OpenAL-like solution exists called ps2al that uses Multistream, and therefore is available to registered PS2 developers only. More information is available at *http://playstation2-linux.com/projects/ps2al*.
3. Although obviously, you should check this first as most proprietary license agreements are more rigid than those in the Open Source world.
4. If the values were unsigned you'd get a similar distortion effect if the value beyond 65535, where 65536 would be represented as 0, for example.
5. To use MP3 playback code requires a license from Thomson (*http://www.mp3licensing.com/*).
6. Ogg is one of the few Open Source formats that has been taken up by hardware manufacturers. Although it is supported by many MP3 players, it is still rare to find it in typical console hardware.
7. Such as the one at *http://www.devmaster.net/articles/openal-tutorials/lesson8.php*.

7 Physics

In This Chapter

- Physics Background
- OD—Open Dynamics Engine
- Collision Detection Routines
- OPAL
- Other Solutions

PHYSICS BACKGROUND

Of all the libraries featured in games software over the past five years, the physics engine is probably the newest kid on the block. Even now, the choice of Open Source physics code is minimal. Furthermore, the type of physics being done in the Open Source world is generally limited to rigid bodies. Soft-body physics, such as fluid dynamics and clothes, are usually used in specific confined areas and not permitted to interact with the rest of the environment. Also, what fluid dynamics code *is* available has generally been ported from Unix mainframes and often understandable only by those who understand the science behind them. Even then, they are only suitable for offline processing simulators and not within real-time engines. Ragdoll physics has been adopted as a cheap way of getting some nonscripted dynamics into games, and can be implemented with Open Source solutions such as ODE, rather than existing as its own customized solution.

There are a couple of possible explanations for the lack of suitable physics code. The first is obvious—it is a very complex area. This complexity scares off many developers, and those remaining few are either too busy to work on the problem or disinterested in the topic. Open Source developers have a history of scratching their own itches. If the physics modeling itch isn't there, it won't get developed until someone pays for it. Indeed, up until very recently there were few enough proprietary games using real physics for anything more than falling crates, so perhaps it stands to reason no one wants that functionality in an Open Source game yet.

The second reason may be due to its lack of visibility. The key word in the Open Source community is *community*. These developers are working on projects in their spare time for peer gratification and kudos in the community. This comes easily, and with great aplomb, on visible projects like 3D engines, web servers, and desktop packages because these are things every user can see and appreciate. Even an operating system kernel, a traditionally academic subject, is visible within the geek world because everyone knows it makes the computer tick. The physics code within a game is not visible, however. Its results can often be implemented just as effectively by using keyframe animations, and there are few games that demonstrate the full capabilities of any physics solution. After all, when physics systems work well it's largely transparent to the end user because a natural reaction is expected, but when it fails, the results are cringe-worthy and not conducive to good peer relations. Despite this, some developers have stepped up to the table to offer their solutions to this problem.

The Problems

The handling of solid body physics is not difficult in the basic case. Simply put, an object moves within the world; this body is checked for collisions (one face, vertex, or polygon at a time) against the other objects and the world; and if it collides with anything, it either rewinds its position to the point of impact or begins to move the object with which it collided.

Simple.

Almost! While the simple case can be implemented with a standard high school textbook and a couple of free evenings, a full solution takes considerably more work. Some of the areas to consider are as follows:

Stability: All floating-point numbers are approximate, so it may not be possible to ensure the numbers mean what they need to. For instance, will a box rock backward and forward forever without ever coming to rest? Or if two objects are supposed to be joined, will they remain joined after being pushed around by the physics engine?

Scalability: Although processing one object in a single cuboid world is simple, when the world is made from arbitrary polygons, the floor is uneven, and there are several other moving objects in the world, collision determination and movement solver becomes exponentially more difficult. However, this complexity cannot be passed onto the game developer because they still expect the physics solver to work in constant time.

Accuracy: Because the real world can only ever be approximated, is it possible to make the physics look real and accurate?

The Structure

The important point about real-world physics is that it does not represent the real world. Instead, it *simulates* the real world by using a series of approximations. Every aspect of the simulation is approximated. This is because an accurate emulation would be far too complex to handle in real time, and be too difficult to program accurately because of the number of variables and interactions. And that ignores quantum mechanics and the fact that scientists do not know how the real world works in its entirety. But that's a story for another day . . .

Your simulation breaks down in three main areas.

Global Simulation Parameters

These parameters will affect everything in the game world, or will control how the simulation, as a whole, will react in particular situations. The most obvious example here is gravity. This is often treated as a world constant and applied to every object equally, and is generally an acceptable approximation. But this is just a simulation, because in the real world gravity is not constant—it changes at altitude. But you can assume it's constant for the purposes of most games.

In those games where it is not constant, and you're researching a physics solution because of that very problem, a variable gravity can be mimicked by one of two methods. The most obvious is to change the gravity parameter. However, this may not always work "out of the box" because the engine may precalculate a number of constants based on this value and apply these derived parameters to all physical objects in the world at the start of the game. Therefore, any change in gravity would need to reapply them. Because this is Open Source, you can determine if this is supported and adapt the code if necessary.

The other main way of simulating a dynamically changing gravity is to treat it as a number of individual forces. Begin by setting the world gravity to zero, but apply a downward force every frame on every object, of 9.81 Newtons. As gravity changes, so does this number.

You should also expect other global parameters that allow you to tweak the simulation by varying the amount of error allowed, how such errors are to be corrected, and the maximum number of objects to process each step. The names of these parameters are likely to vary between engines, but they should all exist.

If you're using physics across different platforms, then it is advisable to abstract the global tweaking parameters away from the common initialization code, because the update loop may need to run differently on each platform, and therefore need different values for the tweak parameters. This includes the amount of time processed for each frame of the game and may not equal the time used for the renderer.

The physics engine will often need to be run faster than the actual frame rate to avoid numerical instability.

TIP

The Physical Objects

Every object whose movement is to be simulated by the physics code must contain additional properties describing how it is to react. This includes existing parameters such as position and orientation, but also new ones like angular velocity, mass, and center of gravity.

Most physics solvers will require both sets of property data to be present and usually in its own internal format. This provides the first dilemma, of whether to duplicate this data or not. This comes with the usual arguments of performance, readability, and design. However, this problem can be solved quite easily by introducing an indirection to the data.

To begin, any physical parameters that are required by your games engine should be removed from the standard game object and replaced with a pointer to a new abstract class, such as

```
class GameObject : public BaseObject {
public:
   PhysicalProperties *pProperties;

   tREAL getMass() {
      return pProperties->getMass();
   }

   void getPosition(sgxVector3 &position) {
      position = pProperties->getPosition(position);
   }
   // etc...
};
```

This new `PhysicalProperties` class is, in fact, abstract. Derived concrete classes represent the original set of properties that were removed from `GameObject`. For example,

```
class Standard_Properties : public PhysicalProperties {
protected:
    tREAL       m_fMass;
    sgxVector3 m_vPositon;
    sgxVector3 m_vLinearVelocity;
    sgxVector3 m_vAngularVelocity;

public:
    virtual tREAL getMass();
    virtual void  getPosition(sgxVector3 &position);
    virtual void  getLinearVelocity(sgxVector3 &velocity);
    virtual void  getAngularVelocity(sgxVector3 &velocity);
};
```

This provides a layer of abstraction to the properties held inside the physics engine, such as

```
class PhysicsEngine_Properties : public PhysicalProperties {
    PhysicsEngine_DataClassPointer props;

public:
    virtual tREAL getMass();
    virtual void  getPosition(sgxVector3 &position);
    virtual void  getLinearVelocity(sgxVector3 &velocity);
    virtual void  getAngularVelocity(sgxVector3 &velocity);
};
```

Any members that only apply to the physics engine are now only allocated if necessary (and are invisible to the rest of the engine), while all common information is held in only one place, incurring only a slight penalty of the virtual indirection. And *in practice*, this will only be a slight overhead because the game and rendering engine will need to reference this information significantly less frequently than the physics engine. This pattern ensures the physics engine has its information in its own personal format.

Because the Properties member of GameObject *abstracts the implementation details of the physical objects away, there is no reason to make it private or provide an accessor function as that would just waste a method call.*

Brave developers can alternatively use multiple inheritance here, deriving GameObject from *both* BaseObject and PhysicalProperties. Although the potential for name clashes and the infamous "diamond problem"[1] are very much reduced, the indirection does not inflict a significant performance overhead in most cases.

Object Geometry

One noticeable peculiarity of the physical properties discussed so far is that it includes no geometry information. That is, you don't know if the game object is a character, a crate, or a car. The fact is, you don't need to know! The properties—such as mass or center of gravity—do not change if the geometry changes. The *values* of the properties change, for sure, but not the properties themselves. Therefore, all object geometry can be stored separately and queried when you need to determine whether two objects have collided. This essentially divides the physics problem into two halves: collision detection and collision resolution. The detection routines look at the geometry of two objects, and, if it determines they would collide, produces a set of contact points. The physics solver then produces a new set of positions, velocities, and orientations for each object that has collided, based on these contact points.

Almost without exception, the geometry of an object used in collision detection is not the same as the mesh used for rendering. In most cases, they will not even be related. Instead, a completely separate collision model will be generated for each game object. An NPC might become a simple cylinder or capsule, or a car might be considered as a cuboid, and so on. The collision model is usually created by the 3D modeler by combining one or more geometric primitives (such as sphere, cylinder, and box) to generate a geometry that fits as snuggly around an object as possible.

This information is typically only of use to the physics solver, so it will be stored in its internal format and created from metadata parameters stored within the object. For example,

```
void GameObject::loadModel(FileStream &stream) {
// ...
stream >> numCollisionModels;

for(int i=0;i<numCollisionModels;++i) {
   stream >> type;
   switch(type) {

      case COMO_CUBE:
         stream >> width >> height >> depth;
         addPhysicsCollisionCube(width, height, depth);
         break;

      case COMO_CYLINDER:
         stream >> radius >> height;
         addPhysicsCollisionCylinder(radius, height);
         break;
```

```
        // etc
    }
}
```

One other general use for these collision models is raycasting (for shadows, projectiles, or line-of-sight calculations). You do not need to duplicate the data or write new code for this. Most physics solutions can perform these calculations, as it is a specialized form of their general mandate, so you can call its existing functions.

Convex hulls and arbitrarily shaped polygonal collision models can be used as collision models in most physics engines, but are substantially slower than the base primitive examples shown previously. In cases where the shadows need to be more complex than the collision model, you can simply use metadata to mark the collision models as a subset of the shadow set.

Object Functionality

One of the main requirements for physics objects is the ability to disable them, or at least limit which objects are processed each frame. Most physics solvers will disable objects that haven't moved recently as an automatic process, but you also need the ability to turn off the physics processing on the crates in the second warehouse when you're still in the first, for example. This is simple functionality, and always included. You just need to be aware of whether the enable/disable pairing is a Boolean control or counted.

It is also very useful to receive messages when one object collides with another. This is so you can trigger sound effects or make other game objects react to the situation.

For more complex physics structures, you need healthy joints. These connect two bodies and constrain their movements. The most typical joint is the hinge joint, as found on doors and doorframes, although in most games this example is handled by a simple keyframe animation. Ragdoll physics is almost entirely derived from joints, and if this is a necessary feature of your game, then the physics solution should contain them. Joints should also have a means to limit their movement in each axis and often a way to break them.

The World

The game world exists solely to contain the physical objects. There are two main parts to it: the world shell (containing the walls, ceilings, and floors) and the static objects within it that react *with* the physical objects, but are immovable and therefore do not react *to* them.

It is also useful to see if the world can be sensibly subdivided so that you can limit the amount of processing done in an intelligent way. Some systems provide a callback mechanism where you can use your knowledge of the world (described in your data format) to limit the collision tests performed using the physics engines' internal data.

Some games will require nested, or hierarchical, worlds. In this case, objects in one world (for example, on a sailing ship) would move within their own world space, but they would all be affected by the general physical motion of the ship as a whole as it sailed across the ocean.

ODE—OPEN DYNAMICS ENGINE

Despite being a sub-1.0 release, this is the most prominent rigid-body physics engine available to the Open Source community. It has a solid history of engineering practice and adopts all the classic principles of physics solvers. It is also focused toward the gaming environment since it prefers to favor speed, and will sacrifice real-world accuracy for performance if the choice ever needs to be made.

It's not short on functionality, either. It contains all the principles necessary (as covered previously in the backgrounder) along with multiple joint types, collision spaces for efficient searching, contact and friction modeling, and collision primitives including arbitrary polygon meshes. It has been integrated into the Ogre 3D graphics engine, and exists as a plug-in for CrystalSpace. It was also used in *Blood-Rayne 2*.

Homepage: *http://ode.org*

License: GNU LGPL version 2.1 (Appendix C) or revised BSD (Appendix D)

Distribution: Source and binary

First release: March 2001

Current version: 0.5 (stable since May 29, 2004)

Platform(s): Windows, primarily, but can also work on Linux and Macintosh, and should be portable to the consoles

Dependencies: OPCODE (integrated)

Other resources: Mailing list

ON THE CD

The ODE package comprises of three parts. The first is ODE itself, and is the physics solver, also known as an *integrator*, which performs collision resolution and handling for the objects in the world. This is available on the CD-ROM.

The second is OPCODE, which stands for OPtimized COllision Detection (see *http://www.codercorner.com/Opcode.htm* for more information). This handles the mathematics of collision for spheres, boxes, cylinders, and meshes against rays, planes, and the primitives themselves. This functionality can be leveraged independently in-game for line-of-sight checks or trajectory collision tests. OPCODE can be replaced with custom and/or optimized collision detection code if desired. It also is on the CD-ROM.

ON THE CD

The third, and final, part is the DrawStuff code. This is a small OpenGL library used to render basic primitives and handle the standard event loop of ODE. It is used in the various demos that accompany ODE, but it is independent of it and can be safely ignored for real games.

NOTE

The combination of ODE and OPCODE is not small (around 1.8 MB for a complete WinTel32 release version), so may be too heavy for some consoles.

Integration

Producing a suitable ODE code base is more complex than most libraries and requires more than a simple file copy. This is because there are a number of compile-time options to decide upon before building the code. It is possible to download binaries of most configuration options, but it is preferable to roll your own.

Preparing the configuration file varies according to platform. Those using Linux-flavored tools can use the `make configure` command to adapt the sample configuration (held as `config/user-settings`) into something compatible, which is automatically placed in the `include/ode` directory. Windows users, on the other hand, can copy an appropriate file from the `VC6\_configs` directory.

The first decision, and the easiest, is whether to use floating-point numbers or doubles. Invariably the answer is floats, so ensure that #define dSINGLE 1 is inside your configuration file, and dDOUBLE is not.

You then have to decide whether to support *trimeshes*. These are collision models using an arbitrary mesh composed of triangles. These are slower to evaluate than the standard sphere, box, and cylinder primitives, but allow a very tight collision model. The primary consideration, though, is whether you really need it enough to support the extra performance headaches caused by them. They are not a bad feature, per se, but there's at least 250 KB of code to support them, and it gives the developers enough proverbial rope with which to hang themselves because of the complexity involved in solving collisions between two trimeshes. Enable trimesh collisions with

```
#define dTRIMESH_ENABLED 1
```

The only other task of the `config.h` file is to prepare the base types. These are the standard types, using yet a different naming convention for 8-, 16-, and 32-bit types, both signed and unsigned. If you're likely to be porting across to different platforms, you might want to define these in terms of your existing types.

Global Properties

ODE conforms well to our set of expectations, providing access to two tweaking parameters, and a global gravity parameter that is specifically applied on each frame.

The first parameter is *constraint force mixing* or CFM. It is similar to the epsilon value in standard floating-point calculations to cover rounding errors. Increasing the CFM value can make the individual surfaces soft, allowing for singular configurations, compliant joints, and can improve numerical stability in places. The latter point is more appropriate when using the quick-step integrator that is discussed shortly. It is set up with

```
void dWorldSetCFM(dWorldID world, dReal cfm);
```

The default[2] is 1.0×10^{-5}.

The *error reduction parameter* (ERP) governs how much error correction is handled on each frame. This defaults to 0.2, but is typically in the 0.1 to 0.8 range. Whenever two joints are out of alignment, an additional force is applied to correct them. This value indicates what proportion of this force is used to bring them back to alignment. The appropriate function is

```
void dWorldSetERP(dWorldID world, dReal erp);
```

However, note that the documentation recommends against zero (because they would continually drift out of alignment) and one (because internal approximations would lead to over- or undershoot and still not be correct).

World Step and Quick Step

In order for the physics to work, an update must occur every frame to integrate all existing forces on the world objects. There are two ways of achieve this. The current favorite is quick step because it uses an iterative method of calculation that uses less memory ($O(m)$ compared to ($O(m^2)$)) and less processing time ($O(m*N)$ versus $O(m^3)$)). In both cases, m refers to the constraint rows, and N is the number of iterations processed.

```
void dWorldQuickStep(dWorldID world, dReal stepsize);
void dWorldSetQuickStepNumIterations(dWorldID world, int num);
```

Additionally, quick step will use less stack space, which is useful on consoles. The trade-off in all cases is that this method is slightly less accurate, although this can be improved by increasing the number of steps and increasing the CFM. This highlights the need, and handling, for tweakable parameters in a physics engine.

Memory Handling

The games market has certainly been considered here because it is all too easy to hook into the memory allocation routines used by ODE internally. To begin, all appropriate objects derive from a common dBase class with its own overloaded new operator. This in turn calls the global function dAlloc that is part of memory.c. It is that memory library that, although simple, provides a mechanism to register call-back functions and replace the standard library calls of malloc, realloc and free.

```
void dSetAllocHandler(dAllocFunction *fn);
void dSetReallocHandler(dReallocFunction *fn);
void dSetFreeHandler(dFreeFunction *fn);
```

All three use the standard prototypes. The only drawback is that you can't correctly determine __FILE__ or __LINE__ to help debug the allocations.

One potential case for performance improvements is the area where temporary joints are created as part of each collision. These joints exist for one frame to help offset the objects so they are no longer colliding. Each joint is allocated and deleted using malloc and free, and would benefit from a reusable memory pool.

Mathematics

With such a reliance on mathematics in a physics solver, it is perhaps inevitable that this can be the largest part to integrate. Whether the integration is necessary is an open question.

The math functionality is held in common.h, and exists to switch between the floating-point versions (such as sinf) of the standard functions, and their double precision counterparts (sin.); for example,

```
#define dSin(x) ((float)sinf(float(x)))
```

If you switch this to a platform-specific version for performance reasons, you may be able to improve the speed somewhat, but due to the complexity of the math in a typical physics engine, you could find it losing (even more) stability in the process.

When faced with a choice between slow accurate physics and an instable game, most producers would be happy to drop the physics component entirely. However, there is one compensatory approach: that is to *not* replace sin with mySin, for example, but with trueSin. In this way, you have two sine functions—one accurate and one fast—and both held in your common code so that the rest of the engine can use it and maintain numeric stability with the physics engine.

You can experiment with the code by switching each individual instance between the fast and accurate methods to see when, where, and if the physics breaks down. This is a slow and laborious process and may never yield appropriate results. Even then, it could still be less efficient than tweaking the CFM and ERP parameters.

In addition to ODE, the OPCODE library also uses these standard trigonometry functions, so they will have to be converted, too.

The ODE World

In ODE, the world is one über-entity with every physical object contained within it. However, there are several mechanisms to limit the amount of collision processing that needs to occur on each frame.

Spaces

This is a way of limiting the number of collision tests by encapsulating several pieces of geometry into one area or *space*. The space can then determine which geometries within it are likely to collide and process only those. It does this by arranging each piece of geometry inside the space to fit within a particular structure, such as a quadtree or an AABB tree. These, in turn, can be nested to create a hierarchical world. For example,

```
space1  = dHashSpaceCreate(0);       // parent
space2a = dHashSpaceCreate(space1); // child 1
space2b = dHashSpaceCreate(space1); // child 2
```

Category-Collide Bits

There is a special feature where each piece of object geometry can be assigned a category and a collision mask, such as

```
void dGeomSetCategoryBits(dGeomID id, unsigned long bits);
void dGeomSetCollideBits(dGeomID id, unsigned long bits);
```

The value of these bits is completely user-definable and used by the spaces mechanism to determine which pieces of geometry will interact.

Enabling-Disabling Objects

Last, but by no means least, there is the tried and tested method of just switching off every object that doesn't appear in the current location. This is an efficient method for games development because through a combination of our level designer and renderers culling routines you will usually know the player's current location and can isolate those objects very efficiently.

ODE Usage

By following the example GameObject structure given earlier, ODE can be integrated very easily. It follows the metaphors well, and adopts the logical split between object and geometry, too. This makes the conceptual structure very simple.

Every game object in ODE is termed a *body* and covers all the physical properties of your object such as position and velocity. This is incorporated into the abstraction properties class.

```
class ODE_Properties : public PhysicalProperties {
    dBodyID bodyID;
    dGeomID *geometryList;

    ODE_Properties(dWorldID worldID) {
        bodyID = dBodyCreate(worldID);
    }
    // etc ...
```

and an implementation of your handler would be,

```
void ODE_Properties::getPosition(sgxVector3 &position) {
    const dReal *pPos = dBodyGetPosition(bodyID);

    position.x = *pPos++;
    position.y = *pPos++;
    position.z = *pPos++;
}
```

You can mirror this with setPosition but, like all physics engines, this can cause instability since these objects are only intended to move under the auspices of the physics solver.

This is the same reason why you shouldn't need to call setVelocity *at any time other than the start of the game. If you want an object to move faster, it should do so because a force is being applied to it.*

You should also provide a back pointer from the body to your game object for when you're "stuck" inside the physics code and need to notify the game about an event, such as when two objects have collided. This is the popular concept of *userdata*, and there is a ready-made function for this:

```
dBodySetData(bodyID, (void*)this);
```

The physical shape of the object is held separately as an array of geometry primitives, and these can be populated with calls such as

```
void ODE_Properties::createComoBox(tREAL32 width, tREAL32 height,
        tREAL32 depth) {

    geometryList = new dGeomID[1];
    geometryList[0] = dCreateBox(space, width, height, depth);
}
```

COLLISION DETECTION ROUTINES

In many games, you don't need a full rigid body solution. Instead, you just need to determine whether the cylinder representing the player has collided with the box representing the car. The physical interaction between the two objects is of no concern—you know the player will stop and get in the car—you just want to know with what they've collided. For these types of game, you can probably avoid large, complex solutions like ODE. Much smaller libraries that solely determine these collisions are sufficient.

Because the focus of these libraries is to provide very specific functionality, their scope is limited and so only briefest technical details need be given.

OPCODE

In addition to providing ODE with its collision detection routines, OPCODE has also been used in the Tokamak physics code, along with the CrystalSpace 3D engine and Orion 3D among many others. Its pedigree is impressive, and if there is the intention to upgrade your development environment to full physics later (especially ODE), then there are few better choices than OPCODE.

Homepage: *http://www.codercorner.com/Opcode.htm*
License: Revised BSD (inferred)
Distribution: Source only
First release: October 2001
Current version: 1.3 (stable since June 1, 2003)
Platform(s): Windows and Linux, but is portable

Dependencies: None

Other resources: Author, and through the support groups of those using it, such as ODE and CrystalSpace

Supports: AABB (axis aligned bounding boxes), spheres, boxes, cylinders, arbitrary meshes, ray tests, and deformable meshes

The OPCODE documentation often compares itself to the RAPID (Robust and Accurate Polygon Interface Detection) library. While it is probably true that OPCODE is both faster and smaller, RAPID is written in a more straightforward manner that makes it more suitable for beginners wanting to learn the background and algorithms behind the routines. Also, RAPID uses `doubles`, instead of `floats`, which contributes to its performances problems. However, because RAPID is only free for noncommercial use, it cannot be detailed here. OPCODE is included on the CD-ROM.

ON THE CD

ColDet

This is a small collision library that can perform basic collision tests between individual objects as well as ray tests. The code appears quite old, however, and has not been updated recently.

Homepage: *http://photoneffect.com/coldet*

License: GNU LGPL 2.1 (Appendix C).

Distribution: Source only.

First release: 2000.

Current version: 1.1 (stable since 2000).

Platform(s): Windows and Linux, but is portable.

Dependencies: None.

Other resources: Mailing list and (low traffic) message board.

Supports: Triangles, spheres, boxes, segments, arbitrary meshes, and ray tests. It also has a timeout feature to limit the amount of processing.

Note: The matrices used are row major, with translations in the fourth row. This follows Direct3D. All matrices are affine 4×4.

OPAL

OPAL stands for the Open Physics Abstraction Layer and originally began as an abstraction layer for ODE. Its intention is to create a framework into which you can slot any compatible physics engine. At the time of writing only ODE is supported, although work is currently ongoing with the port of TrueAxis to OPAL, and both Novodex and Newton are planned in the future.

ON THE CD

In addition to the ODE engine, it also comes with exporter tools for Blender and 3dx max and is supplied on the CD-ROM.

> **Homepage:** *http://ox.slug.louisville.edu/~o0lozi01/opal_wiki/index.php/Main_Page*
>
> **License:** GNU LGPL (Appendix C) or BSD (Appendix D)
>
> **Distribution:** Source and binary
>
> **First release:** November 1, 2004
>
> **Current version:** 0.3.1 (stable since October 19, 2005)
>
> **Platform(s):** Windows, primarily, but can also work on Linux and Macintosh, and should be portable to the consoles
>
> **Dependencies:** An OPAL-compatible physics engine, such as ODE (supplied)
>
> **Other resources:** Wiki, forums, and IRC channel

Although OPAL is a well-thought-out abstraction layer for physics engines, it's unfortunate that only one engine has been successfully ported to the system. Fortunately, the chosen one is ODE, which makes it a worthwhile endeavor. Although many will not need another layer of indirection between their game and the physics code, the OPAL/ODE source can provide a fresh perspective on the API, helping the developer whenever problems arise.

OPAL can also be thought of as an insurance policy against ODE getting too bloated in the future, or as a future-proof upgrade path when and if better proprietary physics engines become available using the OPAL API.

OTHER SOLUTIONS

While there are no other similarly powered Open Source physics solutions to discuss, two alternate options may be available to you. However, neither is Open Source.

Tokamak

This proprietary solution exists only as Microsoft Windows binary and header files, enabling your code to only statically link to the library. It is, however, cost free and so will be of interest to many readers.

As a library, it supports all the usual features of joints, friction, and stacking, and includes its own collision detection routines. There is also available documentation for its integration into the Irrlicht engine, at *http://irrlicht.sourceforge.net/tut008b.html*. Only Microsoft Windows binaries (version 1.2.5) are currently available.

The license requires you to mention Tokamak in *all* materials. This puts it in line with the original BSD license and its "obnoxious BSD advertising clause." While this might appear only as an inconvenience, it does directly oppose the GPL and the work of the FSF. Consequently, Tokamak, like all other software under the original BSD license, is not compatible with the GNU GPL, or the GNU LGPL. Therefore, any usage of Tokamak precludes its ability to be integrated with any GPL or LGPL package. This includes, but is not limited to, SDL, CrystalSpace, and ClanLib.

It can be downloaded from *http://www.tokamakphysics.com*.

Newton Game Dynamics

This too is a proprietary solution. Its SDK can be downloaded for Windows, Linux, and the Macintosh. Again, this is available for free despite its license falling foul of the FSF due to an advertising clause. So, like Tokamak, it cannot be used with any GPL or LGPL code. Additionally, the license requires you to notify the company of any release made with the library.

Functionally, it contains everything you need from a physics engine: joints, friction, and simple out-of-the-box ragdoll handling. It also has a wiki and online forum.

It can be downloaded from *http://www.physicsengine.com*.

ENDNOTES

1. Although oft-quoted, this problem appears so rarely in well-designed systems it's surprising that it's still used as an rallying cry against multiple inheritance!
2. The double precision version of ODE has a default CFM of 1.0×10^{-10}.

8 Networking

In This Chapter

- Background to Networking
- SDL_net
- Torque Network Library
- OpenSSL
- Other Solutions

Of all the game libraries covered in this book, the networking libraries are probably the simplest to implement, abstract, and use. This is partially because the complexity of networking does not come from the abstraction, but from the implementation of the driver and game. In the first instance, the low-level driver code puts arbitrary data into network packets, places them onto the network cable, and checks for collisions and the packets' safe arrival at their destination[1]. To a certain extent, this process has already been abstracted by the sockets code library, network card drivers, and an implementation akin to the ISO seven-layer model[2].

The second part of networking complexity lies within the game itself: how it lets players create and join games, what the game does when it finds itself isolated on the network, how to maintain a fast ping time, and so on. None of these problems is solved by the introduction of middleware. However, it does facilitate a method whereby a connection can be made between two or more machines and messages exchanged between them. The focus will therefore be on how these libraries provide these services, and not on the underlying drivers. This breaks down into the basic areas of:

- Creating a connection
- Sending packets (to single, multiple, or groups of addresses)
- Blocking and nonblocking I/O
- Secure transmission
- Lobby services

BACKGROUND TO NETWORKING

There are many thousands of network specialists in the world today. Unfortunately, very few of them are developing games outside of the traditional networking strongholds of MMOGs. Therefore, the discussion of networking solutions, and your ability to make informed decisions about them, is difficult. To that end, we begin with a brief coverage of networking, sockets, and their role in online games.

Understanding Sockets

With every networking API taking its lead from *sockets*, it makes sense to understand its principles first.

Sockets provide a way for two processes to communicate. For machine A to talk to machine B, A must create a socket and *bind* it to a specific port on machine B. This port is determined by the application itself and can be any number from 49152 to 65535. Any value below 1024 is reserved for the typical, well-known system software, such as HTTP, FTP, or SSH, and those between 1024 and 49151 are registered ports and handled by the IANA. Games should not use any port classified as well known or registered (although some do). A complete list of these ports can be found at *http://www.iana.org/assignments/port-numbers*, along with the procedure for registering ports.

Once the port is bound, machine B must then agree to accept the connection, which it is not obliged to do. Machine B might have enough users already, or the sender's IP address could be banned. After agreeing that a connection is to be made, a second port is automatically allocated. This is used to transfer the data between the machines and will usually have little relevance to the incoming port number. This dual port arrangement allows many different computers to connect to machine B without having to share the port with those machines already connected and transferring data.

After this second port has been assigned (through a connection acceptance), the two computers can communicate through the bidirectional socket just created. Each can poll the socket for new messages and act accordingly.

If the connection is lost, or purposefully dropped, then the sockets on both sides of the network must be closed and deleted.

The Gaming Network

The ante for network games has been upped significantly in recent years. Not only have the games become bigger and more elaborate, but the user experience has improved, too. It is no longer enough to have separate batch files to run client or server games. Nor is it acceptable to ask users to find out their opponent machine's IP address and send it via an instant messaging system to their friends, so they can connect to a game. The code has to be smarter than that.

Local Network Games

The first experience of network gaming for many was on the office, or school, Local Area Network (LAN). Finding games running on a LAN is easy because there are a very limited number of machine addresses upon which players can reside. This range is determined by the subnet of the current machine and is usually derived from the IP address itself.

A local network, for example, will usually have addresses in the 10.x.x.x or 192.168.x.x range. This instantly tells you which addresses can be reasonably probed. In the case of your local host being 192.168.1.43, the subnet range extends from 192.168.1.1 to 192.168.1.254.

A machine may have two or more network cards, each with a different IP address, which can cause problems when trying to determine the appropriate IP of the local host.

Once the user has selected "Find Games," it is therefore simple enough to work through this list, creating and binding sockets to a predetermined game-specific port on each machine until a response is found.

Use a different game port for the query messages to the actual game because this can prevent the strange bugs that occur when a query message gets confused with game data.

Internet-Based Games

Obviously, the brute force method outlined for LAN games cannot work across the Internet. Instead, it is usual to have one or more central servers to which particular games can connect. These servers are stored by name in a configuration file that comes with the game, and resolved to IP addresses automatically by the system and the Internet at large. These servers are generally geographically distinct and are maintained and owned by the developers or, more usually, the publishers. This provides a common meeting point for all players of your game. It also means there's a limited number of IP address to which a connection is likely to be made.

Once a connection to the game server is made, it is up to the server to maintain the list of people who've connected and provide a pairing system for them. Again, a separate port should be used for this lobby system. And once the game players have configured their particular game, new sockets should be created that connect only their machines under the auspices of peer-to-peer networking, relieving the load from your server, and improving ping times for them.

SDL_NET

SDL has many supplementary components. This one provides a thin wrapper around the sockets library to provide networking. The functionality provided is minimal, but can support basic games using either TCP (guaranteed deliverable packets) or UDP (nonguaranteed) and has socket *sets* so that a game server can listen on multiple sockets at the same time. Parts of the API involve blocking I/O, which means that the function will not exit until the requested data has been found or an error or timeout has occurred. While not ideal, it only needs to be used when making the initial connection, but can be eradicated by running the networking code in a separate thread.

> **Homepage:** *http://www.libsdl.org/projects/SDL_net*
>
> **License:** GNU LGPL version 2.1 (Appendix C)
>
> **Distribution:** Source and binary
>
> **First release:** April 22, 2000
>
> **Current version:** 1.2.5 (stable since January 5, 2003)
>
> **Platform(s):** Extensive, including Windows, Linux, Macintosh, and PlayStation Linux
>
> **Dependencies:** SDL 1.2. GUIlib[3] to compile the example chat program
>
> **Other resources:** Various tutorials and examples on the Web

ON THE CD

For whatever faults may be laid at the door of SDL, one thing is truly certain—it has a user base. And a large one at that. This is one of the 137 libraries currently available for download from its site (or from the CD-ROM) and, like many of them, integrates very simply into the existing SDL installation because it reuses the macros and types of the base package. However, because very little of the original functionality is required, it is possible to integrate it into your game engine *without* occurring the overhead of SDL.

Integration

Like SDL_mixer, the binary installation of SDL_net involves copying the header file to c:\devlib\include (*not* c:\devlib\include\SDL because that is reserved for the main package itself), the library file into the lib directory, and the DLL to the Windows system folder. Those compiling the library manually can place this code directly into their game.

If you are compiling from source, you only need to include the source files,

```
SDLnet.c
SDLnetselect.c
SDLnetTCP.c
SDLnetUDP.c
```

plus their respective header files,

```
SDL_net.h
SDLnetsys.h
```

to integrate this directly into your code.

Windows users will need to include the wsock32.lib WinSock library. Other platforms will require linkage with their own sockets library.

If you wish to build SDL_net as a separate library, the archive is supplied with suitable makefiles and a project for Microsoft Developer Studio.

Integration Without SDL

Although it is rare to find an Open Source game that doesn't use SDL in some capacity, it is, nonetheless, a big overhead to endure for the sake of a networking library. If you truly have no other reason for including SDL in your game, then it is recommended you consider one of the alternate libraries covered here, paying particular attention to the networking components of the other all-encompassing libraries covered at the end of the chapter.

If you are adamant that SDL_net is right for your project, then what follows is a brief commentary as to the other integration steps necessary when SDL isn't present. In this case, we shall ignore the binary installations because you do not want the overhead of installing SDL.dll or SDL_net.dll, lest Windows spots the missing dependency and refuses to start the executable. This DLL adds around 232 KB to the total install size.

The first step in building SDL_net without SDL is to, er, install SDL! Or rather, the SDL headers must be available since these contain the type definitions and endian swapping macros you need. The latter are necessary because the network designers refused to suffer the byte ordering problems present in processors to affect data traveling across a network, so a standard order was decided upon—big endian. These macros are therefore necessary on approximately half the platforms to convert the processor endian into one suitable for network data. Because only macros and types are referenced from these header files, no additional code space is used, nor are any dependencies on SDL unwittingly made.

This is, curiously enough, very simple to do because there are only two dependencies on the main SDL package. The first is SDL_SetError. In the original package, this function would populate an SDL_error structure with the details of the error, and print the error message to stderr. This functionality can either be ignored by creating an empty function stub,

```
DECLSPEC void SDLCALL SDL_SetError(const char *fmt, ...)
{
}
```

or modified by passing control to any existing error trace facility. Because the variable arguments marked by the ellipses cannot be portably passed into another function, it is necessary to build the complete string inside SDL_SetError and use this resultant string directly. This uses the slightly more portable code,

```
#include <stdarg.h>

static char buffer[1024];

DECLSPEC void SDLCALL SDL_SetError(const char *fmt, ...)
{
    va_list va;

    va_start(va, fmt);
    vsprintf(buffer, fmt, va);
    va_end(va);

    sgxOutputTraceMessage(buffer);
}
```

This code is not totally ideal because va_list *is not completely portable, and there is no thread safety.*

The other issue that can affect you is due to SDL.h including SDL_main.h. This incorporates a macro to change main into SDL_main and is to facilitate a cross-platform entry point for the code. However, in doing so it can change the real `main` function into `SDL_main` and produce linker problems. This is easily solved by either not including `SDL.h` in the file containing your start-up code, or by prefixing your `main` function with,

```
#undef main
```

Usage

The basic initialization and closedown takes the pairing of

```
SDLNet_Init();
```

and,

```
SDLNet_Quit();
```

From here, the implementation differs depending whether your machine needs to accept connections from other users or not; that is, a peer-to-peer architecture, or all communications occur between your machine and a central server. This latter case is the familiar client-server architecture.

Preparing to Accept Connections

You begin by creating a socket for the server (i.e., us) by finding the local host.

```
#define GAME_PORT 54002

IPaddress serverAddress;
TCPsocket serverSocket;

SDLNet_ResolveHost(&serverAddress, NULL, GAME_PORT);
serverSocket = SDLNet_TCP_Open(&serverAddress);
```

CAUTION

We resolve the local host using the previous NULL parameter. When it has more than one network card, any of its IP addresses may be chosen. To specify a specific server address requires a platform-specific code. Alternatively, we may intelligently guess at any IP that begins 192 or 10, or ask the player to select from a list.

Once a valid socket is found, we can begin to listen for connections. We therefore prepare a list of sockets on which to listen,

```
socketset = SDLNet_AllocSocketSet(2);
SDLNet_TCP_AddSocket(socketset, serverSocket);
```

and call the, admittedly blocking, function,

```
SDLNet_CheckSockets(socketset, ~0);
```

Then, whenever a new player attempts to connect, we can validate them and accept their connection, creating the data transference socket as we do so. This clientSocket would also be added to the current list of players.

```
if (SDLNet_SocketReady(serverSocket)) {
    clientSocket = SDLNet_TCP_Accept(serverSocket);
    SDLNet_TCP_AddSocket(socketset, clientSocket);
}
```

There are additional functions, such as SDLNet_TCP_GetPeerAddress, to retrieve their IP address, which are often useful for debugging and can be found in the API reference.

The server is now ready. It only needs to poll the appropriate socket,

```
length = SDLNet_TCP_Recv(clientSocket, dataBuffer, 512);

if (length > 0) {
    // data has arrived
} else if (length < 0) {
    // error
}
```

to retrieve the last message. The function itself is not blocking, so it can be incorporated into a standard loop. However, if you are building an abstraction layer (or planning on moving to another API in the future), then it can be visionary to place the polling code in a separate thread and use callback functions attached to particular message types. These message types would, in fact, get manually encapsulated in the first byte(s) of the message.

Connecting to Another Machine

This is a much simpler process as you only need to know the server address, and you have a completed socket. This server address is determined by the lobby approach outlined earlier. That is, searching the local area network for anyone that responds on your port or by connecting to a known game server on the Internet.

```
SDLNet_ResolveHost(&serverAddress, szServerName, GAME_PORT);
serverSocket = SDLNet_TCP_Open(&serverAddress);
```

You can then send messages with merry abandonment using,

```
SDLNet_TCP_Send(serverSocket, (void *)pBuffer, bufferLength);
```

Using UDP

Generally, games will use UDP because of the faster throughput, and the fewer message stalls[4] that occur when using it. The UDP protocol only sends data, without first making the formal connection, as was set up earlier. This means that each UDP packet needs to be explicitly addressed before being sent. SDL_net provides a shortcut for this by allowing you to specify a channel and a binding between the UDP socket and the remote host/port pair to prevent the programming overhead, although the packet data sent is identical in either case.

Other Functionality

As far as out-of-the-box functionality is concerned, there isn't very much else. Any secure or encrypted data needs extra code, as does any lobby server, and sending the same data to multiple machines requires the loop iterators to be handled manually. Most of this functionality will need to be provided anyway because machine groups and lobbies are a game-specific problem. However, the lack of security can be a problem if you don't have any other way of authenticating users.

In its favor, however, SDL_net is a very compact library and can be made to work in minutes.

 There is also a Net2 library for SDL at http://gameprogrammer.com/net2/net2-0.html. *It sits on top of SDL_net and provides an event-driven approach to network traffic by running the network code on a separate thread.*

TORQUE NETWORK LIBRARY

The Torque Network Library (TNL) has found a home in the toolbox of many indie developers as it is probably the most powerful and featureful networking library available to the Open Source community. It is part of the larger Torque library created by GarageGames, but available under a separate, and multiple, licenses.

It is a C++ API that provides fast network message passing and control. It does this by using nonguaranteed UDP data packets that are then wrappered with error recovery and resend logic. Since this has been implemented within the library, you have more control over the error handling routines than you would have, had TCP been used directly. This provides TNL with one of its most powerful features—a variable level of data guarantee. It also provides the usual connection and transmission code, which includes inline data compression and aremote procedure call (RPC) framework that allows your game to communicate more efficiently with an online game server.

It is also available on the companion CD-ROM.

Homepage: *http://www.opentnl.org*

License: GNU GPL version 2 (indie and commercial licenses are also available for a fee)

Distribution: Source only

First release: March 20, 2004 (as Open Source)

Current version: 1.5.0 (stable since February 23, 2005)

Platform(s): Windows, Linux, Macintosh, Xbox, and PlayStation 2

Dependencies: None

Other resources: website with good documentation, mailing list, and forums

Integration

As with most cross-platform libraries, the first port of call is the abstraction code for bit-perfect types. With TNL, this is found in tnlTypes.h and is no different to the list of typedefs found in most libraries. It therefore needs a simple remap of your existing cross-platform types into the names used by TNL. This ensures you only need to change one types.hpp file when moving between platforms or compilers.

```
#include "sgx/core/types/types.hpp"

typedef tINT16  S16;    // let TNL use S16 internally
typedef tUINT16 U16;

// and so on...
```

This file also makes decisions concerning other core information, such as the endianness (defined by TNL_LITTLE_ENDIAN) and the supported compiler versions. These should also be wrapped using existing core properties.

Also, this file (curiously) contains math constants—such as pi—that are used in the BitStream code to transmit normalized vectors. While this code does no harm, it is rarely used because the calculations used to normalize vectors involve expensive square roots and arctangents that you would normally want to avoid. You can either transmit vectors using their individual components such as,

```
pStream->write(pPlayer->vOrientationNormal.x);
pStream->write(pPlayer->vOrientationNormal.y);
pStream->write(pPlayer->vOrientationNormal.z);
```

or as blocks of raw data using,

```
pStream->writeBits(sizeof(pPlayer->vOrientationNormal),
    &pPlayer->vOrientationNormal);
```

This makes two savings. Most obviously, it eliminates the mathematics involved in repeatedly recalculating a value you probably already have in your engine. Second, by sending raw binary data packets across the network, you eliminate the need for TNL to convert the component data elements into network (i.e., big) endian format.

Sending raw data is generally better in games development because you know the platform to which you're talking: PC games commonly play with PC games, and Xbox games talk directly to Xbox games. You do not need to be concerned that your game will suddenly begin talk to a PlayStation 2 and need to swap endian. Therefore, the conversion to (and from) network endian is redundant and can be ignored[5].

Console manufacturers have yet to sanction interplatform networking, so this is a safe assumption in the foreseeable future. If the circumstances change (or you're writing a game that works between WinTel and non-Intel Macintosh platforms) you should adopt a higher-level control structure where the sender knows it needs to convert the data for the receiver, and does so before entering the labyrinth of writeBits *or its associated methods.*

Integers can also be written using this method or make use of the templated wrapped version of

```
pStream->write(pPlayer->iScore);
```

that will invoke endian conversion if necessary. While there is no technical problem in mixing the methods you use to send data, you must *always* retrieve them in the same way to avoid unexpected endian swaps occurring.

In TNL, all endian conversion is done during the write phase of transmission. You should consistently adopt this approach.

You can extend the number of types that the template write works with by overloading the convertHostToLEndian function inside tnlEndian.h. This works well for small data types, but, because the function takes an input *value* as an argument—

and returns one as the result—means that a lot of needless copying takes place as arguments are passed onto, and off from, the stack. You could eliminate this by adopting

```
class DataToSend {

    tREAL32 x, y, z;

    virtual bool writeStream(BitStream *pStream) {
        bool result = true;

        result &= pStream->writeBits(sizeof(x), &x);
        result &= pStream->writeBits(sizeof(y), &y);
        result &= pStream->writeBits(sizeof(z), &z);

        return result;
    }
}
```

This solution scales better and endows you with the ability to switch endian inside your own writeStream function, if necessary.

File Handling

One of the easiest tasks in TNL is the elimination of the standard I/O library, as it is only used for retrieving seeds in the pseudo-random number generators (PRNGs) for the encryption portion of the API. Simply add,

```
#define NOFILE
```

to mycrypt_custom.h, or add

```
-DNOFILE
```

to the compile options, and the standard I/O will be removed.

However, this does not eliminate the ability to use the PRNG since there are platform-specific implementations within libtomcrpy/bits.c. The Microsoft Windows version, for example, uses the CryptAcquireContext function, while the PlayStation 2 uses the current state of 10 of its control registers.

Memory Allocation

Unfortunately, integrating your own cross-platform memory allocator will take more work. Despite having an XMALLOC macro in the crypto library, this is not used throughout the library, requiring a thorough global search-and-replace operation.

If you do replace the allocator, you may need to add one additional hook to handle in-place construction. This is a little-used undertaking of the new operator in C++ of the form

```
ClassType var = new(ptr) ClassType;
```

and will result in a newly constructed object whose address is guaranteed to be that of the provided pointer, ptr. This can save a lot of fragmentation and makes memory pools a possibility. Not only that, but because it incorporates the new operator, the class instance will have been instantiated correctly.

The suggested addition here is to amend the constructInPlace method,

```
template <class T>
inline T* constructInPlace(T* p)
{
    return new(p) T;
}
```

to update the memory manager, indicating that a different object is now occupying this memory location. For example,

```
SGX_ALLOC_INPLACE(p, __FILE__, __LINE__);
```

This functionality is mostly used within TNL's own vector class. Because the methods of this and the traditionally STL::vector classes are inline, no memory is saved by coalescing them.

Finally, remember that for every new, there is a delete, and destructInPlace should be adapted accordingly.

Error Handling

Despite the library's C++ architecture, no exceptions are used within it. This is a good thing, since exceptions cause a noticeable speed hit and around a 10 percent increase in code size due to the automatic unwinding code for the stack. Instead, the programmer needs to be continuously vigilant about the return codes, especially on functions such as BitStream::write since the upper limit for UDP packets can be reached quite quickly and no get-out clause is provided.

Usage

TNL has two main mechanisms for transmitting data across the network. The first is through a socket, where the data is formatted into a raw block, wrapped with packet headers, sent across the network, and unpacked by the receiver. This is how

SDL_net and most sockets-based networking works. The second involves RPCs where the packing and unpacking of the data is handled transparently to the game, and the data is only seen as parameters to a specially constructed function, which is also indicated in the RPC header. Both are briefly covered.

Socket Control

Creating a connection for either the client or server is a simple process that is analogous to the other networking libraries covered here. The main difference, however, is that the nomenclature does not reference or acknowledge its sockets heritage, despite following the same binding process. Additionally, its C++ architecture is prevalent throughout, meaning you will need to create a fairly large C wrapper if C++ is not to your liking.

The Server

This is always the easiest since you need only to create an interface that is bound to the address of the current machine.

```
Address bindAddress(IPProtocol, Address::Localhost, GAME_PORT);
NetworkInterface = new NetInterface(bindAddress);
```

Then, because this is a server, you need to allow incoming connections,

```
networkInterface->setAllowsConnections(true);
```

The interface is now ready to accept and process handshaking messages (using the loop you discover shortly). These messages appear in the form of a call made to the derived `processPacket` method, which means you can ban a user's IP by looking at the source address inside this method and refusing to pass the data to the parent class. This feature also allows you to add key exchange and security to the communication chain at this low level.

The Client

The client is built in a similarly simple manner. This uses the same structure, although binds its connection to any available port.

```
Address bindAddress(IPProtocol, Address::Any, 0);
```

From here, the address is bound to a connection in the usual way,

```
networkInterface = new NetInterface(bindAddress);
```

You may also need to include

```
networkInterface->setAllowsConnections(true);
```

for those clients that allow connections from other machines, as is the case in a peer-to-peer architecture.

It's then just a matter of connecting this interface to that of the server. Having previously deduced the server's address and port from your lobby service, you can therefore affect

```
Address serverAddress("ip:192.168.1.100:54002");
```

This uses the standard trio of protocol, address, and port, which can also be stored in an IPAddress class for housekeeping purposes. Note that because the IPAddress class has already nailed its protocol preferences to the mast, the first parameter (ip) is omitted. Once the interface has been created and bound to the server's port with

```
networkInterface = new NetInterface(serverAddress);
```

you can then create a connection:

```
OurGameEventConnection *gameConnection = new OurGameEventConnection;
gameConnection->connect(networkInterface, serverAddress);
```

This involves a special class that derives from EventConnection, which traditionally handles all message posting and returns notify messages to you if packets are dropped (i.e., lost) in transit. In many examples, OurGameEventConnection is derived from the GhostConnection class to include the functionality detailed later.

```
class OurGameEventConnection : public EventConnection {
   typedef EventConnection Parent;

public:
   TNL_DECLARE_NETCONNECTION(OurGameEventConnection);
   // Custom handlers go here
};
```

The uppercase symbol in the pervious code references a macro that declares suitable variables for the class. The implementation requires a similar construct,

```
TNL_IMPLEMENT_NETCONNECTION(OurGameEventConnection, NetClassGroupGame,
true);
```

The base classes give us access to the utility functions such as `packetReceived` and `packetDropped` that are virtual functions, and are called automatically. It also includes the method by which you can send data through the connection to the server. For example,

```
U8 scorePacketType = FirstValidInfoPacketId + 12;

pNotify = new PacketNotify; // generally unused

pStream = new BitStream;   // this uses an automatically resizing buffer
pStream->write(scorePacketType); // so the server knows how to
interpret it
pStream->write(pPlayer->iScore);

gameConnection->writePacket(pStream, pNotify);
```

Regardless of whether the machine is running the client or the server, both must poll for messages using the same familiar code,

```
networkInterface->checkIncomingPackets();
networkInterface->processConnections();
```

To handle these packets, the interface (which exists in the network interface and is therefore common between client and server) examines the packet header and determines if the message is one that controls the internal system (such as `ConnectRequest`, `Disconnect`, or `ConnectChallengeResponse`), or intended for the user. Any user packets are passed to the virtual function,

```
void
handleInfoPacket(const Address &address, U8 packetType, BitStream
*stream)
{
}
```

for processing. Consequently, it is usual to derive your own `GameNetworkInterface` class for this.

One of the overriding benefits of TNL is that it abstracts many of the housekeeping tasks, such as lost connections, away from the user, and uses a number of class methods as callback functions to indicate these conditions cleanly to the user.

TIP

GhostConnection

One strength of the OpenTNL architecture is the ability to derive classes that extend the basic connection functionality. Ghosting is one such example. This allows the game to maintain a set of objects on each side of the connection and transmit only the changes between them. Each of these objects must be specially formatted to conform to a NetObject, and exist within a *scope*. Whenever a GhostConnection sends a packet, any changes recently made to the NetObjects (that are also in scope) are sent to the appropriate clients using a series of masks and dirty flags. The documentation, including the page *http://opentnl.sourceforge.net/doxytree/classTNL_1_1Ghost Connection.html*, covers this well.

Remote Procedure Calls

RPCs have been used in networking for decades, with the method being first described in RFC 707 in 1976. They are used in a number of situations where one computer wishes to call a function on another computer, without a large overhead. In games, they are often used to transmit small pieces of connected information between two computers, since it is more natural to send the server a call such as,

```
setPlayerPos(x,y,z);
```

than it would be to build, and unbuild, a data packet with the same information.

In OpenTNL, RPCs are very easy to set up and use as each RPC function is declared inside an existing connection class, such as

```
class GameConnection : public TNL::GhostConnection { ... }
```

and formally implemented with

```
TNL_IMPLEMENT_NETCONNECTION(GameConnection, TNL::NetClassGroupGame,
true);
```

You then need to attach each specifically named RPC function to the class, describing its formal parameter list. Since both sender and receiver must agree on these arguments, they are defined ahead of time and cannot change between versions. If, after release, an RPC function needs augmenting to support new features you must either have already built the capability into the arguments (by making one of them accept a process string, for example), or replace the RPC with a newly named or versioned function. Because games are likely to use RPCs to query existing games on the local network, this rule needs to be strictly enforced to prevent mismatched data being passed to an RPC function and causing errors. An RPC function can additionally be supplied with a versioning number to assist with this handling.

Unlike normal function calls, an RPC cannot return data. However, you can mimic this feature by creating an additional RPC function that is only used to return results from a particular function.

Each RPC function is defined with a macro called `TNL_IMPLEMENT_RPC`. This hides the complexity of the newly created class that receives network events.

```
TNL_IMPLEMENT_RPC(GameConnection, rpcSetPlayerPos,
    (TNL::F32 x, TNL::F32 y),     // formal arguments
    (x, y),                        // argument names
    TNL::NetClassGroupGameMask,    // group mask
    TNL::RPCGuaranteedOrdered,     // the guarantee of delivery
    TNL::RPCDirClientToServer,     // direction of data travel
    0                              // version number of the RPC call
    )
{
    // Code follows here...
}
```

To invoke this remote function, the client needs only to send a message, such as

```
pNetwork->pConnectionToServer->rpcSetPlayerPos(x, y);
```

for the data to be sent. Note that this requires that both server and client code declare the RPC function. This prototype must be added with the `TNL_DECLARE_RPC` macro, like this,

```
TNL_DECLARE_RPC(rpcSetPlayerPos, (TNL::F32 x, TNL::F32 y));
```

Finally, note that it is impossible to send pointers to data across the network; this includes strings. However, structures can be sent via a bit-by-bit copy. This permits the old C trick of returning a string from a function, by incorporating an array inside a structure and returning an instance of the encompassing structure.

```
struct CheekyString {
    char data[256];
}
```

This technique also works in TNL, provided you override the necessary functions for `read` and `write`. However, if you intend to send actual strings, TNL adopts a more optimal solution of string tables, where each string is assigned an ID and it is the ID that is sent instead of the string.

License

One point to consider when using the TNL is that because it is sold under multiple licenses, any submissions you make to the project, regarding bugs or features, must be available under all three licenses. GarageGames will not accept changes made without a joint copyright agreement (JCA) between both parties. So, although you will be helping your fellow Open Source developers, you will also be effectively working for free on the project. This is not generally a problem because the value you get from Open Source exceeds the few hours work you might put in to a single bug, but the more zealous in the community would attempt to discourage submissions because of this.

However, because it is available under the GPL license, any changes you make must be given back *to the GPL version*. No one can *make* you sign a JCA or include your change in either of the proprietary versions without permission. Unless your change was a bug fix, or some other uncopyrightable change, you are legally obliged to release it only to the GPL version. If your change is wanted in the proprietary version, and no agreement can be reached, the GPL version with your changes will indicate a fork in the project. But unless your change was significant it is likely to be the first and last release of that fork, and the maintainers of the TNL version will continue happily without it.

The Torque Gaming Engine

Because TNL is part of the larger Torque Gaming Engine (TGE), it makes business sense for GarageGames to tempt you into adopting the rest of its engine. However, it has no Open Source version of TGE, and there are specific clauses in the indie and commercial licenses where, for example, it gets all electronic publishing rights to your game.

If you decide to adopt TGE, however, remember that you will need to drop all GPL components from your game because they are not compatible with the licenses on offer for the Torque Gaming Engine. Any code combined with GPL code must become GPL'd itself. LGPL licenses are also incompatible since you cannot dynamically link your game to the TGE *and* LGPL libraries. However, it might be possible to talk directly to the copyright holders (GarageGames) and negotiate a situation where your game is compiled in with TGE and released as a single object file that dynamically links to your die-hard LGPL libraries[6].

BSD- and X11-licensed code can be used as normal with TGE code.

These issues apply only to TGE, not OpenTNL.

OPENSSL

This is probably the most heavyweight package in the book. It is a cross-platform, robust, and commercial-grade implementation of the secure sockets layer (SSL v2/v3). This means it can communicate safely with remote servers (such as https) to diminish the users' fear that their personal details are available to the prying eyes of a cracker.

The encryption works by exchanging public and private keys through means of signed certificates that validates the site issuing the certificate as legitimate. It is normally used on e-commerce sites when transferring personal account details, but could equally be used for the communications between the game and a server when handling player statistics and login details[7].

However, it should *not* be used to encode general-purpose game data (such as character positions) because strong encryption such as this is slow and you would suffer unacceptable latency.

Homepage: *http://www.openssl.org*

License: Custom (pre-1999 BSD)

Distribution: Source and binary (for Windows only)

First release: December 12, 1995 (as SSLeay, version 0.5.0)

Current version: 0.9.8a (stable since October 11, 2005)

Platform(s): Wide, including Windows, Linux, and Macintosh

Dependencies: Perl for the initial configuration process

Other resources: Various examples, tests, and demos on the Web; most are Unix-oriented

ON THE CD

The configuration and build process for *OpenSSL* is complex, so if you want only to experiment with it then it is suggested you make use of the pre-built version referenced from *http://www.slproweb.com/products/Win32OpenSSL.html* or from the CD-ROM. Because this software comes under the banner of strong encryption, there may be issues in regard to your geographic location that prevent you from using this library. These issues are covered more fully later during the discussion on the OpenSSL license. If these binaries do contravene your local laws, you have no choice but to compile it yourself with some more compliant options.

Integration

Adding the libraries and header files to your system is simple enough, although at nearly 2 MB (for the Windows version), you might want to spend time removing the unused encryption algorithms when porting to a console. Normally, the include files, such as `ssl.h`, would be placed directly into `c:\devlib\include` since they are always referred to as

```
#include <ssl.h>
```

However, the number of header files (there are 70 in the Win32 version) introduces unwarranted clutter, and so an `openssl` subdirectory is recommended and the *additional include directories* list amended.

The SSL process itself is relatively complex and beyond the scope of this book. However, the high-level principle works by creating a context,

```
SSL_CTX *pContext = SSL_CTX_new();
SSL_CTX_use_RSAPrivateKey_file(pContext, KEYF, SSL_FILETYPE_PEM);
```

and an SSL handler,

```
SSL *pSSL = SSL_new(pContext);
```

This will be used as a receptacle for all messages being sent across the network. Any traffic sent into, or out of, the SSL connection (through `pSSL`) is decrypted or encrypted before being passed to the user's program. All that is then necessary is to tie this encryption pipeline into the network stream. This is done by creating a standard socket,

```
clientSocket = socket(PF_INET, SOCK_STREAM, 0);
// The usual socket initialization goes here...
clientConnection = accept(clientSocket, 0, 0);
```

and passing this socket onto the SSL handler.

```
SSL_set_fd(pSSL, clientConnection);
SSL_accept(pSSL);
```

The data is then read and written using the functions `SSL_read` and `SSL_write` that transparently decrypt and encrypt the data. Once everything has been transferred, all memory is released with

```
SSL_free(pSSL);
SSL_CTX_free(pContext);
```

The additional steps of certificate signing and validation can be found in the OpenSSL API reference.

Integrating SSL with Other Libraries

Because SDL_net, for example, does not provide a sockets file descriptor (`client Connection` in the previous example) you need to extract one. This can be done by creating an access function to the `TCPsocket` data structure. For example,

```
void SDLNet_ConnectSSL(TCPsocket server, SSL *pSSL)
{
    SSL_set_fd(server->channel, pSSL);
}
```

Technically speaking, OpenSSL cannot be combined with GNU LGPL code as noted in the licenses section below; and SDL_net is LGPL.

The Torque Network Library, by contrast, is able to apply its own encryption algorithms to data in its UDP packets, making this step unnecessary.

Finally, there is an example of OpenSSL being integrated into Windows using asynchronous control at *http://www.jetbyte.com/portfolio-showarticle.asp? articleId=48&catId=1&subcatId=2* with an archive of source at *http://www. jetbyte.com/zips/SSLAsyncClient.zip*.

Licenses and Patents

This is the most painful legal minefield you should have to walk.

About the Licensing

The OpenSSL license is a combination of the SSLeay license from which the project was derived, and its own custom license on top of that. Although the preamble states they are based around the BSD license, the specific version on which they were based was the pre-1999 version with the "obnoxious advertising clause," and not the later, more utopian version. This causes the problems highlighted in Chapter 2, "License Commentaries," because Clause 3 (in both license parts) includes an advertising clause that makes it incompatible with both the GPL and LGPL licenses, since adding attributions on advertising is considered "a further restriction."

As an interesting twist, however, it is possible that you can include OpenSSL in any games you create for the Linux and BSD platforms—but none of the others! This is because the GPL doesn't prevent you from linking into code that comes with the operating system, and OpenSSL is now part of most Linux distributions, meaning it's allowable to link to it without falling foul of the GPL.

Because your games are more likely to sell, and be sold, on more non-Linux platforms, an alternative encryption solution should be found if you also intend to use GPL code.

The text for both parts of the license are included here for reference.

The OpenSSL License

Copyright (c) 1998-2005 The OpenSSL Project. All rights reserved.

1. Redistribution and use in source and binary forms, with or without modification, are permitted provided that the following conditions are met: notice, this list of conditions and the following disclaimer.

2. Redistributions in binary form must reproduce the above copyright notice, this list of conditions and the following disclaimer in the documentation and/or other materials provided with the distribution.

3. All advertising materials mentioning features or use of this software must display the following acknowledgment: "This product includes software developed by the OpenSSL Project for use in the OpenSSL Toolkit. (*http://www.openssl.org/*)"

4. The names "OpenSSL Toolkit" and "OpenSSL Project" must not be used to endorse or promote products derived from this software without prior written permission. For written permission, please contact *openssl-core@openssl.org*.

5. Products derived from this software may not be called "OpenSSL" nor may "OpenSSL" appear in their names without prior written permission of the OpenSSL Project.

6. Redistributions of any form whatsoever must retain the following acknowledgment: "This product includes software developed by the OpenSSL Project for use in the OpenSSL Toolkit (*http://www.openssl.org/*)"

THIS SOFTWARE IS PROVIDED BY THE OpenSSL PROJECT "AS IS" AND ANY EXPRESSED OR IMPLIED WARRANTIES, INCLUDING, BUT NOT LIMITED TO, THE IMPLIED WARRANTIES OF MERCHANTABILITY AND FITNESS FOR A PARTICULAR PURPOSE ARE DISCLAIMED. IN NO EVENT SHALL THE OpenSSL PROJECT OR ITS CONTRIBUTORS BE LIABLE FOR ANY DIRECT, INDIRECT, INCIDENTAL, SPECIAL, EXEMPLARY, OR CONSEQUENTIAL DAMAGES (INCLUDING, BUT NOT LIMITED TO, PROCUREMENT OF SUBSTITUTE GOODS OR SERVICES; LOSS OF USE, DATA, OR PROFITS; OR BUSINESS INTERRUPTION) HOWEVER CAUSED AND ON ANY THEORY OF LIABILITY, WHETHER IN CONTRACT, STRICT LIABILITY, OR TORT (INCLUDING NEGLIGENCE OR OTHERWISE) ARISING IN ANY WAY OUT OF THE USE OF THIS SOFTWARE, EVEN IF ADVISED OF THE POSSIBILITY OF SUCH DAMAGE.

This product includes cryptographic software written by Eric Young (*eay@cryptsoft.com*). This product includes software written by Tim Hudson (*tjh@cryptsoft.com*).

The SSLeay License

Copyright (C) 1995-1998 Eric Young (*eay@cryptsoft.com*)

This package is an SSL implementation written by Eric Young (*eay@cryptsoft. com*).

The implementation was written so as to conform with Netscapes SSL.

This library is free for commercial and non-commercial use as long as the following conditions are aheared to. The following conditions apply to all code found in this distribution, be it the RC4, RSA, lhash, DES, etc., code; not just the SSL code. The SSL documentation included with this distribution is covered by the same copyright terms except that the holder is Tim Hudson (*tjh@cryptsoft.com*).

Copyright remains Eric Young's, and as such any Copyright notices in the code are not to be removed. If this package is used in a product, Eric Young should be given attribution as the author of the parts of the library used.

This can be in the form of a textual message at program startup or in documentation (online or textual) provided with the package.

Redistribution and use in source and binary forms, with or without modification, are permitted provided that the following conditions are met:

1. Redistributions of source code must retain the copyright notice, this list of conditions and the following disclaimer.

2. Redistributions in binary form must reproduce the above copyright notice, this list of conditions and the following disclaimer in the documentation and/or other materials provided with the distribution.

3. All advertising materials mentioning features or use of this software must display the following acknowledgement:

"This product includes cryptographic software written by Eric Young (*eay@cryptsoft.com*)"

The word cryptographic' can be left out if the routines from the library being used are not cryptographic related :-).

4. If you include any Windows specific code (or a derivative thereof) from the apps directory (application code) you must include an acknowledgement: "This product includes software written by Tim Hudson (*tjh@cryptsoft.com*)"

THIS SOFTWARE IS PROVIDED BY ERIC YOUNG ``AS IS'' AND ANY EXPRESS OR IMPLIED WARRANTIES, INCLUDING, BUT NOT LIMITED TO, THE IMPLIED WARRANTIES OF MERCHANTABILITY AND FITNESS FOR A PARTICULAR PURPOSE ARE DISCLAIMED. IN NO EVENT SHALL THE AUTHOR OR CONTRIBUTORS BE LIABLE FOR ANY DIRECT, INDIRECT, INCIDENTAL, SPECIAL, EXEMPLARY, OR CONSEQUENTIAL DAMAGES (INCLUDING, BUT NOT LIMITED TO, PROCUREMENT OF SUBSTITUTE GOODS OR SERVICES; LOSS OF USE, DATA, OR PROFITS; OR BUSINESS INTERRUPTION) HOWEVER CAUSED AND ON ANY THEORY OF LIABILITY, WHETHER IN CONTRACT, STRICT LIABILITY, OR TORT (INCLUDING NEGLIGENCE OR OTHERWISE) ARISING IN ANY WAY OUT OF THE USE OF

THIS SOFTWARE, EVEN IF ADVISED OF THE POSSIBILITY OF SUCH DAMAGE.

The licence and distribution terms for any publically available version or derivative of this code cannot be changed. i.e. this code cannot simply be copied and put under another distribution licence [including the GNU Public Licence.]

About Patents

Depending on which encryption algorithms you choose to include, there may be no patent problems at all. The documentation is very good in this sense, as it tells you straight away that:

- There might be patenting problems.
- It is your responsibility to solve them.
- These are the algorithms that can cause the problems.
  Those algorithms being:
    - RC5, held by RSA Security, *http://www.rsasecurity.com*
    - RC4, held by RSA Security, *http://www.rsasecurity.com*
    - IDEA, held by Ascom[8], *http://www.ascom.ch*
    - MDC2, held by IBM, *http://www.ibm.com*

If you are unwilling or unable to purchase rights to these patents, you must use OpenSSL without them. This is simply achieved by using the configure line,

```
perl Configure VC-WIN32 no-rc5 no-rc4 no-idea no-mdc2
```

and then recompiling the package.

If you have been using a precompiled binary, then check its documentation to determine whether these algorithms have been included.

OTHER SOLUTIONS

Since the abstraction layer provided by these components is generally very thin, it is perhaps surprising that any Open Source projects exist at all. The underlying connection and communications protocol in most cases is sockets, and is available on almost every platform with an RJ45 connection.

Having this abstraction does provide benefits, however. First, it saves you from having to redesign the API to abstract whatever minor differences may exist between platforms. Because API design is usually the difficult part, this is to be welcomed. It even allows you to use the architecture as a base for your own networking library if you decide to roll your own implementation.

Second, by highlighting the simplicity of sockets, and being able to read the code (through the benefit of it being Open Source) allows you to learn involved sockets code much more quickly since you have a fully working example with all the error codes encapsulated into a simple TRUE/FALSE return value.

Finally, it benefits you because network code is often included as part of other libraries because it is easy to do so. This means you can save integration time, because it's likely your existing graphics library (for example) will already contain usable network code.

In practice, there is very little difference in performance or handling of the network code between APIs, so the choice will often revolve around which one integrates well with your naming convention, type definitions, or engine. For this reason, SDL_net has a large following because, although SDL has no real 3D component to speak of, the numerous other modules (for GUI, sound, fonts, and movies) are almost guaranteed to work (since they have generally been developed in the same environment as your SDL engine code), and so are a good choice for the developer.

A list of some of these other networking libraries follow.

Pegasus Network Library

ON THE CD

This is part of Plib, Steve's Portable Game Library, covered in Chapter 10, "Utility Libraries," and available on the CD-ROM. It provides the basic connection and transmission code, relying on the underlying sockets' implementation from the operating system. Plib uses low-level functions akin to SDL_net, but has a more C++-centric approach to API design. So, after initializing the network code with

```
netInit(&argc, argv);  // these can be NULL
```

it is usual to create a class that connects to the server,

```
class GameClient : public netBufferChannel
{
   GameClient(const sgxString &serverName) {
      open();
      connect(serverName.c_str(), GAME_PORT);
   }
}
```

This is then used to retrieve all incoming messages through the event-driven method

```
virtual void handleBufferRead(netBuffer& buffer) {
   char *pData = buffer.getData();
   // process pData
}
```

This works naturally because the `netBufferChannel` class has a base class of `netSocket`, and works identically to an explicit creation of

```
netSocket *pSocket = new netSocket();

  pSocket->open(false);
  pSocket->bind(serverName, GAME_PORT);
```

clanNetwork

ON THE CD

Also featured in Chapter 10 (and on the CD-ROM), this is part of the ClanLib suite and provides the rest of the engine with a client-server architecture. While this has adopted a nice clean C++ interface, its method of passing messages to the game relies heavily on the slots metaphor used throughout the rest of ClanLib and is therefore perfect for use within the library—but very difficult to make effective use of outside it. The initialization and use, however, are very easy to follow, and employ the C++ style used in the previously covered Plib examples.

```
CL_SetupCore::init();
CL_SetupNetwork::init();

CL_Socket *pClient = new CL_Socket(CL_Socket::tcp);
CL_IPAddress *pIPAddress = new CL_IPAddress(szServerName, GAME_PORT);

client->connect(*pIPAddress);
```

To handle the incoming messages you need to register a slot for the current class,

```
CL_Slot readClient = pClient->sig_read_triggered().
   connect(this, &readCallback);
```

This then requires the callback function to query the data in the received buffer, and process it with

```
receivedBytes = pClient->recv(buffer, sizeof(buffer));
```

This slot mechanism is also used to great aplomb because network dropouts can be detected, and the handling function called automatically, by simply registering your interest in the message.

```
CL_Slot remoteDisconnect = pClient->sig_disconnected().
   connect(this, &disconnectCallback);
```

ENDNOTES

1. If you already know about networking, you'll know that UDP packets do not check for safe arrival, but this is meant as an example!
2. Again, if you're an networking expert you'll know that no one has truly implemented the seven layer model, but we're teaching theory here!
3. *http://www.libsdl.org/projects/GUIlib/index.html*
4. If a TCP/IP message is not acknowledged to have arrived, the sender will not send another packet until the original message has been re-sent and acknowledged. This can lead to a backlog of messages.
5. Naturally, the data swapping has a bigger processing hit on little endian machines (such as the PC and Xbox) over big endian (Xbox 360 and PlayStation 2) because the endian swapping operation can be quite expensive. This is more true on floating point numbers because it additionally requires a "float to integer" cast on the sending side, and an "integer to float" process on the receiver.
6. It can been suggested on the forums (at *http://www.garagegames.com/mg/forums/result.thread.php?qt=1687*) that referencing TGE functions in public is acceptable, provided the underlying source code isn't, so the possibilities bode well.
7. Although many would consider this overkill.
8. But only in the countries of Austria, France, Germany, Italy, Japan, the Netherlands, Spain, Sweden, Switzerland, UK and the USA, it seems.

9 Scripting Engines

THE ORIGINS OF SCRIPTING

Scripting libraries are a recent addition to the game developer's arsenal. Most puzzle, platform, and retro games have never seen a need for them. The game is the engine. The engine is the game. And the gameplay is inherent in, or emergent from, the behavior of the engine. If you were writing a *Tetris* clone, for example, then you'd have no need for scripting because once the blocking falling code was written, the gameplay would be complete.

With the advent of mission-based games and the addition of levels where new intricacies were added or set pieces introduced, specific code was needed to implement them. The turnaround cost of hard code became prohibitive, and led to an increase in memory usage. Consequently, developers turned to scripting languages.

ROLLING YOUR OWN

Let us begin by saying that this is a case for the prosecution! There are very few good reasons for writing your own, particularly when several Open Source languages exist and have made their codes available to all. So, what are the problems?

First, the skill required to design a *good* language and maintain an efficient implementation of it, exceeds most developers. Those that are capable are better placed to work on more important areas of the game.

Another problem is the reliance on a single source of information—namely, the original programmer. By adopting an Open Source scripting language, such as Lua, you have access to magazine articles, websites, and forums to ask questions about the language and its use. This limits the questions asked of the leads to game-specific problems that only they can answer.

The usual defense for internal scripting engines is that it allows for better integration into the existing game engine. This is a sign of premature optimization, since all script code that exists outside of the executable will need interpreting at some level, and a layer of bridge code that transitions into the game engine. This is the standard three-layer model of scripting, as shown in Figure 9.1.

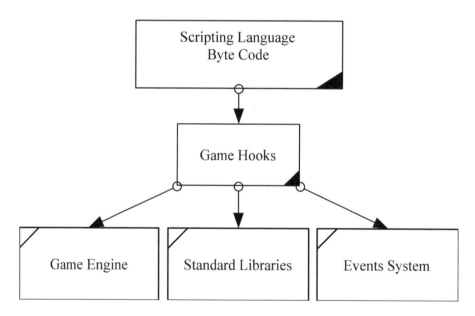

FIGURE 9.1   Three layers of scripting.

Regardless of which scripting engine you choose, you will always need the hooks into the game engine and logic. If you are currently unsure of which language you will employ, they should be written as two sublayers: script-to-hook and hook-to-engine. This will ensure that only half the effort is wasted if you ever change the scripting language and you keep a single point of access to the engine code.

The implementation is split into two, as the first stage of the process will assign a particular callback to a symbol within the script, and implemented like this:

```
CScriptingEngine.Assign("move_character", fn_move_character);
```

Notice that the callback itself forms a small layer of indirection between script and engine so that various design patterns, like singletons, can be used within any of the scripting engines.

```
void fn_move_character(int param)
{
    CScriptingHooks.MoveCharacter(param);
}
```

By adopting this pattern, different scripting engines can be plugged into the CScriptingEngine class to maximize code reuse if you ever need to change.

LUA

ON THE CD

For the bilingual among you, Lua (pronounced LOO-ah) means "moon" in Portuguese. It is a procedural scripting language developed by the Computer Graphics Technology Group (Tecgraf) at the Pontifical Catholic University of Rio de Janeiro in Brazil (PCU-Rio) and included on the companion CD-ROM.

It provides very basic language mechanics with a view that these semantics can be extended in various ways to enrich the use of the language without increasing its raw bulk. Consequently, it can implement classes and inheritance, despite none of them existing explicitly in the language. This enables the memory footprint of Lua to be incredibly small—less than 120 KB for the Windows version. Additionally, it is very portable as it is written in a common subset of both C++ and ANSI C.

Homepage: *http://www.lua.org*

License (version 5) MIT (Appendix E).

License (version 4 and previous): Lua's own (akin to zlib).

Distribution: Source only.

First release: July 8, 1994.

Current version: 5.0.2 (stable since March 17, 2004).

Platform(s): All known, with little to no tweaking.

Dependencies: None.

Other resources: Lua has a very good online presence with documentation covering both the workings of the interpreter and the language itself. There are also books and articles including *Programming in Lua* by Roberto Ierusalimschy and *Game Development With LUA* by Paul Schuytema and Mark Manyen.

Around Lua

You can draw a ring around the concepts of Lua to encompass all three of its basic parts. The first is a parser and compiler that turns ASCII Lua source code into a compact byte code that is executed by the second part: the interpreter. This provides a minimal language subset to perform all the basic tasks of the language, such as loops, function calls, and variable handling. To support this, a number of extensions can be added to tie Lua into hard code that runs natively on the machine. There are several supplied extensions, and it is easy to add your own. For this reason, Lua is sometimes known as an Extensible Extension Language.

The code that handles the environment is delineated in similarly neat fashion, and sections off main code, library code, and standard header files. The code is cleanly modular, so it is only necessary to include those files necessary for the functionality you require. To demonstrate this, the default Lua package comes with lua (a standalone Lua code interpreter) and luac (a compiler). The latter outputs binary byte code that can be loaded and processed directly by the interpreter if you do not wish to make your Lua source code available within the game.

Internally, all Lua code works within a *state*. This state contains all the code and data necessary for the program. You begin by creating a state, into which the Lua source code is loaded. All execution then takes place within this state. This initialization process is simply

```
m_LState = lua_open();
```

To use the extensions, they too must be loaded into this state. So, to load the base library you use

```
luaopen_base(m_Lstate);
lua_settop(m_LState, 0);
```

The second function is used to discard the result of the library load function.

Throughout the examples here, the state variable is given as m_LState *instead of the more usual* L, *which appears throughout the Lua code, for clarity.*

Compatibility Notes

Although the current version of Lua (5.0.2) has been available for some time, there is still a lot of tutorial source code available from previous versions. The API changes have been minor and documented in the HISTORY file.

Signals

Lua has a number of features that involve *signals*. These Unix-derived features exist on the PC and some consoles, but may not be available in a truly cross-platform environment. However, in all cases these are optional, and the language works very well without them. Although the Lua source itself doesn't use them, much of the demonstration code does, but it is safe to remove such calls without adversely affecting the functionality.

Integration

There are two important differences to consider when integrating Lua into a predominantly C-oriented code base. The first is that Lua is a dynamically typed language. This means that the variables are able to change their type, according to what value they hold. That is, the *values* hold the type, not the variable.

The second point of note is that, internally, Lua works as a stack-based language. This information is hidden within the implementation of the language itself, so the scripting programmers do not need to worry about it. However, this becomes important when integrating the Lua interpreter into your engine as all the hook code must pop the data from the stack, its type interrogated, and the appropriate conversion made. This can feel unnatural and lead to bugs when the stack order or state is not understood.

Compiling Lua

Compilation of the standard packages are painless since the code is clean, and while there are generally no problems when integrating it into a larger code base, there are some points to note.

As with all third-party libraries, you should begin by creating a new header file to wrapper the supplied ones. This will unify the point of entry for all Lua hooks. Despite being C++ compatible, these header files are still pure C that dictates luacore.hpp should appear as:

```
extern "C" {
    #include "lib/lua/include/lua.h"
    #include "lib/lua/include/lauxlib.h"
    #include "lib/lua/include/lualib.h"
}
```

The three header files given above are the ones you will generally need for all Lua programs. All the basic type information and structures exist within lua.h, making this essential. lauxlib.h contains the prototypes for those functions that bridge the gap between Lua and its extensions. Because the Lua script code interfaces with the game engine through your own extensions, this is a necessity. Finally, lualib.h provides access to the standard libraries such as math, string, and debug. While not necessary, they are very useful to have.

The Lua code base comes in a number of C source files that share these three headers. They need to #include the same set of headers. Consequently, you will need to do one of the following:

- Make duplicate copies of the files for the interpreter and compiler.
- Add additional include directories within your development environment and compiler so the headers can be found.
- Use a monolithic directory structure so that all Lua-oriented files exist in the same directory.
- Modify the Lua code so that the header files are referenced with explicit paths.

Console Considerations

Lua began life in an environment where double precision calculations did not have a speed implication. In games, especially consoles, they do. Consequently, it is necessary to modify Lua to use single-point precision. This is easy to do, since the designer discovered this necessity and provided a suitable mechanism for changing the type used for noninteger values. Namely,

```
#ifndef LUA_NUMBER
    #define LUA_NUMBER      float
#endif
```

Such code must appear before lua.h is included by any of the source files so that the same type is used throughout the code. Consequently, it is usually best to write this code directly into lua.h itself. If you are using your own repository for Open Source code, the updates can be localized, although in Lua's case updates are so few that they cause no problems.

Note that it is technically possible to use fixed-point calculations within Lua by defining LUA_NUMBER to be a class with overloaded numeric operators. However, since this abstracts away a very critical aspect of the code and can unwittingly slow your game down, it is best to *not* hide the fact you're running fixed point under the hood. Instead, define the number as an integer, and provide an explicit fixed-point library as an extension.

Executing Lua Code

Lua works best when running short blocks of code in their entirety, as opposed to time-sliced fragments. To this end, it is best suited to event-based systems where one message will execute an entire block of Lua code. Each block of code runs within a Lua state that contains all the variables and tables necessary for the code.

Executing Lua code is a two-stage process beginning with a call to lua_cpcall, which starts the execution process, and the callback function it calls once preparation has completed. Although the Lua state is passed to both functions, transmitting additional information between class methods must be done through global variables or user data. In the latter case, you can simply pass a recast this pointer to the function, which it will duly pass back to your static class method. At this point it can call an instanced class method, like so:

```
tBOOL CLuaScriptState::Run()
{
   int status;
   status = lua_cpcall(m_LState, &StateMain, this);
   return status==0 ? TRUE : FALSE;
}

static int StateMain(lua_State *l)
{
CLuaScriptState *pLState = (CLuaScriptState *)lua_touserdata(l, 1);

   return pLState->LuaCall(0, TRUE);
}
```

In order to call the Lua code itself, you need to apply the standard code given as

```
tBOOL CLuaScriptState::LuaCall(int num_arg, tBOOL clear)
{
   int status;
   int base = lua_gettop(m_LState) - num_arg;  /* function index */
```

```
      lua_pushliteral(m_LState, "_TRACEBACK");
      lua_rawget(m_LState, LUA_GLOBALSINDEX);  /* get traceback function
*/

      lua_insert(m_LState, base);  /* put it under chunk and args */

      status = lua_pcall(m_LState, num_arg, (clear ? 0 : LUA_MULTRET), base);

      lua_remove(m_LState, base);  /* remove traceback function */

      return status;
}
```

An example of this architecture in action can be found on the accompanying CD-ROM in the *bookcode/sgxcore/source/sgx/scripting* directory.

Thead Safety

Because Lua values the ability to be cross-platform over the ability to be thread-safe, there is no mutex code within Lua itself. However, the functionality is possible because those critical areas have been surrounded with the macros lua_lock and lua_unlock. These are defined to be NULL by default, but can be replaced with your own methods.

Dynamic Code Execution

While it is rare for scripting code to be generated on the fly, it can happen. Lua makes this possible by providing a function to evaluate a single expression by compiling it on the fly and then executing it.

```
      lua_dostring(m_LState, "lua code goes in here");
```

This still acts on a preexisting state, but because it has to parse the code into its internal byte language first, this will take slightly longer than normal to execute and will generate a larger executable because the game must also incorporate the parsing code.

The Memory System

Lua only requires you to supply two new functions should you wish to change the method by which memory is allocated and freed. Those are l_realloc and l_free. This uses the ANSI C requirement that reallocating a block of memory is equivalent to allocating a complete new block. These symbols should both be #defined at the top of lmem.c or in lua.h.

```
#define l_realloc(block_ptr, old_memory_size, new_memory_size)  \
   myalloc(block_ptr, old_memory_size, new_memory_size)

#define l_free(block_ptr, old_memory_size) \
   myfree(block_ptr, old_memory_size)
```

You may decide to add a `lua_config.h` file to include this (and the `LUA_NUMBER` macro) that can in turn be added to all the appropriate files.

Memory management within Lua is completely automatic and works by running a garbage collector periodically to collect and dispose of all *dead objects*. When an object is no longer referenced, it is scheduled for garbage collection at the next opportunity. All objects, such as tables, threads, strings, function, and user data are handled automatically.

File I/O

Due to the nature of scripting, you need to consider the issue of loading external data from disc. This comes in two very simple parts. The first is the technical code to load a specific file from disc into memory, which is accomplished with the `lua_load` function call. The second involves those cases where the standard I/O routines need to be overwritten, for example, on the consoles to use the specific loaders.

The latter problem is also solved with `lua_load` since it accepts a `lua_Chunkreader` callback function that you should write that calls the appropriate file system functions manually. This must also makes use of `userdata` to provide the necessary class pointer. For example:

```
#define SGX_LUA_BUFFERSIZE   1024

typedef {
   CSGXFile *pFile;
   char buff[SGX_LUA_BUFFERSIZE];
} LoadLuaFile;

const char *LuaLoadGetBuffer(lua_State *, void *userdata, size_t *size)
{
   LoadLuaFile *lf = (LoadLuaFile *) userdata;
   *size = lf->pFile->Read((tBYTE *)lf->buff, SGX_LUA_BUFFERSIZE);
   return (*size > 0) ? lf->buff : NULL;
}
```

As you can see, the function fills an arbitrary buffer with as much data as possible and returns the size in the *size input parameter. It then returns a pointer to that buffer if there is data in it, or NULL if the end of file has been reached. This is called indirectly with a simple function such as this:

```
tBOOL CLuaScriptState::LuaLoad(const sgxString &filename)
{
CSGXFile file(filename);
LoadLuaFile lf;
int status;

    if (!file.IsValid()) {
        return FALSE;
    }

    /* index of filename on the stack */
    int fnameindex = lua_gettop(m_LState) + 1;

    lua_pushfstring(m_LState, "@%s", filename.c_str());
    lf.pFile = &file;
    status = lua_load(m_LState, LuaLoadGetBuffer, &lf,
        lua_tostring(m_LState, -1));
    file.Close();

    if (status) {
        lua_settop(m_LState, fnameindex);
        return FALSE;
    }

    return TRUE;
}
```

Debugging

Lua has a number of different debugging utilities, all of which can be abstracted away into your standard tools. The first is the LUA_DEBUG macro, which must be switched on with

```
#define LUA_DEBUG
```

and placed in either lua.h or at the head of ltests.c. This activates a suite of debugging functionality including memory tracers, limit testers, and state queries. The memory tracers, for example, make use of an alternative set of memory allocation and free functions.

To ease debugging of the scripts themselves, however, the same functionality can be accessed through Lua itself by using the *ldblib* extension, which is supplied with the standard Lua package. This only needs to be initialized once in the C code with:

```
luaopen_debug(m_lState);
```

From here, new commands are available to query the local variables and stack trace. At the time of writing, these functions are:

- `getlocal`
- `getinfo`
- `gethook`
- `getupvalue`
- `sethook`
- `setlocal`
- `setupvalue`
- `debug`
- `traceback`

All of this functionality can also be accessed through C directly with your usual game debugging tools. And naturally, there is nothing to prevent you from including your own debugging code alongside the game-specific output.

Lua also provides replacement debugging functions that can be called explicitly by the C code. One such example is `luaD_pcall`, an equivalent of `lua_pcall`, which allows you to specify an error function that will get called at every invocation of `lua_error` so you can add trace messages.

The License

The Lua license is almost as liberal as they come, and from version 5 (the one you will most likely be using) it follows the MIT license, which doesn't need reexplaining to the management and legal teams.

GUILE

This is a library intended for developing plug-ins and modules, and so fits nicely into your requirements for a scripting language. Guile stands for the GNU Ubiquitous Intelligent Language for Extensions and has been used in heavyweight projects like GNU Emacs and The GIMP (the Free equivalent of Adobe Photoshop, detailed in Chapter 12, "Graphics Production Tools"), but it also fits in with smaller projects, too. You also have full access to the Guile interpreter itself, so even that can be extended as needed.

The project is an implementation of a Scheme interpreter, which is a version of LISP and so comes with an unmatched history of literature on the subject, particularly in the field of AI. However, Guile is more than just an interpreter. It also comes with a threading library, exceptions, a portable Scheme library, and a Posix and regular expression library. This makes Guile a heavyweight in every sense of the word. The complete library, under Windows, is just under a megabyte, although this could be pruned of unused features if necessary.

There are also plans to provide language translators for Scheme that will allow the script writers to develop in other languages (such as Tcl or Python), which will then be converted automatically, although this is not yet ready.

The software itself is stable and portable, although the developers admit they're not focused on maintaining 100 percent interface compatibility between releases. But past experience has shown that they're no worse than any other project and have maintained as much compatibility as one could expect. Also, if you're working with your own repository, this will not even be an issue. Version 1.8.0 is available on the CD-ROM.

ON THE CD

Homepage: *http://www.gnu.org/software/guile*

License: GNU GPL[1] (Appendix B) and GNU LGPL (Appendix C). See commentary for details.

Distribution: Source only (although binary versions for Cygwin and AIX exist).

First release: June 13, 1995.

Current version: 1.6.7 (stable since December 21, 2004).

Platform(s): Linux (gcc) and Windows (MingW32).

Dependencies: None.

Other resources: Guile has a several online tutorials to supplement the immense material available on both Scheme and LISP. There are also at least five mailing lists on the GNU site alone, with at least two of these being useful to end users.

Integration

The initial hurdle in developing with Guile is its Linux heritage. As with a lot of recent GNU software, it uses the autotools system that ensures solid cross-platform compatibility across most flavors of Unix. Such software follows the rules of `configure`, `make`, and `make install`. That is, before you can build the code, you must configure it using the existing script. This usually generates custom header files like `config.h`, and builds a suitable `Makefile`. Naturally, this configuration script is written for Bash, not the Microsoft Windows command prompt; so any initial development is best suited to MingW32 or Cygwin.

Its heritage also raises the bar to entry for console development, since you will need to make changes directly to the source code because there are no hooks for filesystem handling. You should simplify this process by creating your own repository. However, the scope of Scheme as a language is superior to Lua and has a greater wealth of past literature, and so is often worth the extra up-front effort.

With any system of this size, it is inevitable there will be some overlap of the base functionality. The only other concern is that Guile's implementation of SCM_ASSERT can prevent your game from exiting cleanly. This macro can be safely redirected to your own code, however.

Guile or Scheme

The first thing to consider when building a Guile-based scripting engine is whether you need high- or low-level control. These are referred to as *gh* (Guile High) and *scm* (Scheme, sometimes called *libguile*) access, respectively. You can include the high-level libraries (where each function begins with gh_) with

```
#include <guile/gh.h>
```

while libguile has its own header:

```
#include <libguile.h>
```

Inclusion of the Guile high-level library automatically includes the header files for libguile. When using Guile in either of these forms you must remember to link with the Guile library.

There is no memory trade-off in using the low-level scm libraries, since they're needed in all cases, and the time consumed passing data from the gh wrapper to the scm code underneath is negligible. Even the stability consideration is moot since both are robust pieces of code with a good heritage. Ultimately, the selection is governed by personal choice, so we shall use the high-level gh library for initialization and the majority of functions, dropping into Scheme where necessary.

The Guile initialization procedure appears slightly odd, since it expects the standard C command line arguments to be passed in

```
gh_enter(argc, argv, inner_main);
```

However, this can be replaced with

```
void stub(int argc, char *argv[]) { /* empty */ }
...
gh_enter(0, NULL, stub);
```

The reason for this construct is that most high-level Guile-enabled applications were intended to run in their own loop in much the same way that GLUT does in the OpenGL field.

The Guile environment is very similar to Lua insomuch as the environment is initialized, and program code (given as strings) is then evaluated within that environment. One important difference here is that Guile has no localized state, which makes every variable essentially global. This is not as bad as the formal methods lecturers would have you believe because of the way Scheme works as a language. Consequently, the process for reading and writing Scheme variables from C is much easier because the concept of scope doesn't apply, as you are only ever handling global variables.

Creating Function Hooks

As is typical for C, all function hooks are registered with the symbol-callback pair giving a human readable name to be used in the Scheme code, and a function pointer indicating what C code should be executed when that symbol is invoked.

```
gh_new_procedure("move_character", fn_move_character, 3, 0, FALSE);
```

In Guile, you have three additional parameters to consider. They are:

■ The number of required arguments.
■ The number of optional arguments.
■ Whether the function takes a "rest" list. This can be ignored for your purposes.

There are macros to hide these parameters, but they go by the equally opaque names such as gh_new_procedure1_0 so are not used here.

These arguments always use the SCM type and must be decoded, as you see next.

Data Types

Guile follows the ideas of a weakly type language. While this has the potential of making problems when it is integrated with a (relatively) strongly-typed language such as C, it only means you have to be more careful with your wrapper functions. To cope with this singularity, the parameter types involved in a function are always termed SCM. This new type holds the internal description of every Scheme variable and whatever C type might be its equivalent. This is then used in all functions that are used by Scheme. A typical callback function would begin as:

```
SCM fn_move_character(SCM scmIndex, SCM deltaX, SCM deltaY)
{
```

You can then extract a C-compatible integer from this variable with the code:

```
int objIndex = gh_scm2int(scmIndex);
int dx = gh_scm2int(deltaX);
int dy = gh_scm2int(deltaY);
int distanceMoved = AIManager::MoveCharacter(objIndex, dx, dy);
```

and return that value with

```
    return gh_int2scm(distanceMoved);
}
```

Note that every C function called by Guile must have a return type. If it would usually be `void`, you must return `SCM_EOL`.

The mappings of each type can be found in Table 9.1, along with the predicate functions to determine whether the value inside the Scheme variable truly is of the required type.

TABLE 9.1   Guile Type Mapping

Data Type	Convert From Guile	Convert To Guile	Validity Check
void	N/A	SCM_EOL	N/A
bool	gh_scm2bool	gh_bool2scm	gh_boolean_p
char	gh_scm2char	gh_char2scm	gh_char_p
short	gh_scm2short	gh_short2scm	gh_number_p
unsigned short	gh_scm2ushort	gh_ushort2scm	gh_number_p
int	gh_scm2int	gh_int2scm	gh_number_p
long	gh_scm2long	gh_long2scm	gh_number_p
unsigned long	gh_scm2ulong	gh_ulong2scm	gh_number_p
char *	gh_scm2newstr	gh_str2scmii or gh_str02scm	gh_string_p
double	scm_num2dbl	gh_double2scm	scm_real_p
size_t	N/A	N/A	N/A

Additionally, there are macros to wrap these functions, but longhand is used for the sake of explanation.

There appear to be some issues in retrieving real numbers from the SCM type when using the gh *library. Therefore, we have elected to suggest the Scheme equivalent,* scm_num2dbl.

The character type in Guile is unsigned, *so all C chars must be cast before any conversion takes place. Otherwise, the value will be sign extended.*

You can use the macros SCM_BOOL_T and SCM_BOOL_F as an analog to the Boolean values of true and false, although since ANSI C (pre C99) doesn't have a base Boolean type, Guile uses int for all Boolean operations.

The SCM_BOOL_NOT *macro has a peculiar construction due to an issue in the Borland suite of compilers. Should similar oddities appear in this area, you should employ an inline function in your local version of the code.*

Because the comparison procedure of opaque SCM types can be costly (as it involves two conversions from SCM into native C types, an evaluation of the types to determine the appropriate comparison routine, followed by the comparison itself) there are built-in predicates available for use by your C code. They are gh_eq_p and gh_equal_p, and both take two SCM as their arguments and return a Boolean result.

Executing Code

Scheme code can be executed directly in the interpreter by filling a string and calling

```
gh_eval_str("(define value 123)");
```

Larger scripts can be run directly from a file with

```
gh_eval_file("filename.scm");
```

Unfortunately, this will use the standard I/O libraries and should be avoided since reprogramming Guile to redirect the I/O to custom code is tricky. Instead, create your own loop to read from the file in whatever manner is suitable for the game, and evaluate each string in turn with gh_eval_str.

Some of the standard Scheme commands, like define, have their own C functions to make initialization easier.

```
gh_c_define("health", value);
```

Alternatively, you can set these variables using the SCM type. This gives you greater scope since SCM can handle many types that C cannot, such as vectors and lists. It is invoked like this:

```
gh_define("health", gh_int2scm(value));
```

You can later retrieve a handle to this variable with

```
SCM scmHealth = gh_lookup("health");
sgxTrace("The current health is %d.", gh_scm2int(scmHealth));
```

All Scheme symbols are case insensitive.

The Use of Inum

Throughout many Scheme discussions the phrase INUM will appear. This is short for immediate numbers and describes any integer that fits inside a Scheme word. The size of this word, however, is nonobvious. It is two bits less than `sizeof(long)`. So, to save memory on PS2 (where a `long` is 64 bits) you should define `LONG_BIT` as 32 in `scmconfig.h`.

Exceptions

Guile is also capable of handling exceptions in a safe, controlled manner. All operations that would normally cause a processor exception (such as the infamous divide by zero) are emulated and handled within Guile as the internal stack unwinds. Additionally you can capture these exceptions from within your C code to perform debugging and diagnostics on the scripts. This requires two additions. The first is a special callback function that is invoked on each Scheme exception:

```
SCM cbCatchException(void *data, SCM tag, SCM throwArgs)
{
    int length;

    sgxTrace("Caught %s exception.", gh_symbol2newstr(tag, &length));
    return SCM_EOL;
}
```

The second is a special call to the interpreter to redirect the *catch handler* to this new function:

```
gh_eval_str_with_catch(szCodeLine, cbCatchException);
```

Testing this involves throwing an exception manually. For example,

```
gh_eval_str_with_catch("(throw 'badex)", cbCatchException);
```

Memory Handling

While the Guile developers have made some effort to create modular garbage collection code, the low-level allocation code does not provide any direct hooks. Instead, you must replace all instances of `malloc`, `calloc`, and `realloc` with calls to your own allocation code. This must be done across the whole code base, but only amounts to six different files.

Additionally, there is new functionality in the form of `alloca`, an implementation of the PWB library code that allocates memory from the runtime stack, and reclaims it when the function exits.

The License

As noted previously, the Guile license allows developers to make use of its primary functionality without succumbing to the full GPL. This puts the Guile library (`libguile`) under an effective LGPL license.

The only exception to note is that the Guile `readline` module (which parses command line arguments) is not part of this exclusion and is still controlled by the full GNU GPL. Consequently, you should remove readline if you're planning on releasing as LGPL.

OTHER LANGUAGE POSSIBILITIES

This is by no means the extent of the available scripting languages. What follows is a short appraisal of other languages that loosely fit the genre or might be suggested for use.

Java

This is not yet free, and so should not strictly appear in this book. However, the continued belief that it is free requires an explanation of that fact.

In short, the Java language and its Java Virtual Machine (JVM) specification is under the control of Sun, and only it has the right to change the language or its workings in any way. This prohibits you from extending it, should you need to, and therefore is not free. This was legally proven when Microsoft added extensions to Java and was sued. Microsoft was then forced to withdraw Java from all its products within seven years.

The only case where Java can be used in FLOSS is when the byte code (as generated by any Java compiler) is interpreted by an independent JVM. There are currently several Open Source JVMs in existence that would give the developer an ability to use Java code to script a game, and those are covered here.

Kaffe

Kaffe is probably one of the best well-known of all Open Source JVMs currently available. It also comes with the main Java classes necessary to run it. In order to allay any legal fears, it is a clean-room implementation of the JVM, although it is unlikely that this is a major deciding factor. It has been released under the GNU GPL and has numerous ports in production, including one for PlayStation2-Linux, which should port to the official console quite easily.

Its own website claims it is not yet powerful enough for debugging or serious development work, but as a means of incorporating prewritten Java code into a free environment it is stable and very encompassing, being able to run even large applications, such as the Eclipse IDE.

The current version is 1.1.6 and can be found at *http://www.kaffe.org*. It has its own mailing lists and forums, and has inspired many similar projects based on its own C99 (but C++-compatible) source code, such as Latte, JanosVM, KaffeOS, JESSICA, Gilgul, Alta, Guaraná, and Kangaroo.

SableVM

This project, hosted at *http://jcvm.sourceforge.net*, benefits from being released under the GNU LGPL. It too is a clean-room implementation of the JVM and is capable of running Java byte code within your game. Its primary mechanism for doing this is to compile the Java class files into C, using your local toolchain, before running it natively. While this doesn't help the turnaround time of script development work, it does allow Java code that would usually be processed at runtime (with say, Kaffe) to be precompiled for the final release candidates.

JamVM

Available from *http://jamvm.sourceforge.net*, JamVM is a very small JVM focused on Unix platforms. Windows users will have to compile from source, although it is certainly the most compact JVM available, so this extra effort might be worth it.

Like all the other JVMs presented here, it has been created in a clean-room environment and is comprised of its own garbage collection and class loading code. Consequently, this means there is some work to effectively integrate them with your abstracted memory manager and file system.

GNU Classpath

While this is not a JVM in itself, it is used within many of the other Java-based solutions covered. Classpath provides the basic system libraries that a typical JVM will use during its execution. This includes stalwart methods like `System.Array.copy`.

Classpath is GNU software in the genuine sense of the word by coming from the Free software Foundation. While being released under the GPL (from *http://www.gnu.org/software/classpath*), it has an exception allowing you to include it with independent modules to produce executable code.

C#

This was born out of Microsoft's need for a cross-platform write-once, run-anywhere programming language. It follows the same principles as Java, employing a Common Language Runtime (the CLR, similar to Java's JVM) and a set of standard libraries. Also, like Java, it is not free despite being submitted to the ECMA standards group. The only Open Source implementation of note is the Mono project from Ximian, *http://www.mono-project.com/CSharp_Compiler*. It contains the C# compiler, CLR, and class libraries each released under a different license; that is, the GPL, LGPL, and X11 licenses, respectively. Incorporating C# code into a game requires only the latter two.

Parrot

Of all the possibilities provided here, this is the outsider. It follows the familiar idea whereby a host language is compiled into byte code, which then runs on a virtual machine. One benefit of Parrot is that the host language can involve dynamic types (Java and C# are both statically typed languages). Additionally, the source itself is not fixed to any specific language, so C, Python, and Perl could all be compiled into identical byte code. This allows them all to be combined within the same project and run from a single virtual machine.

At the present time, work is progressing slowly on Parrot, although the basic virtual machine is available (and Open Source) and programs can be written and executed using Parrot byte code. While this appears too hardcore for a basic scripting language it is perfectly feasible to adapt Lua byte code, although for the short term this is impractical. More information can be found at *http://www.parrotcode.org*.

Python

This language never began with its eye on the game scripting market. Instead, its purpose was to provide an extensible language that made effective use of exceptions. This extensibility led to a number of useful modules (encompassing Internet protocols, software engineering, and operating systems) that grew its user base in the Linux and Unix environments. While Python was originally chided by many for its judicious and pedantic use of whitespace, this hostility has since cooled, enabling the true beauty of the language to be appreciated.

Its first introduction to the games community came through PyGame, an LGPL wrapper module that inaugurated multimedia support to Python using SDL. Its reputation was further enhanced by the introduction of the Python Game Programming Challenge that asked developers to write a game in a week. The results showed a greater maturity than their seven-day gestation period defined, and so it entered the consciousness of Open Source game developers.

The currently favored implementation for games developers is stackless Python. This version runs faster that the original implementation (a.k.a. CPython) and, as the name suggests, requires no stack space, enabling much deeper recursion than the preliminary version (which could only manage "a few thousand levels").

The home page for the Python language, *http://python.org*, also includes the full FAQs for extending and embedding the language into existing C code. The stackless variant lives at *http://www.stackless.com*.

ENDNOTES

1. But with the exception that allows software to be linked with GUILE without it being classed a derivative work.
2. This takes a char * and length. Use `gh_str02scm` for nul-terminated strings, or `gh_set_substr` for substrings.

10 Utility Libraries

For many, the power of Open Source in game development is being able to take a complete graphics engine and begin work. But in reality, most game developers spend more time solving a number of more fundamental problems, such as implementing efficient storing mechanisms for the data, or developing fast-sorting and search algorithms. This functionality can be acquired instead from Open Source repositories.

LANGUAGE EXTENSIONS

As a language, C++ is well stacked with features, mostly through the Standard Template Library (STL). But as developers always strive for more, we begin with a source library that adds to the base language itself. By introducing functionality at this level we know the new library will be available across different platforms, and will work reliably on them.

STLport

This is probably the most fundamental language extension available under an Open Source license. STLport, which is included on the CD-ROM, is an open implementation of the STL library that normally comes bundled with your compiler, along with some useful improvements of its own.

For those using a non-Free compiler you might wonder about the rationale behind using a free solution that performs the same job as something for which you've paid money. There are a couple of reasons. First, the implementation quality of STLport is higher than most commercial offerings due to its peer-reviewed approach and focus on standards-compliant code.

Second, having a single STL implementation across all platforms eliminates a number of problems that would otherwise arise. For example,

```
m_Vertices.clear();
```

is not obliged to release the memory held by m_Vertices, which can vary the memory footprint on different platforms[1]. This is especially true in the console field.

Finally, with the STL source living outside of the compiler's standard directories it is easier to upgrade, change, and experiment with the STL implementation without breaking any other software you build on that machine.

> **Homepage:** *http://www.stlport.org*
>
> **License:** Custom, BSD-style.
>
> **Distribution:** Source only.
>
> **First release:** 1997.
>
> **Current version** 4.6.2 (stable since April 10, 2004).
>
> **Platform(s):** Visual C++ 4.0 and above, gcc and most Unix-based systems. See also *http://www.stlport.org/doc/platforms.html*.
>
> **Dependencies:** None.
>
> **Other resources:** Forums and mailing lists.

The validity of STL within games is hotly debated, and there is no place for such debate here. Even if you decide against STLport as a solution you should still peruse the source code, as there are a number of useful comments pertaining to best-practice C++ development within particular environments. For example, the file _msvc_warnings_off.h is a good reference of the Visual Studio warning messages that produce a lot of unwarranted noise in the compiler output.

STLport originally comes from the good people at SGI and so is sometimes referred to as SGI STL, especially within the code itself.

Integration

Being a replacement for the native implementation of STL, as provided by your compiler vendor, there is some minor magic to perform before you can seamlessly use STLport in your game. The first step, as outlined in the install notes, is to *not* overwrite the system STL header files, but place them into their own directory and add this directory at the *top* of your additional include directories list. This will ensure that any STL-oriented references will be directed to those in STLport and not the original header files, so every

```
#include <string>
```

will first find `devlib/include/stlport/string`, for example.

Overwriting your native STL will not work because the STLport implementation of iostreams has some caveats requiring the native versions.

It may be tempting to place STLport in the root of your `devlib/include` directory and move it to the top of "additional includes" list, saving on another entry in the list. This is not valid for two reasons. First, it gives higher priority to libraries that are not language extensions, and therefore allows a library that uses its own `math.h` to hide the one provided by the compiler. This is a general problem and should be avoided elsewhere, too. The second issue is specific to STLport, but can also apply to other languages. That is, STLport uses the native header files for some of its functionality. One example of this is in `stlport/math.h`, where the construct of

```
#include _STLP_NATIVE_C_HEADER(math.h)
```

attempts to include the original implementation of `math.h`. If the STLport-equivalent file is in the root of the directory that the compiler searches first, it will not find the native version and instead include itself. Recursively. This is the only library featured in this book that has such an issue, but is an important consideration for the future with other libraries of this ilk.

All users are directed toward the documentation with STLport for other compilation problems and information, especially those working under a multithreaded environment.

Since STLport is incorporated as part of the language, you can use

```
#include <string>
```

as usual, within your code. However, when using a library that is as unchanging as STL, and with precompiled headers turned on, it is often more convenient to create a new header file, such as `stl.hpp`, and reference all the oft-used files from within it. This allows you to make specific enhancements, as can be seen from the SGX Core file that follows, which follows this idea.

```
#ifndef SGX_CORE_STL_HPP
#define SGX_CORE_STL_HPP    1

#include <string>
#include <vector>
#include <map>
#include <algorithm>

#define sgxString    std::string
#define sgxVector    std::vector
#define sgxMap       std::map

#endif /* SGX_CORE_STL_HPP */
```

This allows for the basic abstraction of the STL libraries and permits additional STL features to be handled transparently.

One issue to bear in mind with STLport is whether you wish to use native or STLport iostreams, because unlike the rest of the package, it is not a drop-in replacement. There is work to be done, whether you decide to keep the native implementation or not, with the main controlling mechanism inside `stl_user_config.h`. This should be used in preference to local amendments of `stl.hpp` since the web of header files in STLport is quite complex and difficult to trace.

Native *iostreams*

This is the simplest, as STLport passes control directly to the native implementation. The compilation method can be a complex one, however, and depends on your precise setup and needs. There are three controlling macros inside `stl_user_config.h` that need attention.

_STLP_NO_OWN_IOSTREAMS: Allows you to switch on STLport iostreams, which requires the compilation of the iostream library, for which code is supplied.

_STLP_NO_NEW_IOSTREAMS: Suppresses new-style streams, even if available.

_STLP_NO_IOSTREAMS: Disable all forms of iostreams. Used on embedded systems, such as consoles.

The most useful switch for game developers is _STLP_NO_IOSTREAMS. This still permits operator<< and operator>> to control iostreams, but it doesn't bloat the code with any of the standard code you will never use. Even on the Microsoft Windows platform, you will generally adopt an abstracted, cross-platform file-handling library to facilitate the more complex I/O games require, such as asynchronous loading.

Because the basic string functions are inside standard headers you might arrive at the situation where functions like sprintf are not available when using STLport. This generally should only occur in misconfigured compilations, but can be fixed by using alternate header files. For example,

```
#include <stdio.h>
```

becomes

```
#include <cstdio>
```

and

```
#include <stdlib.h>
```

becomes

```
#include <cstdlib>
```

and so on.

STLport iostreams

This requires an additional library to be compiled in with the code. This is built from the files in the src directory. Naturally, it uses the code from its sibling stlport directory; so any changes you wish to make to stl_user_config.h, for example, must be done *after* the library is compiled.

Compilation generally occurs in Windows with

```
C:\Program Files\Microsoft Visual Studio\VC98\Bin\vcvars32.bat
nmake -f vc6.mak
nmake -f vc6.mak install
```

This produces libraries in combinations of debug/release and static/dynamic. Being an I/O library, minimal time is spent redirecting into DLL code so, given the memory footprint, this might be a good option for Windows code. Console developers will not use the supplied iostreams anyway, and it therefore is not an issue.

The last command in this build process copies the libraries, headers, and DLLs into specific locations: namely, those belonging to the Microsoft Developer Studio development environment and Windows System directory, respectively. While this is a good general-purpose solution, it often doesn't fit your requirements because you'll often keep your third-party libraries in a separate directory tree. Therefore, you need to copy these files to the appropriate directories manually.

Always clean and rebuild your code when changing fundamental components such as STLport, otherwise strange, unfathomable, errors will appear.

You do not need to manually reference the libraries, however, because the `stlport/config/stl_select_lib.h` file includes `#pragma` instructions (compatible with Visual Studio and .NET) to do this automatically.

STLport Namespaces

By default, STLport will replace your native implementation of STL as `std::` with its own code, also under `std::`. You can replace this with your own namespace by massaging the configuration macros, such as `_STLP_USE_OWN_NAMESPACE`. This is useful when the native STL implementation produces conflicts with your own namespace, or you need both.

STLport also uses the `stlport` namespace (which is an alias to its internal `_STLP_STD` namespace).

Extensions

The purpose of STLport is to provide an independent, cross-platform implementation of the existing STL specification. It does not contain other utility libraries, unlike Boost. However, it does add some extensions to the traditional STL containers and types where domain-specific improvements can be made. They are as follows:

New Hashed Containers: Four new hashes are available in STLport—`hash_set`, `hash_multiset`, `hash_map` and `hash_multimap`.

Single-Linked List Container: This removes the overhead of storing back pointers when, most of the time, they will not be used. It is called `slist`.

Ropes: These are for big strings and should be used be used in preference to string when very long text strings are used. While game code itself is unlikely to use ropes, offline tool processing with XML and/or base64 encoding (see later) may benefit from this type.

License

The license presented in the STLport archive states that any program compiled with STLport can be distributed without "any royalties or restrictions." The propagation of source implementations (whether modified or not) must be supplied with the permission notices given in the license.html.

This is compatible with GPL, LGPL, BSD, and X11 licenses.

LOW-LEVEL CONTROL

Most senior programmers have a toolbox of code that they have collected over the years. This code is usually very simple in nature, but implements some of the fundamental principles in computer science. Unlike the language extensions you saw at the beginning of the chapter, this code actually performs a useful task on its own. The code can act as a copy-and-paste template that demonstrates best practice, or a piece of drop-in functionality for any project. Most of the time, this code comes (and goes) with the programmer in question because it is usually too simple to be considered worthy of a full release or warrant keeping secret. Fortunately, some programmers have released such code under open licenses and so save everyone else reinventing the same proverbial wheels.

XML Parsing

On February 10, 1998, XML (Extensible Markup Language) 1.0 was officially recommended by the W3C and was being heralded as the new silver bullet that would cure all ills. It is a text-based hierarchical file format for describing data. Its textual nature ensures it can be read and written by any number of prewritten tools, while the parent-child hierarchy allows complex data structures to be represented within it. XML was not the first format of this type, however. HTML, its more famous cousin, was introduced in 1991 enabling people to develop web pages with ease; and *its* grandfather, SGML, was standardized as far back as 1978[2]. However, the introduction of XSLT (Extensible Stylesheet Language Transformations) that describe how to convert one XML file format into another, heralded the belief that no file format would become obsolete and that XML would aid data cross-pollination.

In the right hands, XML provides a very powerful mechanism for representing the structure of data. Unfortunately, in many instances, this does not always happen since the complexity involved in creating good file formats comes from the understanding, abstracting, structuring, and documenting the data in a precise, insightful, manner. This is a hard problem and is not directly connected with the implementation because, despite common conceptions, XML is not self-describing in the general case. The hot buzz of XML soon simmered to that of any other software tool.

Unlike other tarnished silver bullets, XML remained in use because, while it wasn't perfect, it was still the best tool available to the average developer. There are a few reasons for this. First, it is plain text. As developers spend most of their time debugging, this provided a very simple mechanism to spot problems with broken files, formats, and parsers. Second, by the time the limitations of XML were realized, a slew of tools, development suites, and libraries had been released that made the task much easier. And finally, it *is* a good mechanism for storing information in a structured manner.

Open file formats like Collada use XML, as do many toolchains and level editors.

Storing Data

As can be seen from the following snippet, XML follows a very simple format. It is comprised primarily of elements (descriptive terms, such as player and position) and attributes (parameters that quantify those elements, like x and y.) These can be nested as desired. Each element (or tag) should describe only one class of item within your data set. That is, it is inadvisable (although technically possible in most cases) to have two elements called "position" (one of which describes a Cartesian location, the other holding an AI's rank) in a single XML file. However, by maintaining unique names throughout ensures that the data can be transformed and parsed much more simply when required.

```
<?xml version="1.0" encoding="utf-8"?>
<map>
 <player>
  <start>
   <position x="12" y="132" z="0"/>
   <health value="100"/>
  </start>
 </player>
</map>
```

While the format might appear like HTML, it is not to be treated as such. XML deserves much more respect since HTML has very lax parsing rules! It is possible to forget to close tags or omit the quotes from attributes, and the HTML will still load and parse. HTML also allows you to mismatch tags, and (to a very large extent) it will still work. One of the reasons web pages look different in assorted browsers is due to the poor-quality HTML on most sites, which requires the browser to interpret the meaning of the code despite it being technically broken. XML will not work with such sloppiness. Every XML file must be perfect. So, although this makes the coding of the XML harder, the parser is much simpler as it needs no error-recovery code and as a consequence, is faster and simpler. The main points to remember with XML files are:

- There is only one element in the main body of the XML (`map`, in the previous example).
- All element tags that are opened must be explicitly closed.
- Element tags must match.
- Attributes must surround their values with quotes.
- You cannot include tags and data within a single element; that is, `<tag>some text<illegal/></tag>` is not allowed.

One apparent limitation with XML is that binary data, a stalwart of computer games, is seriously lacking from the format. However, there are several different mechanisms by which it can be stored, depending on the source material.

Graphic Images

Large blocks of binary data are best stored by referring to their filename. This is true for graphics, meshes, and compiled script files. Any file that is exported from an external tool will generally be formatted in binary (say as a PNG), so no information is lost by storing it as binary in the XML. And the most efficient form of storing binary data is with a filename.

Floating-Point Numbers

Floating-point numbers are only accurate to a certain extent. When saving data with one level of accuracy, it is not possible to know whether the program loading the data will be satisfied with the accuracy at which you've chosen to save.

There are two primary solutions to this problem. The first involves storing an ASCII representation of the number, being output with code, such as

```
sprintf(string, "<x = \"%f\"/>", position.x);
```

This, while functional, is reliant on the `sprintf` implementation to maintain enough accuracy for the next application. Because many floating-point numbers cannot be represented exactly, a value of 1.5 might get exported as 1.4999999. This is turn could get read back by the application as 1.49998. Over time, this margin of error could increase to unacceptable proportions.

A better method is to write the bit pattern according to the IEEE-754 specification for floating point numbers, thus,

```
sprintf(string, "<x = \"0x%x\"/>", *(tUINT32 *)&position.x);
```

While the result isn't as easy to read as straightforward ASCII (the number 1.1 becomes 0x3f8ccccd, for example), it doesn't lose any of the precision of the text version, and it is much faster to parser than a series of digits. You can always add comments to the XML to provide human-readable numbers if you wish.

Base64

This encoding scheme originates from the Multipurpose Internet Mail Extensions (MIME) system described in RFC 2045. It uses 64 different characters (A-Z, a-z, 0-9, + and /) to represent binary data. You may additionally see = used; this is for padding and special processing. The method of encoding is very simple: three 8-bit bytes are read from the binary source and split into four 6-bit bytes. These 6-bit values are then mapped onto the characters given previously and padded with = for any nonmultiples of three found at the end of the file.

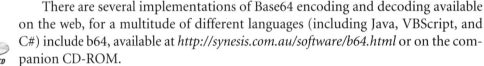

```
<code dt:dt="bin.base64">R29zaCEgQmFzZTY0IG1zIHJlYWxseSBlYXN5IQ==</code>
```

ON THE CD

There are several implementations of Base64 encoding and decoding available on the web, for a multitude of different languages (including Java, VBScript, and C#) include b64, available at *http://synesis.com.au/software/b64.html* or on the companion CD-ROM.

This method is only recommended when you need to encapsulate all data within a single XML file or have very small binary files.

XML-binary Optimized Packaging

This method (shortened to XOP) adopts the ideas of both MIME and Base64 to remove the binary components of the document into separate components and handled as a multipart MIME message. This allows serialization using separate containers without interrupting the singular text-only approach of XML. Because little to none of your game data would be serialized in this manner, or need to be interfaced with systems that do, this is of limited use.

This W3C recommendation can be found at *http://www.w3.org/TR/2005/REC-xop10-20050125*.

Converting Data

With the vast multitude of free and Open Source software available it is not surprising that most of it uses incompatible file formats. Collada (as seen in Chapter

11, "The Tools Pipeline") is the exception that proves the rule. In most other cases, an XML project file from one application cannot be used directly by another. If you are producing a toolchain using two of these applications, you may need to convert between them.

XML to XML Conversion

This requires the use of Extensible Stylesheet Language Transformations (XSLT) and allows you to transform a single XML document into another single document[3]. The conversion process parses each element *node* from the XML file and transforms it into something else according to the rules laid down in the transformation file, which is also a valid XML file.

ON THE CD

Transforming XML requires additional software, but there are many translators available. The tool supplied on the CD-ROM is called Saxon, and has been implemented in Java using Xerces, the Apache XML parser. It is run simply with

```
java -jar saxon.jar mapdata.xml newplayer.xsl
```

If you have a full Java install for your Microsoft Windows platform you can also associate .jar files with the javaw program to run them automatically from a double-click.

ON THE CD

The sample transformation demonstrated here is also available in the bookcode directory of the CD-ROM.

NOTE

Although Saxon is Open Source, it is not compatible with the GPL. However, since the code is in Java and should only appear in the toolchain, it should not hinder your production.

There are many guides to the syntax and structure of XSL files, such as the canonical *http://www.w3.org/TR/xslt*, that a full tutorial need not be given here. However, the salient points are featured to demonstrate a typical transformation of the previous XML.

```
<?xml version="1.0" encoding="ISO-8859-1"?>
<xsl:stylesheet version="1.0"
xmlns:xsl="http://www.w3.org/1999/XSL/Transform">

<xsl:template match="/">
  <newlevel>
    <xsl:apply-templates select="map"/>
  </newlevel>
</xsl:template>
```

```
<xsl:template match="player">
 <player x="{start/position/@x}" y="{start/position/@y}"
z="{start/position/@z}">
    <xsl:apply-templates/>
 </player>
</xsl:template>

<xsl:template match="health">
   <health value="{@value}"/>
</xsl:template>


<xsl:template match="ai">
 <ai x="{position/@x}" y="{position/@y}" z="{position/@z}"/>
</xsl:template>


</xsl:stylesheet>
```

The structure of XSL is very simple, with this example moving the position data into attributes of the player element, transforming

```
<ai>
  <position x="100" y="132" z="20"/>
</ai>
```

into

```
<ai x="100" y="132" z="20"/>
```

The first section of note is the *template match* operation. Whenever a node matches the element given here, the XSLT will process all the text in that template block to output a new version of that node. The text may consist of instructions (such as apply-templates) or text to output that, in your case, is the new XML format.

Because the XML format is essentially tree-like, there needs to be a way of referencing alternate branches on the tree. This is achieved with XSLT's use of Xpath and is highlighted in the previous example with the term start/position/@x. This indicates that the parser should traverse into the child node called start, then into its position child node, and read the x attribute from position. The braces are used to embed this Xpath into a traditional XML line. It could be written identically with the standalone instruction

```
<xsl:value-of select="start/position/@x"/>
```

Once the new position has been written, the `apply-templates` instruction causes the parser to recurse through every child node of this tag. This instruction may optionally contain filters to only enumerate a particular element, as shown with the `select` attribute near the beginning of the file. If no tag for the present node exists (as is the case with `position`, in this example) then an implied line of

```
<xsl:apply-templates/>
```

is executed, and no filtering occurs. Consequently, you can terminate the parser descending beyond specific nodes with the code

```
<xsl:template match="position">
</xsl:template>
```

Throughout the processing you should consider the hierarchical nature of the XML file and rely on its recursive nature. XSLT provides a `for-each` instruction to support iterative processing, but while this construct is unavoidable at times, some purists consider it the XSLT equivalent of C's `goto` statement!

One final output method to mention is the mechanism used to output XML control characters, such as <, >, and &. These are all handled identically to their counterparts in HTML with the entities < > and &, respectively. However, in order to write them into the output stream you must disable escaping (otherwise it will appear literally, as <) thus,

```
<xsl:text disable-output-escaping="yes">&lt;</xsl:text>
```

ON THE CD

An example of these transformations can be found in the `bookcode` folder on the CD-ROM.

Sometimes you will want to output multiple files from a single XML, such as when one tool requires each game level in a separate XML file. This introduces a problem, since such transformations then require some understanding about filesystems, which is outside the scope of XML. However, it is possible in specific cases.

The simplest way is to process the XML file multiple times, passing a parameter into the XSLT process that determines which part of the nodes should be handled. The mechanism by which these are passed in will be determined by your XSL processor. However, internally you will always use

```
<xsl:param name="level"/>
```

and the value accessed with

```
<xsl:value-of select="$level"/>
```

An alternative implementation is by introducing platform-specific code embedded in the XSL, but that is not covered here.

Combining multiple XML documents into one requires some preprocessing on the XML that must occur before the XSLT program because the stylesheet can, by definition, only process one file. The output format you require will govern the solution employed. However, in most cases a simple concatenation will work by removing the duplicate headers, and wrapping each file in its own element tag because XML can only have one root element. One solution is by using two BASH scripts as follows,

combine.sh
```
# Creates the main header and root tag.
# It then handles every xml file in the directory.
echo \<?xml version="1.0" encoding="ISO-8859-1"?\>
echo \<combined\>
ls *.xml | xargs -i ./wrap.sh {}
echo \</combined\>
```

wrap.sh
```
# This encases a single XML file into an element tag
TAG=`echo $1 | tr -c [:alnum:] _`

echo \<$TAG\>
tail +2 $1
echo \</$TAG\>
```

ON THE CD
These are available on the CD-ROM in the `software/chapter10/scripts` folder.

XML to Binary Conversion

There are two main reasons for converting source XML into binary beyond the traditional need to create a compatible file format. The first is to improve loading speed. This might be through the implementation of a binary-based XML format, or a conversion into a custom format that maps directly to the end platform. Console games will often use this latter approach to generate vertex buffers that are binary-compatible with the graphics hardware. The second reason is to obfuscate the meaning of the XML and hide the game logic from the prying eyes of bored crackers.

However, these aren't necessarily *good* reasons for doing so. In the first instance, the loading speed may not be limited by the XML processing, disk speeds and caching generally play a larger role in I/O systems than the parsing that occurs on the CPU. There have been several debates as to whether XML should include a binary version for this reason, but the general thought is that it should remain as

ASCII as this maintains the cross-platform nature of the data format and keeps the benefits of having a directly editable format.

Converting XML into binary for the purpose of security also has issues insomuch as it adds an extra step to the toolchain, thereby increasing your turnaround time. Should your game import and process XML files, a better solution would be to compress these files for the final build and store them in a password-encrypted Zip file or similar.

The other remaining case, to build platform-compatible binary data, is worthy and shall be considered next. Unfortunately, it is a long process since XSLT doesn't provide any functionality to generate binary output streams. It *can* be coaxed into providing most of the necessary functionality, however, by generating the output in base64, or similar, and then process this in an external tool. The most common method, however, is to parse the XML with a separate program and let it intelligently produce the blocks of binary data, which is covered next.

Parsing XML

There are two basic ways in which to parse an XML file: DOM and SAX. DOM stands for Document Object Model, and these parsers build the complete hierarchical XML structure in memory when loading the file, so that afterward code can recursively process each node as it sees fit. This is the more powerful of the two mechanisms as arbitrary parts of the tree can be ignored, reprocessed, or studied ahead of time to produce the most exacting result necessary. The biggest downside has already been alluded to. That is, it is all built in memory, which can result in a lot of memory and large parsing structures. Additionally you may need to write extra code to save the XML file back to disk from the internalized DOM tree structure, should it change.

The SAX parser is the Simple API for XML. This parser triggers callbacks to user code that describe a parsing event whenever a tag is opened or closed. The callback indicates the element tag, the attributes present along with their values, and the textual data inside it, if any. It is a specific form of stream parser that works sequentially through the file, stopping at each new element. Consequently, tree information for a tag's subelements cannot be included. SAX is good for processing very large XML files and extracting small pieces of data from them, or for use in small memory environments. One of the biggest problems with SAX is the bulk of the code that can result from having each element handled explicitly in long switch statements. This bulk increases if you need to know the parent tags, or need to recall any contextual information from them.

Well-Formed and Valid XML

There are two levels of strictness involved with XML. Well-formed XML means that every opened element tag is correctly closed, no tags mismatch, and that no other similarly obvious XML-based problems occur. It performs no validity checks on the context or specifics of the data itself; that is, if the XML is supposed to describe a mesh, but begins with the element tag sound, no error will be raised if the sound tag is correctly formatted. Therefore, this is the easiest and simplest verification check to add.

Valid XML, on the other hand, requires a schema or DTD to verify the element tags and attributes used within the XML are applicable to that particular type of XML file. This has a much broader scope and has additional checks that ensure the correct child elements are present, and that attributes fit within a particular range, for example.

In either case, you can verify the validity of your source XML using xmllint, a small program available from *http://www.mame.net/downmain.html.* Although this is not generally needed in the toolchain, since all XML will be generated by machines, it does provide a quick sanity check of the data, especially because some programmers and artists will amend the XML by hand to overcome shortfalls in the tools, and break the format.

To check for well-formed XML, the invocation is simply

```
xmllint —noout level.xml
```

By default, xmllint will echo the input back to the screen; so you suppress this with noout. If the XML is correct, no output will be generated and a zero return code will be returned.

For valid XML, you should use

```
xmllint —valid —loaddtd level.dtd —noout level.xml
```

or

```
xmllint —valid —schema level.xsd —noout level.xml
```

In both cases, you can omit the reference to the validating schema if the XML file indicates what it is, which it should do, but most internal developers omit this for simplicity.

Expat

ON THE CD

Expat is James Clark's popular Open Source stream parser, and is featured on the CD-ROM. It has been used as the basis for XML parsing in both Perl (as XML::Parser::Expat) and Python. It functions as a basic SAX parser, invoking specific callbacks as each tag is either opened or closed. It can also be used to create a DOM tree, and although this code is not included in the standard package, many different implementations have been contributed by various third-party authors.

Both DOM and SAX have formal definitions of the interfaces required to access XML data from them; therefore, Expat is more correctly referred to as a stream parser.

Homepage: *http://www.jclark.com/xml/expat.html* (original page) and *http://www.libexpat.org*

License: MIT-based

Distribution: Source and binary only

First release: 1998

Current version: 1.95.8 (stable since July 23, 2004)

Platform(s): All known, with little to no tweaking

Dependencies: None

Other resources: Mailing lists, books, articles, forums

Integrating Expat

The source for *Expat*, while often impenetrable in places, works well in a confined space, and compiles cleanly with only a minimum of effort. The parser itself is split into three basic parts. The first, XMLParse, comprises of a single file (of nearly 4,000 lines) that scans the source file to find tagged elements and their attributes. The information it needs to do this comes form the second part, XMLTok, the tokenizer. When incorporating Expat into an existing project you should note that two of the source files (`xmltok_impl.c` and `xmltok_ns.c`) must not be compiled into the project directly as they are `#include`d from existing source files.

The third part of the Expat trilogy involves the user-supplied callbacks. Being a stream parser, no DOM tree is created, and so nothing happens to the data at all if this section is omitted. There are three callbacks that cover the important features of the parser: `startElement`, `endElement`, and `dataHandler`.

Expat is initialized, and these callbacks prepared with the basic scaffold of

```
XML_Parser parser = XML_ParserCreate(NULL);
XML_SetElementHandler(parser, startElement, endElement);
XML_SetCharacterDataHandler(parser, dataHandler);
```

The XML file on the disk is processed by manipulating a copy of the data in memory. This makes it trivial to adopt XML files on consoles or other systems without the standard I/O library. The parsing happens by repeatedly calling the `XML_Parse` function with consecutive parts from the file. This works by allocating a buffer, filling it, and then returning the amount of data filled. The size of this buffer is completely arbitrary and doesn't have to worry about whether an element tag is entirely encased within the buffer, since Expat will automatically track this for you. This can be declared with

```
char buffer[1024];
```

A typical read loop is then implemented like this:

```
do {
    int len = file.Read(buffer, sizeof(buffer));

    done = len < sizeof(buf);

    if (!XML_Parse(parser, buf, len, done)) {
        /*
        Error,
        Line: XML_GetCurrentLineNumber(parser)
        File : XML_ErrorString(XML_GetErrorCode(parser))
        */
        return FALSE;
    }
} while (!done);
```

ON THE CD   An example of this code in action can be found on the accompanying CD-ROM in the `bookcode/sgxcore/source/libraries/expat` directory.

Handling the memory is not as simple, however, because the `xmlparse.c` file contains no less than 27 different dynamic memory allocation points. Despite being the only file of the package that uses dynamic memory, it is preferably to make the changes outside of it. This can be accomplished by simply placing macros in `xmldef.h` to redirect the standard memory allocators with macros. For example,

```
#define malloc(x)    customMalloc(x)
```

This is the mechanism used by the Mozilla client to integrate Expat, which has alternate allocators. Note that you must replace all standard memory functions—`malloc`, `calloc`, `realloc`, and `free`—for *Expat* to work correctly.

Creating a DOM Tree

During development, it is often more usual to parse game files from an XML DOM tree, than it is to simply watch the tags appear as `startElement` is repeatedly called. This is because there is no sense of depth held within a SAX parser, and with each game object likely to have many identical elements in its tree (e.g., position or properties) a SAX parser would be saddled with code such as

```
if (bInsideHumanElement) pHuman->properties = properties;
if (bInsideAlienElement) pAlien->properties = properties;
if (bInsideSpaceshipElement) pShip->properties = properties;
```

Therefore, it is simpler to generate and recursively parse a DOM tree.

Building your own tree from SAX events will normally use as much memory as switching to a normal DOM parser.

The first port of call is the callback functions, which must have the prototypes of

```
void startElement(void *userData, const char *name, const char **atts);
void endElement(void *userData, const char *name);
void dataHandler(void *userData, const XML_Char *string, int len);
```

When each callback handler is executed, there is almost enough information to add a new tag into a DOM tree. Almost—because the pointers to the DOM tree itself are unknown. The userData argument is used to replenish this shortfall, as it can point to any structure you should desire and is assigned to the parser before the first call to XML_Parse. Usually a suitable structure is created and its pointer used.

```
struct expat_state {
   sgxXMLNode                  *pCurrentRoot;
   sgxVector<sgxXMLNode *>   NodeStack;
};

expat_state state;
// ... as before
XML_SetUserData(parser, &state);
```

Each callback can then pick up this information easily and add the tag to the appropriate tree. The node stack is kept so that it is possible to assign the correct root node when the recursion unwinds with each call to endElement. This partners

```
void startElement(void *userData, const char *name, const char **atts)
{
   expat_state *pState = (expat_state *)userData;
   sgxXMLNode  *pTag = new sgxXMLNode;

   pTag->SetElement(sgxXMLElement(name));
```

```
const char **p = atts;
while(*p) {
   pTag->AddAttribute(sgxString(*p), sgxString(*(p+1)));
   p+=2;
}

pState->pCurrentRoot = pState->pCurrentRoot->AddNode(pTag);
pState->NodeStack.push_back(pState->pCurrentRoot);
}
```

and

```
void endElement(void *userData, const char *name)
{
   expat_state *pState = (expat_state *)userData;

   pState->NodeStack.pop_back();
   pState->pCurrentRoot = pState->NodeStack.back();
}
```

This is supplemented only by the `dataHandler` that adds textual data into the current node, thus,

```
void dataHandler(void *userData, const XML_Char *s, int len)
{
   expat_state *pState = (expat_state *)userData;

   pState->pCurrentRoot->AppendData(sgxString(s, len));
}
```

It is possible to receive two calls to `dataHandler` *for the same node, therefore the string should be appended, not replaced.*

NOTE

ON THE CD

This implementation features in the SGX Core by way of a demonstration. An alternative Open Source approach can be found with scew on the CD-ROM, which is released under the LGPL.

Compression

Storing data in a compressed format provides a couple of benefits. First and most obviously, it occupies less disk space. This is generally more useful on console games with fixed disk limits than those destined for PC, but it can also be useful when downloading dynamic content in MMOGs. Second, it provides a thin layer of protection or obfuscation to those who delight in cracking the game data. And finally, it gives the potential for faster loading times. This is not only because less information needs to be loaded from the disk, but also due to the lower number of disk seeks that need to occur when loading sequential blocks from a single file, compared to the loading of many different physical disparate files. This latter point is primarily true when reading from CD- and DVD-based media because the disc structure can be specified by the developer; files copied onto a user's hard drive is often fragmented by the operating system.

Zlib

Zlib implements a lossless, general-purpose compression algorithm. It is Open Source (under its own license) and not covered by any patent. The bulk of the work rests with two developers, Jean-loup Gailly (compression) and Mark Adler (decompression), both of whom have good pedigree in the field of compression having worked on `gzip` and `UnZip`, respectively.

> **Homepage:** *http://www.zlib.net*
>
> **License:** Zlib (BSD-like, but less stringent).
>
> **Distribution:** Source and DLL.
>
> **First release:** 1995.
>
> **Current version:** 1.2.3 (stable since July 18, 2005).
>
> **Platform(s):** All known, with little to no tweaking. The DLL package only includes VisualStudio link library stubs, however, so you will need to use `implib` (for Borland) or `dlltool` (gcc).
>
> **Dependencies:** None.
>
> **Other resources:** Mailing lists for developers. Information is also available on the general-purpose comp.compression newsgroup.

Installation

ON THE CD

The easiest way to start using zlib under Windows is to use the binary DLL package from the CD-ROM and copy the header files into one of your include directories. The DLL (`zlib1.dll`) should be placed in the `windows/system32` folder (which may be called `winnt` or `win2k`, depending on your installation). Then add the `zlib1.lib` file to your project, and you're ready to go.

In its simplest form, zlib consists of one algorithm for compression and one for decompression. It is possible to enhance zlib with different decoms because the interface is identical in all cases. From here, additional layers of functionality can be added to handle streaming decompression (that occurs in discrete chunks to reduce memory) or file-based decompression. Zlib supports of all this—although no file handling occurs inside the library itself. This is good news for most developers because it allows you to use the best file operations available on your platform of choice. The only losers here are the tutorial writers who have to reinvent the wheel with standard file operations each time, but the positives far outweigh the negatives.

One hook that zlib does require from the end user is for memory allocation, although this is only required for streaming decompression.

Finally, note that zconf.h holds the abstractions for types; uInt must be at least 16 bits and uLong must be at least 32. All current consoles and development platforms can fulfill this clause.

Memory Compression and Decompression

This is the simplest method to process compressed data. The compress function performs a one-off compression routine on a raw memory buffer. It doesn't give you any control over memory allocation and doesn't provide much in the way of feedback as to the resultant data, but it does work very fast and is suitable for many applications.

```
char compressedBuffer[1024];
int compressedSize = sizeof(compressedBuffer);

int errorCode  = compress(compressedBuffer, &compressedSize,
        inputBuffer, inputBufferSize);
```

The errorCode will return 0 (Z_OK) for success, with negative values indicating error codes and positive numbers highlighting exceptional, but normal events. When using simple compression in this way, the only errors you are likely to get are Z_BUF_ERROR, indicating the output buffer is not large enough to hold the compressed data, or Z_MEM_ERROR for out of memory.

In addition, there is a little-used compress2 function that works identically to the one earlier, but takes a final integer argument describing the method by which the data should be compressed. This may be one of Z_DEFAULT_COMPRESSION, Z_NO_COMPRESSION, Z_BEST_SPEED, or Z_BEST_COMPRESSION. With data blocks less than 2 KB in size there is not usually more than 30 bytes difference in the resultant compressed sizes. However, with larger block sizes this facility becomes more significant.

The numeric values of the compression type, like Z_BEST_SPEED, give away a secret on zlib's implementation. On a scale of 1 to 9, a compression of 1 gives the best speed, while 9 gives worst speed but best compression. This is truly scalable between both extremes, with the default compression considered a level 6.

To decompress a memory block you need to feed the same parameters back to uncompress using the pointer-size metaphor.

```
int errorCode = uncompress(decompressedBuffer, &decompressedSize,
        compressedBuffer, compressedBufferSize);
```

In reality, both functions are wrappers to the streamed versions called inflate and deflate. If your game must avoid malloc and free, then you will be using the streamed versions directly, anyway.

Streaming Compression and Decompression

To make effective use of the compress routines on large data sets, it is necessary to switch to the streaming compression routines. These allow input data blocks to be passed into the compression code piecemeal, allowing application developers to determine how much memory they wish to budget on buffers. This technique is also used to decompress files saved on disk.

The structure of the streaming implementation is very simple. It begins with the two-part initialization of the stream, then it performs deflate (compression) or inflate (decompression) on presized blocks, and finally tidies itself up by closing the stream.

The first part of the initialization process is to correctly create a z_stream structure with the necessary data. The example that follows is for compression and is identical to the memory-based code you previously saw:

```
z_stream stream;
stream.next_in = (Bytef*) inputBuffer;
stream.avail_in = (uInt) inputBufferSize;
stream.next_out = compressedBuffer;
stream.avail_out = (uInt)* compressedSize;
```

The z_stream structure holds everything that is necessary for zlib to do its job. This allows the library to be fully reentrant should it be required by the application.

Then the memory handlers are redirected to your own code:

```
void *customAllocator(void *opaque, uInt items, uInt size);
void  customFree(void *opaque, void *pAddress);

stream.zalloc = customAllocator;
stream.zfree = customFree;
stream.opaque = NULL;
```

Alternatively, by setting the `zalloc` and `zfree` values to NULL, zlib will use the default implementations of `malloc` and `free` from inside C's standard library. At least one of the previous two steps must occur, lest the uninitialized function pointers get dereferenced. These memory allocators must obviously be reentrant if the application is to be multithreaded in any way.

The opaque pointer allows you to thread custom data from the initial stream structure to any call of the memory functions. This will often be a reference to the specific allocator necessary for this type of compression. It matches the standard element of user data found in many libraries.

From here, it is a simple matter to deflate the stream and cleanly exit:

```
errorCode = deflate(&stream, Z_FINISH);
if (errorCode != Z_STREAM_END) {
   deflateEnd(&stream);
   return errorCode == Z_OK ? Z_BUF_ERROR : errorCode;
}
errorCode = deflateEnd(&stream);
```

Although WinZip, gzip, Zip-it, and so on, all use zlib compression internally, each adds its own headers to the data making them incompatible to other high-level applications. The files in `contrib/minizip` *may be used if you need .zip compatibility.*

The License

To quote the documentation,

> /* zlib.h — interface of the 'zlib' general purpose compression library
>
>   version 1.2.2, October 3rd, 2004
>
>   Copyright (C) 1995-2004 Jean-loup Gailly and Mark Adler

This software is provided 'as-is', without any express or implied warranty. In no event will the authors be held liable for any damages arising from the use of this software.

Permission is granted to anyone to use this software for any purpose, including commercial applications, and to alter it and redistribute it freely, subject to the following restrictions:

1. The origin of this software must not be misrepresented; you must not claim that you wrote the original software. If you use this software in a

product, an acknowledgment in the product documentation would be appreciated but is not required.
2. Altered source versions must be plainly marked as such, and must not be misrepresented as being the original software.
3. This notice may not be removed or altered from any source distribution. Jean-loup Gailly *jloup@gzip.org*
Mark Adler *madler@alumni.caltech.edu*
*/

License Commentary

As you can see, the license is very liberal. If you incorporate zlib in an executable of any form, it's yours to do with as you wish. As Clause 1 says, acknowledgment is not required. If you release the source—either intentionally or because you're combining it with GPL code that requires you to—then you must indicate that you've changed the code, and keep the license notice.

STANDARD LIBRARIES

Despite the rabid insistence of some developers, games follow the rules of most general-purpose applications. Therefore, it is not surprising that each game will need some measure of some all-purpose libraries.

Localization with GNU gettext

With games playing on the world stage, there is no reason why they should not be localized for the gamers' home territory. This process covers several areas, namely:

- Translating text on a per-language basis
- Changing graphics that contain language-specific text
- Changing in-game text strings to include translations
- Adjusting UI to cope with the size of the new text
- Adjusting other game elements, such as the currency, to match the locale

The issues we're concerned with here involve getting new text strings into the game. However, you must also implement a workflow structure so that you can determine which strings those are, and produce a simple mechanism for delivering this content to the translators.

Because the language is often selected from the first menu in the game, it is generally unknown at compile time; so the mechanism used must use runtime translation, and is therefore always the same. That is, the game requests a string using a unique identifier and the translation module uses this to determine the correct string from a language-specific catalog. The difference is in the implementation and the data type used for that unique identifier.

Games with limited memory can use the simple implementation of an integer ID that indexes a table of strings. This table is generally loaded from disc, but can be stored as an internal 2D array. The code is simple to write and fast to execute, but is problematic for larger games because the maintenance costs increase. Consider the basic code in this case:

```
Gfx.textOut(getString(TXT_GAME_OVER));

// ...

const char *getString(int id) {
    return pCurrentStringBank[id];
}
```

Every time you add a new piece of text to the game, a new, unique ID must be created (usually in a common header file, which requires a large recompile) and the string to each language file added. While this does not sound like a lot of work, it doesn't scale well when several people are adding text strings to the game, particularly as each check-in requires a hand-merge to prevent ID collisions.

Also, the implementation presented here lacks many of the features necessary to correctly handle foreign languages. Unfortunately, many developers consider it complete! Handling plurals, for example, differs greatly between languages—even more so than it does in English. In English, most people are happy to pluralize words by adding an *s*, although some cases require *es*. But some words change entirely, like from *goose* to *geese*. And some don't change at all. With English-speaking developers it is usual to code this logic into the game itself:

```
if (deadGeese == 1) {
    pScore = getString(TXT_DEAD_GOOSE);
} else {
    pScore = getString(TXT_DEAD_GEESE);
}
```

But this, then, requires either some horrible additional logic or duplicated text strings for every single other foreign language. Needless to say, this is not a good solution.

Further problems occur when building strings dynamically. The sprintf function is still most game developers' favorite for inserting absent nouns into a string like

```
sprintf(string, "The %s sat on the %s", szFeline, szFloorCovering);
```

However, some languages translate this as the equivalent of

```
sprintf(string, "The %s was sat on by the %s", szFeline,
szFloorCovering);
```

This is wrong. Again, you either have to produce two separate text strings or surround the piece of problem text with

```
if (language == FRENCH)
```

or other similar monstrosities. Not only that, but you have to implement a lot of error checking within the tools to catch mismatched string formatting characters, too. All of these problems can be solved by changing the way in which you think about the identifiers, and by moving to gettext.

The `Gettext` Package

The purpose of gettext is to provide a complete localization solution for all Free software. It does this by providing two sets of components. The first is the `gettext` library. This is linked into your game and provides a number of functions that translate text string into foreign versions by means of an externally-loaded catalog of translations. It includes enough functionality to handle problematic plurals and differing word orders.

The second part includes a set of tools to extract text from source code, maintain the text during development, and build binary text catalogs suitable for the gettext library. In the best tradition of data-driven development, these catalogs can be used and tested for completeness without recompiling the code.

> **Homepage:** *http://www.gnu.org/software/gettext*
>
> **License:** GNU LGPL (Appendix C) for the library; GNU GPL (Appendix B) for the tools
>
> **Distribution:** Source and binary
>
> **First release:** July 8, 1994
>
> **Current version:** 5.0.2 (stable since March 17, 2004)
>
> **Platform(s):** All known, with little to no tweaking
>
> **Dependencies:** iconv (depending on port)
>
> **Other resources:** Mailing lists, books, articles, forums

Coming from GNU, the gettext package is very Unix oriented, and as such, you won't find a Windows port on its website. However, there are at least three people maintaining versions on our behalf. They are:

Tor Lillqvist, who handles the GTK+ port for Windows, which includes the version available from *http://www.gimp.org/~tml/gimp/win32/gettext-dev-0.14.5.zip*

Franco Bez, whose page at *http://people.freenet.de/franco.bez/gettext/gettext_win32_en.html* is still available, although fairly inactive

The anonymous group at *http://gnuwin32.sourceforge.net*, which maintains a fairly active port

There is little difference among them, as they all stem from the same software; however, the specific version of each varies. The version on the CD-ROM comes from *http://www.gimp.org*.

Integration

Linux users will normally have gettext installed by default or find it trivial to build the source packages from the homepage. For Windows users, the prebuilt library and DLL aren't any more difficult to incorporate. Installation follows the traditional trinity of header-library-DLL, with the header being copied into your include directory structure, the library getting included with the project files, and the DLL being placed in the windows/system32 directory.

Foreign text is retrieved using the same catalog idea you saw earlier, but in this case the unique ID is a string; not an integer. This is the first secret move that improves productivity in localization since no external files need to be rebuilt for the English version. The second is that the function call that performs the translation will return the input string argument if no translations exist for that term. This means you should determine the string ID for best practice by picking the same text that should appear on-screen—hyphens, commas, and all! Then the default game will work normally until the translations are ready. And when they are, it means that any missed translation strings will appear obvious as the English text is displayed, instead of the more usual scenario where nothing is rendered and no bug can be logged.

CAUTION
You should always ensure the text used in the IDs is good enough to be displayed on-screen. This means no profanity or libel. Even if you create a completely separate English catalog to hide these strings, they will still be present in the code since they're used as identifiers. A simple scan of the executable by a bored cracker may get you enough negative publicity to damage your reputation.

The function calls that perform the translations are also used to determine which strings in the code need translating as the extraction tool (xgettext, as you see later) searches for instances of those functions.

gettext

This simple function translates the input string to another, based on the globally initialized catalog. It is a very simple "one in-one out" principle. The string returned should be considered constant, as the pointer dereferences a string from the catalog:

```
pString = gettext("High Score:");
```

This can only be used in active code because of the function invocation.

gettext_noop

This variation of the previous code is used for text strings that appear in initializers such as

```
char *pHighScore = gettext_noop("High score:");
```

This symbol is also recognized by the tools as a variant of gettext, so the text within it will also be added to the catalog to be translated. However, the compiler sees it as a null operation, and so evaluates to

```
char *pHighScore = "High score:";
```

Therefore, no translation occurs until the string is called with gettext proper:

```
Gfx.textOut(gettext(pHighScore));
```

It is therefore correct to think of each pointer, or string literal, as the translation ID and only consider the result from gettext (or ngettext, but not gettext_noop) as translated text.

You do not have to worry about called gettext twice on any particular string because if foreign text is passed through, it won't exist as a key and will get passed straight back out again.

ngettext

This is used to translate plurals, so any text that has the potential of needing to differentiate between one and many, should use this function:

```
pString = ngettext("You killed %d goose!", "You killed %d geese", kills);
```

The benefit of this structure is that the *gettext* library switches between the different variations of text, not the game logic. Since *gettext* knows more about the locale than the game, it can make an improved judgment.

This interface works because the game is assumed to have been written first in English, where there are only two variations: plural and singular. If your mother tongue is not English, then add two placeholder cases for plural and singular and add the translations to the catalog file for your own language as if it were a foreign language.

Note that the plural mechanism is more complex than a simple

```
if (n == 1) {
    return pSingular;
} else {
    return pPlural; /* "You have 0 bullets" is caught here */
}
```

because natural language is more complex than that. French, for example uses a singular noun when discussing "zero" items, which would break the traditional logic. Most languages in the Baltic family take this idea one step further by having separate words for zero, one, and two. Trying to retrofit this logic into the game—in all cases—would be troublesome at best. Therefore, gettext understands that in the case of n==2, and language==Baltic it needs an additional string. The tools know this, too, and will check for their inclusion when processing such language files.

In all cases, do not change the string identifiers without good reason, as this will cause synchronization problems with the translators.

The Text Pipeline

The focus of gettext is the supporting tool set that generates the resulting language catalogs. This multistage process begins with the source code.

Creating a Template

The template is a list of all text strings in the game, along with some brief data on how they're used. This allows gettext to make a distinction between words used in standard translations and those that require plurals to support ngettext. Running the xgettext tool on each file in the project like this,

```
xgettext maingame.cpp hud.cpp menu.cpp
```

will produce a template file called messages.po. It does this by searching the source files for any use of the strings gettext, gettext_noop, and ngettext and extracts quoted strings from within them. It makes no changes to the source files. However, it understands the basic structure of the C language (and C++, Java, and Python, among others) and so will not extract calls to gettext hidden inside comments, or variables called ngettext. You can request that xgettext produces a menutext.po instead of the default name by using the -d switch like this:

```
xgettext –d menutext maingame.cpp hud.cpp menu.cpp
```

This switch also has another important function as it dictates the textdomain for this set of strings, which is declared at runtime.

xgettext cannot evaluate any of the preprocessor instructions, so any gettext function references appearing within #if-#endif blocks will always be included. If this is not desirable, you can ask xgettext to read the text from standard input and feed a preprocessed version of the source to it. With gcc compilers, this is done using

```
xgettext –C < (gcc –E maingame.cpp)
```

Visual Studio[4] supports this with

```
cl /EP maingame.cpp
```

although you will generally have to use temporary files to transfer the output data from the preprocessor to xgettext because of the comparatively limited command shell in Windows.

If you now examine the language template file (messages.po by default), you will notice that every translation string is ready in the following format. Each string is supplemented with filename, line number, the string identifier, and a gap (msgstr) ready for translation.

```
#: maingame.cpp:432
msgid "Game Over"
msgstr ""
```

You should then copy this template file (to say french/maintext.po) so that it can be edited by the translators.

TIP

Depending on your engine design, xgettext *can also report on which assets are still accessed from within the game. This can help your company avoid getting into hot water!*

Building the Catalogs

Despite the speed of modern machines, having random access to a large chunk of textual data is always going to be suboptimal. Just searching for a matching ID will take a noticeable amount of time. Therefore, it is necessary to build these translated string tables into binary catalogs where the IDs are stored in, say, a hash table for fast access. This requires an additional tool that is also supplied. It's called `msgfmt`.

```
msgfmt -o french.mo french.po
```

The `-o` flag ensures the binary version avoids the default `messages.mo` name.

In addition to a straightforward conversion, `msgfmt` will also check the format of the messages and deliver any warnings it feels necessary. For example, if the format specifiers (such as `%d` and `%s`) present in the text differ, or if one string ends with \n and the other doesn't, then a message to that effect will be given.

This translated catalog must then be copied into a suitable directory structure, so that different languages can be incorporated without conflict.

```
copy french.mo game\locale\fr_FR\LC_MESSAGES\maintext.mo
```

This catalog can then be loaded, and used, with the simple inclusion of

```
#include <locale.h>

char *pPackage = "maintext";
char *pDirectory = "locale";

setlocale(LC_ALL, "");
bindtextdomain(pPackage, pDirectory);
textdomain(pPackage);
```

Voila! A translated game.

Text that doesn't appear as part of the normal gameplay, such as credits, instructions, and so on, can be added to a manually created po *file, converted and accessed as normal. The IDs in this case would be numbered sequentially from CREDIT_0001, for example.*

Maintenance

The aforementioned functionality is enough on its own to sell `gettext`, but it would have the same problems as any other solution if, and when, new text is added. The solution to this problem is covered with the `msgmerge` tool. This takes the existing, part-translated, text file (french.po, for example) and combines it with the latest po from the xgettext tool. This then adds any new strings that have been created since the original was built, but leaves the already translated text as it was.

```
msgmerge -o newfile.po french.po new_maintext.po
```

One alternative method that is often discussed is to keep the original po file as a template for future comparisons. This template is the same as the normal output from xgettext.

```
xgettext -d menutext -o menutext.pot maingame.cpp hud.cpp menu.cpp
```

The benefit of using a separate template file (pot) is that it allows the standard po file to be used for English translations. While having an English translation (when the IDs are already in English) might sound unexpected, it does allow dynamic text changes to occur without a recompilation of the standard game code. This gives you a get-out clause for those developers whose IDs are written in poor English, or have accidentally misspelled the text.

Safe Integration

Gettext has a very small library; the intl.dll weighs in at around 44 KB and even in those distributions where iconv.dll is also required, there's still less than a megabyte of additional DLLs.

There is an additional bonus for Windows users insomuch that the DLL can be loaded dynamically and, if it doesn't exist, the game will use the identifier strings (which are also valid text) as the output. Dynamic DLL handling is included by default in Franco's version of gettext, but can be ported to the other implementation if desired.

Missed Strings

Throughout the localization process, it is assumed that all translatable strings will be encased with calls to gettext. This should always be the case. But occasionally text will get missed, and while the English version looks fine, the foreign versions will be lacking in several areas and it will take someone fully familiar with the game to spot the omissions. Therefore, another tool is required to check for anything in quotes that doesn't get passed to the gettext function. This can be achieved with

```
perl -n -e
  'print "$. : $1$2\n" while /(n?gettext(?:_noop)?\()?\"(.*?)\"\)?/g;'
  - filename.c |
  grep -v gettext
```

Naturally, this will produce false positives in the form of filenames, but it is a good final check before the text is sent for translation.

License

As noted earlier, this is split into two. Any game that uses the gettext library must be compatible with the LGPL library. Therefore, any changes made to the library should be fed back into the community, while the game-only code needs appear as object files linkable with a free compiler. However, this is a comparatively small part of the package as you only generally use the gettext and ngettext functions. Therefore, it is feasible to rewrite these functions if you are desperate to avoid the LGPL connotations.

In contrast, the tools have been made available under the GNU GPL. This means you can use them within your tools pipeline provided they are not recompiled or linked with your other tools, as this constitutes a derivative work. If they are, and you distribute the toolchain to anyone else, then you must make the entire source available. However, if you only ever call xgettext from a system call, then the GPL does not apply.

The only issue to raise is that software under the LGPL can be rereleased under the GPL at the whim of a developer. Therefore, make sure that the version of gettext you use, particularly if it's a Windows port, is still under the LGPL and has not accidentally (or purposefully) changed its license to that of the GPL.

GAME-SPECIFIC LIBRARIES

While much of the engine developers' work is applicable to many fields in computing, the world of the game programmer is not. To a database programmer, or a bank worker, an A* search algorithm is meaningless. Here then are a number of libraries whose use outside of games is fairly limiting. This means that in the general case there are fewer support groups and mailing lists available. The flip side is that because the only people using it are games developers, the focus is much greater, and those involved can provide more in-depth assistance.

Plib

This project, Steve's[5] Portable Game Library, is the mutant love child between an enhanced version of GLUT and SDL. It utilizes the rendering facilities of OpenGL to produce a suite of game tools, without generating a monolithic engine like CrystalSpace. The Plib source archive, included on the CD-ROM, builds 12 different libraries that encompass separate parts of the development spectrum such as joystick handling, GUI functionality, a scripting language, and an OpenGL scene

ON THE CD

graph. Each library builds into a separate .lib file and is completely self-contained (although some header file sharing does occur) enabling you to incorporate only the libraries you need.

OpenGL and GLUT are needed for the graphic-based enhancements, such as the GUI and the fonts, but their use is localized to around 12 files and would be easy to change. As it stands, the Plib UI library (pui, which nonintuitively stands for Picoscopic User Interface) also supports SDL and native rendering giving the user enough template code to implement a replacement driver, should the need arise.

Homepage: *http://plib.sourceforge.net*

License: GNU LGPL (Appendix C) with an exception for embedded systems such as games consoles

Distribution: Source only

First release: April 1, 1999

Current version: 1.8.4 (stable since January 2005)

Platform(s): Windows, Linux, and MacOS X

Dependencies: OpenGL and GLUT

Other resources: Three mailing lists: announce, users, and developers

Plib follows the convention initiated by the Linux kernel where the even point release version number (8 in version 1.8.4, for example) indicates stable versions and odd numbers are used for versions that are deemed unstable, experimental, or for developers only.

Integration

Considering the originator and maintainer of this project doesn't use Windows, Plib is surprisingly well supported under the Microsoft platform. The supplied archive includes .dsp project files for Visual Studio 6.0 and will compile out of the box, with .NET automatically converting the project on load. No workspace is given, however, so a batch build is necessary to compile all the libraries. This build process will put all the libraries (in both debug and release versions) and the appropriate header files in the root of the Plib directory from which you have just built. It is then your responsibility to manually copy them into the appropriate directories. To ease compilation of the examples, and to follow the guidelines laid out at the start of Part B, all headers should go into devlib/plib. So you can reference the sublibraries with

```
#include "plib/sg.h"
```

One of the disadvantages of individual, self-contained libraries is that there are no common elements to help limit code size. However, the approach taken by Plib is that any common types and classes should be kept in specific header files, with their methods written as inline functions. This applies only to specific functions that would hold little sway on the total executable size (such as the endian swapping functions) or those that would be traditionally inlined for speed in most cases anyway.

In addition, larger methods are generally presented as global functions, external to the classes on which they operate. In this way, those methods will be compiled into the library to reduce code size when used, but can be ignored entirely when they're not. Consequently, any other library may use their functionality without affecting the dependencies. That said, only pw (the plib windowing library) and ul (utility library) are completely independent, as will be covered in the library breakdown later.

A customized memory manager is absent from Plib; so those wanting stricter control over their allocations than `stdlib` provides will have to amend the existing calls to `new` (of which there are, unfortunately, several, constructing both classes and native types like `char`) and the single remaining call to `malloc`!

Furthermore, there is no abstraction to the filesystem. This means console developers will have to replace the 50 `fopen` calls to something more suitable. Plib works like most other libraries insomuch as it parses its file formats in the engine (as opposed to loading ready-to-use resources provided by the toolchain). Consequently, the file I/O routines are more involved than they need to be, so once Plib has been proven to work in a PC environment, it would be prudent to move all the format parsing code into the toolchain and purge it from the Plib source itself. This will automatically remove the vast majority of `fopen` calls, thereby simplifying the problem.

Finally, be aware that none of the standard types is abstracted (except for `sgFloat`).

The Libraries

Each library has the same loosely coupled ethos. This allows individual library components to be included or ignored as appropriate. This is fortunate because there is usually a better, more full-featured implementation available for some individual libraries. For example, Plib includes a sound library, but it falls short of the facilities offered by those you saw in Chapter 6, "Audio," such as SDL_mixer. Employing SDL_mixer will introduce an overhead that Plib/SL will not because it also requires SDL to be present. This overhead may be minimal in terms of final executable size, but the management of the code will be that much larger because the SDL headers will need to exist and be correctly pathed in. This, in turn, will increase the chance of name collisions and require more libraries to be linked and/or installed. And an increase in libraries means longer compile times because the linker is working harder to remove the redundancies (assuming it can) and has more Open Source licenses to worry about. This includes both the legal aspect of ensuring each license is mutually compatible and the acknowledgment angle making sure each library is mentioned in the documentation as is often required by the BSD and X11 licenses. There is no right answer—only what is right for a specific project.

Joystick

This is a simple cross-platform library to handle joystick input. It uses platform-specific code to extract the appropriate data and keep it in common structures. The benefit of this approach is that it is no longer tied to other native-like APIs (such as Glut) that are too old to handle the "modern" advancements in joystick design, such as the hat. This is a fairly small library that automatically handles one of the most important parts of game-based joystick handling, namely the dead zone.

It depends on ul (utility library).

PUI

Pronounced pooh-ey, this is the Picoscopic User Interface Library and handles simple interface widgets like buttons, sliders, and menus. Each widget is derived from a simple puObject class, which uses a virtual draw method to handle the rendering, and doHit for the control.

It depends on ul (utility library), sg (standard geometry), and fnt (font).

There is also puiaux, with follows on from pui to provide more interface widgets, including a file selector, combo box, and compass.

SG

This is the standard geometry module that contains the math code. Despite being common to many of the plib libraries, this code does not adopt the best practices for a modern game as the implementation of most functions are not the faster methods available, so time should be allotted to improving this code in this area. Or, more likely, replacing it entirely.

However, the biggest problem in using this library is that the angles are measured in degrees, and not standard radians. In the short term, you can amend the sg.h file to begin,

```
#undef  SG_DEGREES_TO_RADIANS
#undef  SG_RADIANS_TO_DEGREES

#define SG_DEGREES_TO_RADIANS   1
#define SG_RADIANS_TO_DEGREES   1
```

This convinces the functions they are working in radians and should help the compiler eliminate the instructions. You then need to end the file with

```
#undef  SG_DEGREES_TO_RADIANS
#undef  SG_RADIANS_TO_DEGREES

#define SG_DEGREES_TO_RADIANS    (SG_PI/SG_180)
#define SG_RADIANS_TO_DEGREES    (SG_180/SG_PI)
```

so that other parts of Plib that use these functions can still work in degrees, although the number of cases where this happens is minimal.

It is recommended that this library becomes a wrapper to an existing math library, and it remains solely for Plib code that depends on it.

The standard geometry library depends on ul.

SL

This is a functioning, but minimal, sound library that supports basic wave playback and MOD trackers out of the box. However, the slDSP class only supports a single wave at the time, which is not good enough for most games. Furthermore, its multiwave scheduling code can only handle 8-bit waves. Unless your needs are ultra-basic, this is not the solution you're looking for.

Its control over the mixer device is also less than stellar, meaning you must resort to CPU-based mixing placing a heavier burden on the processor than would happen with SDL_mixer or OpenAL, which performs a lot of work on the sound card.

It depends on ul.

FNT

This is a bitmap font handler that sits on top of OpenGL and uses preformatted textures to draw text as quickly as possible onto the screen. These textures are generated separately with the gentexfont program, samples of which are provided in the Plib archive.

While this is certainly quicker that using TrueType fonts, the results are not as attractive. Therefore, these are best kept for brief in-game messages. Larger bodies of text may need the extra anti-aliasing support that FreeType gives you, or the extra text formatting capabilities because fnt only understands the newline character; the use of tabs, or non-left-justified text will require extra code.

It depends on ul and sg.

PW

The Plib Windowing library is very small, but only truly useful for those using OpenGL in a Windows environment as it provides an abstraction to open a window and access the mouse and keyboard.

This library is independent of the others.

PSL

For those daunted by the integration of Lua or Guile into the toolchain, Plib provides a surprisingly complete scripting language. It is able to take source programs, looking like C, and compile them internally before running the byte code through its own virtual machine. The PSL source can come from memory or disk, although the latter uses FILE * meaning it will need a work-around for console.

```
pslInit();

pslExtension extensions[] = { { NULL, 0, NULL } };
pslProgram *pProgram = new pslProgram(extensions, "psl test");

pProgram->compile(pProgramSource, "ai_grunt");

pProgram->step();
```

The virtual machine itself is stackless, with 64 KB of code space and 256 variables. These variables can hold any type, and are held internally as pslValues. You can also provide C++ functions that can be called from inside the PSL code itself. These are registered as extensions and are declared as

```
pslValue setHealth(int argc, pslValue *argv, pslProgram *pProgram) {

    int aiRef = argv[0].getInt();
    float delta = argv[1].getFloat();

    AIManager::Get()->getAI(aiRef)->changeHealth(delta);
    return 0;
}
```

They are then initialized by filling the extensions array like this:

```
pslExtension extensions[] = {
{ "ai_SetHealth", 0, setHealth},
{ NULL, 0, NULL }
};
```

This is the best way to communicate information between the C and PSL code, as accessing specific member variables is difficult. Also, there is no current way to pass arguments into the script when it starts; however, you can assign user data to the pProgram pointer that indicates the current object.

```
pProgram->userData = (void *)pAIObject;
```

All extensions must be prepared before the program is compiled because it uses the extension information to build the byte code. Therefore, if you extend PSL so that the byte code can be loaded separately, you will need to ensure the extension list is identical in both cases.

It depends on ul.

SSG

This is the simple scene graph handler, and is comprised of a tree containing leaves and branches. Each leaf contains something to render (such as a mesh), while the branches contain transformations and other geometry management. As the renderer recurses through the tree, the current states and textures are noted by the scene graph to prevent wasted state changes. The ssg also contains loaders for numerous image and mesh formats, including MD2 (the *Quake* animation format), 3DS, and VRML!

At every stage of the graph, Plib's OpenGL-centric perspective is obvious. The state and texture monitoring code, for example, can only use OpenGL parameters. If you are building a game that has an OpenGL engine, this is a good library that very quickly provides a working scene graph implementation[6]. However, you must then use the ssg library exclusively because it relies on knowing the last state and texture before every object is drawn, and any extraneous calls to OpenGL from either you, or an abstracted graphics engine, can result in broken rendering due to inaccurate state information. Potential solutions are either:

- Add any special rendering, such as the front end, in its own leaf node at an appropriate point in the scene graph. Your constructor can then call setState to indicate the appropriate states for this object so that the scene graph can prepare the states before it invokes your leaf's callback function. This is the preferred method for adding special effects.
- Handle the rendering outside of the scene graph, and flush the states before calling it. This is the better approach for the front-end and in-game menus, since it only happens once, and at the end of each frame.
  The ssg library depends on ul and sg.

In addition, ssgaux exists to supplement ssg by providing special effects (such as fire and lens flare) and worldly matter such as sky domes, clouds, and stars. These exist as ssg-compatible nodes and are ready to be dropped into the standard scene graph, although the rendering routines themselves can be freely taken (under the terms of the LGPL) and used in other OpenGL engines.

NET

This is the Pegasus Network Library and provides a means to create client-server network applications. It is effectively a thin wrapper around the platform's native sockets library because it requires identical setup steps in each case. While this has little benefit over any of the larger libraries covered in Chapter 8, "Networking," it does provide a basic interface that can be used as a template for implementing a similar library on other platforms, and because it is already integrated into Plib there is no need to repeat the integration process with another library that doesn't gain you any real functionality.

The example programs demonstrate simple UDP message passing with both client and server projects, which highlight the unexpected low barrier to entry involved in basic network programming, which will help demystify the field.

It depends on ul.

Util

This is a general grab bag of useful abstractions to the operating system. Although the functionality presented here is not new, it is fundamental to the rest of Plib. This includes high-resolution timers, trace output, lists and linked lists, and RTTI handling.

However, this is a very spartan library with just enough functionality to support the existing Plib code. This means that any other libraries that support similar functionality will contain all this functionality, and much more, making this library redundant. Although it's only 100 KB in size, this memory could still be better spent so these functions can become wrappers to an external library. With the exception of the high performance counters, everything that features here is not likely to be time critical or called within a tight loop, so it is feasible to write a brand-new ul.cxx file that massages any necessary parameters and calls out to your existing code.

CAUTION

This library contains a cross-platform implementation for stricmp called ulStrEqual but it is not interface-compatible with it.

This library is independent of the others.

License

All libraries have been released under the LGPL, so you are free to use them provided you include your game in a prelinkable form (that is, the object file from an Open Source linker) so that it may be relinked against newer versions of the library.

One exception, as previously noted, is that console and embedded developers may use the library without releasing the object files.

AI with GGTL

GGTL stands for Generic Game-Tree Library, and as the name suggests, it is a generalized implementation for creating and evaluating game-tree searches. Its focus is to facilitate two-player, zero-sum games, although it also provides additional features for N-player games. This type of library is best suited to puzzle and board games where a simple decision tree can be easily generated describing the current state of play. However, it is possible to use the same pruning techniques to evaluate the best gameplay options for AI in FPS games by generating suitable heuristics for the current game state. The method employed by GGTL is to perform *minmax* search trees with *alpha-beta pruning*, although other algorithms may be possible.

Homepage: *http://brautaset.org/software/ggtl*

License: GNU GPL (Appendix B)

Distribution: Source only

First release: May 7, 2003

Current version: 2.1.1 (stable since December 24, 2005)

Platform(s): Windows (under Cygwin), Linux, and MacOS X

Dependencies: SL, linked list library, also from the above site

Other resources: Direct to the author, and the university report from which the project is taken

To experiment with this package it is advisable to trial the Reversi demo (examples/reversi-demo.c) that includes a text-based front end and controls the basic engine logic of ggtl/reversi.

Integration

The library was originally written in pure C under Linux, and as such requires an occasional tweak to compile. This involves creating a dummy config.h header file to replace the one that ./configure would normally build. You must also copy the ggtl.h and sl.h header files from their respective directories to wherever your header files are stored.

Being written in C means the only memory allocation used is from the `malloc` family, which is mercifully easy to spot with a quick text search. The only gotcha in GGTL comes from the mechanism to free the move cache data because of its interaction with the linked list library SL. Here, the two functions `state_cache_free` and `move_cache_free` need to be amended so that they pass in a callback function containing the appropriate function to free the cache memory.

The file I/O portion of the integration is simple because it is all handled externally to the library. This means you are required to implement the loading and saving of the whole cache states, if you want the minmax state trees, and therefore the AI's thinking, to be preserved between games.

Finally, there are two operating system calls to retrieve the time hiding in `ggtlai.c`. They have been wrapped by the abstraction functions of `setstarttime` and `havetimeleft`, and are used to limit the duration over which the minmax search tree can run. As it stands, this implementation works in milliseconds. Given that each frame of a typical action game must complete in under 17ms to achieve the magical 60 FPS, this doesn't give a lot of scope to process the AI. Therefore, this time scale is several orders of magnitude too large and will need to be adapted. This can either be done by changing the unit in which it works (e.g., milliseconds to nanoseconds) or changing the type to `floats` and using fractional seconds.

Preparing the State

Using GGTL requires you to prepare a state describing the condition of the game at a specific moment in time. This state is used to determine the best "move" when prompted. Designing the game state is probably the hardest part of the integration. If you're writing a board game, then this step is suitably easy as you can simply represent each square in an array. In this example, the state will also indicate whose turn it is.

For a more abstract game, such as a shooter, you need to describe the possible scenarios in which the AI actors could find themselves, with their potential options, and how their scenario consequently changes. The state could, for example, approximate the game level in a logical fashion with a connection graph. These nodes would be abstract concepts and indicate how important it was that the AI attained it. This could include either a location to reach, or objects to collect (e.g., ammo or other weapons). The connections between them would be described as a heuristic indicating how likely the AI is of accomplishing it, based on gunfire, obstacles, and so on.

The basic initialization construct is

```
GGTL *g = ggtl_new();
```

```
PrepareCallbacks(g);
state = buildGameLevelState();

ggtl_init(g, state);
```

This state must include a specific key that indicates which AI character is try-ing to find a good move. The scope the AI is given to make that particular move is governed by the parameters set by

```
ggtl_set(g, TYPE, FIXED);   // AI type
ggtl_set(g, MSEC, 1);       // Limit each search to 1 ms
ggtl_set(g, PLY, 5);        // the maximum depth search
```

When you need to process the AI, it's then a simple call to

```
state = ggtl_ai_move(g);
```

The state is a game-specific structure indicating how the game appears, but is passed around GGTL opaquely using `void *`. This is supplemented by a move structure that, again, is game-specific and describes a single move for a specific transition between two game states.

Once `ggtl_ai_move` completes, the state will be in the optimal position, as gen-erated by the minmax algorithm.

While this may appear simple, all the complex work is done in the callbacks!

Creating AI Callback Functions

There are six callbacks essential for GGTL to work, and each one is called auto-matically by the GGTL engine.

```
void *game_move(void *state, void *move, GGTL *g);
```

This applies the given move to the existing state. If the move cannot take place, it will return NULL. Otherwise, the `state` pointer is returned.

```
GGTL_MOVE *game_get_moves(void *state, GGTL *g);
```

This asks the program to produce a linked list of every valid move from this state. These are later used to evaluate the board position at each of these moves, and thereby produce a single `GGTL_MOVE` that should be considered when the move is ready to be made.

```
int game_eval(void *state, GGTL *g);
```

Evaluate the positional benefits of the current state, according to the current AI, and produce a score relating to its fitness. Higher values mean that this is a good position for the character. Although there is no limit on its range, the numbers should not lie near the edge of MAX_INT, in case the numbers overflow when the scores for subsequent, deeper, positions are evaluated.

```
void game_state_free(void *state);
```

Release any memory associated with the current state.

```
void *reversi_state_clone(void *state, GGTL *g);
```

Make and return an exact copy of the current state. This must be the same size as the state passed in through state. This is used by the GGTL engine when it replicates each new node.

GGTL is based entirely around a single processor. With the Xbox 360 and PlayStation 3 starting the proverbial ball rolling for multithreaded and multiprocessor game development this solution may become outmoded. One possible solution may lie with APHID (*http://www.cs.ualberta.ca/~games/aphid/index.html*), which stands or Asycnhronous Parallel Hierarchical Iterative Deepening that uses PVM (Parallel Virtual Machine).

ClanLib

ClanLib is a collection of large modules connected within a framework based around its core module, clanCore. This core library features a lot of the standard functionality you would want from any game engine, such as XML parsing, mathematics, resource handling, and system abstractions. In addition it contains a sound library, an OpenGL engine and abstraction layer, and networking code. This is all available on the CD-ROM.

ON THE CD

Homepage: *http://www.clanlib.org*

License: ClanLib License (as Zlib, for 0.8.0), LGPL (version 0.7.8 and earlier)

Distribution: Source and binary

First release: 1998

Current version: 0.8.0 (stable since October 20, 2005)

Platforms: Windows, Linux, and Mac OS X

Dependencies: zlib; Service pack 5 if you're using Visual Studio 6; other libraries needed for some modules (notably libjpeg, libpng, and DirectX 8.0)

Other resources: Mailing lists, books, articles, forums

The most obvious thing to note is the number of dependencies. However, do not worry, as they are all supplied in binary-readable formats for Windows users, and they compile cleanly.

Installation

Installation of ClanLib is a three stage-process. Linux users will not be surprised by this, as they are used to the ./configure, make, make install procedure. However, it is something of a rarity under Windows. The first phase is to generate suitable project files for ClanLib itself. This is handled by a program called configure that you must first compile using the configure.dsw workspace. This program allows you to specify the type of workspace you need (Visual Studio 6 or 7) along with the supported functionality, as shown in Figure 10.1.

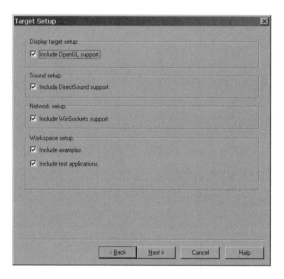

FIGURE 10.1 Configuring ClanLib.

You are then asked for the target directory of where the resultant library and header files will be stored. If you are using the c:\devlib hierarchy, then specify c:\devlib\include as the target for the newly generated header files as this will cause all of ClanLib's files to be placed c:\devlib\include\ClanLib.

ClanLib has its own gl.h *and* sdl.h *include files, which are not equivalents of the official headers. You must therefore maintain the directory structure as ClanLib provides it, and make sure that the additional include directory for ClanLib is specified separately, and after, the other directories.*

After the configuration wizard has completed, you can build all the projects in the `ClanLib.dsw` workspace, and they will automatically copy their library and header files into the previously declared directories. There are also workspace files for the example and test programs to confirm the build went smoothly.

If you want to review the API without configuring and building the libraries, you should peruse the directory structure underneath `ClanLib-0.8.0-RC1\Sources\ API`. This corresponds closely to the files that are copied into the user-specified include directory. From here you can see that each module has a master header file, such as `network.h`, in the root, with the individual header files inside the equivalently named directories. Not all of these directories are used, however, just Application, Core, GL, GUI, GUIStyleSilver, Network, SDL, and Signals.

While the header filenames use only lowercase and the underscore, the directory names do feature uppercase characters. Therefore, be precise with your naming if you are likely to migrate to a case-sensitive filesystem (such as Linux) in the future.

Integration

All of the ClanLib modules have been written, almost exclusively, by the same small team. This leads to a lot of commonality in design. So, although there is no type abstraction present in the code (everything uses `int`'s and `float`'s, for example) anything the libraries do, they do consistently.

The first point to note are the memory allocators—there aren't any. For those working with consoles, and/or wanting to keep a tight quantifiable reign on memory, you will need to do some extra work. There are around 400 instances of the `new` operator in the source base; so it is feasible to replace these, or (preferably) overload the `new` operator in those cases.

It is inadvisable to replace the global new operator, as this will replace the memory allocation that occurs in external libraries and could break their code.

Second, the endianness of the code is determined at compile time, although no macros are to be found in the header files. Instead, the configure process adds `USE_BIG_ENDIAN` as a preprocessor definition to the invocation of the compiler where appropriate. GCC users would specify this with

```
gcc -DUSE_BIG_ENDIAN clanfile.cpp
```

Finally, you should note that in ClanLib terminology, *Core* is *common*. That is, it is the core of the ClanLib feature set and includes the XML and math libraries, along with general system handling (mutexes, threads, and so on), a reference counting data resource manager, and basic filesystem I/O. The data resource manager is fundamental to most of the other libraries and is difficult to remove or wrapper effectively.

ClanLib is const safe throughout. While this is a good thing generally, it can mean that non-const-safe third-party libraries need casting or wrapping to prevent const-based compiler errors.

TIP

The Modules

Each module can be invoked separately from the others, enabling you to limit the overall footprint of your game. Each module has its own initialization method, in addition to the general core initialization that is needed first in any case,

```
CL_SetupCore::init();
```

This is followed by the initialization of the other modules. The order doesn't matter here because they are all independent, relying only on core. The de-initialization procedure is handled in reverse order, ending with

```
CL_SetupCore::deinit();
```

There have been reported problems, on some platforms, that this causes a crash on shutdown when the destructor is called. One suggested problem is to create the object on the stack, and let the destructor handle deinit thus,

```
CL_SetupCore setup_core;
```

This mechanism is used throughout ClanLib, so this problem may reappear in other modules.

Ideally, you would be able to initialize all your engine components in any order. Alas, that is not always possible when combining components from different vendors, although the ClanLib core itself is very good at preparing only the data structures it needs. However, should you need to initialize structures at the same time as ClanLib or change the behavior of it (to use a different event dispatcher, for example), then you will need to change the init_system function inside Core/ System/Win32/init_win32.cpp and rebuild the library.

clanSignals

Despite its small size, this library is fundamental to the communications process in ClanLib. The implementation uses the *slots* and *signals* metaphor. This is a good way of loosely coupling modules because neither needs to know about the other. What happens is that each object sends a signal when it does something that might be of interest to the outside world, such as when it changes its state, or completes an operation. Then, any object that is interested in this signal creates a slot and connects to it. The typical construction for such a signal appears as

```
Class MySignallingClass {
public:
   CL_Signal_v1<int> signalStateChanged;
};

// State is changed here
void setState(int newStateValue) {
   signalStateChanged(newStateValue);
}
```

Then, the connection involves a local callback that is called whenever the signal occurs.

```
class MySlotClass {
private:
   CL_Slot slotValueChanged;
   void onStateChanged(int newState);
};

MySlotClass::MySlotClass() {
   slotValueChanged = MySignallingClass.signalStateChanged.connect
      (this, &MySlotClass::onStateChanged);
}

void MySlotClass::onStateChanged(int newState) {
   // Do something useful here
}
```

Because this callback is local, type safety can be maintained, and knowledge of the function doesn't extend to other methods that shouldn't know about it, ensuring good encapsulation.

The adoption of this mechanism should be encouraged, particularly as ClanLib cannot work without it.

clanCore

This comprises of general-purpose functionality needed for the other modules. It features:

XML: Load and saving capabilities, using its own parser, but is DOM only.

Maths: A basic library with vectors and matrices. None of this is optimized, however, so you may want to replace this with a faster and more expansive implementation.

IOData: A filesystem implementation capable of handling Zip files. It also supports memory files and cross-platform directory enumeration.

Resources: This is a resource handler and manager employing reference counting to prevent the same object being loaded twice unnecessarily. All of the other ClanLib libraries that retrieve assets from disk (such as samples, sprites, and images) use this code to manage themselves. That makes this an essential part of the ClanLib package.

System: Platform-specific operations are abstracted here, such as mutexes, threads, event listeners, and debugging. This section has a very good crash reporter class for Windows that would be useful to many other projects.

clanApp

This is a basic class that wraps the `WinMain` function and handles the standard initialization of the ClanLib core. It is good as an initial test bed for your game and doesn't add any real weight to it. You can use it by declaring your game as:

```
class MyGame : public CL_ClanApplication {
   int main(int argv, char **argv)
   {
      // do usual initialization, and run game, here
      return 0;
   }
} app;
```

The game will start automatically when `WinMain` is called.

There is a Unix implementation in `Sources\Application\Unix` that can be copied for use with any of the major consoles. The only change is that you may need to remove the `std::cout` stream.

clanNetwork

As with all other network libraries covered here, this abstracts the socket handling code into a couple of well-thought-out functions that can work as either a client or server. The basic initialization involves

```
CL_SetupNetwork::init();
CL_Socket *pClient = new CL_Socket(CL_Socket::tcp);
CL_IPAddress *pAddress = new CL_IPAddress("www.bluedust.com", "1103");
```

From here, you can connect the socket to the remote machine,

```
pClient->connect(*pAddress);
```

and send requests as normal. As with the other libraries, this uses the slots metaphor to read the messages and pass control information between the two hosts, which prevents it from being used effectively outside of ClanLib.

clanDisplay

Additional Dependencies: libjpeg, libpng, and DirectX 8.0 or above. However, the dependency on DirectX is, in fact, for the DirectInput component only.

This combines the input and output attributes of the display. For input it details where the mouse is on the current window and the current key presses.

For output it provides a basic canvas, font handling, image loading, and sprite functions. It also covers the basic draw surface, and supports rendering and capability queries. However, in each case control is actually passed through the abstraction layer to the device handling it.

clanSound

Additional Dependencies: DirectX 8.0 or above

This is a well-featured library that includes the usually sample playback facilities, in addition to audio recording, runtime filters, and CD audio.

The library runs on a separate thread that combines each currently playing sample into the primary buffer, and apply any filters that have been set up. This means all sample processing must occur on the CPU because the hardware has been abstracted away. Perhaps because of this there is no dynamic pitch control on any particular sample. To achieve this effect (useful for making repetitive sounds, like footsteps, sound slightly different) you will need to write a custom filter and apply it to the appropriate sounds. Again, this introduces a greater load on the CPU.

clanGL

Additional Dependencies: DirectX 8.0 or above. As with `clanDisplay`, DirectX is only here to support the DirectInput.

This thin wrapper hides the OpenGL functionality, but provides nothing in the way of scene management or high-level concepts such as alpha sorting. But it does map the arguments and return types into something more C++ oriented, such as Booleans. Each OpenGL function call is bound to a dynamic pointer, retrieved through `GetProcAddress`, to directly access the function inside the DLL. This introduces two indirections per OpenGL call, and provides only cosmetic differences to the API. If you want an easy-to-use wrapper, this is certainly a good one; however, for speed purposes you're advised to use either OpenGL directly or a static wrapper.

clanVorbis

Additional Dependencies: The ogg vorbis codec

Like clanGL, this is a cosmetic wrapper around the standard Vorbis codec. Again, if you're using an existing library or engine, then clanVorbis invokes the overhead of using the ClanLib library and may be considered unwarranted, and you may directly integrate the Vorbis reference code yourself.

clanMikMod

Additional Dependencies: MikMod, the MOD playing library

Soundtrack MODs are as good as dead at the moment. Although the principle is good, the temporal granularity is not. Furthermore, the tools available to generate them are firmly in the old school camp. Much better results can be achieved through MIDI sequences, linked to sample playback code.

License

The most recent version has been released under a Zlib-inspired license, enabling you to do anything with the source you like and, if you release an executable, do nothing in return. It is even unnecessary to credit ClanLib for its part. If you redistribute the source (either through munificence or law—because you're also using GPL code) then you cannot you claim you wrote it and must mark your changes.

ENDNOTES

1. One solution, as covered in *Cross-Platform Game Programming,* is to use m_Vertices.resize(0) instead.
2. Although its predecessor, GML, was developed by IBM in the late 1960s.
3. It can also transform XML into plain text or HTML, but they are not useful for our purposes.
4. VisualStudio can be used from the command line quite easily, but requires you to explicitly run C:\Program Files\Microsoft Visual Studio\VC98\Bin\vcvars32.bat beforehand.
5. Because all programmers appear to be called Steve, this should be qualified as Steve J. Baker!
6. A more encompassing scene graph implementation can be found at *http://www.openscenegraph.org.*

11 The Tools Pipeline

In This Chapter

- Image Manipulation
- Sound Conversion
- Open Source File Formats
- Source Control
- Auditing Tools

For many, the process of writing a graphics engine is comparatively easy because it is a well-understood discipline. It's also a very sexy area in which to work, and so many man-hours have been spent learning the nuances of each new console, or graphics card, to produce the stunning eye candy gamers now expect. By contrast, the role of the tools programmer has been a lonely, and generally unappreciated, one. This is beginning to change, with many companies realizing the key to good game development lies within their tools, and the pipeline that streamlines them, bringing them all together, is their most powerful asset. Specialists in this area are hard to find, and with each tool (such as image manipulation or level editors) being a field of study unto itself, means the required expertise in this area is larger than any other single topic in games development.

The Open Source community appears to care very little about the tools pipeline for game developers because there is no prebuilt solution in this area and only a few attempts at creating common, open file formats for its data[i]. Consequently, you will still need to write scaffold code that describes how to manipulate each asset into a game-ready format, and what parameters to pass into the appropriate tools. This can take some effort, employing XML project files, attribute editors, and the like. However, most of the individual problems inherent in data processing within the toolchain have been solved, and Open Source developers have made that software available to all.

For the purposes of our discussion, we shall assume the toolchain is the means by which the game's data assets (such as meshes, animations, sounds, etc.) are categorized and grouped in preparation for the game engine. Each asset will generally be supplemented with metadata, describing the method by which it will be built into a platform-ready resource. This data either exists inside the asset as a separate file with the same stem name, or aggregated into a single project file with every other asset. The location or specifics of this data are unimportant for our discussions. Instead, we shall concentrate only on the operations that a typical pipeline would need to perform and how Open Source tools can facilitate it.

IMAGE MANIPULATION

One of the largest areas of data processing is with textures. In the cross-platform field especially, the artist will generate a large reference image to be used within the game, while each platform (including the PC) will use a specialized version of this texture. In most cases it will be smaller and held in a custom format, but it may also use a different bit depth and require the inclusion of metadata. While there are no existing tools for configuring these format requirements automatically, there is one very special tool that performs the actual processing required.

ImageMagick

ImageMagick is a package of utility software for converting and processing images. It comes as a number of command-line utilities that can be run from within batch files or larger tool-chain applications, to perform most of the standard image processes found within Adobe® Photoshop®, the GIMP, or other such software. It is supplied with a very large number of image format handlers (known as *delegates*) that can convert almost any file into a common, internal format. The standard ImageMagick filter routines can then process this data—using common code— before employing the appropriate delegate to resave the file.

ON THE CD

This software can be found on the accompanying CD-ROM.

Homepage: *http://www.imagemagick.org*
License: Custom (similar to BSD).
Distribution: Source and binaries.

First release: August 1, 1990.

Current version: 6.2.6 (stable since March 1, 2006).

Platforms: Windows, Linux, Mac OS X.

Dependencies: libxml and zlib, included in binary distribution. Other formats can be handled with additional delegates but place no direct dependency on ImageMagick itself.

Other resources: ImageMagick has a very good online presence with at least four mailing lists and numerous tutorials.

The Package

There are several tools living under the singular banner of ImageMagick. Each has its own purpose and documentation, which are briefly covered here.

Convert

This is probably the most used tool of the suite. As the name suggests, it will convert images from one file format to another. As part of this conversion process, it can apply a number of parameterized filters to the image. This includes palette remapping, resizing, and gamma correction. The specifics of some of these commands are covered later by way of demonstration.

Mogrify

This command is essentially the same as convert. It takes the same set of parameters and performs the same tasks. The main difference is that the output filename is identical to the input filename in all cases. This is generally less useful for the games developer who generally wants to keep a set of source images and generate build-ready textures from them. However, you can achieve some performance gains by copying the file to your target directory and running mogrify over what you can achieve by using convert. This will become apparent to those running a distributed toolchain.

Display

This simple utility allows you to render the supplied image to the screen. Because it uses the ImageMagick delegates it can display formats that most image viewers, or your web browser, cannot. The only caveat with this program is that it requires an X server to be running on your machine. This is fairly standard with Linux and Mac OS X machines, but is not so common under Windows. The easiest way to get a fully working X server is to install the one supplied with Cygwin or download one from Red Hat at *http://sources.redhat.com/win32-x11*. Alternatively, the current

Windows installer comes with `imdisplay`, an alternate image viewer with basic editing facilities.

Display has a sister program called `animate` that displays animating images (such as multi-image GIF and PNG files) and allows its parameters (such as speed and direction) to be controlled in real time. It also requires an X server and has no Windows GDI-compliant version.

Composite and Combine

These two tools are actually the same one, but depending on your version may be named differently. Its job is to overlay one image onto another and includes much of the same functionality as `convert`. The only stipulation in this case is that both images must be same size when performing a direct composite.

One newly useful feature is the ability to include watermarks in your image. In contrast to other composite processes, these watermark images do not have to be the same size as the source image. And although they are not useful within the game, per se, they should be added to any game screenshots you release to magazines or websites. A typical command such as

```
composite -watermark 75% -gravity SouthWest mylogo.png source.png
target.png
```

would combine Figure 11.1 and Figure 11.2 into Figure 11.3.

FIGURE 11.1 The source image.

FIGURE 11.2   The identifying logo.

FIGURE 11.3   The resultant image.

You may additionally want to include a *hidden* watermark into the image. This is accomplished through steganography, which means "hidden in plain sight." It melts the watermark image into the source image without being visible in any way. This is naturally a more compute-intensive procedure and can take over 30 seconds to hide a single watermark. Figure 11.4 contains such a watermark.

Because no one knows this watermark exists, or how to extract it, it becomes a useful tool for tracking the route by which images of your game travel. As you may be aware, this can also be used to determine leaks of confidential information. The basic command for adding this is

```
composite -stegano 14022006 hidden.png source.png target.png
```

FIGURE 11.4 The main watermark in this image is completely hidden. The company logo misdirects attention away from the fact there may be other marks in the image.

The number used here is a magic number to determine the specific instance of that watermark in that specific image. Because these watermarks are added automatically, it is very easy to use different numbers for each person to whom you give these images.

You can only extract the logo by knowing the magic key and the size of the original watermark image. Keep this information safe. You can then use

```
display -size 99x92+14022006 stegano:target.png
```

or

```
convert -size 99x92+14022006 stegano:target.png decodedlogo.png
```

This technique is not foolproof, as it is possible to destroy the watermark through destructive editing techniques such as cropping. However, it is a good basic precaution, although getting steganography to work effectively can be problematic.

Compare

This allows you to determine how similar two images are. Each file is compared pixel for pixel, and if they match, the resultant comparison pixel is drawn in white. The concept of "identical" can be user adapted. This command can take some time to run, but is useful for overnight processing to provide feedback on other image-processing commands or checking automatic test suites.

```
compare source.png target.png difference.png
```

Conjure

This magical utility is the closest prewritten tool there is for specifically automating ImageMagick. It handles the Magick Scripting Language (MSL), which is an XML script format for ImageMagick.

Other Tools

Additionally, ImageMagick comes with the following tools:

identify: This parses the header of an image and displays those properties. It also infers properties from this data to provide a more complete picture (no pun intended) of the image. It can be a useful debugging tool to check for, and parse, metadata.

import: This requires the X Window System and performs basic screen capture.

montage: This combines multiple images into a single larger one. This large image can be supplemented with captions.

Using ImageMagick

There are two basic ways in which ImageMagick can be invoked within your toolchain. The first is to compile the source into an existing piece of software and call it internally, while the second is to invoke it as a normal executable.

Recompiling ImageMagick

Very few tool developers want to waste time spawning an extra process when they have source code that they can integrate; so this would appear to be the natural solution. Particularly since the amount of offline processing is increasing with each new generation of console, and each new game.

You should never consider compiling the ImageMagick source into your game as it is too bulky. The toolchain should process all data into platform-ready assets so that your game can have the smallest possible footprint to enable faster loading times and smaller code sizes. All file conversion, therefore, should be performed offline.

The first stage in recompiling the source is to download the appropriate delegates for the formats you will be using. ImageMagick comes with a large set of file formats built in, but to handle PNG files, for example, you also need the sources to the libpng library.

Additionally you need to compile the ImageMagick source if the supplied binaries do not support the particular file formats you will be using. Granted, they can be called as external delegates but this is not to everyone's taste. You can determine which formats are supported by typing

```
convert -list delegate
```

Full compilation details can be found in the documentation, but in most cases you will be calling the ImageMagick tools externally. This is because the image processing and file operations will be the slow part of the process, not the separate invocations of the convert tool, particularly since the operating system will have generally cached the convert program in memory eliminating most of the start-up time. Consequently, you shall assume you are calling ImageMagick externally.

Using ImageMagick Directly

The start-up time of the ImageMagick applications is very fast, and so most people are unconcerned with the effort involved in recompiling and embedding ImageMagick into their toolchain. The process is very simple, and a binary installation works out of the box.

For utilizing the command-line utilities in your toolchain you must first determine the configuration. This establishes the delegates in use, the amount of disk space it may use, and so on. There are several directories in which ImageMagick will look for this configuration information, starting with the MAGICK_CONFIGURE_PATH environment variable, followed by MAGICK_HOME, and .magick in the current user's home directory. To ensure uniformity across all machines, your toolchain should standardize on one of the environment variables, say MAGICK_HOME, and check that it has been initialized. The Windows API allows you to do this with the code

```
char buffer[32767];    // the maximum size for a buffer
if (GetEnvironmentVariable("MAGICK_HOME", buffer, sizeof(buffer)) == 0) {
    // Success! We now know where ImageMagick lives
```

```
} else if (GetLastError() == ERROR_ENVVAR_NOT_FOUND) {
    // No such variable — is IM installed?
}
```

Developers with a Linux toolchain should instead use

```
char *pEnvironmentValue = getenv("MAGICK_HOME");

if (pEnvironmentValue == NULL) {
    // No such variable — is IM installed?
}
```

From here it is a simple matter of putting the ImageMagick executables in the path, or calling it explicitly and applying the correct parameters. The executables in a Windows install are in the root of the ImageMagick directory (c:\Program Files\ImageMagick-6.2.6-Q8, for example).

Basic Conversion

The most common operations will generally involve resizing and changing the bit depth of textures. This is achieved simply with

```
convert —scale 64x64 source.png target.png
```

and

```
convert —colors 16 source.png target.png
```

This is of primary use for the PlayStation 2, where 4-bit textures are the norm. Note that you must specify the number of colors required, not the number of bit fields. You can also convert other images into a palletized version with

```
convert -type palette source.png target.png
```

It is also possible to take the palette from one image and remap all colors in another image to match. This is handled with

```
convert —map palette_image.png source.png target.png
```

But unfortunately, the order of the palette is not maintained in the current version of ImageMagick. You can, however, use the identify program to determine what colors were chosen for the remapping by using the identify command,

```
identify -verbose target.png
```

Image scaling is a deceptively complex field and it is not enough to blindly scale an image to the appropriate size in all cases because one pixel in the resultant image may be the amalgamation of, say four, in the original. The method by which these pixels are combined is called filtering, and here the idea of "one size fits all" most certainly does not apply.

The simplest alternate to scale is *sample*. It performs a more complex algorithm than scale, but accomplishes the same task.

```
convert —sample 64x64 source.png target.png
```

Both sample and scale in these examples do not use a filter. Or, more correctly, they use a simple internalized default filter to process the data. However, ImageMagick has at least 15 different filters that can be applied like this:

```
convert —sample 64x64 —filter catrom source.png target.png
```

Determining the best filters for any particular image can only be done empirically, although some guidelines are available from Anthony Thyssen's online tutorial[2].

You should always keep your source images in a high-resolution, lossless format and convert down in as few steps as possible to ensure the highest possible quality. PNG is recommended, as it has lossless compression, transparency, and can contain metadata.

Metadata

Adding metadata to the file itself is possible provided the right file formats are used. Again, PNG scores well here. There are two main approaches: either you store the metadata within the file and use ImageMagick to extract it into a game-specific format that your engine or toolchain will understand, or you keep it within the file format and let the engine parse it out directly. This is an ecumenical matter for your lead and engine programmers. The process of handling this data, though, is identical in both cases.

```
convert -comment "metadata here" source.png target.png
```

The metadata for images has to be a text string, so it is not as flexible as a custom image packer. However, it is simple to use and parse. Additionally, the comment string may include attributes about the file, such as its size and resolution. The format characters used are typical of printf and include %x, %y, and %f. A full list of these can be found in the ImageMagick documentation. You can retrieve this metadata with the all-seeing eye of

```
identify —verbose target.png
```

Finally, you may want to remove all metadata from the images. This can eradicate any special "Created by . . ." tags that the original software added, and remove your own control data to reduce the size of the data in the final build. This is achieved with

```
convert -strip source.png target.png
```

Drawing Tools

ImageMagick additionally includes some basic rendering facilities, allowing you to draw directly onto the image. In most cases, this is but a curiosity, but for the toolchain this provides a means to add large red crosses to textures that fall foul of one or more guidelines, for example:

```
convert –size 128x128 –stroke red –fill red –linewidth 5 \
  -draw "line 0,0,128,128 line 128,0,0,128" source.png target.png
```

You could even add the offending filename to the texture, too:

```
convert –pointsize 24 –stroke red –annotate 0x0+5+24 %f \
    source.png target.png
```

Both invocations can be combined by simply concatenating the commands. As always, the manual pages and Google can provide many other tutorials on this topic.

Writing Delegates

One of the most obvious omissions is the lack of Xbox and PlayStation image formats within ImageMagick. This is not surprising, however, since the FLOSS community frowns on such closed proprietary formats, but such support is possible through delegates that convert one custom format into another.

Each delegate is a simple command-line program that is called by ImageMagick when it is asked to perform a conversion it doesn't understand. The program can be an executable or script, and is triggered by a line in the configuration file delegates.xml such as

```
<delegate decode="" encode="tm2" mode="bi"
    command=""c:\bin\tm2make.exe" "%i" "%o""/>
```

The arguments %i and %o represent the input and output filenames, respectively. Other parameters can also be added, of course, provided your application supports them.

SOUND CONVERSION

Like the graphics toolchain, the primary purpose of the audio tools is to get the data into an engine-ready, platform-friendly format. The primary difference between them is that there are usually fewer supported formats in the audio sphere than in graphics. A cursory examination of the audio APIs in Chapter 6, "Audio," will remind you that WAV is supported by them all; in some cases exclusively. However, this doesn't eliminate the need for audio tools—it merely changes their focus. In the games environment, you're more likely to modify the data within the format (its sampling rate, bit depth, etc.) as opposed to the format itself. Consoles complicate this by requiring proprietary formats, but you come to those later.

SoX

SoX stands for Sound eXchange, the universal sound sample translator. It began life as a converter for the popular audio files of its day, but has expanded to include basic audio effects, such as chorus, echo, and low-pass filters. SoX has been through many revisions over the years, and the number of filters and file formats has increased substantially. But the interface and focus have remained consistent. It is the audio equivalent of ImageMagick.

There are three main parts to SoX. The first is the conversion program itself, `sox`, that allows you to resample individual sounds and process them with specific effects. Every input file provided on the command line is processed with exactly the same arguments. The second part is a special `soxmix` tool that mixes each of the sound files given on the command line together into a single output, if the files are in the same format. And finally, it comes with libst, a library of sound tools that can read and write any of the file formats handled by SoX and perform the same selection of effects. These are all supplemented with documentation (albeit slightly dated) and sample scripts, and can be found on the CD-ROM.

ON THE CD

Homepage: *http://sox.sourceforge.net*

License: GNU GPL (for the utility), GNU LGPL (for the sound tools library[3])

Distribution: Source and binary

First release: 1991 (although probably earlier)

Current version: 12.17.9 (stable since December 5, 2005)

Platform(s): Windows, Macintosh, and most flavors of Unix, including Linux

Dependencies: None

Other resources: SoX-users mailing list

During the birthing pains of the Internet, SoX was instrumental in allowing the users of the many disparate operating systems to share music clips and audio snippets from cult TV shows such as *Star Trek* and *Monty Python*. With the introduction of MP3 and OGG Vorbis, and de facto WAV support in most applications, the number of different file formats has been reduced, and the opportunity for conversion utilities consequently dwindled. Not surprisingly, the maintenance of SoX faltered in this time, too. However, it has never truly been orphaned because its continued use as a command-line (and therefore batchable) tool is second to none. This has kept SoX in the toolbox of many developers. Releases are, admittedly, infrequent, but because there's little functionality missing (proprietary formats excepted) this should not be problem.

Integration

For the games developer, SoX provides the best means of creating a cross-platform audio toolchain without relying on the sound designer to process sounds individually. The first part of the toolchain should allow metadata to be applied to each class of sound. This parameter is used within the engine to determine, on a quantitative basis, where higher priority sounds replace the lower, should it run out of available channels. This generally breaks down with an in-game priority of (from low to high):

- Bullet impacts
- Footsteps
- Music (main and incidental)
- General sound effects (doors, windows)
- Special effects (gunfire, ricochet)
- Ambient
- POV (such as an FPS weapon, or something always played on center speaker)
- GUI sounds
- Explosions
- Speech

The sounds can then be individually subassigned a *quality* priority based on their specific importance to the game. So for example, all the footsteps will be of low importance, by default, except for those of the player and his assistant, as they are of high importance. This priority is then used to determine how far each sound may be automatically down-sampled so that it fits into the audio memory assigned for that specific platform. This is only a guide, however, and can vary on a game-by-game basis since a stealth game would place a greater importance on footsteps and whispered voices than would a loud and brash first-person shooter.

Features

SoX works using a standard command line of

```
sox [ general options ] [ format options ] infile
    [ format options ] outfile [ effects ]
```

All options are detailed in the manual page, which exists as a text file for Windows users. We shall now cover the important elements of this document, as it pertains to toolchain development.

Down-Sampling

For the most part, SoX will be used to down-sample audio files from a high-quality wave to a lower-quality one. There are two parts to the sound's quality: playback frequency (a.k.a. sampling rate) and bit depth. Generally speaking, the playback frequency should be at least twice the highest frequency in your source wave. This is known as the *Nyquist limit*. So most of the low-frequency sounds, such as footsteps, can be kept at 22,050 Hz and converted with the command line

```
sox -r 22050 infile.wav outfile.wav
```

Bit depth holds the number of discrete volume levels a sample may have. This is rarely anything other than 8 bits (256 levels) or 16 bits (65536 levels). Down-sampling to 8-bit is achieved with

```
sox -b infile.wav outfile.wav
```

Unfortunately, there is no good universal algorithm for down-sampling, so you should give the audio designer the opportunity to apply specific algorithms to different samples. You may even need to permit unique samples for each platform to balance tight memory requirements and audio clarity. There is a discussion on this topic, and the generally unused up-sampling options, at *http://leute.server.de/ wilde/resample.html*.

One of the more common audio correcting procedures is to change stereo samples into mono ones. This is because most sounds (everything except music and stings) will be placed in the stereo field by the audio engine. Therefore, 50 percent of the space can be saved with

```
sox source.wav -c 1 mono-target.wav avg
```

Standard Effects

Pregenerating special effects is a good way of adding extra sonorous depth to your game. If the player, upon entering the cave, hears an echo on each footstep and gunshot sound, it adds an extra dimension to the game. Similarly, any gunshot atop the mountain also echoes, but in a different way. This can be achieved through in-game DSP audio code or by generating partnered samples that have been preeffected.

On the next generation of consoles, and the ones after that, the use of pregenerated sound effects is likely to become passé and fall from grace. The chips have powerful DSPs and can handle special effects accurately enough to make SoX's preprocessed effects redundant. Furthermore, engine development is advanced enough to determine *which* of those sounds needs the effects in such a way as to make best use of the processing power available. Consequently, this section is of primary interest to handheld and PC developers (where a high-quality sound card cannot be guaranteed, as it is on the consoles) and those working on the current generation of consoles.

Games with a large audio palette should be careful to prebake only those necessary sounds to save memory. This is usually done manually with metadata, since the time necessary to write intelligent code that searches each level to determine what sounds *could* play inside each environment is uneconomical.

```
sox normal.wav mountain.wav echo 0.8 0.6 400.0 0.2 800 0.17 \
        1200 0.1 1600 0.05  2000 0.01
```

These effects could be extended to speech, such as a voice talking on the telephone:

```
sox voice.wav phone.wav band 3000 700
```

The sound effects available in SoX are operative, but difficult to program effectively. You should allow your audio designer to contour most sounds in their sample editor and only use the effects shown here when batch processing is not otherwise possible.

To ensure the best quality audio possible you should normalize all sounds in the toolchain, making them as loud as possible, and then quiet them down in software. This ensures the maximum dynamic range is available for each sample. You can determine the maximum extents of a wave using

```
sox source.wav -e stat
```

which will produce output like

```
Samples read:                48462
Length (seconds):         1.098912
Scaled by:           2147483647.0
Maximum amplitude:        0.337433
Minimum amplitude:       -0.337280
Midline amplitude:        0.000076
Mean      norm:           0.017194
Mean      amplitude:     -0.000047
RMS       amplitude:      0.043522
Maximum delta:            0.405945
Minimum delta:            0.000000
Mean      delta:          0.020852
RMS       delta:          0.047316
Rough     frequency:          3815
Volume adjustment:           2.964
```

The two important pieces of data here are maximum and minimum amplitude. Extract these and applying formula:

```
tREAL32 gain = 2.0f / (max – min);
```

You can then pass this value to SoX in order to normalize the sound.

```
sprint(normalizeCommand, "sox –v %f %s %s", gain, inFile, outFile);
system(normalizeCommand);
```

As an alternative, there is a single tool that can perform the normalize operation if your toolchain cannot support the previous. It's located at *http://www1.cs. columbia.edu/~cvaill/normalize.*

You should store an additional piece of metadata for each sound, or sound group, to indicate the volume of the sound in-game to counteract the normalization process. These values are best determined by the ears of the audio designer.

TIP

Console Audio

For console development there is an extra stage to this process—the conversion into a suitable proprietary format. Developers working cross-platform can omit this step because the sound designer can be given a PC build of the game into which his sounds are included by means of simple WAV files. In all other cases, you either need to rebuild the SoX code in order to add the appropriate formats, or trigger an external build process. Because these formats are covered by NDAs, they cannot be discussed further.

One rare case you may need to consider is the endian swapping of samples. This is rare because most consoles will provide their own code that takes audio information in standard WAV format and generates data in its own correct format. In cases when you are handling this yourself, or you are moving raw data between platforms of a different endian, you should use the endian swap option,

```
sox -x original.wav swapped_endian.wav
```

Using SoX Source

To make use of the SoX source within your own code you must build the library yourself, as no prebuilt Windows library currently exists, although project and workspace files for Microsoft Developer Studio version 6 are available in the standard source package.

The SoX program is essentially a command-line wrapper to the functionality contained within stlib. You will therefore need to compile this library before anything else.

The only file to be careful of is `ststdint.h`. This contains the data types usually generated by `./configure` in the Linux world. It is a simple case of:

```
typedef int int32_t;
typedef unsigned int uint32_t;
```

and so on, so only users on 64-bit machines should be aware.

The usage is straightforward, although the only real demonstration is to be found in `sox.c`, the main stub program for `sox` and `soxmix`.

The Sound Tools License

The sound tools license follows the GNU LGPL. If you *only* release the tools internally, *and* you include the source code with the executable then you are complying wholly with the license. If you include the FFT code, then your internal release will be considered GPL (not LGPL) because of the license included with that piece of code, but it can remain safely behind closed doors.

However, if you forget to include the source with the license, then it is possible for any third party (including external developers) to request the source. This anomaly is covered in Chapter 2, "License Commentaries."

The Unix Benefit

The heritage that SoX owes to Unix is immense. Apart from the clutter of near-obsolete file formats like .au, SoX is able to make use of the /dev/dsp device under Unix-like operating systems to play sounds in a uniform manner. Whereas Microsoft Windows requires sound drivers and numerous API calls before a sound can be played (review the source code to any of the libraries featured in Chapter 6 to learn how many). Unix treats everything on the machine like a file. The file for the sound card is /dev/dsp, so any file output to this file causes the speaker to make a noise. This has enabled SoX to contain some unique functionality, when run on Unix machines, with its self-contained playback mode. While this is not useful in the processing phase itself, it is a useful test when adding individual samples to your game database because if SoX is able to play the sample, you can be sure it's able to effectively convert it. Also, it allows the sound designer to tweak the actual values that will be used in the postprocessing stage. If you are unable to run these tools on a Unix machine, the traditional solution of temporary files can always be used to achieve the same effect.

Mencoder

This is the transcoding component of the mplayer package, which is probably the most well-respected media player in the Open Source community. It has been voted "favorite media player" in most readers' awards across many countries. Its primary focus was as a media player capable of handling all the basic movie formats[4], but has grown to include other audio facilities. This makes it a good work-horse tool for conversion and playback, particularly when dealing with formats generated by external third parties.

Both mencoder and mplayer are command-line programs that work using plug-in codecs. These introduce a lot of dependencies and special code, making it unsuitable for inclusion within games software itself. However, using it as a precompiled binary for offline conversion is very pertinent. Since most platforms have their own proprietary movie formats, the focus here is on the utility functions that mencoder can perform.

> **Homepage:** *http://www.mplayerhq.hu*
>
> **License:** GNU GPL (Appendix B)
>
> **Distribution:** Source and binary
>
> **First release:** November 11, 2000 (although the preceding code, mpg12play, was released September 22, 2000)
>
> **Current version:** 1.0 (pre7) (stable since April 16, 2005)
>
> **Platforms:** Windows and Linux

Dependencies: Many, but all included in Windows binary

Other resources: Six user-oriented mailing lists, plus an additional 11 for developers

It is recommended that mplayer and mencoder be used only within the toolchain using the supplied, statically linked binaries. Conversion into proprietary formats (such as are often found on the consoles) is obviously not supported here and will probably require the use of the manufacturer's toolset.

Portions of the Windows port are maintained with the help of specialized device drivers (such as mapdev.vxd on Win9x), which obtain pointers directly into the hardware. This is not a problem, but it is something of which you should be aware.

Mplayer

This is the basic playback engine of the package. Its use in the toolchain is limited because its method for movie playback relies on the mapdev.vxd, which cannot be easily redirected into a window. However, it has one useful feature in that it can identify the full properties of a particular file when run as

```
mplayer -identify filename.mpg
```

This will show you the full statistics of the movie, including bit rate, size, and format. This information is repeated at least twice on the standard output, so you can retrieve it in the best way for your pipeline. One typical fragment is

```
VIDEO: MPEG1 320x240 (aspect 12) 29.97 fps 1500.0 kbps (187.5 kbyte/s)
ID_VIDEO_FORMAT=0x10000001
ID_VIDEO_BITRATE=1500000
ID_VIDEO_WIDTH=320
ID_VIDEO_HEIGHT=240
ID_VIDEO_FPS=29.970
ID_VIDEO_ASPECT=1.3333
```

The Windows port of mplayer has no GUI and so you are limited to the command line throughout, although you may drag movie files onto the mplayer.exe icon if you wish. When using mplayer under Linux, you may want to install gmplayer, which provides a graphical interface.

Basic Conversion

mencoder handles an abundance of movie formats and does so very well. Alas, much of this wonderful technology is lost on us because the movies we handle are generally cut-scenes generated by ourselves using known (and standards-compliant) formats. Ultimately, we may only need the very basic of processing routines to convert between PAL and NTSC, or to supplement our cut-scene with a letterbox surround. As always, having a capable command-line tool to do these tasks is a boon to productivity.

The best place to look for detailed information regarding encoding methods is the official documentation available at http://www.mplayerhq.hu/DOCS/HTML/ en/encoding-guide.html.

PAL and NTSC

Ideally, games would have an identical movie for both territories, but unfortunately, they always differ in terms of screen size and frame rate, as shown in Table 11.1.

TABLE 11.1 Resolution and Refresh

TV Standard	Frame Size	Refresh Rate	Movie FPS	MPEG-1 Frame Size
NTSC	640 × 480	60 Hz	29.97 Hz	352 × 240
PAL	640 × 528	50 Hz	25 Hz	320 × 240

Although it's possible to have one movie for both territories and change the frame rate during playback to keep the audio in sync, the drop in quality is noticeable to most developers. Therefore, you should be begin with a high-resolution movie clip and down-sample into two separate movies. For example,

```
mencoder -oac copy -ovc lavc -lavcopts vbitrate=5000 —ofps 25  \
        original.mpg —o ntsc.mpg
```

One common approach to this PAL/NTSC problem is to produce the original cut-scene in letterbox format that is, say, 400 pixels high, and generate a full-screen movie from this to fill the 480 NTSC screen. This can be done with the output filters of mencoder. For example,

```
mencoder —oac copy -ovc copy —vop expand=640:480:0:40 \
    original.mpg —o letterbox_ntsc.mpg
```

for NTSC, and

```
mencoder –oac copy -ovc copy –vop expand=640:480:0:64 \
    original.mpg –o letterbox_pal.mpg
```

for PAL. However, if your approach to movie making is to adopt the pan-and-scan mechanism, you can crop any portion of the movie using the `crop` command and the –vop set.

Movie Bit Rates

When loading movies from the hard drive, it is generally fast enough that you rarely have to worry about the transfer rate. In the console world, move playback generally runs from the CD-ROM or DVD, making this a more time-critical task. When using a cut-scene to mask a level load, for example, there will be strict guidelines as to the maximum duration of the level load; so there is some juggling as the bandwidth must be shared between the level data and cut-scene movie, and so the movie bit rate must be specified to come in under this ceiling.

Adjusting the bit rate can only be done by reencoding the movie. Therefore, you should always reencode from the *original* movie to maintain quality. The necessary flags will vary depending on the codec you use to encode the movie. DivX, for example, uses `br` in

```
mencoder –oac copy -ovc divx -divxopts br=5000 original.mpg –o output.mpg
```

while mpeg (using `lavc`, the internal AV codec) will use the `vbitrate` option shown previously in PAL and NTSC conversions.

Splits and Joins

Both of these tasks are very simple and can allow you to add SKU-specific movie fragments to existing footage. The join is simpler and uses the pipe feature of the BASH shell:

```
cat clip1.mpg clip2.mpg | mencoder –oac copy –ovc copy –o result.mpg
```

The split is no harder, and works by extracting a timed segment from the film. This can be given in seconds, minutes and seconds, or hours and minutes and seconds. The program will deduce which you mean by the number of colons in the description.

```
mencoder –oac copy –ovc copy –ss 1:52 –endpos 2:14 full.mpg –o
snippet.mpg
```

The most important point to note is that to extract movie data based on time, there *must* be a time index in the film in the first instance. Mpeg-1 and -2 should automatically have this, but AVI-based formats (such as DivX) might not. To add this index you can simply run

```
mencoder —oac copy —ovc copy —idx movie.mpg —o movie_plus_index.mpg
```

Two Pass Encoding

While getting the best quality movie is one important consideration, making sure it is small enough to fit on the disc is equally so. Indeed, many would argue it is *more* important because a game can ship with a mediocre-quality cut-scene, but would never ship if said cut-scene was missing altogether!

Reducing the movie's size is done by reducing the bit rate. There are two main approaches to bit-rate encoding: constant and variable. Constant, as the name suggests, uses the same rate throughout the clip, and is covered earlier. It performs lossy compression on the data until the frame fits within the bit-rate headroom given to it. A variable bit rate allows you to take advantage of the lower bit rates possible in slow-moving scenes. Consequently, variable is the better option in most cases.

The overhead of variable bit rate (VBR) files exists offline because the encoding routines cannot reduce the bit rate on one pass, since at any given time it doesn't know how the movie frame changes from the current scene onto the next. The solution is to use dual pass encoding.

```
rm frameno.avi
mencoder —oac copy -ovc lavc -lavcopts vcodec=mpeg4:vpass=1 \
    original.mpg —o resultant.mpg
mencoder —oac copy -ovc lavc -lavcopts vcodec=mpeg4:vpass=2 \
    original.mpg —o resultant.mpg
```

The first pass generates a log file describing the bit rates necessary for each section of the clip when encoded using the prescribed codec. The second then applies the values from that log when it encodes the file for real. In reality, the first pass will also generate an output mpg, but this can be safely discarded.

CAUTION

The seemingly isolated `frameno.avi` *file is generated automatically by certain mencoder operations. This, like the log file it generates during the first pass, can affect the result of VBR compression and must be removed before any multipass operation.*

Foreign Cut-Scenes

When working with foreign-language versions, the need to dub an existing movie with a new soundtrack will often present itself. `mencoder` makes short work of this by supporting both halves of the process. It can remove the original audio track from a movie,

```
mplayer -vo null -ao pcm -hardframedrop original_film.avi
```

producing an audio file called `audiodump.wav`. This can then be edited with new voices using perhaps Audacity, which is featured in Chapter 13, "Audio Production," and then recombined with the original movie by dubbing it directly with

```
mencoder original_film.avi -ovc copy -oac copy \
    -audiofile new_audio.wav -o completed_film.avi
```

ffmpeg

ffmpeg is a converter for audio and video data, with a strong bias toward those in the MPEG family, include Xvid. Although its origins are firmly with Linux, ports to Windows have been well received, providing a range of till now unavailable functionality to the platform. `ffmpeg` complements `mencoder` well, and in areas where one appears lacking, the other is able to fill the void. Their development appears to be linked symbiotically since as one develops further, so does the other. This is no surprise, however, because they share many of the same developers and much of the same code.

> **Homepage:** *http://ffmpeg.sourceforge.net*
> **License:** GNU LGPL (Appendix C)
> **Distribution:** Source primarily, although binaries do exist
> **Current version:** 0.4.9-pre1
> **Platforms:** Cross-platform, including Linux and Windows
> **Dependencies:** None, unless other codecs are required
> **Other resources:** Mailing list, IRC channel, and website

The focus between `mencoder` and `ffmpeg` is different. While the former is aiming for maximum penetration, by incorporating every available codec, regardless of philosophy, `ffmpeg`'s approach is of maximum performance and conversion. This has meant that most codecs are implemented natively and embedded in the software itself.

Basic Conversion

Like all conversion software, its competence is determined by the quality of the conversion and how fast it works. `ffmpeg` scores well on both counts, with real-time transcoding available in many situations.

The simplest case of direct conversion works by

```
ffmpeg -i infile.mpg outfile.mpg
```

Although the format is usually determined by the file extension, with so many utilizing the same (mpg) three letters, an explicit target may need to be given.

```
ffmpeg -i infile.mpg —target dv outfile.dv
```

This example has been chosen because Kino requires its source material in DV format, and this is generally the best tool for that conversion.

This conversion process can be supplemented with parameters to resize the clip:

```
ffmpeg -i infile.mpg —s 320x200 outfile.mpg
```

A portion of the movie can be extracted by specifying the start time and duration. Note that, unlike mencoder, these numbers must be in strict hours:minutes:seconds format.

```
ffmpeg -i infile.mpg —ss 00:01:12 —t 00:00:10 outclip.mpg
```

Overdubbing

Like mencoder, it is easy to extract the video track,

```
ffmpeg -i infile.mpg -an silent_video.mpg
```

and audio track,

```
ffmpeg -i infile.mpg -vn audio_track.wav
```

from a single file, and then recombine them at a later time, perhaps after editing in Audacity.

```
ffmpeg -i silent_video.mpg -i audio_track.wav dubbed_video.mpg
```

Being able to handle these tasks in more than one program gives you the flexibility of choice.

To learn about other media players, consult the Wikipedia page at http://en.wikipedia.org/wiki/Comparison_of_media_players.

OPEN FILE FORMATS

Having Open Source software solves one of the problems of extensibility, but it only *helps* with the issue of interoperability. Despite having the code to handle a particular file format, it is still quite difficult to extract that code for use in a new program. Tools to import different file formats, or convert between them, are still quite rare, and only the more prominent applications have them, such as Microsoft Word.

Most applications use a combination of open, but binary, formats or custom XML files. Some formats, like 3DS, have become fairly standard, thanks to Autodesk releasing the file structure so that other developers could understand and apply their data. But for data stored in a proprietary format, it forces vendor lock-in, and can become obsolete very easily. Free software at least provides access to the "source chain" from on-disc format to in-memory asset. Consequently, open formats are the best approach and save us from a future of digital archeology.

Collada

Heralding from the R&D labs at Sony, Collada is an open interchange format being championed by Sony, Autodesk, and others as a means to exchange digital assets (such as meshes) between tools and applications in a common manner. In addition to basic polygonal mesh data, the XML of Collada can also detail the textures, scene graph, and animations it uses that encompass the basic asset requirements in most current games.

It is hoped that the XML describing a 3D object can be saved from any Collada-compatible tool, get processed by another, and then reimported without any loss of information. This process should remain lossless even if the tools do not understand a particular XML tag. This will enable larger, more powerful, and elaborate toolchains to be built from individual components by different vendors—and consequently, different Open Source projects.

The Collada specification is not "open" in the correct sense of the word. Its structure and content are completely governed and controlled by Sony, and changes can only be made through its Collada division. Sony has said it will hand control over to a steering group once its uptake and dominance is assured. For the time being, however, Sony is not independent as it has its PS2 and PS3 interests to take care of which might limit its uptake with other console developers. So, although the PC is currently supported, you should consider the implications of employing Collada on other platforms where Sony is not in control.

Despite being a new technology, Collada assets can be exported by 3ds Max 7.1 (service pack 1) and this data used with other tools in the pipeline.

Its home page is at *http://collada.org*.

The Collada Format

The important point to remember is that Collada is a data exchange format for digital content creation (DCC) packages, such as 3ds Max. This means it contains a generalized description of an object; it is not meant to be used as an in-game object format. Instead, an external tool should load the XML into memory and convert it into an engine-ready binary format. This tool will be specific to the platform and engine of the game, and generally will be custom-written.

Like many open formats, Collada uses XML to provide an easily understood hierarchical data structure. It describes each asset in terms of specific categories. These cover the types of data that can be exchanged using Collada, and include the following:

Animation: This supports basic keyframe animations, and functional curves. In the case of the latter, a 1D curve is specified using sampled points, and the technique by which the position is interpolated between them.

Cameras: Multiple cameras can be included in a single file, each supporting the usual parameters. Additionally, you can specify the optics of the camera itself. This allows you to specify a mirror or chrome ball, which can be used in the generation of environment maps.

Controllers: This is used to control other elements; for example, the animation sequences to provide skinning.

Geometry: The most common and often-used part of Collada is that which holds the mesh data. It supports the usual geometric primitives such as polygons, tristrips, and fans. Each vertex in the mesh contains the traditional compliment of position, normal, color, and UV texture coordinates.

Images: This references an external asset via URL. In all but the most advanced web-savvy toolchains, this will be a local bitmap file. The binary data is not encoded in the XML in any way.

Library: This is a mechanism to organize content by modularizing it into particular Collada types. Each library can contain data from one (and only one) type. The types match those given here; that is, controllers, geometry, images, and so on.

Lights: As found in any graphics engine, the light element stores the usual information such as color, attenuation, falloff, and, of course, position.

Material: As used by the graphics engine, this describes additional rendering and shader information, above and beyond the basic concept of texture. Multipass shaders are supported, and the `program` subnode allows you to reference them with specific parameters.

Scene: This singular node specifies every object that exists within a Collada file, and their relationships. The method used is a directed acyclic graph (DAG) that contains transformations for the scene, and a hierarchical tree containing nodes that will be instantiated within the toolchain.

Textures: These reference the images already specified, allowing multitexturing support.

CAUTION

The left- or right-handed coordinate debate has not been settled by the introduction of Collada. Instead, it provides an `up_axis` *element that can indicate either* `Y_UP` *or* `Z_UP`.

Development Support

With such a wide array of functionality supported by the file format, it is not surprising that this needs a correspondingly large toolchain to support it. If unfettered, the Collada approach is detrimental to a games team; instead of reinventing the wheel on a small subset of exported features, it now seems you have to reinvent a much larger one. Fortunately, this is not the case due to an existing API, source code, and profiles.

Profiles

There is scope for many profiles in Collada. The one that is of primary interest is the *common profile*. This indicates which specific features must be supported for the tool to be considered compliant with Collada. The COLLADA 1.1 Common profile includes "Geometry, Transform hierarchy, Materials, Textures, Shaders, Lights, Camera, Techniques, Procedural Elements, Multi-representations, Assets, Skinning, Animation, and User data." Version 1.2 adds instancing to this list.

The common profile also stipulates that any data that a tool cannot process must be retained and transparently honored when the file is exported back to disc.

The API

Sony has provided a SourceForge project, linked from *https://collada.org/public_forum/viewforum.php?f=10*, with an archive of sample code that generates a complete DOM tree from a Collada file into C++ instanced code. This is standalone code and contains its own XML parser and DOM structures. Note, however, that this will bulk up the toolchain slightly because you're likely to have an existing XML parser. But being offline, it's not a big issue.

TIP

With Collada being an XML file format, not an API, it can be parsed in any language that has an XML parser. This includes Java and C#, both of which are becoming prominent in game development toolchains.

This source code has been released under the SCEA Shared Source License and can be found in the archive.

Tools

Without a means of generating Collada data, any new format—no matter how well thought out—is dead in the water. To aid this, 3ds Max includes an exporter. Furthermore, one of the developer exponents of Collada, Feeling Software, has provided a free-cost viewer that can be downloaded from *http://www.feelingsoftware. com*.

Each Collada file uses the DAE extension (Digital Asset Exchange) and sample files can be found at *http://www.collada.org/public_files/COLLADA_1.3_Sample-Data.zip*. This will enable you to see the specificity involved in such files.

Engines

At the end of the toolchain comes the game engine. Provided your toolchain is building binary-ready assets, there is no more work to do here than usual. Indeed, if you have an existing engine, then you can generate identically formatted data and begin instantly.

The Open Source approach to engine development generally involves importing models directly from the format supplied by the DCC. Irrlicht and Ogre (see Chapter 5, "Graphics," for details) both currently support Collada, but they load the models directly from their XML. This, however, provides a good practical introduction into Collada parsing.

SOURCE CONTROL

One of the most marked jumps between personal and professional development is the use of source control. Most developers' first connection with source control comes from their first time working within a team, perhaps using Microsoft Source Safe. Over recent years, the entry level for source control has been lowered. The granddad of free source control software, CVS, has been joined by free cost versions of proprietary software like Bitkeeper and Perforce for single developers and small teams. This gives them the opportunity to experience the benefits of source control in lesser projects and has, in turn, stimulated development into new and improved software.

CVS

Standing for Concurrent Versions System, CVS is the oldest, and most well known of free source control software. It was born out of the frustration with RCS (Revision Control System) that supported the same ideas, but was limited to changes being made on a single local machine. With development teams growing, CVS was designed from the outside to extend across many remote machines and work with many different users.

CVS is still in use at many companies and is a good and stable piece of technology. Unfortunately, it is showing its age rather badly and has been superceded by Subversion. Consequently, many new Open Source projects and teams are starting afresh with a clean Subversion repository.

Subversion

Subversion was intended to replace CVS by with a newly designed architecture, removing the various design flaws from CVS, including the lack of atomic commits, the inability to rename files while maintaining their history, and cheap branching and tagging. This it has successfully done with a number of stable releases and good community support.

> **Homepage:** *http://subversion.tigris.org*
>
> **License:** Custom (Similar to Apache and BSD).
>
> **Distribution:** Source and binaries.
>
> **First release:** October 20, 2000.
>
> **Current version:** 1.3.0 (stable since January 1, 2006).
>
> **Platforms:** Windows 2000/NT (the clients will run on Windows 9x, but not the server), Linux, Mac OS X, BSD, and Solaris.
>
> **Dependencies:** BerkeleyDB 4.3 on Windows. Apache is recommended but not required, although some binary distributions are compiled on the assumption you will be using them with Apache.
>
> **Other resources:** Mailing list, online forum, and O'Reilly & Associates, Inc. book on Subversion is available free at *http://svnbook.red-bean.com*.

Subversion is one of the few Open Source projects that has lived up to its initial hype. Even while still at point zero releases, it was stable and being put to use in professional organizations. The developers have had enough confidence in the project to self-host the Subversion source code since August 30, 2001.

Requirements

The minimum requirements for Subversion are very modest because it is able to store its repository on the local filesystem. However, this is not recommended as not all filesystems (notably those under Windows) can lock files effectively, which can temporarily break the repository. It is far better (and not particularly difficult) to make use of one of the versioning filesystems that Subversion uses to store its data. This can either be a database, such as Berkeley DB or Apache webDAV. Where available, the latter option certainly scales better. By using the Apache web server (version 2.x is required) you instantly gain remote access and authentification for free[5].

Integration

Used as part of the workflow solution, Subversion is like any other source code manager (SCM). Where it differs from CVS and the proprietary Perforce is that all its functionality can be accessed through specific library calls, and need not be achieved by calling out to the command-line binaries. This allows you to incorporate "Check in" and "Check out" into your art tools without burdening other members of the development team with the technical details of the command-line switches or command shell boxes.

Migration

Since its inception, Subversion has been touted as a "CVS killer." Consequently, the migration guide from CVS to Subversion is very simple, with well-rehearsed scripts performing all the necessary donkey work automatically. The first port of call for this information is *http://cvs2svn.tigris.org/cvs2svn.html*, followed by *http://search. cpan.org/perldoc?VCP::Dest::svk* and *http://lev.serebryakov.spb.ru/refinecvs*.

Migration has two time sinks of which to be aware. The first is the technical migration time. Moving to Subversion can be a large task since the entire CVS history is kept and transferred into Subversion history. This is an automatic process, however, and a typical game project can be left for the weekend. Naturally, the larger the project, the larger the history; and consequently, the longer the migration. This can lead to downtimes in the region of a week, which is unacceptable for many companies who will refuse to switch because of this alone.

The second cost is the retraining of users. It is easier for most users to go from CVS to Subversion because many are used to the terminology, command-line commands, or preintegrated CVS control that comes from its long legacy. But for those used to GUIs, such as Perforce, this might take a little longer. Fortunately, the Tortoise project (*http://tortoisesvn.tigris.org*, released under the GNU GPL) was created to give Windows users a graphical tool that adds Subversion control directly into Explorer through Windows shell extensions. This supports most of the functionality available from the command line and allows users to right-click a file, or selection thereof, and commit them directly, update to the latest versions from the repository, or branch the source tree.

License

As given at *http://subversion.tigris.org/project_license.html*, the license reads:

* Copyright (c) 2000-2005 CollabNet. All rights reserved.

* Redistribution and use in source and binary forms, with or without modification, are permitted provided that the following conditions are met:

1. Redistributions of source code must retain the above copyright notice, this list of conditions and the following disclaimer.

2. Redistributions in binary form must reproduce the above copyright notice, this list of conditions and the following disclaimer in the documentation and/or other materials provided with the distribution.

3. The end-user documentation included with the redistribution, if any, must include the following acknowledgment: "This product includes software developed by CollabNet (*http://www.Collab.Net/*)." Alternately, this acknowledgment may appear in the software itself, if and wherever such third-party acknowledgments normally appear.

4. The hosted project names must not be used to endorse or promote products derived from this software without prior written permission. For written permission, please contact *info@collab.net*.

5. Products derived from this software may not use the "Tigris" name nor may "Tigris" appear in their names without prior written permission of CollabNet.

THIS SOFTWARE IS PROVIDED ``AS IS'' AND ANY EXPRESSED OR IMPLIED WARRANTIES, INCLUDING, BUT NOT LIMITED TO, THE IMPLIED WARRANTIES OF MERCHANTABILITY AND FITNESS FOR A PARTICULAR PURPOSE ARE DISCLAIMED. IN NO EVENT SHALL COLLABNET OR ITS CONTRIBUTORS BE LIABLE FOR ANY DIRECT, INDIRECT, INCIDENTAL, SPECIAL, EXEMPLARY, OR CONSEQUENTIAL DAMAGES (INCLUDING, BUT NOT LIMITED TO, PROCUREMENT OF SUBSTITUTE GOODS OR SERVICES; LOSS OF USE, DATA, OR PROFITS; OR BUSINESS INTERRUPTION) HOWEVER CAUSED AND ON ANY THEORY OF LIABILITY, WHETHER IN CONTRACT, STRICT LIABILITY, OR TORT (INCLUDING NEGLIGENCE OR OTHERWISE) ARISING IN ANY WAY OUT OF THE USE OF THIS SOFTWARE, EVEN IF ADVISED OF THE POSSIBILITY OF SUCH DAMAGE.

This software consists of voluntary contributions made by many individuals on behalf of CollabNet.

This follows the basic BSD license where, provided you acknowledge Collab.Net, and do not misappropriate its name in any advertising or literature about your product, you can do as you wish with it. However, all copyrights in the project remain vested with CollabNet.

Patch and Diff

Although not a source control tool, per se, the two Unix-derived programs `patch` and `diff` are indispensable when it comes to version control. Particularly if you are submitting bug fixes back to the Open Source community in source code form (as opposed to emailing bug reports).

Patch files list differences between two specific versions, say 1.1 and 1.2. They generally end in the `.diff` extension, and can contain descriptions of many files within them. This patch file is the preferred method for passing patches back to the developers as changes are easier spot in this format. If accepted, these patches will be combined and released in combination with all the other patches submitted for that release. It used to be the case that both a combined `.diff` file (labeled `program-1.1-1.2.diff.gz`) and completely new source archive (`program-1.2.gz`) would be released with each new version. This limited the bandwidth costs because the difference files were invariably orders of magnitude smaller. With cheaper server hosting, and faster home broadband, this is becoming increasingly less common.

Using Diff

This program is a very simple file comparison tool. It only works on text files, but is clever enough to generate contextual differences from them. This means that if line 100 of your program doesn't match line 100 of the maintainer's program it doesn't matter, because it can find an equivalent matching line nearby.

Patches can consist of one or more files, but `diff` will generate a single file containing all their changes for ease of use. To compare two source trees, go to the directory *above* your source code and type:

```
diff —cr original-dir new-dir > changes.diff
```

An examination of `changes.diff` is now pertinent. This will verify that only the necessary changes are included. Remember that you do not want to have a series of changes that differ only by whitespace, include meaningless test comments, or other such morbidities that you don't want to submit. Including too many superfluous changes will very likely result in your patch being quietly refused. Some maintainers receive many patches and may only apply those that require the least effort to verify, so ensure yours is one of them!

From here you should test your `.diff` file by applying it to a clean version of the original source tree using `patch`.

There is also an Open Source program for comparing binary files (called `bdiff`) and a cost-free (although not Open Source) difference program available from the Perforce download web page called `p4diff`.

Using Patch

This takes a suitable `.diff` file and the original code to rebuild a patched version of the source. The first important point to remember is that you should `patch` (and `diff`) from the original version. Although the contextual differencing algorithm is clever, it is not miraculous; so you want to mimic the maintainer's version as closely as is possible. You can verify your patch by typing,

```
cd clean-dir
patch -p1 —i changes.diff
```

The change of directory is important because you will be operating on the source files directly. Also, since your diff file listed the changes present in the `new-dir` directory (which makes no sense to any other machine) you must ignore the first element of the path: thus the `-p1` option.

Once you have applied this patch, you should perform another `diff` between your newly patched version, and the original version from which you built the patch. If no differences are given, you have a successful patch that can be sent to the maintainer, or placed on your own website to fulfill any licensing agreements you may have.

AUDITING TOOLS

In those cases where you must provide access to your source, it is strongly advised you audit the code before releasing it. The auditing process itself should give confidence that the code you're giving out is suitable for external developers. Whereas closed source is only ever seen by the developers themselves, and perhaps the publisher (depending on the deal), Open Source can, in some instances, be visible to everyone. So one sly comment about the boss could find its way into the code, and consequently appear in the source archive on your website. This comment can then find its way to a fan site, or Slashdot, or any number of news sites. Word of mouth spreads very fast on the Internet as the Hot Coffee mod demonstrated in 2005. Even if the comment appears in someone's Open Source code, and is about *their* boss, an overzealous fan-boy is unlikely to know or care about the difference. And many Slashdot posters are unlikely to RTFA! For them, it's the joy of breaching the inner sanctum and kudos in the blogosphere[6].

Auditing encompasses a number of different areas and generally means:

- No third-party software has been included.
- No Open Source software has been included without appropriate license accreditation.
- No profanity, slurs, libel, or suspect content has been included.

This can involve as much, or as little, work as you're prepared to give it but as always, there are tools to help.

To be truly honest to the license you must audit the code before compiling the final version since the source you release should compile into the exact same executable that you release.

Unlicensed Software

There is no simple way to find unlicensed source among a large base of self-written code. Instead, it is best to adopt safe working practices for the code as you develop it and not try to audit in retrospect. Any existing Open Source code you adopt is assumed to be licensed correctly unless attention is made in the documentation to the contrary. This latter point usually consists of comments regarding patents.

License Blocks

You should begin each new source file with a very specific declaration of the source code's license. The specific license is unimportant, as is the format in which it is stored. However, by knowing that each new file starts in a precise fashion allows you to quickly determine which have been written by your staff, and which have been copied wholesale into the source tree to perform some other task.

A typical license template might appear as:

```
/*
** File: myfile.cpp - 14/02/2006
** Author: Holly
**
```

```
** This file is copyright 2006 by A&C Software Incorporated.
** All rights reserved. It is released under the license
** dictated by the supplementary file, LICENSE.TXT
*/
```

The inclusion of the initial date gives the legal department some recourse and leverage in the event of dispute, and the filename is used to trap developers that fall foul to the copy and paste brigade.

Copied Code

Alexandria was insignificant compared to the Internet. This, coupled with the indexing power of Google, provides a resource the likes of which the world has never seen. Almost every compiler error, warning, algorithm, and data structure has a number of useful web pages describing it in prodigious detail. But with this information comes the responsibility to use it correctly. Everything written on the web is under copyright unless explicitly detailed otherwise. This includes posts on most forums and mailing lists. Code snippets, bug fixes, and basic vendor sample code don't usually fall under this category, and can be incorporated under the terms of fair use. Most other code is placed on the web so that you can use it, so you are unlikely to find problems using it, but you should always read the text surrounding the code for any gotchas or extra permissions.

To ensure correct attribution, each developer should prefix any copied algorithm with an easy-to-recognize comment such as COPYCODE, and a URL to the website from which it was taken.

```
// COPYCODE: Algorithm from http://www.bluedust.com/pub/sources/
/* something really cool here */
// COPYCODE-END
```

In all cases, the comment can serve as documentation and direct other programmers to the background information describing the algorithm used. It also provides an easy method to generate a list of contributors automatically.

Libelous Text

Retrieving text strings from source code is a comparatively easy process. You saw, in Chapter 10, "Utility Libraries," how xgettext can be used to extract translation strings from a body of source. This provides a single text file that can be audited for problematic words. However, any string that isn't targeted for translation does not appear in this file. Nor do comments. Both of which are more likely candidates for the suspect phrases that a nefarious programmer would attempt to hide. Consequently, you need to search in both types of text. This can be done in two passes. A basic string extraction can be performed using Perl (either as part of Cygwin or using ActivePerl) by checking for matching quotation marks using

```
perl -n -e 'print "$. : $1\n" while /\"(.*?)\"/g;' -- filename.cpp
```

Then, a list of all text within comments can be extracted from the source separately, regardless of whether they use the /* */ or // variety.

This can produce a lot of text, but is worthwhile considering your reputation as a developer can be at stake, particularly if unprofessional developers or disgruntled ex-employees have had a hand in the source code.

A quick, automatic check of the source can be performed by searching the resultant list against a set of known words. This would include:

- A dirty word list. With new words and alternate misspellings coming to the fore with regular abandon this can never be truly up to date, but it is usually a good "early out." *Wikipedia* is attempting to maintain a canonical list at *http://en. wikipedia.org/wiki/List_of_profane_words.*

- The names and nicknames of existing and past workers. You should also include tiles such as "boss" and "producer."

- Words describing the work environment. It's not uncommon to find phrases like "I could fix this, but they don't pay me enough, so I won't" in source code comments, so check for "pay", "overtime", and so on.

- Religion concerning both online and offline deities. While few people are truly offended by the "vi versus emacs" religious war, a comment like "Micro$oft $ucks" would be highly embarrassing and could cool a good relationship. This type of search requires something a little more custom, as it is common to replace particular characters with supposedly humorous variations (such as the "s" for "$" in the Microsoft example). This also applies to religion, because some people will refer to God as G-d, since there is a belief that anything containing the Lord's name can never be destroyed or deleted. They therefore refer to Him as G-d, to prevent that.

- Leetspeak. This is an alternate method of misspelling words used originally in the underground cracking communities so simple text scanners wouldn't spot their communications. This essentially replaces letters with physically similar numerics. For example, "this" could be written as "7h1$". The number of potential transliterations is staggering and is generally limited only by the imagination and perversions of the author. A good starting point, however, is the page at *http://en.wikipedia.org/wiki/Leet#Common_transliterations.*

Obviously, this will never eradicate those strings that are encrypted in some fashion or those which are intentionally obfuscated to avoid detection. These can only be found through an exhaustive audit of the source code and play-testing.

TIP

Searching binary data for text strings can be achieved using the strings

ENDNOTES

1. Although many have discovered the benefits of plain ASCII and XML, these are but container formats. The structure of the data within them usually differs radically, and often originates from the software's internally data structures.

2. *http://www.cit.gu.edu.au/~anthony/graphics/imagick6/resize/#filter* with examples at the graphics-heavy page of *http://www.dylanbeattie.net/magick/filters/result.html*

3. With the exception of the fft code, which is under the GPL.

4. All video codecs include some form of audio playback, so standalone audio handling is essentially available for free.

5. Subversion also comes with its own small portable Web server, svnserve, but this provides none of the extras of Apache. Its use is generally limited to experiments and sandboxes.

6. In contrast to professional developer studios, the Open Source community appears to care very little for niceties in comments, as a quick profanity search of the Linux kernel source code will attest.

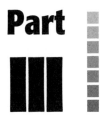

Part

III

Not all Open Source needs to be supplied with its source to be useful. Many of the big open source projects are distributed primarily in binary form because the time and effort required to compile them outweighs the patience of most developers. This section covers those tools; they are all are Open Source and provide the game developer with enough scope to create game-ready content in all disciplines—art, music, and design—without the need to understand or compile the source code.

If you are not redistributing these applications, you can modify them to fit in with the tools pipeline involved in your game without having to release any source code changes. Similarly, you do not need to agree to the license if you are merely using the product.

In all cases, we cover the tools briefly to demonstrate their scope and how they fit into the development environment because the documentation is sometimes lacking in the idiosyncrasies of game development. For more general assistance, however, the existing help files and documentation that come with the package, and that which can be found on Internet, should be referenced to give a complete understanding of the tool and its usage.

12 Graphics Production Tools

In This Chapter

- The GIMP
- Object Modeling
- Movie Editing

THE GIMP

GIMP stands for the GNU Image Manipulation Program. It was created to retouch photographs, create images, and perform a wide range of graphical manipulations. It is often called the Linux version of Adobe Photoshop due to its marked similarities to that product, although the GIMP is a truly cross-platform project with at least 20 different supported operating systems.

It was begun as part of a college project in 1995 by Peter Mattis and Spencer Kimball, and in Peter's original email[1] he refers to a *graphical* image manipulation program he's planning on writing. From the beginning it grew through grass-roots support, with separate mailing lists for developers and users, although at this time its user base was still largely limited to academics. This was due to its reliance on Motif, a nonfree graphics interface that was popular in the last century. However, this artificially restrictive market encouraged Peter to write his own graphical toolkit, called GTK. This has been the basis of GIMP and much other software ever since.

Despite some turbulent years with frequently changing maintainers, the project continued to grow, thanks to its plug-in architecture and the patronage of community celebrities like Larry Ewing, who drew Tux (the Linux penguin mascot) using the GIMP. It even acquired a mascot of its own, called Wilbur.

Homepage: *http://www.gimp.org*

License: GNU GPL (Appendix B)

Distribution: Source only; binaries available elsewhere (see later)

First release: November 21, 2005 (first public release in January 1996)

Current version: 2.2.11 (stable since April 14, 2006, but changing frequently)

Platforms: Extensive desktop platforms, such as Windows, Linux, and Macintosh

Dependencies: Several, but included in Windows binary

Other resources: Several mailing lists, forums, online tutorials, books, and IRC channels

Installation

By default, the developers provide GIMP only as a source package, although most distributions of GNU/Linux will provide a binary package as standard. Microsoft Windows users, however, do not have a standard repository from where they can download software, and so must rely on the kindness of strangers to compile and package the source code for them. These are available on the CD-ROM, although for a more recent version you should visit the GIMP Windows page at *http://gimp.org/windows* or the current downloads page at *http://gimp-win.sourceforge.net/stable.html*. Because GIMP uses the GTK+ toolkit, you will need to download and install both packages.

ON THE CD

The GTK+ package contains everything necessary for the GIMP to work under Windows. This includes a large collection of utility DLLs—some of which you might have previously compiled for use by your game—such as `zlib1.dll` (for zlib compression), `intl.dll` (for localized translations), and `freetype6.dll` (font support). If you are using these libraries, then you will need to manually confirm that the new versions are binary compatible with your link libraries. However, since there have been relatively few releases of these packages, and it's generally unnecessary to make changes to them, there shouldn't be a problem.

During installation you will be presented with the GNU GPL license. When you are, just click *Continue*. This is not the typical EULA agreement asking you to agree to an arbitrary set of unknown preconditions before you're permitted to use the software. Instead, it is merely letting you know that this software is under the GPL. As mentioned in Chapter 2, "License Commentaries," mention of the license agreement must be made somewhere within the package, and instead of including it solely within the Help>About menu, the GIMP developers decided to be more blatant. Note, however, that there is no EULA with GPL software at all, giving everyone the right to *use* the software freely without agreeing to anything.

Under recent incarnations of the Windows operating system, software can usually be installed as either the current user or the administrator. Although the GIMP can be installed for a single user, the GTK+ toolkit requires administrator privileges. Many developers set up their Windows machines to run with administrator privileges, so they can more easily install software and change settings. The artist-oriented machines are generally not so configured, and need one extra step to run the installer as the administrator user. This is done by simply pressing Shift and holding it down while you right-click the installer's icon. A menu will appear with the additional item, Run As, which you should select. You must then type the local machine's administrator username and password to install as that user.

If you elect to install GIMP as an administrator, then remember to install all upgrades and new versions as an administrator also. Otherwise the older files will be not be overwritten by the (lower privileged) local user and you'll get lots of version mismatch errors.

When the installation has completed, you can execute GIMP as normal and will be greeted by the splash screen, followed by the standard toolbar shown in Figure 12.1.

In addition to the program executable, a number of auxiliary files, such as brushes and plug-ins, are installed. To adopt the cross-platform nature of GIMP, these files are stored in a directory structure that is common with all other platforms, instead of a structure that makes obvious sense on the current platform. Therefore, the only difference in structure is the root directory. So, for example, the `lib/gimp/2.0/plug-ins` directory would have an absolute path of `C:\Program Files\GIMP-2.0\lib\gimp\2.0\plug-ins` under Windows, and `/usr/lib/gimp/2.0/plug-ins` under most Unix machines. All subsequent examples shall use the Unix naming convention.

Usage

The GIMP is like any other paint program and, although its interface isn't as polished when compared side by side with Photoshop, it is a fully functional and stable piece of software. The toolbar, shown in Figure 12.1, provides all the standard functionality you'd expect from the editing tools, such as marquee selection, zoom, and paint.

FIGURE 12.1   The GIMP toolbar.

If you open the Layers dialog panel (by pressing Ctrl+L, or using the Dialogs >Layers menu), you will notice that the onionskin layers from Photoshop are also available here. To maintain this information, you should save all images in XCF format, which is the GIMP equivalent of PSD. When you're ready to export an image for use within the game, you should use File>Save a copy and agree to the Export procedure, which will flatten all layers into one making it compatible for the game's format of either PNG or BMP.

Postmigration retraining is one of the biggest obstacles for Open Source software, and despite its artist-friendly demeanor, GIMP is no different. While much of the interface is oriented more toward a technical artist or programmer, there is still one area that belies its Linux background—the file requester. While it is a well-designed and functional requester, it is not the one expected when most users select Open File. To that end, a plug-in has been written that replaces the existing one (which is GTK+ styled) with the native Windows requester. This plug-in, available from *http://registry.gimp.org/plugin?id=3908* adds a new option to the File menu, which can then be associated with the Ctrl+O shortcut by changing the preferences.

Coming to grips with the GIMP can take time, particularly if you start exploring all the filters and plug-ins provided. The web is full of tutorials on the GIMP, and many are collated at *http://www.gimp.org/tutorials*. They are all recommended.

You can also personalize your copy of the GIMP by creating your own 400 × 300 splash screen by changing `share/gimp/2.0/images/gimp-splash.png`.

Plug-Ins and Extensions

One of the things that makes the GIMP so usable is its plug-in architecture. No longer does a developer have to write a (half-baked) paint program for the sole purpose of demonstrating his new cloud-generation algorithm. Instead, he can write a small piece of code for an existing program so both gain benefit. This is the Open Source idea at work again.

There is such a wide range of plug-ins, it is difficult to make any generalizations about them. Because there is no enforceable style guide, there are some problems with a unified interface—or rather, the lack of one. For example, it is not always possible to determine how much of the canvas any particular plug-in will affect without first trying it. The expected case is that the image-processing tools will only work on the current layer and within the selection boundary, but this is not always the case. In addition, there is a range of rendering plug-ins, that you come to later, that will generate an image that covers the whole canvas, confusing the issue further. Fortunately, many plug-ins have a preview feature to guide you, and there's always the undo option of GIMP itself.

But plug-ins are useless unless people know about them, and the GIMP project has been good enough to collate all those known on its website at *http://registry.gimp.org*. It contains both types of plug-ins, which are covered here.

Executable Plug-Ins

This was the first form of extensibility written into GIMP. They are platform-specific executable files and live in the `lib/gimp/2.0/plug-ins` directory. Due to the Linux origin of GIMP, not every plug-in has been ported to exist as a Windows executable, although the situation is very much better than it was, and the most useful ones are available across most platforms.

You can install plug-ins, or any type of extension, in any folder by adding new paths to the preferences from the menu, `File>Preferences>Folders>Plug-Ins`.

Plug-ins are installed by copying the executables into the `plug-ins` directory and restarting GIMP. They will appear in one of the submenus, off `Filters`. Which menu, however, is a decision of the specific developer. Again, there is no style guide here; so the location might not be obvious. Furthermore, this information is sometimes omitted from the readme file and documentation; so you must find it using the `Xtns>Plug-in Browser` menu option, from the main GIMP tools panel. This opens a dialog, as shown in Figure 12.2, that lists every plug-in currently loaded. You only need to type the name, or part of it, and the dialog will show you a list of the extensions that match the given text.

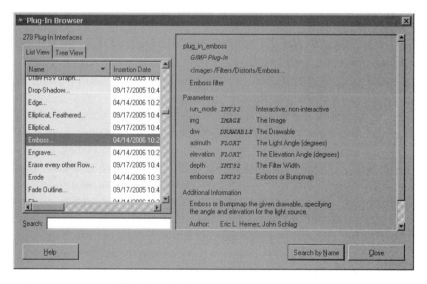

FIGURE 12.2 Searching for plug-ins.

The third line on the right-hand panel describes the submenu under which the plug-in can be found. The `<Image>` declaration means it's available in the window containing an editable image. In the example given, it can be found in the `Filters` menu, in the `Distorts` submenu, and is called "Emboss . . ." The ellipses refer to the fact that an additional dialog box will open as a consequence of selecting this item. No ellipses means it executes immediately.

The ellipses are an adopted convention, although it is not enforced it is likely that some plug-ins will not conform.

The browser dialog also contains a Tree view tab on the left. This will show the position of the selected plug-in in its true relative position, inside the menu.

Script-Fu Extensions

These extensions are generally more lightweight than their executable counterparts, and are written as script files held in `share/gimp/2.0/scripts`. Because of the power present in the GIMP API, a lot of functionality can be provided from basic scripts, which is one reason why there are so many available. Writing scripts is also a very quick and safe way of experimenting with GIMP because you do not need to reload the GIMP for any changes to take place, and it is more difficult to crash the program as a whole when using them.

To load (or reload) a script, simply copy the file (it will generally end in `.scm`) into the previous directory, and select `Xtns>Script-Fu>Refresh scripts`. The script will now appear on the `Script-Fu` menu in an appropriate submenu.

Like the executable plug-ins, if you are unaware of the submenu, and do not care for eyeball searches, then a search facility is provided from the toolbar menu in `Xtns>DB_browser`.

The search facility for script-fu is different from the search used for plug-in modules.

The scripting language used is called Scheme, and is a variant on Lisp (and the basis for Guile, as covered in Chapter 10, "Utility Libraries"). It is also possible to develop scripts in Perl or Python, which is becoming increasing more popular as a GIMP language, and is covered at *http://www.gimp.org/docs/python/pygimp.html*.

All scripts are in plain text, so you can study them at your leisure.

Typical Extensions

A search of the *http://registry.gimp.org* website can result in many hours of happy experimentation. What follows are a selected few of the extensions you may find useful.

Image Manipulation

The usual lighten/darken combinations are present in abundance inside GIMP, including AutoLevels and gamma correcting utilities. Additionally, there are plug-ins, such as photofilters[2] that will make the image appear as if it were black and white or viewed through an infrared camera.

File Format Handlers

There are separate internal mechanisms for loading and saving images, so not all extensions will automatically handle both. The dds (DirectDrawSurface) plug-in (*http://registry.gimp.org/plugin?id=3475*), for example, will only *load* images. With the more exotic file formats used in games, such as TM2, being proprietary, it is more likely you will either need to write your own plug-ins or save all the graphics in a standard format (such as PNG) and let the toolchain take the strain.

Automatic Rendering

GIMP provides a specific menu for those features that generate complete swaths of graphic as a basis for your work.

Along with the usual faire of plasma clouds and chessboards, there is also the facility to overlay jigsaw lugs on the image and generate fractals. This latter can provide some nice menu backgrounds when zoomed in beyond the conventional image.

TIP

Some plug-ins, such as Clothify, can produce nice rendered backdrops on their own when applied to a black canvas.

There is also a suite of simple scripts (like `draw-box.scm` and `draw-ellipse.scm`) to provide pixel-perfect primitives. They are sized, unfortunately, by typing screen coordinates!

GIMP Forks

There are at least two popular forks of the GIMP project. The first is CinePaint, originally called Film GIMP, which is used for manipulating still movie frames and covered later in this chapter. The second is GIMPShop. This is self-effacingly called a "hack," and reorganizes the tools, options, and menus within the GIMP to more closely resemble Photoshop. This is an attempt to overcome the perceived interface problem of the GIMP, which is often touted as the biggest migration issue with this software. The author's intentions are to "convert a Photoshop *pirate* into a Gimp *user.*"

The software can be downloaded from the pages at *http://plasticbugs.com/ ?page_id=294*, or through the links at the "fan" site at *http://www.gimpshop.net*.

OBJECT MODELING

There are so many parts of modern 3D games that require modeling; chairs, tables, animals, humans, spaceships, prison cells, and so on, that it is rare that any one package can author all of the above models in a manner that's agreeable with the artist creating them. Even the professional packages, such as 3ds Max and Maya, have holy wars from time to time. Here then, are some Open Source tools that can generate game-friendly meshes.

The most well-known tool of this kind is Blender, but that is covered separately in Chapter 14, "World Editors," when discussing design tools.

JPatch

JPatch is a work-in-progress modeling tool for splines and patches. Despite the early version number, it is a very usable and stable product that can handle keyframe and morphing animations, extrusion, five-sided patches, and various export facilities. It also supports lip-syncing when used in combination with timesheets from Jlipsync. UV mapping and bones are planned for future versions.

The benefit, and purpose, of splines and patches is to generate smooth curves in either two or three dimensions. This is done by creating a number of control points that dictate the path of the curve, without specifying any particular point along it. This path can be extruding into a solid, or rotated around an axis (like a lathe.) Using patches alone, you can create human characters, pillars, cars, and terrain meshes. JPatch even ships with some demonstrations that include a cartoon-like human.

Patches and splines allow the data to be represented as equations, which is more efficient in terms of memory, and can improve the resolution of rendering since it is not confined to prebuilt individual polygons.

Homepage: *http://www.jpatch.com*

License: GNU GPL Version 2 (Appendix B)

Distribution: Java JAR file;. source from CVS

First release: 2004

Current version: 0.4 preview 1 (stable since May 9, 2005, although later development versions are available)

Platform(s): Windows, Linux, and any other compliant Java platform

Dependencies: Java 2, Standard Edition; and Java Runtime Environment 1.5

Other resources: Online forum, tutorials, and wiki

Using JPatch

The screenshot in Figure 12.3 show the three main interface areas of JPatch. The main central portion of the window shows the current spline. This view can be moved or rotated by the controls along the top, while the form of the object within it is controlled with the tools down the left edge.

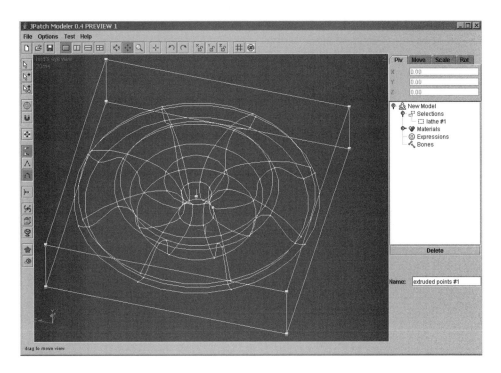

FIGURE 12.3 A UFO test model in JPatch.

Creating an object such as this is easy. First, create a curved shape by selecting the Add Multiple Points option on the left, and then click and drag a number of points to make up the edge of the object, as shown in Figure 12.4.

Next, select all the points, and choose Lathe. This will rotate all the points around a central axis. The number of segments indicates the resolution and will use that many patches to encompass one revolution. You can then scale this new object to suit, constraining the appropriate angles where necessary, as shown in Figure 12.5.

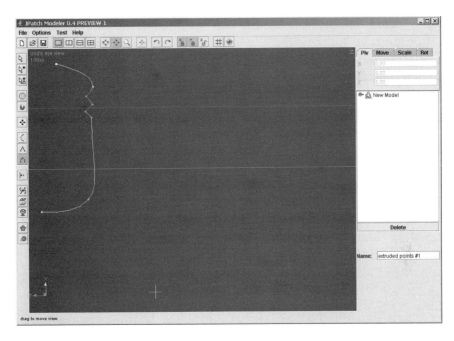

FIGURE 12.4   The edge of a candlestick, prior to the lathe.

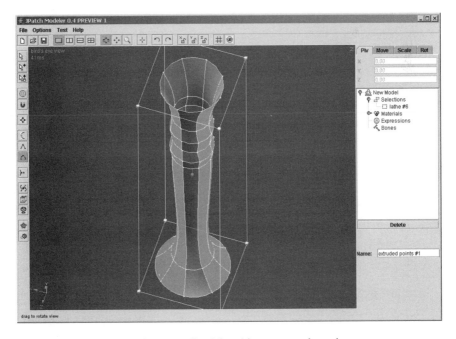

FIGURE 12.5   The resultant candlestick, with computed patches.

From here you can modify individual points on the surface, if necessary, or export ready for the game.

Integrating Patch Data

Depending on the type of modeling you're doing, and the engine present within your game, there are two potential forms of data to consider: raw and cooked.

Raw data consists of the *description* of the object so that it can be rebuilt at run-time. In the example of the candlestick, this would include a list of the control points and the lathe settings. It is then up to the game engine to derive polygons from this data.

Although there is no formal exporter for raw data, the JPatch program uses a very simple format for its own use. It is in XML, and describes each mesh in terms of the control points for the curves, for example,

```
<curve>
   <cp x="-0.24048893" y="17.562702" z="3.6227725"/>
   <cp x="0.021832207" y="19.812843" z="2.106671"/>
   <cp x="0.31883985" y="36.963943" z="1.9751331" mode="peak"/>
   <cp x="0.2913019" y="38.260433" z="2.1668909" mode="peak"/>
   <cp x="0.4050497" y="39.686573" z="1.9222019" mode="peak"/>
   <cp x="0.3895431" y="41.50166" z="2.117763" mode="peak"/>
   <cp x="0.50655276" y="43.316746" z="1.8941522"/>
   <cp x="0.48257133" y="48.24341" z="3.0523896"/>
</curve>
```

When combined with the other data in the file, this gives enough information for a suitable graphics engine to render the object directly.

Cooked data decomposes the surface into individual polygons, and is more suitable for a standard polygonal mesh renderer. This data is available through the JPatch exporters; one for each for Alias/Wavefront[3], POV-Ray, and RenderMAN. Immediately prior to export, you are asked to select a Mesh Density, which indicates the number of polygons used to represent each patch. Naturally, the higher the density, the larger the data, the slower the render, but the better the quality. You can see examples of these formats in the bookcode directory of the CD-ROM. Note

ON THE CD

that JPatch does not support Collada, which is supported directly by engines such as Irrlicht, although conversions can be made using a tool, such as the one at *http://earth.whoola.com:8080/space/collada*. Therefore, you must convert from one of the previous formats into something suitable for your engine. Fortunately, all of these exportable file formats exist as plain ASCII, and it is therefore simple to extract the polygon data from them.

Freyja

This is a new 3D modeling package that supports UV mapping, mesh editing, and surface generation. Animation is also intended for inclusion. As it stands currently, Freyja is an early adopter project with potential. It is capable of producing textured meshes (see Figure 12.6), and exporting them in a variety of formats (including the text-only format, ASE) although the interface is currently a little rough around the edges, and there are several bugs.

Homepage: *http://www.icculus.org/freyja*

License: GNU GPL Version 2 (Appendix B)

Distribution: Source only; binary snapshots available

First release: 2004

Current version: 0.3.5 (stable since August 10, 2005, but the repository changes more frequently)

Platform(s): Linux and Windows

Dependencies: Several, but included in Windows binary

Other resources: Online forum

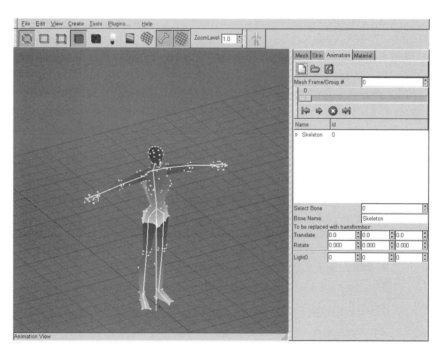

FIGURE 12.6   An example mesh in Freyja.

To experiment with Freyja, it is recommended you take the latest binary snapshot from *http://www.icculus.org/freyja/files/freyja-win32-20050810-snapshot.zip*. It *must* be extracted to `c:\freyja` and run from the same directory.

MOVIE EDITING

This section, above all others, disproves the myth that Linux can't make money. In the movie industry, around 90 percent of all postproduction work is handled using computers running Linux. The compositing tools Nuke and Shake, although closed source, run on Linux systems with major films like *Titantic* (which used only Linux renderfarms) and *Shrek 2* (the first feature film to use Linux end to end) being prime examples. However, the software being run on these machines is mostly proprietary, which leads to the interesting dichotomy, as the amount of Open Source available in this area is rather limiting. But, it is available, and with a little extra legwork you can edit and manipulate movie-driven cut-scenes with entirely Open Source tools. The short film *Cenobitic*[4], for example, was the first made entirely using Open Source technology and creative commons content in this way.

Kino

Kino is a digital video-editing suite for Linux. It integrates with IEEE 1394 hardware to capture raw and DV-quality images from cameras which it can then manipulate internally. It can also load presaved DV clips from other sources. These clips can then be edited and resequenced into an edit decision list that indicates which portion of which clips are to be played in what order. This list is stored in XML, and contains only references to film data, making the entire editing process nondestructive. The resultant film can then be exported, through Kino, into various different formats, including DV, IEEE 1394, and MPEG.

In its current incarnation, Kino is a usable package for the editing and manipulation of existing footage. It is not as powerful or flexible as many proprietary solutions, such as Final Cut Pro, since its ability to handle soundtracks is lacking, but for the manipulation of game cut-scenes (where prerendered clips are placed into order, and a completely new audio track is overdubbed), Kino is worth investigating.

> **Homepage:** *http://www.kinodv.org*
>
> **License:** GNU GPL (Appendix B) incorporating portions of LGPL and BSD code.
>
> **Distribution:** Source only. Binaries available in many distributions.
>
> **First release:** October 8, 2000.
>
> **Current version:** 0.8.1 (stable since April 15, 2006).

Platform(s): Linux only.

Dependencies: GTK, Glib, Gnome, xdevel, imlib, libxml, audiofile. All generally provided through the Linux package manager. Libdv, libraw1394, libavc1394, and libsamplerate are also needed.

Other resources: Mailing lists, discussion forums, and online user guides.

Installation

The Linux bias is so heavy in Kino that unless you're running a Linux distribution where Kino has prepackaged binaries, it is unlikely you would want to recompile it yourself[5]. In reality, it's no worse than any other large, complex, piece of software, but because it's a multimedia application, the dependencies are more exotic. After all, an operating system whose focus has generally been web servers and the routing of networking packets will find media editing outside its traditional remit. The most vital of these dependencies is IEEE 1394 support, which is necessary to handle digital video (DV) and must be provided as part of the kernel, although the program will still work if no such devices are available. More information on this can be found at *http://www.linux1394.org*.

At the present time, compilation under Windows is unrealistic.

Editing a Film

Once the individual clips have been converted or captured into DV format, they can be inserted into the storyboard list, as seen in the left-hand column of Figure 12.7.

FIGURE 12.7 A typical editing session in Kino.

These clips can be reordered with the familiar click-and-drag notion within the list. You will notice the bar under the preview image reflects the relative duration of each clip and highlights the current playback position.

For a finer granularity, you can split each clip into several parts and reorder those independently. You can split at the current position with the Split menu option, or switch to the Trim view (through the right-hand tabs), and specify the beginning and end of each clip according to the specific frame. Kino uses nondestructive editing throughout; so although these clips appear separate in the list, they in fact reference the same file, as it has not been altered in any way.

TIP

Although the audio facilities are limited in Kino, it is best to keep the soundtrack intact while editing. This enables you to extract the entire completed (and modified) audio track at the end of the project and import it directly into a sound editor, such as Audacity. This will give your sound engineer enough audio cues to synchronize special effects to the existing sound track, without using timecodes.

Special Effects

Kino supports a small number of wipes and fades for the transitions between clips. Again, this is nondestructive, and no effects are applied to your original footage. Instead, each effect is processed in pseudo real time in the preview window and then generated to a new DV file. This is then placed into your storyboard list, and the start and end frames of the clips on either side of the transition are then modified to accommodate this new sequence.

The controls for the special effects, as shown in Figure 12.8, allow you to prepare separate audio and video transitions, or filters, for the clips. This is a purely exclusive operation, as you cannot filter *and* perform a transition with a single special effect since there is no interface to dictate the order of the two processes. However, you can generate a filtered image clip that is *then* used in a transition as a separate step.

The video filters affect each frame as a whole, and those available include sepia, black & white, mirror, blur, and kaleidoscope. The quality is as good as you'd get from GIMP; so there is no need to export individual frames for postprocessing, although there is usually a small range of options available in Kino.

The list of available transitions is fairly small, but usable. They include the standard fade, barn door wipe, differences, and luminance changes. They always apply data from both the preceding and following clips. Being Open Source, it is possible to write your own code here, but in practice you're likely to make do with those provided or that come as prepackaged plug-ins. Such is the case with *timfx* (from *http://www.k-3d.com/kino*) and *dvtitler* (*http://dvtitler.sourceforge.net*).

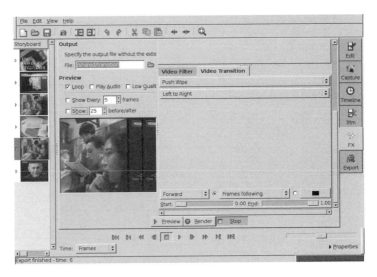

FIGURE 12.8   Special effects in Kino.

It is also possible to use Kino to generate static color washes and fades using this set of options.

Exporting the Film

Once the movie has been edited and ordered correctly, you can export it using the simple View>Export menu option. This panel, shown in Figure 12.9, supports many different formats, but you are unlikely to need anything other than MPEG, as this can be played with the SDL-MPEG library covered in Chapter 5, "Graphics."

Note that those working on consoles with custom file formats may need to perform a secondary transcoding step. In this case, you export the movie using the highest quality format available, which the proprietary tool also supports, since each transcoding step reduces the clarity.

The movie used in the examples is an episode of Computer Chronicles from 1988 about computer games. It has been placed into the public domain by the Prelinger Archives at http://www.archive.org/details/prelinger. *The program itself can be downloaded freely from* http://www.archive.org/details/games2.

CinePaint

Originally called FilmGimp, this project forked from the granddaddy of free media applications, the GIMP, in 1998. Its original purpose was to provide a high-resolution

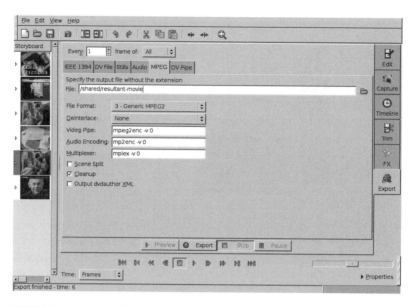

FIGURE 12.9 Exporting movies from Kino.

editing tool for the film industry because the 8-bit color support of the original GIMP didn't offer enough clarity for high-resolution movie stock. Furthermore, touching up a *motion* picture in a *static* image editor is not easy because artists need to move between consecutive frames quickly and easily see how their changes affect the film *in situ*. CinePaint was bourn from these two main needs.

For many game developers, having a paint program like this is an unnecessary luxury. Many cut-scenes are prerendered in the correct storyboard order using the existing game engine, giving a complete digital chain from source to screen. Furthermore, any necessary film edits can be done in Kino, with postproduction effects being handled by cleverly scripting mencoder, ImageMagick, or a combination of the two.

Homepage: *http://www.cinepaint.org*

License: GNU GPL (Appendix B) incorporating portions of LGPL and BSD code

Distribution: Source only; binaries available elsewhere (see below)

First release: 1998 (as the Hollywood branch in the GIMP 1.0.4 CVS repository)

Current version: 0.2.1 (stable since April 4, 2006)

Platform(s): Linux primarily, although a Windows port is available

Dependencies: Several, but included in Windows binary where available

Other resources: Three mailing lists (announcements, users, and developers) and online tutorials

Installation

Like Kino, this package has many compile dependencies and is a complex task to build from scratch. It is strongly recommended, therefore, that you use a prebuilt version with a bias toward those on the Linux platform, as this is invariably more stable than its Microsoft Windows counterpart.

Once installed and run, CinePaint looks like an older version of the GIMP, for that is what it was when it was forked at version 1.0.4. However, because none of GIMP's newer features have been ported across, it looks like the ugly sister of the group. In their place is the functionality necessary for film work.

Using CinePaint

The important functionality divides into the following areas.

Deep Color

This is the term given when the bit depth of any color channel (i.e., red, green, or blue) exceeds 8 bits. Most traditional paint packages stop at 8-bit because that is the highest resolution available on a standard computer monitor. Higher-end software, such as Photoshop, goes beyond this because it is targeted at print magazines and books.

CinePaint goes even further because of the increased resolution required by filmmakers. In addition to 8-bit channel data, it can also work with images in 16-bit (in both integer and RnH short float formats) and 32-bit color (IEEE 754 float).

All the painting operations work identically in these new modes, although it can be difficult to notice the improved resolution on a standard (8-bit color) monitor using typical game cut-scene data that has been rendered by an in-game engine—also running 8-bit color. However, you will notice differences in the Color Picker dialog box, if proof were needed that you're running with deep color. If you need to support this increased color range, you should save using the XCF format (an expanded version of that used in the normal GIMP) or OpenEXR. This latter format was developed by the world-renowned Industrial Light & Magic (ILM) to exchange images with a high dynamic range between computer imaging applications. The source code to handle OpenEXR files is freely available from *http://www.openexr.com/downloads.html*, along with some sample images. It has been released under the revised BSD license (Appendix D).

The Frame Manager

For the nonprofessional user, this is CinePaint's most useful feature. It allows you to flip between consecutively numbered files to spot discontinuities. It then allows you to fix them in a similarly simple manner.

If you're starting with a movie file, you first need to extract each frame into it own image file. This can be done using the `mencoder` package you saw in Chapter 11, "The Tools Pipeline." First, you must remove the audio track,

```
mplayer -vo null -ao pcm -hardframedrop original_film.avi
```

This saves a file called `audiodump.wav`, which you reapply later. You must then extract each still frame into sequentially numbered files using, for example,

```
ffmpeg -y -i movie.mpg -vframes 200 -ss 00:00:00 -an frame%7d.png
```

This saves the files as `frame0000001.png` *et al in the current working directory, not that of the original film.*

NOTE

You then start CinePaint and load the first file in the sequence, `frame0000001.png`. From here, you can create a frame manager through that image's `File` menu, and you're ready to begin editing.

The store frame manager, as shown in Figure 12.10, contains a list of the images you're going to be editing in this session. Because this list exists outside of the image files themselves, this list (and the associated information) is not stored anywhere, and is therefore lost when CinePaint is closed down.

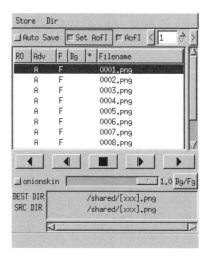

FIGURE 12.10 The frame manager in CinePaint.

The list is populated with the sequentially numbered images by selecting the File>Add menu option, which opens the dialog box shown in Figure 12.11. These images can then be selected and modified on an individual basis. You can use the transport controls and the onionskin option, along the bottom of the Store Frame Manager dialog to preview these images to see how each individual edit affects the film as a whole.

FIGURE 12.11   Adding new still images to the store frame manager.

The AofI option is short for Area of Influence, and is a simple mask. This area is protected, on all frames from accidental edits within CinePaint. This area is determined by selecting the SetAofI option and invoking the traditional marquee tool. It can be controlled as usual.

Once the images have been touched up, make sure they are all saved to disk and then rebuilt into a movie with,

```
ffmpeg -i %8d.png -r 25 -an fixed_film.mpg
```

The audio track is then overdubbed, as covered in Chapter 11, with,

```
mencoder fixed_film.mpg -ovc copy -oac copy \
    -audiofile audiodump.wav -o completed_film.mpg
```

ENDNOTES

1. *http://groups.google.com/group/comp.os.linux.x/msg/ffa0c060f527159b?
   output=gplain*

2. Also available from *http://registry.gimp.org/plugin?id=7495*
3. Described briefly at *http://www.eg-models.de/formats/Format_Obj.html*
4. *http://www.cenobitic.org*
5. This is also true of the other prominent video-editing tool, Cinelerra (*http://heroinewarrior.com/cinelerra.php3*) where pre-packaged binaries are only available for the Fedora Core distribution of Linux.

13 Audio Production

In This Chapter

- Sample-Based Audio
- MIDI Sequencing
- Software Synthesis

When comparing the range and depth of Open Source software there is a very marked difference between the availability of audio APIs and the equivalent audio tools. While there are several solutions and APIs available for developing audio software, remarkably few tools exist to make use of them. And even fewer tools that are capable of handling a professional workload. This is unfortunate, but expected. After all, you can't build a sample editor without libraries for sample loading, user interface, and audio playback. The Open Source community is solving these problems in a progressively logical order. This can only mean the quality of user-related (as opposed to developer-related) tools will improve over time.

Some of the command line audio tools have been covered as part of the greater tools pipeline in Chapter 11, "The Tools Pipeline." This chapter focuses on end-user productivity tools.

SAMPLE-BASED AUDIO

The process of managing samples in games development splits into three main areas. To begin, you have the gathering of raw material from either local microphones or sample CDs. You then process them with particular effects (such as echo, reverb, or normalization) so that they conform to the auditory aesthetics of your particular game. Finally, each sample is formatted to fit within the technical limitations of your platform. The second point is of interest here.

Audacity

The primary sample-editing tool in the Open Source world has to be Audacity. It has good sound import facilities that allow you to edit MP3 and OGG files directly, the traditional collection of editing tools to cut and splice sounds together, and a wide range of effects such as compressors, equalizers, and noise-removal tools.

As an extension over most other basic editors, Audacity also has a multitrack facility. This allows several sample tracks to be placed along side one another and played together, enabling audio designers to hear their work *in situ*. This feature even allows Audacity to be used as a composition tool, as shown in Figure 13.1, because the tracks can be either samples or MIDI-based data, which can be supplemented with label and timing tracks enabling music to be composited and then exported as WAV, MP3, or OGG.

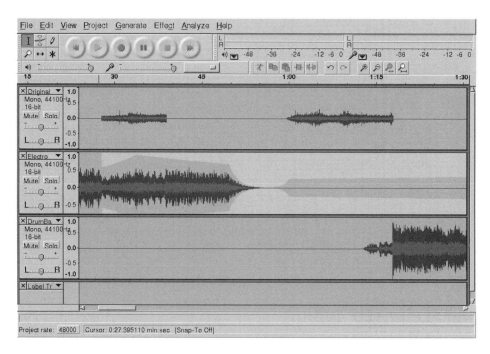

FIGURE 13.1   Building the soundtrack for *Cenobitic* with Audacity (Linux version).

Homepage: *http://audacity.sourceforge.net*

License: GNU GPL (Appendix B)

Distribution: Source and binary

First release: 2000

Current version: 1.2.4 (stable since November 28, 2005)

Platforms: Windows, Linux, and Macintosh

Dependencies: Several, but included in Windows binary

Other resources: Mailing list and website forum

Audacity is a prime example of Open Source foundations being used to build other projects. The main program itself draws on the code from no less than 11 other Open Source projects to provide its functionality, and in doing so becomes greater than the sum of its parts. It has been included on the companion CD-ROM.

ON THE CD

Sample Editing

For basic sample editing, Audacity stands tall against its peers. The manipulation process is much the same as it is for any sample editor. That is, you load the sample into the editor, use the left mouse button to click and drag a selection region for the sample, and then operate on that area, as shown in Figure 13.2. Clicking the

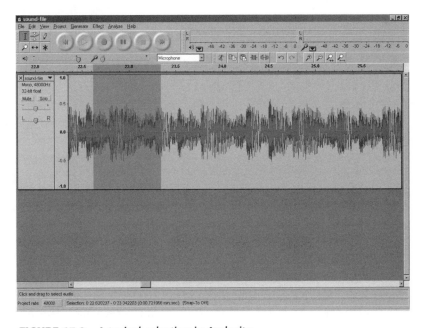

FIGURE 13.2   A typical selection in Audacity.

left- or right-hand edge of the region will move these selection boundaries. When the mouse is in the appropriate area, the cursor will contextually change to the hand icon, and the status text (in the bottom left of the window) will update, as it does for all commands.

The usual cut and splice tools are kept in the Edit menu, with Trim being used to "remove everything outside of the current selection." For fine control, you can always zoom into the appropriate area and modify the sample in place; however. Audacity also has a Split option that allows you to extract the selection into a separate window and modify it there. When you Export that as a WAV file, it reappears in its original position. This is useful for affecting artifacts of the original sound and experimenting with them in isolation because it is easier to apply affects to an entire track (of pre-Split data) than individual portions embedded in another waveform.

For basic effects, a separate volume envelope can affect each sample. This gives you a way to bake basic mixer settings into the waveform itself, as shown in Figure 13.3.

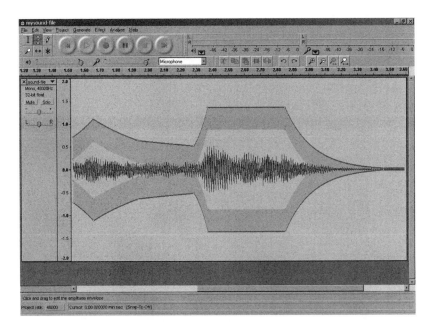

FIGURE 13.3   A basic volume envelope.

Each handle allows you to change the volume of the sound at that point in time. It can also be moved in time, too, to make the sound fade up earlier or later. For fine control around the zero line, it is best to move the cursor into the left-hand range bar (showing -1 to 1, by default) and zoom in with the left click.

To add a handle at the start or end of the sound, it is easier to create one near the extent and drag it into position.

Once all editing is complete you need to save the new waveform. This is done with Export—not Save[1]—which is also on the File menu. The format of the WAV export is governed by the sample rate of the sample itself (shown as Project rate at the bottom of the window) and the `Edit>Preferences` setup in the File Formats dialog. This is the only way to export 8-bit wave files from Audacity, for example.

Multitrack Editing

The two main uses for multitrack editing in games are cut-scenes and music composition. Cut-scenes are better suited to Audacity because they generally involve a number of separate pregenerated samples (each extracted from the source cut-scene movie), which are then mixed down together to form a single stereo waveform. The only editing generally required is envelope shaping to correct the volume of each component. This works exactly as it does for single sounds.

The more complex scenario of multitrack music composition is also possible with Audacity, but is not its forte. This is because each of the tracks can only represent one sample. This limitation should perhaps label Audacity as a multi*sample* editor, instead of multi*track*. Traditionally, you would have a track labeled "percussion," and into this would be placed every drum fill, timpani roll, and cymbal crash. However, to accomplish this using the Audacity metaphor you would need to copy each drum fill individually into the percussion track, or create separate tracks for each percussion part and copy the sample within itself.

In both cases you lose the best benefit of a multitrack editor, which is that each sound in the track is a reference to the *same* sample. This is not possible here because both examples require you to *copy* the data. Because Audacity is focused as a sample editor, it means that if you amend one of the drum rolls it will *not* change any of the other drum rolls you have copied into the other tracks. Some of the time this is useful, but when sequencing music it is generally not. Consequently, Audacity should be kept for the postproduction of existing music tracks.

Loading multiple sounds into Audacity is achieved through Import. Each sample that you import is loaded into the existing project and creates a new block for itself. The timings for this block are only as long as the sample you imported—not the duration of the project. This is to enable quicker turnaround times because only short samples are being processed.

For those combining samples with other media, you can also import MIDI files, although they cannot be edited. And for those wanting to synchronize with video, the timing bar can work in PAL or NTSC h:mm:ss:ff format from the `View>Set Selection Format` menu option.

File Formats

The natural format of Audacity files is AUP. This is an XML file that describes the state of the editor at any particular time. It does not, however, include any audio data. Instead, it references the original file, along with newly created data that represents particular editable audio blocks inside the editor. The project shown in Figure 13.4 has 3 blocks, for example.

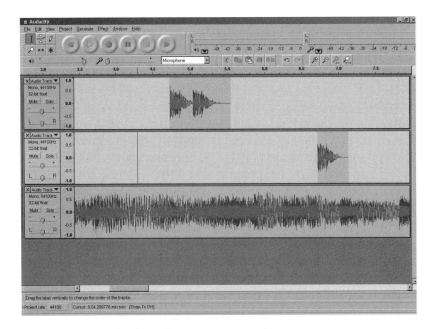

FIGURE 13.4   Each of the fills here is a copy of the others.

Each block is an audio file in its own right, and is stored in a newly created subdirectory. This directory has the same name as the project file, but appended with the word *data*. E.g. `sound-file_data`. The files in this directory are chosen and controlled by Audacity, so it's best not to mess with them, although they are valid samples (in `.au` format) so can be previewed elsewhere.

Wherever the Audacity project file references the sound files, it will save disk space by aliasing one sample to the original WAV file, if it hasn't changed. This filename is specified with an absolute path, however, which means there is some manual work involved if you intend to edit the data on more than one machine. Fortunately, the DOS command `subst` is still supported in current versions of Windows allowing you to use,

```
subst m: d:\projects\music\rawwaves
```

This creates a pseudo-drive letter called `m:`. If you load all your samples through this drive, the paths will be absolute to `m:`, not `d:\projects\music\rawwaves`. This then means you can move projects between machines and only need to execute a single `subst` command to replicate identical paths. Linux users can use the familiar `mount` command.

Being XML, the AUP format can be read by humans and toolchain parsers alike, and it is certainly possible to reinterpret the data within it to build tracker or sequence data. Additionally, Audacity has the ability to export the entire work as WAV, MP3, or OGG. All options are available from the File menu.

The MP3 format is patent encumbered, so does not feature in many Open Source tools by default, although conversion is usually available with the installation of extra tools. A better approach is to export in a more open standard format, such as WAV, and use the toolchain to encode accordingly.

Should you need a sequencer-like approach to in-game music—and were considering developing an AUP to MIDI converter—you will certainly do better by creating an audio sample palette in Audacity, and then use another tool to build the composition because of the multitrack limitations mentioned earlier. There is an option from `File>Export Multiple` to help export individual WAV files to aid you.

GunGirl Sequencer

This is a basic multitrack sample sequencer that can take any file from disk and play and manipulate it any number of times on any track. Unlike Audacity, any editing occurs nondestructively on the files, so it doesn't affect the waveform data stored on disk. It supports full ADSR volume envelopes on each sample, along with basic trimming and whole-track volume control. However, in many respects it is a cut-down version of the multitrack editing facilities present in Audacity because it cannot add effects to any of the sounds and only lets you control references to existing sounds, which matches the MIDI sequencer methodology of composition as shown in Figure 13.5. This is comparatively new software, and its limited feature set is representative of its age, although it's still useable, with the current version supplied on

the CD-ROM.

Homepage: *http://ggseq.sourceforge.net*
License: GNU GPL (Appendix B)
Distribution: Source and binary
First release: 2005
Current version: 0.3.1

Platform(s): Windows and Linux

Dependencies: None

Other resources: None

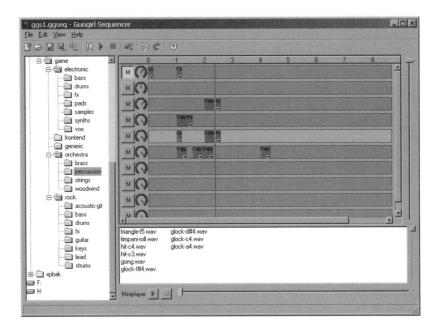

FIGURE 13.5 A basic editing session (Windows version).

Creation and Editing

The basic handling works through a drag-and-drop interface. Samples are taken from the file manager and placed onto the playback grid. Once on the grid, you can move the samples around by employing the familiar click-and-drag mechanism. A left click moves the sound in time, snapping to the current grid size, measured in frames, while holding the Shift key down at the same time avoids the snap.

It is best to set this snap timing before you start because there is no current facility to repeat a sound, so you have to manually duplicate it and place it at the end of the preceding sample. This is easily done with the `Edit>Copy` and `Edit>Paste` combination, or by using the right mouse button to click and drag. To move samples accurately, you need a specific snap size for your music. Therefore, find or create a sample that matches your ideal snap size (this will often be one quaver beat) and view it in *GunGirl*. Clicking the right central button shows you for how many frames the current sample lasts. Enter this into the properties and begin working.

Don't make the snap too small because it can be difficult to click on the handle that opens the Sample Properties dialog.

The handle in the bottom right of each sample instance allows you to control options for this specific instance. They are:

Edit Sample>Timestretch: This lets you slow down, or speed up, the rate at which the sound plays. This doesn't change the pitch—just the duration.

Edit Sample>Trimmer: This is so you can use a smaller portion of the sound than exists on disk. This can provide a cheap way of isolating individual drum sounds.

Envelope: This provides a traditional four-phase ADSR envelope: attack, decay, sustain, and release. When this option is selected you see four white boxes indicating the volume at each phase of the envelope. You can click and drag these to affect the sound. This matches the functionality of the Audacity envelope shaper.

File Formats

There are two ways of saving sequence data from *GunGirl*. The first is as a ggseq file. This is an XML data file listing each sample used in the composition, along with the track and the time at which each sample is to be played. Additionally, because the sample data is never modified, this also contains the envelope processing and sample trim settings applied to each instance. It is comparatively easy to extract pertinent information from this file to build an in-game engine or format for music playback.

The other method is to export a *package*. This is a Zip file containing the ggseq file, along with all the individual samples. This requires a copy of zip in the ggseq/ bin directory, but it is not supplied. Because the main purpose of packages is to transport files elsewhere, it should be noted that you can achieve the same effect by adopting a sensible workflow structure (for example, all WAV files are stored in the same, known, directory) and manually copying the ggseq file. Also, review the subst tip given previously for Audacity as this comes in useful, too.

Finally, although not a method for saving sequence data, you can save the entire composition out as a single WAV file. This can then be encoded by mencoder or sox (as shown in Chapter 11) into an OGG or MP3 file.

MIDI SEQUENCING

Like sample processing, MIDI sequencing software arrived comparatively late in the Open Source timeline. Even the more mature of its offerings have many years

of catching up to do with the most popular proprietary offerings such as Cubase®
or Cakewalk. Furthermore, its comparatively late arrival has meant that ports for
Microsoft Windows can be a significant way behind its GNU/Linux counterparts.
It is difficult to explain the true reason for this. However, one plausible explanation
is that the MIDI device in Linux is much easier to program accurately than the one
in Microsoft Windows and, being such a fundamental part of a MIDI sequencer has
meant that porting requires a larger up-front effort that many Linux-based developers have been reluctant to begin.

Rosegarden-4

Whenever good MIDI-sequencing software is mentioned in Linux circles, they are
generally referring to this sequence, as shown in Figure 13.6. The UK magazine
Sound on Sound has called it "the closest native equivalent to Cubase for Linux" for
good reason. It has a complete sequencer, matrix editor, score editor, and all the
usual editing capabilities found in proprietary sequencers costing many hundreds
of dollars. It even has support for audio samples to be multitracked alongside the
MIDI data.

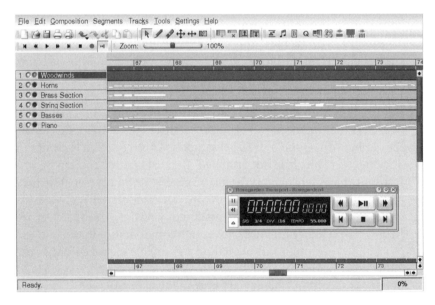

FIGURE 13.6   An example of Rosegarden-4.

Homepage: *http://www.rosegardenmusic.com*

License: GNU GPL (Appendix B).

Distribution: Source only, but see the following.

First release: 2000.

Current version: 1.2.3 (stable since February 14, 2006).

Platform(s): Linux only.

Dependencies: Linux. JACK, and ALSA, most importantly. Your Linux package manager will take care of them, though.

Other resources: Mailing list and website forum.

While it is true that many Open Source development projects are only ever released as source, Rosegarden is one of the very few that embrace these same principles for end-user applications. This means a composer cannot simply download the latest version and get started without first asking a developer to compile it. Instead of inflicting this pain on everyone, most Linux distributions have a *packager* who periodically takes the source, and compiles binary versions suitable for their version of Linux. For them it is not a big job, since the dependencies, build environment, and configuration settings are preprepared as part of their system. Windows users are not so lucky, which is probably why there is no prebuilt binary for the Microsoft platform. Those wishing to experiment with Rosegarden are advised to trial the VMWare Player with Linux distributions, as detailed in Chapter 4, "Development Environments."

Operation

The current version, Rosegarden-4, handles much like any other sequence on the market. Each sequencer track is assigned a MIDI channel, an instrument, and incorporates a stream of MIDI events. These events are represented as one or more blocks on-screen, with each representing an individual passage of music. These passages are not explicitly created by the software, but are introduced by the composer to mark logical phrases in the piece. Consequently, each passage can be moved between channels, or played at a different point in time, without disrupting the rest of the music. Additionally, these copied passages can refer to the original score, so that common phrases can be repeated many times and maintained so that if the original sequence is changed, then so do all the references.

TIP

Deselect the Scroll to Follow Playback option if you are merely reviewing the score, otherwise the staff display will continually revert to bar 1.

But ultimately, there is little difference between Rosegarden and any other sequence in its operation, and once installed there is little that needs relearning.

File Formats

Although the MIDI standard is followed within Rosegarden, it—like most other sequencers—goes beyond what is available in the standard. Consequently, there is still a need for its own format (rg), in addition to the facilities to import and export standard MIDI.

Its own format is of very little use to the game developer because MIDI is already such a well-defined standard that converters and playback engines for MIDI already exist in many forms. However, for interest sake, you might be keen to know that the rg format is in fact a Zip file, inside of which is a single XML document describing every setting, note, and parameter of the music. If you are intending to make use of an XML structure in some fashion, you are advised to export in MusicXML and use that as a basis from which to work.

SOFTWARE SYNTHESIS

Software synthesis applications, a.k.a. soft synths, fall into two main categories. First, there are the emulations of real instruments, like the infamous 808 or 303. They come mostly in freeware, shareware, and proprietary versions because those producing them like to keep their synthesizing algorithms, and therefore their sources, secret. These tools are focused at musicians and retro fans, and faithfully follow the interface of the original instrument. The second category features arbitrary sound generators that can be coaxed into producing nice sounds. These are generally more programmer-oriented but are no more difficult to program than a DX7! Additionally, libraries of sounds are often available for both categories of soft synths to aid those who need it.

Csound

This is the archetypal soft synth. It generates music algorithmically using two specially formatted text files: one describes the timbre of the instruments in the virtual orchestra (.orc), while the other dictates the score (.sco) that they will perform. The combination of these two files then generates a WAV file either to disk or directly to the computer's sound card. There is also a combined version of these two files ending in the .csd extension. This latter format is similar to XML but not close enough to be sensibly parsable with *expat* (from Chapter 10, "Utility Libraries.")

The general usage of Csound has been to generate both text files manually, and run the supplied command line tool over them. However, recent versions allow you to import MIDI files in place of the score file, and some sequencers (such as

Rosegarden) will export Csound score files directly to make this task easier. Additionally, Csound can be used as a real-time instrument using a MIDI controller or scripted with Python.

Homepage: *http://csounds.com*

License: GNU LGPL (Appendix C)

Distribution: Source and binary

First release: 1991

Current version: 5.0 beta (stable since November 9, 2005)

Platform(s): Windows, Linux, and Macintosh

Dependencies: None, but Python is useful

Other resources: Mailing lists, forums, ezines, and website

It's undeniable that programming Csound orchestra files can be difficult. But those wanting to learn—rather than downloading prewritten patches from the Internet—should read the online tutorial at *http://www.csounds.com/toots* and the other articles on the same site. Some documentation is also available in the source archive included on the CD-ROM.

Windows Installation

When using the command line version, you need to prepare the following environment variables like this:

```
set OPCODEDIR=C:\csound5\lib
set OPCODEDIR64=C:\csound5\lib64
set PATH=%PATH%;C:\csound5\bin
set CSOUNDRC=C:\csound5\.csoundrc
```

The final variable specifies the default options for the csound command, which, in the standard installation, pipes all output to the sound card.

It is also advisable to install Python and copy the py.dll *into the* csound5/lib64 *directory to prevent warnings.*

You can then verify your installation by running one of the examples, such as

```
csound c:\csound5\src\examples\xanadu.csd
```

This should generate a file called Xanadu.wav in the current directory.

Basic Csound Construction

The simplest example to give at this point is a basic sine wave, playing a single note. Here you only need a single instrument set to a specific frequency. So, create a file called `sine.orc` containing:

```
; The semicolon is a comment
; The following are global set-up variables
sr     = 44100
kr     = 4410
ksmps  = 10
nchnls = 1


       instr 1   ; define the first  instrument
a1     oscil 10000, 440, 1  ; use the oscil function with 3 params
       ; of amplitude, frequency, and function table
       out   a1
       endin
```

This is supplemented with the score file (`onenote.sco`), thus,

```
; preparation of a sine wave
f1   0   4096   10 1

; The notes : each has three parameters
; instrument - starting time - duration
i1  0       1
e ; end
```

The three fixed parameters in the instrument definition would imply that you need a separate definition for every note. Not so! It is possible to pass a parameter from the score to the instrument by amending the line to read:

```
i1    0    1    10000 440
```

and then changing the `.orc` to read,

```
a1      oscil p4, p5, 1
```

You can then realize this composition with the command:

```
csound sine.orc onenote.sco
```

This will either play the sound to your speakers or generate a file called `test.wav`, depending on your configuration. To force a WAV-based output just use:

```
csound -W —oonenoteplaying.wav sine.orc onenote.sco
```

There are many more instructions available to describe orchestra sounds, but they are covered in the manual and online, including the Cmusic music page at *http://mitpress.mit.edu/e-books/csound/fpage/Csmus/Csmus.html* that also contains various original compositions.

ENDNOTE

1. Save will save an Audacity project, not the current wave file. This distinction is to facilitate the multitrack editing that Audacity also supports.

14 World Editors

BLENDER3D

For full-scale 3D modeling work, Blender is the heaviest of the heavyweight Open Source contenders right now. It is a powerful cross-platform tool that supports mesh generation and editing using polygons, NURBS, Bezier, and B-spline curves, and vector fonts. It also supports Boolean operations, animations, and Python scripting. Blender has also been focused as a game content generation tool because, in addition to the standard editing facilities, it also incorporates a suite of tools for object behavior, collision detection, and dynamic simulation. Much of this content can be tried without compiling or preprocessing.

The community effort behind Blender3D has been immense, and it has an interesting history. Originally, Blender was developed by NaN (Not a Number) between 1998 and 2002. It was intended to be free and to provide inexpensive access to powerful tools. However, due to differences between developers and investors, the business was restarted several times, then shut down. Soon afterward, the original rights to Blender were bought from the now defunct NaN for 100,000 Euros by the community as a whole under the auspices of the Blender Foundation and released under the GPL.

Blender is also suitable for generating in-game character meshes.

Blender is also available on the accompanying CD-ROM.

Homepage: *http://www.blender3d.org*

License: GNU GPL Version 2 (Appendix B).

Distribution: Source and binaries available.

First release: 1998. First GPL version on October 13, 2002.

Current version: 2.4.1 (stable since January 23, 2006).

Platform(s): Windows, Linux, MacOS X, and others.

Dependencies: Several, but included in Windows binary. A full Python install is optional, but recommended.

Other resources: Tutorials in text and video format, manuals, books, and an online forum.

Creating Assets

The basic screen is awash with controls and features, as shown in Figure 14.1, so you'd do well to read the many tutorials at *http://www.blender3d.org/cms/Tutorials.243.0. html* and *http://www.blender3d.org/cms/Using_Blender.80.0.html* first. If you're in a hurry, there is also a well-crafted quick-start PDF installed with the product.

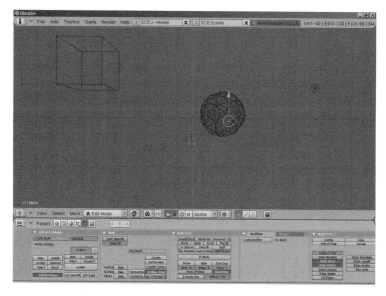

FIGURE 14.1 A simple example.

In essence, the main view displays a scene, and objects are created on a number of different layers. Each layer can be toggled on and off to hide any object placed upon it, thus supporting to the concept of groups. There are a number of different operating *modes*, and the reaction of the objects and their vertices differ accordingly.

In Object mode, for example, right-clicking an object makes it the active selection so that it can then be moved along an axis (by a left-click and drag on the red-, green-, or blue-axis arrow), rotated (by pressing R) or scaled (by pressing S).

The mesh of an object can also be edited vertex by vertex by entering edit mode, at which point you can drag an arrowhead along its appropriate axis to move the currently selected vertex. You can also paint onto the mesh directly, and edit the UV coordinates or vertex color the mesh using the various other modes available.

Python

Outside of the basic mesh handling capabilities of Blender, the most talked about feature is its integration with the Open Source language Python. This is an interpreted object-oriented language with a strong community following. It appears throughout Blender and is used to export meshes and scenes into additional formats, manipulate existing data, trigger (and be triggered from) animations, and even generate algorithmic meshes on the fly.

Blender achieves this extensibility by making new Python modules and submodules available[1], providing a link between the scripts and the back-end engine. These modules provide access to all the internal data and the majority of all necessary functionality. It does not, however, include the standard Python libraries that a typical programmer might expect, such as os or math. To add those, you must install the standard Python packages of the same version as used by your version of Blender.

For information about Python as a programming language please visit http://python.org.

The supplied scripts are mostly exporters, including ones for Collada and Alias/Wavefront. It is still likely, however, that you will want to export directly into your game engine format and create your own exporter. While this is possible, it is not recommended. Despite its power, Python is a language for fast development—not binary data munging. Therefore, it can get very frustrating very quickly to try and build platform-specific binary data inside a Python script. Instead, export the world data from Blender into an XML format, and convert this data using the methods and tools covered in Chapter 10, "Utility Libraries." This has the added bonus that mesh processing can occur outside of Blender in another part of the toolchain. Some game engines have already adopted this approach and created a suitable XML exporter, such as Ogre.

In the `Tools\BlenderExport` directory of your Ogre installation you will find a script called `ogreexport.py` that, if copied into the `Blender\.blender\scripts` directory, will add a new export option called `Ogre XML` to the scripts menu.

The current version of the Ogre blender export tool only works with Blender versions 2.4 and upward.

These meshes should be written using local coordinates only, in order that the game level can reposition them in the world if appropriate, so ensure that the `World Coordinates` button is not highlighted on the export configuration panel, as shown in Figure 14.2.

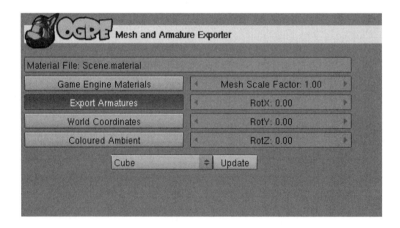

FIGURE 14.2   The suggested mesh export format.

This then allows you to export meshes into individual XML files that look like this:

```
<mesh>
 <submeshes>
   <submesh material="Material" usesharedvertices="false"
       use32bitindexes="false" operationtype="triangle_list">
     <faces count="12">
       <face v1="0" v2="1" v3="2"/>
       <face v1="2" v2="3" v3="0"/>
       <face v1="4" v2="5" v3="7"/>
```

and so on. It then contains the geometry, in the traditional fashion:

```
<geometry vertexcount="24">
  <vertexbuffer positions="true" normals="true">
    <vertex>
      <position x="1.000000" y="1.000000" z="-1.000000"/>
      <normal x="0.000000" y="0.000000" z="-1.000000"/>
    </vertex>
    <vertex>
      <position x="1.000000" y="-1.000000" z="-1.000000"/>
      <normal x="0.000000" y="0.000000" z="-1.000000"/>
    </vertex>
```

This makes the conversion process into game-ready binary very simple.

CAUTION

If the mesh does not have any materials assigned, the export will produce errors, although the XML will still appear correct.

To handle these objects effectively in-game you need to know the scene from which they came, with references to the mesh objects rather than their full list of vertices and faces. This is achieved through the Ogre add-on *dotscene*. It can be downloaded from *http://ogre.cvs.sourceforge.net/ogre/ogreaddons/blendersceneexporter* and should be copied to the same directory as the previous plug-in. The new menu option, Ogre3D Scene, will then open a dialog asking which objects in the scene are to be exported. When Export is selected the scene is saved to disk as scene.xml and will describe each selected object with its name, position, rotation (using quaternions), and scale. For example:

```
<node name="Mesh">
    <position x="2.883078" y="-0.466103" z="2.243039"/>
    <rotation qx="0.481707" qy="0.212922" qz="0.334251" qw="0.781600"/>
    <scale x="1.000000" y="1.000000" z="1.000000"/>
    <entity name="Mesh" meshFile="Mesh.mesh"/>
</node>
```

As you can see, it writes only a reference to the mesh into the file, allowing for a good level of indirection, and the ability to replace specific meshes on particular platforms to cope with their performance differences.

Through a workflow-induced naming convention, these meshes can also be used as placeholders for other features not exported from Blender, such as special effects or level change triggers.

Despite including these export routines, Ogre itself does not load from them. Instead, it provides another tool called `Tools\XMLConverter\src\OgreXMLMesh Serializer.cpp` to create binary-ready assets for its engine. This code can provide good inspiration for converting the XML into your own custom format, if you're not using Ogre.

These tools are under the LGPL and can be used and modified, even if you have no use for Ogre at all in your pipeline.

One very useful game-oriented feature is the ability to assign properties to each object in the scene. This can be seen in Figure 14.3.

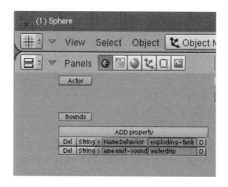

FIGURE 14.3 Applying game-specific properties.

The only data types available are string, integer, float, Boolean, and timer, and are stored in the scene node of `scene.xml`, thus:

```
<node name="Cube">
    <position x="-2.793663" y="-1.148865" z="0.102899"/>
    <rotation qx="0.000000" qy="0.000000" qz="0.332595" qw="0.943070"/>
    <scale x="1.000000" y="1.000000" z="1.000000"/>
    <entity name="Cube" meshFile="Cube.mesh"/>
    <userData>
      <property type="STRING" name="behavior" data="exploding-tank"/>
      <property type="STRING" name="emit-sound" data="waterdrip"/>
    </userData>
</node>
```

The range of properties is, alas, fairly minimal, and it is not obvious how to make an internal connection between two or more different objects. Because C++ pointers cannot be exported anyway, the best solution to this problem is to assign each object a unique id or name, and create a property called *tied*. This is then converted in the toolchain to the serialize method used by the game engine. Each object is automatically given a name during creation, but these are usually confined to unhelpful names such as "Cube.001", so you might care to use the `Scripts>Object>Object Name Editor` option. Or you can use a property (again) called *id* and specify it there.

You do not need to reload Blender for recently copied plug-ins to be acknowledged. Just select the Scripts>Update Menu option.

TIP

TILE MAP EDITORS

While most game worlds will need the 3D editing power of Blender, some can suffice with simpler 2D tile maps. That isn't to say the game will be visually limited to a top-down 2D scene, merely that the world data can be represented by a simple tile map, such as a racetrack. After all, there are many ways to generate a 3D world environment from simple 2D data, as these levels do not need the workload involved in creating a full 3D environment. This section looks at those 2D editors.

With most tools, it isn't particularly important to have an Open Source variant because you're unlikely to change it regularly. However, unlike GIMP and Audacity, the file formats of most world editors are in closed proprietary formats, making it much harder to import their data into your engine or adapt the editor to include game-specific triggers and features. Even when the format is in plain ASCII, or even XML, it is helpful to have access to the source so that vagrancies in the format can be understood.

The RPG toolkit

This is an all-encompassing tile map editor, sprite editor, and logic control system that intends to govern the entire game pipeline and game playback method. The package comes in two halves. First, there is the main editor, as shown in Figure 14.4, which allows you to build each individual game component and connect them together in suitable configurations for your game. The second part is the playback engine. This allows the game files to be run independently of the editor. The game data itself is well organized into separate files, and many of the freeware games using the toolkit are provided in this format. For those who prefer to close access to these data files, you can also export your game directly to an EXE.

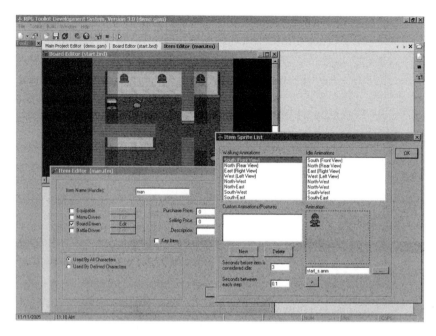

FIGURE 14.4 The main editor in use.

In many cases, the RPG Toolkit succeeds in providing an end-to-end solution, but only for those making smaller and retro-RPG games using 2D or isometric boards, as can be demonstrated by the large community surrounding it. The main website provides links to many games built by it, along with freely available sound and graphic resources[2].

Unfortunately, while more involved and complex games are certainly possible, it takes a large amount of work to go beyond the basic configurations. And this is time that should probably be spent elsewhere, because for games of a larger scope the scripting language provided cannot compete with a custom C++ engine and can lead to designer frustration. It is expected that most readers will consider using the tile and animation editors, but write their own engine to control the characters and render their in-game map. You can experiment with the toolkit by using the installation available on the accompanying CD-ROM.

ON THE CD

Homepage: *http://www.toolkitzone.com* and *http://sourceforge.net/projects/rpgtoolkit*

License: AC Open License v 1.0 (similar to revised BSD)

Distribution: Source and binaries

First release: 2004

Current version: 3.0.6 (stable since April 2005)

Platform(s): Windows only

Dependencies: None

Other resources: Online forum, galleries, sample games, and tutorials

The toolkit editor is written in Visual Basic 6. So, naturally, unless your game is one of the few that also uses this language, you will need to write custom importers and renderers for its data. Although the output format is in binary, the authors made the sensible step to keep the data as clean as possible by using raw binary, unfettered by self-describing blocks or parent-child hierarchies. The `saveBoard` subroutine in `CommonBoard.bas` provides all the necessary information. Similar routines are available for the rest of the data, so it is expected that the toolchain will convert this data into an engine-ready format.

Creating Levels

As with most tile-based editors, creating a level is a two-stage process. To begin, you need to create, or import, a tileset. This will represent each square on your map visually. If you are using the toolkit to only generate map data, these tiles need not be accurate or final.

Generating a Tileset

Each tile is generated individually through the built-in tile editor, as shown in Figure 14.5. This has a small set of standard drawing tools; therefore, it is more likely that you'll create the images in GIMP and import them. You can then save the image from the editor as a tileset so the board editor can use it. You can generate any number of tiles or tilesets in this fashion, although you can also save new tiles into an existing tileset, appending the last image to tiles that were already there, to collate similar images.

The tiles are previewed at the bottom of the window in both 2D and isometric views because the one tile can be used in both types of board. The isometric tile is generated from the standard 2D image by the editor automatically. If your game is truly isometric and you're using final artwork within this editor, you may wish to convert the tiles to isometric at this stage so that the level previews are correct. In performing this conversion, you are now able to edit the pixel-perfect final version of the isometric tiles but are unable to switch back to the simpler 2D axonometric tiles.

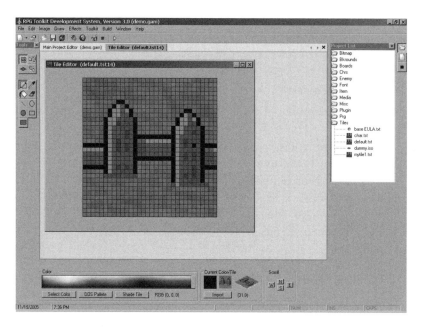

FIGURE 14.5   The tile editor.

Generating a Board

Each board is comprised of up to eight layers, each presenting a series of tiles from any number of different tilesets. Each tile is loaded by double-clicking the current tile icon. You must then select the appropriate tileset to load, from which the individual tile itself can be selected, from all the tiles present in that set.

As each tile is placed, there are two properties that may be assigned, aside from the tile image itself. Both have a heavy bias to the RPG games they were intended, but can be reappropriated if necessary because there is no other mechanism for introducing property data to the tiles.

The first is a shading property. This was originally intended to add shadows and lighting to existing tiles, eliminating the need for additional (slightly shadowed) graphics. The shade parameter exists as *either* a color or a brightness value given by the range of -255 and 255.

The second tile property indicates the type and is programmed with hardcoded references include normal, solid, under, and stairs. There are a total of 13 types available. You cannot change the naming of these properties, but their meaning can be changed within the game engine. Visual Basic users may, of course, rebuild the editor with amended names and properties, such is the promise of Open Source.

In addition to the per-tile properties, you can assign board-wide properties indicating which level would be loaded when you move to the left, right, top, or bottom of the current board, for example. Again, these can be reappropriated according to the needs of your game.

Event Triggering

The mechanism for triggering events on particular squares is carried out by the RPGCode facility. This allows you to run a small piece of code whenever the player is standing on, or presses activate while standing next to, a particular square. Although this logic requires suitable gameplay code, you can still make use of the data as the program references are saved into the board, along with their X, Y, and layer information. This can provide an additional mechanism for incorporating attributes into the level file.

Tiled

This is a generic map editor that is capable of producing 2D maps using arbitrary tilesets. These maps can be represented in several additional formats, including isometric and hexes. It supports multiple layers, each with its own set of properties, zoom, multiple levels of undo, and a plug-in architecture to provide alternate import and export routines.

The focus with this editor is to be general in all cases. Consequently, there is no facility to provide events, or assign data to specific objects or instances of any tile. However, you can cover this situation yourself by creating a layer for each class of object that requires events, and use the layer-specific properties to describe them. This editor is available on the accompanying CD-ROM.

ON THE CD

> **Homepage:** *http://mapeditor.org*
>
> **License:** GNU GPL (Appendix B)
>
> **Distribution:** Source and binaries
>
> **First release:** 2004
>
> **Current version:** 0.6.0 (stable since June 23, 2006)
>
> **Platform(s):** Any supported by Java
>
> **Dependencies:** Java 2 Standard Edition
>
> **Other resources:** Mailing list, online tutorial, and website

This, like most other Java software, is run with a command line, such as

```
java -jar dist/tiled.jar
```

and provides a large amount of functionality for handling the individual tiles on the map, as shown in Figure 14.6, although there is comparatively little editing provision for tilesets, their generation, or the graphics within them. This means the artists will need to generate the completed tilesets before work can begin on the level design.

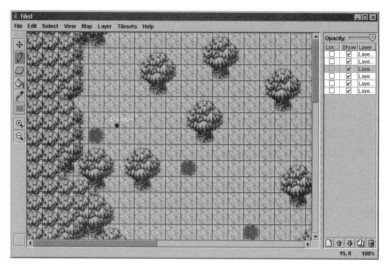

FIGURE 14.6 Tiled in operation.

Unlike the RPG Toolkit, Tiled writes all its data into an XML format, allowing for the parsing methods you saw in Chapter 10 to be utilized. However, there are several possibilities for output format, as shown by the export preference dialog box shown in Figure 14.7.

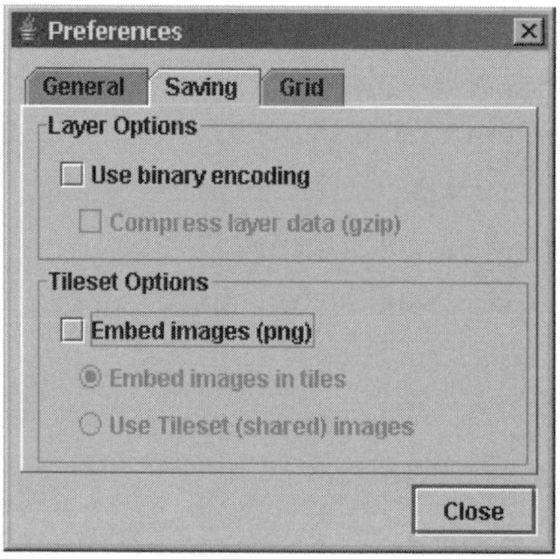

FIGURE 14.7 Export preferences.

The preferred export method is as given in Figure 14.7 because each tileset image is referenced by filename, and each tile is given explicitly in the XML description within the TMX file. This requires no other libraries and produces a level file similar to this:

```
<?xml version="1.0"?>
<map version="0.99b" orientation="isometric" width="64" height="64"
tilewidth="32" tileheight="16">
 <tileset firstgid="1" source="water.tsx"/>
 <tileset firstgid="34" source="water.tsx"/>
 <layer name="Layer 0" width="64" height="64">
  <data>
   <tile gid="1"/>
   <tile gid="6"/>
   <tile gid="12"/>
```

and so on.

In comparison, embedded images will be stored inside the XML file using base64 (see Chapter 10 for suitable decode libraries), and the map data will be compressed into gzip format and stored in base64. Although this saves quite significantly on disk space and can often be parsed quicker (because there is less XML text processing occurring), the openness of the data format is compromised and therefore less effective.

ENDNOTES

1. A full API reference can be found at *http://www.blender.org/modules/ documentation/228PythonDoc/Blender-module.html*.
2. Although the licenses of some assets are not quoted.

Appendix

A About the CD-ROM

The contents of this disc provide a complete suite of tools for game developers working, or wanting to work, with Open Source software. This includes compilers, debuggers, sound editors, 3D modeling tools, and art packages.

FOLDERS

The files on this disc are organized into folders as follows:

Figures: All of the figures from the book, organized in folders by chapter.

Software: This folder contains over 120 software packages; all are mentioned in the text and grouped according to chapter. It includes the libraries and engine code from the components covered in Part B, such as SDL, ODE, and Lua, along with user-end software such as Blender, Subversion, Audacity, and ImageMagick. Each is accompanied by its license and, where appropriate, source code. The specific requirements and usage guidelines are given in the main text.

Bookcode: This contains various examples from the book, such as the XML transformations in Chapter 10 and example object models from Chapter 12. It also contains the SGX core mentioned in many places throughout the book as an independent standard for providing low-level functionality and cross-platform abstractions.

SYSTEM REQUIREMENTS

The software on this disc requires an IBM PC compatible with 256 MB of RAM, 200 MB of available hard drive space, and a copy of Microsoft Developer Studio, version 6 or above. Some software can be compiled using the MinGW32 compiler, which is supplied. An Intel Pentium Processor is required, although Pentium II or higher is recommended. A Windows 98 operating system or later is required.

Appendix

B

The GNU General Public License (GNU GPL)

GNU GENERAL PUBLIC LICENSE
Version 2, June 1991

Copyright © 1989, 1991 Free Software Foundation, Inc. 51 Franklin St, Fifth Floor, Boston, MA 02110-1301 USA

Everyone is permitted to copy and distribute verbatim copies of this license document, but changing it is not allowed.

Preamble

The licenses for most software are designed to take away your freedom to share and change it. By contrast, the GNU General Public License is intended to guarantee your freedom to share and change free software—to make sure the software is free for all its users. This General Public License applies to most of the Free software Foundation's software and to any other program whose authors commit to using it. (Some other Free software Foundation software is covered by the GNU Library General Public License instead.) You can apply it to your programs, too.

When we speak of free software, we are referring to freedom, not price. Our General Public Licenses are designed to make sure that you have the freedom to distribute copies of free software (and charge for this service if you wish), that you receive source code or can get it if you want it, that you can change the software or use pieces of it in new free programs; and that you know you can do these things.

To protect your rights, we need to make restrictions that forbid anyone to deny you these rights or to ask you to surrender the rights. These restrictions translate to certain responsibilities for you if you distribute copies of the software, or if you modify it.

For example, if you distribute copies of such a program, whether gratis or for a fee, you must give the recipients all the rights that you have. You must make sure that they, too, receive or can get the source code. And you must show them these terms so they know their rights.

We protect your rights with two steps: (1) copyright the software, and (2) offer you this license which gives you legal permission to copy, distribute and/or modify the software.

Also, for each author's protection and ours, we want to make certain that everyone understands that there is no warranty for this free software. If the software is modified by someone else and passed on, we want its recipients to know that what they have is not the original, so that any problems introduced by others will not reflect on the original authors' reputations.

Finally, any free program is threatened constantly by software patents. We wish to avoid the danger that redistributors of a free program will individually obtain patent licenses, in effect making the program proprietary. To prevent this, we have made it clear that any patent must be licensed for everyone's free use or not licensed at all.

The precise terms and conditions for copying, distribution and modification follow.

GNU GENERAL PUBLIC LICENSE

TERMS AND CONDITIONS FOR COPYING, DISTRIBUTION AND MODIFICATION

0. This License applies to any program or other work which contains a notice placed by the copyright holder saying it may be distributed under the terms of this General Public License. The "Program", below, refers to any such program or work, and a "work based on the Program" means either the Program or any derivative work under copyright law: that is to say, a work containing the Program or a portion of it, either verbatim or with modifications and/or translated into another language. (Hereinafter, translation is included without limitation in the term "modification".) Each licensee is addressed as "you".

Activities other than copying, distribution and modification are not covered by this License; they are outside its scope. The act of running the Program is not restricted, and the output from the Program is covered only if its contents constitute a work based on the Program (independent of having been made by running the Program). Whether that is true depends on what the Program does.

1. You may copy and distribute verbatim copies of the Program's source code as you receive it, in any medium, provided that you conspicuously and appropriately publish on each copy an appropriate copyright notice and disclaimer of warranty; keep intact all the notices that refer to this License and to the absence of any

warranty; and give any other recipients of the Program a copy of this License along with the Program.

You may charge a fee for the physical act of transferring a copy, and you may at your option offer warranty protection in exchange for a fee.

2. You may modify your copy or copies of the Program or any portion of it, thus forming a work based on the Program, and copy and distribute such modifications or work under the terms of Section 1 above, provided that you also meet all of these conditions:

a) You must cause the modified files to carry prominent notices stating that you changed the files and the date of any change.

b) You must cause any work that you distribute or publish, that in whole or in part contains or is derived from the Program or any part thereof, to be licensed as a whole at no charge to all third parties under the terms of this License.

c) If the modified program normally reads commands interactively when run, you must cause it, when started running for such interactive use in the most ordinary way, to print or display an announcement including an appropriate copyright notice and a notice that there is no warranty (or else, saying that you provide a warranty) and that users may redistribute the program under these conditions, and telling the user how to view a copy of this License. (Exception: if the Program itself is interactive but does not normally print such an announcement, your work based on the Program is not required to print an announcement.)

These requirements apply to the modified work as a whole. If identifiable sections of that work are not derived from the Program, and can be reasonably considered independent and separate works in themselves, then this License, and its terms, do not apply to those sections when you distribute them as separate works. But when you distribute the same sections as part of a whole which is a work based on the Program, the distribution of the whole must be on the terms of this License, whose permissions for other licensees extend to the entire whole, and thus to each and every part regardless of who wrote it.

Thus, it is not the intent of this section to claim rights or contest your rights to work written entirely by you; rather, the intent is to exercise the right to control the distribution of derivative or collective works based on the Program.

In addition, mere aggregation of another work not based on the Program with the Program (or with a work based on the Program) on a volume of a storage or distribution medium does not bring the other work under the scope of this License.

3. You may copy and distribute the Program (or a work based on it, under Section 2) in object code or executable form under the terms of Sections 1 and 2 above provided that you also do one of the following:

a) Accompany it with the complete corresponding machine-readable source code, which must be distributed under the terms of Sections 1 and 2 above on a medium customarily used for software interchange; or,

b) Accompany it with a written offer, valid for at least three years, to give any third party, for a charge no more than your cost of physically performing source distribution, a complete machine-readable copy of the corresponding source code, to be distributed under the terms of Sections 1 and 2 above on a medium customarily used for software interchange; or,

c) Accompany it with the information you received as to the offer to distribute corresponding source code. (This alternative is allowed only for noncommercial distribution and only if you received the program in object code or executable form with such an offer, in accord with Subsection b above.)

The source code for a work means the preferred form of the work for making modifications to it. For an executable work, complete source code means all the source code for all modules it contains, plus any associated interface definition files, plus the scripts used to control compilation and installation of the executable. However, as a special exception, the source code distributed need not include anything that is normally distributed (in either source or binary form) with the major components (compiler, kernel, and so on) of the operating system on which the executable runs, unless that component itself accompanies the executable.

If distribution of executable or object code is made by offering access to copy from a designated place, then offering equivalent access to copy the source code from the same place counts as distribution of the source code, even though third parties are not compelled to copy the source along with the object code.

4. You may not copy, modify, sublicense, or distribute the Program except as expressly provided under this License. Any attempt otherwise to copy, modify, sublicense or distribute the Program is void, and will automatically terminate your rights under this License.

However, parties who have received copies, or rights, from you under this License will not have their licenses terminated so long as such parties remain in full compliance.

5. You are not required to accept this License, since you have not signed it. However, nothing else grants you permission to modify or distribute the Program or its derivative works. These actions are prohibited by law if you do not accept this License. Therefore, by modifying or distributing the Program (or any work based on the Program), you indicate your acceptance of this License to do so, and all its terms and conditions for copying, distributing or modifying the Program or works based on it.

6. Each time you redistribute the Program (or any work based on the Program), the recipient automatically receives a license from the original licensor to copy, distribute or modify the Program subject to these terms and conditions. You may not impose any further restrictions on the recipients' exercise of the rights granted herein. You are not responsible for enforcing compliance by third parties to this License.

7. If, as a consequence of a court judgment or allegation of patent infringement or for any other reason (not limited to patent issues), conditions are imposed on you (whether by court order, agreement or otherwise) that contradict the conditions of this License, they do not excuse you from the conditions of this License. If you cannot distribute so as to satisfy simultaneously your obligations under this

License and any other pertinent obligations, then as a consequence you may not distribute the Program at all. For example, if a patent license would not permit royalty-free redistribution of the Program by all those who receive copies directly or indirectly through you, then the only way you could satisfy both it and this License would be to refrain entirely from distribution of the Program.

If any portion of this section is held invalid or unenforceable under any particular circumstance, the balance of the section is intended to apply and the section as a whole is intended to apply in other circumstances.

It is not the purpose of this section to induce you to infringe any patents or other property right claims or to contest validity of any such claims; this section has the sole purpose of protecting the integrity of the free software distribution system, which is implemented by public license practices. Many people have made generous contributions to the wide range of software distributed through that system in reliance on consistent application of that system; it is up to the author/donor to decide if he or she is willing to distribute software through any other system and a licensee cannot impose that choice.

This section is intended to make thoroughly clear what is believed to be a consequence of the rest of this License.

8. If the distribution and/or use of the Program is restricted in certain countries either by patents or by copyrighted interfaces, the original copyright holder who places the Program under this License may add an explicit geographical distribution limitation excluding those countries, so that distribution is permitted only in or among countries not thus excluded. In such case, this License incorporates the limitation as if written in the body of this License.

9. The Free Software Foundation may publish revised and/or new versions of the General Public License from time to time. Such new versions will be similar in spirit to the present version, but may differ in detail to address new problems or concerns.

Each version is given a distinguishing version number. If the Program specifies a version number of this License which applies to it and "any later version", you have the option of following the terms and conditions either of that version or of any later version published by the Free Software Foundation. If the Program does not specify a version number of this License, you may choose any version ever published by the Free Software Foundation.

10. If you wish to incorporate parts of the Program into other free programs whose distribution conditions are different, write to the author to ask for permission. For software which is copyrighted by the Free Software Foundation, write to the Free Software Foundation; we sometimes make exceptions for this. Our decision will be guided by the two goals of preserving the free status of all derivatives of our free software and of promoting the sharing and reuse of software generally.

NO WARRANTY

11. BECAUSE THE PROGRAM IS LICENSED FREE OF CHARGE, THERE IS NO WARRANTY FOR THE PROGRAM, TO THE EXTENT PERMITTED BY APPLICABLE LAW. EXCEPT WHEN OTHERWISE STATED IN WRITING THE COPYRIGHT HOLDERS AND/OR OTHER PARTIES PROVIDE THE PROGRAM "AS IS" WITHOUT WARRANTY OF ANY KIND, EITHER EXPRESSED OR IMPLIED, INCLUDING, BUT NOT LIMITED TO, THE IMPLIED WARRANTIES OF MERCHANTABILITY AND FITNESS FOR A PARTICULAR PURPOSE. THE ENTIRE RISK AS TO THE QUALITY AND PERFORMANCE OF THE PROGRAM IS WITH YOU. SHOULD THE PROGRAM PROVE DEFECTIVE, YOU ASSUME THE COST OF ALL NECESSARY SERVICING, REPAIR OR CORRECTION.

12. IN NO EVENT UNLESS REQUIRED BY APPLICABLE LAW OR AGREED TO IN WRITING WILL ANY COPYRIGHT HOLDER, OR ANY OTHER PARTY WHO MAY MODIFY AND/OR REDISTRIBUTE THE PROGRAM AS PERMITTED ABOVE, BE LIABLE TO YOU FOR DAMAGES, INCLUDING ANY GENERAL, SPECIAL, INCIDENTAL OR CONSEQUENTIAL DAMAGES ARISING OUT OF THE USE OR INABILITY TO USE THE PROGRAM (INCLUDING BUT NOT LIMITED TO LOSS OF DATA OR DATA BEING RENDERED INACCURATE OR LOSSES SUSTAINED BY YOU OR THIRD PARTIES OR A FAILURE OF THE PROGRAM TO OPERATE WITH ANY OTHER PROGRAMS), EVEN IF SUCH HOLDER OR OTHER PARTY HAS BEEN ADVISED OF THE POSSIBILITY OF SUCH DAMAGES.

END OF TERMS AND CONDITIONS

Available at *http://www.gnu.org/licenses/gpl.txt*

Appendix

C

The GNU Lesser General Public License (GNU LGPL)

GNU LESSER GENERAL PUBLIC LICENSE
Version 2.1, February 1999

Copyright © 1991, 1999 Free Software Foundation, Inc. 51 Franklin St, Fifth Floor, Boston, MA 02110-1301 USA

Everyone is permitted to copy and distribute verbatim copies of this license document, but changing it is not allowed.

[This is the first released version of the Lesser GPL. It also counts as the successor of the GNU Library Public License, version 2, hence the version number 2.1.]

Preamble

The licenses for most software are designed to take away your freedom to share and change it. By contrast, the GNU General Public Licenses are intended to guarantee your freedom to share and change free software—to make sure the software is free for all its users.

This license, the Lesser General Public License, applies to some specially designated software packages—typically libraries—of the Free Software Foundation and other authors who decide to use it. You can use it too, but we suggest you first think carefully about whether this license or the ordinary General Public License is the better strategy to use in any particular case, based on the explanations below.

When we speak of free software, we are referring to freedom of use, not price. Our General Public Licenses are designed to make sure that you have the freedom to distribute copies of free software (and charge for this service if you wish); that you receive source code or can get it if you want it; that you can change the software and use pieces of it in new free programs; and that you are informed that you can do these things.

To protect your rights, we need to make restrictions that forbid distributors to deny you these rights or to ask you to surrender these rights. These restrictions translate to certain responsibilities for you if you distribute copies of the library or if you modify it.

For example, if you distribute copies of the library, whether gratis or for a fee, you must give the recipients all the rights that we gave you. You must make sure that they, too, receive or can get the source code. If you link other code with the library, you must provide complete object files to the recipients, so that they can relink them with the library after making changes to the library and recompiling it. And you must show them these terms so they know their rights.

We protect your rights with a two-step method: (1) we copyright the library, and (2) we offer you this license, which gives you legal permission to copy, distribute and/or modify the library.

To protect each distributor, we want to make it very clear that there is no warranty for the free library. Also, if the library is modified by someone else and passed on, the recipients should know that what they have is not the original version, so that the original author's reputation will not be affected by problems that might be introduced by others.

Finally, software patents pose a constant threat to the existence of any free program. We wish to make sure that a company cannot effectively restrict the users of a free program by obtaining a restrictive license from a patent holder. Therefore, we insist that any patent license obtained for a version of the library must be consistent with the full freedom of use specified in this license.

Most GNU software, including some libraries, is covered by the ordinary GNU General Public License. This license, the GNU Lesser General Public License, applies to certain designated libraries, and is quite different from the ordinary General Public License. We use this license for certain libraries in order to permit linking those libraries into non-free programs.

When a program is linked with a library, whether statically or using a shared library, the combination of the two is legally speaking a combined work, a derivative of the original library. The ordinary General Public License therefore permits such linking only if the entire combination fits its criteria of freedom. The Lesser General Public License permits more lax criteria for linking other code with the library.

We call this license the "Lesser" General Public License because it does Less to protect the user's freedom than the ordinary General Public License. It also provides other free software developers Less of an advantage over competing non-free programs. These disadvantages are the reason we use the ordinary General Public License for many libraries. However, the Lesser license provides advantages in certain special circumstances.

For example, on rare occasions, there may be a special need to encourage the widest possible use of a certain library, so that it becomes a de-facto standard. To achieve this, non-free programs must be allowed to use the library. A more frequent case is that a free library does the same job as widely used non-free libraries. In this case, there is little to gain by limiting the free library to free software only, so we use the Lesser General Public License.

In other cases, permission to use a particular library in non-free programs enables a greater number of people to use a large body of free software. For example, permission to use the GNU C Library in non-free programs enables many more people to use the whole GNU operating system, as well as its variant, the GNU/Linux operating system.

Although the Lesser General Public License is Less protective of the users' freedom, it does ensure that the user of a program that is linked with the Library has the freedom and the wherewithal to run that program using a modified version of the Library.

The precise terms and conditions for copying, distribution and modification follow. Pay close attention to the difference between a "work based on the library" and a "work that uses the library". The former contains code derived from the library, whereas the latter must be combined with the library in order to run.

GNU LESSER GENERAL PUBLIC LICENSE

TERMS AND CONDITIONS FOR COPYING, DISTRIBUTION AND MODIFICATION

0. This License Agreement applies to any software library or other program which contains a notice placed by the copyright holder or other authorized party saying it may be distributed under the terms of this Lesser General Public License (also called "this License"). Each licensee is addressed as "you".

A "library" means a collection of software functions and/or data prepared so as to be conveniently linked with application programs (which use some of those functions and data) to form executables.

The "Library", below, refers to any such software library or work which has been distributed under these terms. A "work based on the Library" means either the Library or any derivative work under copyright law: that is to say, a work containing the Library or a portion of it, either verbatim or with modifications and/or translated straightforwardly into another language. (Hereinafter, translation is included without limitation in the term "modification".)

"Source code" for a work means the preferred form of the work for making modifications to it. For a library, complete source code means all the source code for all modules it contains, plus any associated interface definition files, plus the scripts used to control compilation and installation of the library.

Activities other than copying, distribution and modification are not covered by this License; they are outside its scope. The act of running a program using the Library is not restricted, and output from such a program is covered only if its contents constitute a work based on the Library (independent of the use of the Library in a tool for writing it). Whether that is true depends on what the Library does and what the program that uses the Library does.

1. You may copy and distribute verbatim copies of the Library's complete source code as you receive it, in any medium, provided that you conspicuously and appropriately publish on each copy an appropriate copyright notice and disclaimer of warranty; keep intact all the notices that refer to this License and to the absence of any warranty; and distribute a copy of this License along with the Library.

You may charge a fee for the physical act of transferring a copy, and you may at your option offer warranty protection in exchange for a fee.

2. You may modify your copy or copies of the Library or any portion of it, thus forming a work based on the Library, and copy and distribute such modifications or work under the terms of Section 1 above, provided that you also meet all of these conditions:

a) The modified work must itself be a software library.

b) You must cause the files modified to carry prominent notices stating that you changed the files and the date of any change.

c) You must cause the whole of the work to be licensed at no charge to all third parties under the terms of this License.

d) If a facility in the modified Library refers to a function or a table of data to be supplied by an application program that uses the facility, other than as an argument passed when the facility is invoked, then you must make a good faith effort to ensure that, in the event an application does not supply such function or table, the facility still operates, and performs whatever part of its purpose remains meaningful.

(For example, a function in a library to compute square roots has a purpose that is entirely well-defined independent of the application. Therefore, Subsection 2d requires that any application-supplied function or table used by this function must be optional: if the application does not supply it, the square root function must still compute square roots.)

These requirements apply to the modified work as a whole. If identifiable sections of that work are not derived from the Library, and can be reasonably considered independent and separate works in themselves, then this License, and its terms, do not apply to those sections when you distribute them as separate works. But when you distribute the same sections as part of a whole which is a work based on the Library, the distribution of the whole must be on the terms of this License, whose permissions for other licensees extend to the entire whole, and thus to each and every part regardless of who wrote it.

Thus, it is not the intent of this section to claim rights or contest your rights to work written entirely by you; rather, the intent is to exercise the right to control the distribution of derivative or collective works based on the Library.

In addition, mere aggregation of another work not based on the Library with the Library (or with a work based on the Library) on a volume of a storage or distribution medium does not bring the other work under the scope of this License.

3. You may opt to apply the terms of the ordinary GNU General Public License instead of this License to a given copy of the Library. To do this, you must alter all the notices that refer to this License, so that they refer to the ordinary GNU General Public License, version 2, instead of to this License. (If a newer version than version 2 of the ordinary GNU General Public License has appeared, then you can specify that version instead if you wish.) Do not make any other change in these notices.

Once this change is made in a given copy, it is irreversible for that copy, so the ordinary GNU General Public License applies to all subsequent copies and derivative works made from that copy.

This option is useful when you wish to copy part of the code of the Library into a program that is not a library.

4. You may copy and distribute the Library (or a portion or derivative of it, under Section 2) in object code or executable form under the terms of Sections 1 and 2 above provided that you accompany it with the complete corresponding machine-readable source code, which must be distributed under the terms of Sections 1 and 2 above on a medium customarily used for software interchange.

If distribution of object code is made by offering access to copy from a designated place, then offering equivalent access to copy the source code from the same place satisfies the requirement to distribute the source code, even though third parties are not compelled to copy the source along with the object code.

5. A program that contains no derivative of any portion of the Library, but is designed to work with the Library by being compiled or linked with it, is called a "work that uses the Library". Such a work, in isolation, is not a derivative work of the Library, and therefore falls outside the scope of this License.

However, linking a "work that uses the Library" with the Library creates an executable that is a derivative of the Library (because it contains portions of the Library), rather than a "work that uses the library". The executable is therefore covered by this License. Section 6 states terms for distribution of such executables.

When a "work that uses the Library" uses material from a header file that is part of the Library, the object code for the work may be a derivative work of the Library even though the source code is not. Whether this is true is especially significant if the work can be linked without the Library, or if the work is itself a library. The threshold for this to be true is not precisely defined by law.

If such an object file uses only numerical parameters, data structure layouts and accessors, and small macros and small inline functions (ten lines or less in length), then the use of the object file is unrestricted, regardless of whether it is legally a derivative work. (Executables containing this object code plus portions of the Library will still fall under Section 6.)

Otherwise, if the work is a derivative of the Library, you may distribute the object code for the work under the terms of Section 6. Any executables containing that work also fall under Section 6, whether or not they are linked directly with the Library itself.

6. As an exception to the Sections above, you may also combine or link a "work that uses the Library" with the Library to produce a work containing portions of the Library, and distribute that work under terms of your choice, provided that the terms permit modification of the work for the customer's own use and reverse engineering for debugging such modifications.

You must give prominent notice with each copy of the work that the Library is used in it and that the Library and its use are covered by this License. You must supply a copy of this License. If the work during execution displays copyright notices, you must include the copyright notice for the Library among them, as well as a reference directing the user to the copy of this License. Also, you must do one of these things:

a) Accompany the work with the complete corresponding machine-readable source code for the Library including whatever changes were used in the work (which must be distributed under Sections 1 and 2 above); and, if the work is an executable linked with the Library, with the complete machine-readable "work that uses the Library", as object code and/or source code, so that the user can modify the Library and then relink to produce a modified executable containing the modified Library. (It is understood that the user who changes the contents of definitions files in the Library will not necessarily be able to recompile the application to use the modified definitions.)

b) Use a suitable shared library mechanism for linking with the Library. A suitable mechanism is one that (1) uses at run time a copy of the library already present on the user's computer system, rather than copying library functions into the executable, and (2) will operate properly with a modified version of the library, if the user installs one, as long as the modified version is interface-compatible with the version that the work was made with.

c) Accompany the work with a written offer, valid for at least three years, to give the same user the materials specified in Subsection 6a, above, for a charge no more than the cost of performing this distribution.

d) If distribution of the work is made by offering access to copy from a designated place, offer equivalent access to copy the above specified materials from the same place.

e) Verify that the user has already received a copy of these materials or that you have already sent this user a copy.

For an executable, the required form of the "work that uses the Library" must include any data and utility programs needed for reproducing the executable from it. However, as a special exception, the materials to be distributed need not include anything that is normally distributed (in either source or binary form) with the major components (compiler, kernel, and so on) of the operating system on which the executable runs, unless that component itself accompanies the executable.

It may happen that this requirement contradicts the license restrictions of other proprietary libraries that do not normally accompany the operating system. Such a contradiction means you cannot use both them and the Library together in an executable that you distribute.

7. You may place library facilities that are a work based on the Library side-by-side in a single library together with other library facilities not covered by this License, and distribute such a combined library, provided that the separate distribution of the work based on the Library and of the other library facilities is otherwise permitted, and provided that you do these two things:

a) Accompany the combined library with a copy of the same work based on the Library, uncombined with any other library facilities. This must be distributed under the terms of the Sections above.

b) Give prominent notice with the combined library of the fact that part of it is a work based on the Library, and explaining where to find the accompanying uncombined form of the same work.

8. You may not copy, modify, sublicense, link with, or distribute the Library except as expressly provided under this License. Any attempt otherwise to copy, modify, sublicense, link with, or distribute the Library is void, and will automatically terminate your rights under this License. However, parties who have received copies, or rights, from you under this License will not have their licenses terminated so long as such parties remain in full compliance.

9. You are not required to accept this License, since you have not signed it. However, nothing else grants you permission to modify or distribute the Library

or its derivative works. These actions are prohibited by law if you do not accept this License. Therefore, by modifying or distributing the Library (or any work based on the Library), you indicate your acceptance of this License to do so, and all its terms and conditions for copying, distributing or modifying the Library or works based on it.

10. Each time you redistribute the Library (or any work based on the Library), the recipient automatically receives a license from the original licensor to copy, distribute, link with or modify the Library subject to these terms and conditions. You may not impose any further restrictions on the recipients' exercise of the rights granted herein. You are not responsible for enforcing compliance by third parties with this License.

11. If, as a consequence of a court judgment or allegation of patent infringement or for any other reason (not limited to patent issues), conditions are imposed on you (whether by court order, agreement or otherwise) that contradict the conditions of this License, they do not excuse you from the conditions of this License. If you cannot distribute so as to satisfy simultaneously your obligations under this License and any other pertinent obligations, then as a consequence you may not distribute the Library at all. For example, if a patent license would not permit royalty-free redistribution of the Library by all those who receive copies directly or indirectly through you, then the only way you could satisfy both it and this License would be to refrain entirely from distribution of the Library.

If any portion of this section is held invalid or unenforceable under any particular circumstance, the balance of the section is intended to apply, and the section as a whole is intended to apply in other circumstances.

It is not the purpose of this section to induce you to infringe any patents or other property right claims or to contest validity of any such claims; this section has the sole purpose of protecting the integrity of the free software distribution system which is implemented by public license practices. Many people have made generous contributions to the wide range of software distributed through that system in reliance on consistent application of that system; it is up to the author/donor to decide if he or she is willing to distribute software through any other system and a licensee cannot impose that choice.

This section is intended to make thoroughly clear what is believed to be a consequence of the rest of this License.

12. If the distribution and/or use of the Library is restricted in certain countries either by patents or by copyrighted interfaces, the original copyright holder who places the Library under this License may add an explicit geographical distribution limitation excluding those countries, so that distribution is permitted only in or among countries not thus excluded. In such case, this License incorporates the limitation as if written in the body of this License.

13. The Free Software Foundation may publish revised and/or new versions of the Lesser General Public License from time to time. Such new versions will be similar in spirit to the present version, but may differ in detail to address new problems or

concerns. Each version is given a distinguishing version number. If the Library specifies a version number of this License which applies to it and "any later version", you have the option of following the terms and conditions either of that version or of any later version published by the Free Software Foundation. If the Library does not specify a license version number, you may choose any version ever published by the Free Software Foundation.

14. If you wish to incorporate parts of the Library into other free programs whose distribution conditions are incompatible with these, write to the author to ask for permission. For software which is copyrighted by the Free Software Foundation, write to the Free Software Foundation; we sometimes make exceptions for this. Our decision will be guided by the two goals of preserving the free status of all derivatives of our free software and of promoting the sharing and reuse of software generally.

NO WARRANTY

15. BECAUSE THE LIBRARY IS LICENSED FREE OF CHARGE, THERE IS NO WARRANTY FOR THE LIBRARY, TO THE EXTENT PERMITTED BY APPLICABLE LAW. EXCEPT WHEN OTHERWISE STATED IN WRITING THE COPYRIGHT HOLDERS AND/OR OTHER PARTIES PROVIDE THE LIBRARY "AS IS" WITHOUT WARRANTY OF ANY KIND, EITHER EXPRESSED OR IMPLIED, INCLUDING, BUT NOT LIMITED TO, THE IMPLIED WARRANTIES OF MERCHANTABILITY AND FITNESS FOR A PARTICULAR PURPOSE. THE ENTIRE RISK AS TO THE QUALITY AND PERFORMANCE OF THE LIBRARY IS WITH YOU. SHOULD THE LIBRARY PROVE DEFECTIVE, YOU ASSUME

THE COST OF ALL NECESSARY SERVICING, REPAIR OR CORRECTION.

16. IN NO EVENT UNLESS REQUIRED BY APPLICABLE LAW OR AGREED TO IN WRITING WILL ANY COPYRIGHT HOLDER, OR ANY OTHER PARTY WHO MAY MODIFY AND/OR REDISTRIBUTE THE LIBRARY AS PERMITTED ABOVE, BE LIABLE TO YOU FOR DAMAGES, INCLUDING ANY GENERAL, SPECIAL, INCIDENTAL OR CONSEQUENTIAL DAMAGES ARISING OUT OF THE USE OR INABILITY TO USE THE LIBRARY (INCLUDING BUT NOT LIMITED TO LOSS OF DATA OR DATA BEING RENDERED INACCURATE OR LOSSES SUSTAINED BY YOU OR THIRD PARTIES OR A FAILURE OF THE LIBRARY TO OPERATE WITH ANY OTHER SOFTWARE), EVEN IF SUCH HOLDER OR OTHER PARTY HAS BEEN ADVISED OF THE POSSIBILITY OF SUCH DAMAGES.

END OF TERMS AND CONDITIONS

Available at *http://www.gnu.org/licenses/lgpl.txt*

Appendix

D The BSD License

Available at *http://www.opensource.org/licenses/bsd-license.php*

Appendix E

The MIT License

Copyright © <year> <copyright holders>

Permission is hereby granted, free of charge, to any person obtaining a copy of this software and associated documentation files (the "Software"), to deal in the Software without restriction, including without limitation the rights to use, copy, modify, merge, publish, distribute, sublicense, and/or sell copies of the Software, and to permit persons to whom the Software is furnished to do so, subject to the following conditions:

The above copyright notice and this permission notice shall be included in all copies or substantial portions of the Software.

THE SOFTWARE IS PROVIDED "AS IS", WITHOUT WARRANTY OF ANY KIND, EXPRESS OR IMPLIED, INCLUDING BUT NOT LIMITED TO THE WARRANTIES OF MERCHANTABILITY, FITNESS FOR A PARTICULAR PURPOSE AND NONINFRINGEMENT. IN NO EVENT SHALL THE AUTHORS OR COPYRIGHT HOLDERS BE LIABLE FOR ANY CLAIM, DAMAGES OR OTHER LIABILITY, WHETHER IN AN ACTION OF CONTRACT, TORT OR OTHERWISE, ARISING FROM, OUT OF OR IN CONNECTION WITH THE SOFTWARE OR THE USE OR OTHER DEALINGS IN THE SOFTWARE.

Available at *http://www.opensource.org/licenses/mit-license.html*

This is more correctly known as the X11 license, since MIT have several licenses. However, most people will understand the phrase MIT License.

Appendix F

The Apache License, Version 2.0

Apache License Version 2.0, January 2004 *http://www.apache.org/licenses/*

TERMS AND CONDITIONS FOR USE, REPRODUCTION, AND DISTRIBUTION
    1. Definitions.
    "License" shall mean the terms and conditions for use, reproduction, and distribution as defined by Sections 1 through 9 of this document.
    "Licensor" shall mean the copyright owner or entity authorized by the copyright owner that is granting the License.
    "Legal Entity" shall mean the union of the acting entity and all other entities that control, are controlled by, or are under common control with that entity. For the purposes of this definition, "control" means (i) the power, direct or indirect, to cause the direction or management of such entity, whether by contract or otherwise, or (ii) ownership of fifty percent (50%) or more of the outstanding shares, or (iii) beneficial ownership of such entity.
    "You" (or "Your") shall mean an individual or Legal Entity exercising permissions granted by this License.
    "Source" form shall mean the preferred form for making modifications, including but not limited to software source code, documentation source, and configuration files.
    "Object" form shall mean any form resulting from mechanical transformation or translation of a Source form, including but not limited to compiled object code, generated documentation, and conversions to other media types.
    "Work" shall mean the work of authorship, whether in Source or Object form, made available under the License, as indicated by a copyright notice that is included in or attached to the work (an example is provided in the Appendix below).
    "Derivative Works" shall mean any work, whether in Source or Object form, that is based on (or derived from) the Work and for which the editorial revisions, annotations, elaborations, or other modifications represent, as a whole, an original

work of authorship. For the purposes of this License, Derivative Works shall not include works that remain separable from, or merely link (or bind by name) to the interfaces of, the Work and Derivative Works thereof.

"Contribution" shall mean any work of authorship, including the original version of the Work and any modifications or additions to that Work or Derivative Works thereof, that is intentionally submitted to Licensor for inclusion in the Work by the copyright owner or by an individual or Legal Entity authorized to submit on behalf of the copyright owner. For the purposes of this definition, "submitted" means any form of electronic, verbal, or written communication sent to the Licensor or its representatives, including but not limited to communication on electronic mailing lists, source code control systems, and issue tracking systems that are managed by, or on behalf of, the Licensor for the purpose of discussing and improving the Work, but excluding communication that is conspicuously marked or otherwise designated in writing by the copyright owner as "Not a Contribution."

"Contributor" shall mean Licensor and any individual or Legal Entity on behalf of whom a Contribution has been received by Licensor and subsequently incorporated within the Work.

2. Grant of Copyright License.

Subject to the terms and conditions of this License, each Contributor hereby grants to You a perpetual, worldwide, non-exclusive, no-charge, royalty-free, irrevocable copyright license to reproduce, prepare Derivative Works of, publicly display, publicly perform, sublicense, and distribute the Work and such Derivative Works in Source or Object form.

3. Grant of Patent License.

Subject to the terms and conditions of this License, each Contributor hereby grants to You a perpetual, worldwide, non-exclusive, no-charge, royalty-free, irrevocable (except as stated in this section) patent license to make, have made, use, offer to sell, sell, import, and otherwise transfer the Work, where such license applies only to those patent claims licensable by such Contributor that are necessarily infringed by their Contribution(s) alone or by combination of their Contribution(s) with the Work to which such Contribution(s) was submitted. If You institute patent litigation against any entity (including a cross-claim or counterclaim in a lawsuit) alleging that the Work or a Contribution incorporated within the Work constitutes direct or contributory patent infringement, then any patent licenses granted to You under this License for that Work shall terminate as of the date such litigation is filed.

4. Redistribution.

You may reproduce and distribute copies of the Work or Derivative Works thereof in any medium, with or without modifications, and in Source or Object form, provided that You meet the following conditions:

1. You must give any other recipients of the Work or Derivative Works a copy of this License; and
2. You must cause any modified files to carry prominent notices stating that You changed the files; and
3. You must retain, in the Source form of any Derivative Works that You distribute, all copyright, patent, trademark, and attribution notices from the Source form of the Work, excluding those notices that do not pertain to any part of the Derivative Works; and
4. If the Work includes a "NOTICE" text file as part of its distribution, then any Derivative Works that You distribute must include a readable copy of the attribution notices contained within such NOTICE file, excluding those notices that do not pertain to any part of the Derivative Works, in at least one of the following places: within a NOTICE text file distributed as part of the Derivative Works; within the Source form or documentation, if provided along with the Derivative Works; or, within a display generated by the Derivative Works, if and wherever such third-party notices normally appear. The contents of the NOTICE file are for informational purposes only and do not modify the License. You may add Your own attribution notices within Derivative Works that You distribute, alongside or as an addendum to the NOTICE text from the Work, provided that such additional attribution notices cannot be construed as modifying the License.

You may add Your own copyright statement to Your modifications and may provide additional or different license terms and conditions for use, reproduction, or distribution of Your modifications, or for any such Derivative Works as a whole, provided Your use, reproduction, and distribution of the Work otherwise complies with the conditions stated in this License.

5. Submission of Contributions.

Unless You explicitly state otherwise, any Contribution intentionally submitted for inclusion in the Work by You to the Licensor shall be under the terms and conditions of this License, without any additional terms or conditions. Notwithstanding the above, nothing herein shall supersede or modify the terms of any separate license agreement you may have executed with Licensor regarding such Contributions.

6. Trademarks.

This License does not grant permission to use the trade names, trademarks, service marks, or product names of the Licensor, except as required for reasonable and customary use in describing the origin of the Work and reproducing the content of the NOTICE file.

7. Disclaimer of Warranty.

Unless required by applicable law or agreed to in writing, Licensor provides the Work (and each Contributor provides its Contributions) on an "AS IS" BASIS, WITHOUT WARRANTIES OR CONDITIONS OF ANY KIND, either express or implied, including, without limitation, any warranties or conditions of TITLE, NON-INFRINGEMENT, MERCHANTABILITY, or FITNESS FOR A PARTICULAR PURPOSE. You are solely responsible for determining the appropriateness of using or redistributing the Work and assume any risks associated with Your exercise of permissions under this License.

8. Limitation of Liability.

In no event and under no legal theory, whether in tort (including negligence), contract, or otherwise, unless required by applicable law (such as deliberate and grossly negligent acts) or agreed to in writing, shall any Contributor be liable to You for damages, including any direct, indirect, special, incidental, or consequential damages of any character arising as a result of this License or out of the use or inability to use the Work (including but not limited to damages for loss of goodwill, work stoppage, computer failure or malfunction, or any and all other commercial damages or losses), even if such Contributor has been advised of the possibility of such damages.

9. Accepting Warranty or Additional Liability.

While redistributing the Work or Derivative Works thereof, You may choose to offer, and charge a fee for, acceptance of support, warranty, indemnity, or other liability obligations and/or rights consistent with this License. However, in accepting such obligations, You may act only on Your own behalf and on Your sole responsibility, not on behalf of any other Contributor, and only if You agree to indemnify, defend, and hold each Contributor harmless for any liability incurred by, or claims asserted against, such Contributor by reason of your accepting any such warranty or additional liability.

END OF TERMS AND CONDITIONS

Available at *http://www.opensource.org/licenses/apache2.0.php*